STRATEGIC ARENA SWITCHING IN INTERNATIONAL TRADE NEGOTIATIONS

Strategic Arena Switching in International Trade Negotiations

Edited by

WOLFGANG BLAAS
Vienna University of Technology, Austria

and

JOACHIM BECKER
Vienna University of Economics and Business Administration, Austria

ASHGATE

Published by
Ashgate Publishing Limited
Gower House
Croft Road
Aldershot
Hampshire GU11 3HR
England

Ashgate Publishing Company
Suite 420
101 Cherry Street
Burlington, VT 05401-4405
USA

Ashgate website: http://www.ashgate.com

British Library Cataloguing in Publication Data
Strategic arena switching in international trade
    negotiations
    1. Foreign trade regulation 2. International trade
    3. Diplomatic negotiations in international disputes
    I. Blaas, Wolfgang II. Becker, Joachim, 1960-
    382.9

Library of Congress Cataloging-in-Publication Data
Strategic arena switching in international trade negotiations / edited by Wolfgang Blaas and Joachim Becker.
        p. cm.
    Includes bibliographical references and index.
    ISBN-13: 978-0-7546-4916-8   1. International trade. 2. Commercial
policy. 3. Commercial treaties. I. Blaas, Wolfgang. II. Becker, Joachim, 1960-

    HF1379.S766 2006
    382'.9--dc22

                                                                        2006031452

ISBN-13: 9780754649168

Printed and bound in Great Britain by MPG Books Ltd, Bodmin, Cornwall.

Contents

List of Figures

List of Tables

Notes on the Contributors

Joachim Becker is Associate Professor of Economics at the Vienna University of Economcis and Business Studies in Austria. He got his Diploma in Economics and his PhD in Political Science at Philipps-Universität in Marburg (Germany). He also taught at the Universidad de Buenos Aires. His research and teaching areas include political economy, theory of régulation, international development and regional integration.

Wolfgang Blaas is Associate Professor of Economics. He got his Diploma in Mathematics and his PhD in Public Economics at the Vienna University of Technology, Austria, where he is currently employed. His research and teaching areas include economic policy, regional economics, international economics and real estate economics.

Nitsan Chorev is an Assistant Professor at the Department of Sociology, Brown University, USA. She got her PhD at New York University, after which she worked at Central European University (Hungary) and was a fellow at the UCLA International Institute (USA). Her main area of interest is the politics of globalization. In addition to an extensive study of the domestic and international politics of trade policy-formation, she is currently studying the history and politics of international health.

Muchkund Dubey is currently President of the Council for Social Development, a research and advocacy NGO. He was former Foreign Secretary, Government of India, former Professor, Jawaharlal Nehru University. After obtaining his Master's Degree in Economics from Patna University, he taught Economics for a brief period. He studied Economics in Oxford and New York University and joined the Indian Foreign Service and served as India's High Commissioner in Bangladesh and India's Permanent Representative to U.N. organizations in Geneva.

Luiz Augusto E. Faria earned his Doctor of Sciences in Economics at the Federal University of Rio de Janeiro. He is one of the pioneers employing the Regulationist Approach to understand the Brazilian economy. His current research is on international economics, integration and the MERCOSUR. Now he is Associate Professor of Economics at the Economics Department of the Federal University of Rio Grande do Sul and Research Economist of the Economics and Statistics Foundation in Porto Alegre, Brazil.

Weiyu Gao is currently Chief Economic Analyst at Shanghai Development Research Center, China. His research area covers Macroeconomics, International Trade, and Applied Econometrics. He is now an associate research fellow.

Xiaoling Ji is currently a lecturer at Shanghai Normal University in China. With a graduate degree in Political Science and English, her research fields are International Relations and Teaching of English as a Foreign Language.

Werner Raza earned a doctorate in economics from the University of Economics and Business Administration in Vienna, Austria, where he worked as assistant professor of international economics from 1998–2002. His research interests include international trade, liberalization/privatization of (public) services, and international political economy. He currently works as an economist at the Austrian Chamber of Labour and is a lecturer at the University of Economics and Business Administration in Vienna.

Gottfried Wellmer studied evangelical theology at the universities of Göttingen and Heidelberg, Germany. Furthermore he studied at the University of Botswana, Lesotho and Swaziland social aspects of the migratory labour system of South Africa, and he was trained in the economy of developing countries at Heidelberg and served as advisor to the Evangelical Church in Germany on German investments in South Africa. He was then editor of the Information Service on Southern Africa in Bonn, Germany, and later on free lance journalist on Southern Africa. From 1983–1990 he was a member of the Southern Africa group in the Centro de Estudos Africanos at the University Eduardo Mondlane in Mozambique. On his return to Germany he worked first in adult education on South Africa for the trade union federation DGB, later he turned to freelance research. Main research areas are European trade policy towards Southern Africa, Private-Public Partnerships in water services, and postwar relations between Germany and South Africa.

Gaye Yılmaz got her MA degree of Political Sciences at Kassel University and Berlin School of Economics (Germany), and her Bachelor degree from the School of Economics of Marmara University in Istanbul (Turkey). Her main research areas are ongoing processes of international trade in WTO, globalization and regionalization with particular focus on EU, historical development of social dialogue in the EU, international division of labour in the globalization process, service labour and Marxist theory of value. Currently she is working in the International Relations Department of United Metalworkers' Union and starting a PhD programme in Development Economics of Marmara University.

Foreword

Wolfgang Blaas and Joachim Becker

This book is dedicated to the late Egon Matzner, an economist by profession and a homo politicus by passion, whose scientific curiosity paired with social responsibility were productive driving forces throughout his life.

During the last years of his life he worked intensively on various issues of globalisation (Matzner 1997, Matzner 2000, Matzner 2001), and shortly before his all-too-early death in 2003 he initiated a research project "Global Rule Making". The aim of this study was to demonstrate by international contributions that "globalisation" is no law of nature which mankind has to accept as an unavoidable destiny, but that it is a man-made process which is therefore under the control of human beings. The complexity of the who, why and how questions in terms of globalisation control was approached by Matzner via the issue of rule-making on a global scale.

The editors of the book had the privilege to take up the research project which Egon Matzner was no longer able to carry out. We believe that our book, by focusing on forum-switching in international trade negotiations, touches upon one important agenda of global rule-making, i.e. the strategic context-making for trade negotiations. We think, therefore, that our work might be considered as further extending and developing Matzner's intellectual legacy.

We would like to thank the authors of the country chapters who patiently kept a constructive attitude during a long process of production and revision of the respective contributions. We furthermore want to thank the Austrian National Bank (ÖNB) who funded the research project.

References

Matzner, E. (1997), 'Zur Sozioökonomie der Globalisierung und der noch ausstehenden Antwort der EU', in Werner Fricke (Hrsg.), *Jahrbuch Arbeit und Technik*, Köln, Dietz Nachf., pp. 42–58.

Matzner, E. (2000), 'Monopolar World Order – On the Socioeconomics of US Dominance', *Savaria Books on Politics and Society*, (Szombathely: Savaria University Press).

Matzner, E. (2001), 'Argumente für eine Neuregulierung der globalen Finanzen', in *WISO – Wirtschafts- und sozialpolitische Zeitschrift*, Jg. 24 (2001), H. 3, pp. 79–98.

On April 3, 2006, House Ways and Means Committee Chairman Bill Thomas (R-CA) said that the Bush Administration should turn its focus away from the conclusion of the Doha Round and instead negotiate with certain key partners to conclude bilateral and regional trade agreements that Thomas argues would ultimately be more beneficial to the U.S. Thomas was particularly critical of the European Union's (EU) position in the Doha Round and said that the EU and the U.S. have "irreconcilable differences" in their views on trade. Though he conceded that the U.S. cannot simply walk away from the WTO negotiations, he believes the talks should not be its primary focus over the coming months.

WorldTrade\Interactive, Volume 13, Issue 68, Wednesday, 5 April 2006

Abbreviations

ACP	African Caribbean Pacific (group of states)
AGOA	African Growth and Opportunity Act
AIDS	Acquired immunodeficiency syndrome
ANC	African National Congress (South Africa)
APEC	Asia-Pacific Economic Cooperation
ASEAN	Association of South East Asian Nations
AU	African Union
BIMSTEC	Bangladesh India Myanmar Sri Lanka Thailand Economic Cooperation
CAFTA	Central American Free Trade Agreement
CBD	Convention on Bio-Diversity
CCP	Common Commercial Policy
COMESA	Common Market for Eastern and Southern Africa
COSATU	Congress of South African Trade Unions
CSO	Civil Society Organisation
DDA	Doha Development Agenda
DG	Directorate General
DTI	Department of Trade and Industry
EBA	Everything But Arms (EU system of preferences for LDCs)
EC	European Community
ECJ	European Court of Justice
EFTA	European Free Trade Area
EP	European Parliament
EPAs	Economic Partnership Agreements (between the EU and the ACP)
ESA	Eastern and Southern Africa (states negotiating an EPA with EU)
EU	European Union
FDI	Foreign Direct Investment
FIRE	Finance, insurance and business services
FTA	Free Trade Agreement
GATS	General Agreement on Trade in Services
GATT	General Agreement on Trade and Tariffs
GDP	Gross Domestic Product
GEAR	Growth, Employment and Redistribution (South African programme)
GEIS	General Export Incentive Scheme
GSP	Generalized Sytem of Preferences
HIV	Human immuno-deficiency virus
IDC	Industrial Development Corporation (South Africa)
IDDA	Industrial Development Decade for Africa

ISI	Import Substituting Industrialization
IMF	International Monetary Fund
LDCs	Least Developed Countries
LPA	Lagos Plan of Action
MERG	Macro-Economic Research Group
MFN	Most Favoured Nation
MIGA	Multilateral Investment Guarantee Agency
MVA	Manufacturing Value Added
NAMA	Non-Agricultural Market Access
NEPAD	New Partnership for Africa's Development
NF	Non ferrous
NICs	Newly Industrialized Countries
NP	National Party (South Africa)
OECD	Organization for Economic Co-operation and Development
PTA	Preferential Trade Area
QB	Quarterly Bulletin
Q.Rs	Quantity Restrictions
RCA	Revealed Comparative Advantage
RDP	Reconstruction and Development Programme
REC	Regional Economic Community
RoO	Rules of Origin
RSA	Republic of South Africa
RTA	Regional Trade Agreement
SACP	South African Communist Party
SACU	Southern African Customs Union
SADCC	Southern African Development Co-ordination Conference
SADC	Southern African Development Community
SAFTA	Singapore-Australia Free Trade Agreement
SAP	Structural Adjustment Programme
SARB	South African Reserve Bank
SDT	Special and Differential Treatment
SIC	Standard Industrial Classification
SME	Small and Medium Enterprises
SPS	Sanitary and Phytosanitary Measures
SSA	Sub-Saharan Africa
TDCA	Trade and Development Cooperation Agreement
TFP	Total Factor Productivity
TNC	Transnational Corporation
TRIPS	Trade Related Intellectual Property Rights
UNDP	United Nations Development Program
UN-ECA	United Nations Economic Commission for Africa
USTR	Unites States Trade Representative
WTO	World Trade Organization

Chapter 1

Introduction

Joachim Becker and Wolfgang Blaas

Contested arenas

The World Trade Organisation held a ministerial summit in Cancún in September 2003 in order to map the future negotiation agenda. However, the negotiations failed. A number of Third World governments formed the G-20+ and successfully opposed the US- and EU-led agricultural proposals. Furthermore, they were reticent with regard to widening the WTO agenda (Jawara and Kwa 2004, XV ss). Similar criticisms were voiced by NGOs. "It should not be forgotten that some foreign ministers, like those of the Group of the 20+, utilized coincidences (with the NGOs, B/B) on some issues in order to strengthen their position" (Gudynas 2003a, 39).

Similar disputes were to surface again in the debate on an Área de Libre Comercio de las Américas (ALCA) and in the negotiations on a free trade agreement between the European Union (EU) and Mercado Común del Sur (MERCOSUR). It was similar protagonists – the US (and their allies) and the EU on the one hand, Brazil and its allies on the other – and they were similar issues (agriculture, opening up to foreign capital) that came to the fore. In the case of the ALCA negotiations in November 2003, the governments agreed on envisaging an "ALCA light" agreement with a few common provisions and the option to make additional plurilateral agreements among willing governments (Gudynas 2003b). Both the US government and the Brazilian government have contested the South American middle ground. The US government gained a bilateral Free Trade Agreement with Chile and has pressed hard for similar agreements with other Andean states. These (proposed) agreements stretch far beyond goods trade and encompass issues like protection of investments and property rights (Acosta 2004). Brazil promoted the signature of association agreements between MERCOSUR and a number of Latin American Countries and an inter-bloc agreement between MERCOSUR and the Comunidad Andina that is to bring about a Comunidad Sudamericana de Naciones. The latter is to be confined to issues of goods trade (Ruiz Caro 2004). Parallel to these Inter-American and Intra-South-American trade negotiations, the EU was engaged in negotiations on a free trade agreement with MERCOSUR. By the end of October 2004, these negotiations stalled on the issue of agricultural goods and issues of government procurement, public monopolies and some other investment related measures (Pagina/12,

13/10/2004, Raza 2004). While several of the bilateral or plurilateral negotiations were stagnating or entering into a phase of crisis, the negotiators forged a (shaky) compromise in the WTO which opened the way for re-launching global trade negotiations at the end of July of 2004 (Evia/Gudynas 2004). In an almost parallel move, Third World governments attempted to reinvigorate the UN Conference on Trade and Development (UNCTAD) as an alternative negotiation arena at the XI UNCTAD summit in São Paulo in June 2004 (Gudynas 2004).

This short outline of just a couple of months of just a part of the international trade negotiations demonstrates that similar agendas are pursued in multiple negotiation arenas. If one avenue is closed, another one is tried. *This is the issue dealt with in this book*. We use both the term *arena switching* and *forum shifting* for this phenomenon.

Recent trade negotiations have displayed a significant degree of arena switching. Though "very few actors in the context of global regulation have the capacity to run strategies of forum-shifting" (Braithwaite and Drahos 2000, 565), these have not been confined to the two main players – i.e. the US government and the EU Commission. Some Third World middle powers, like Brazil, have occasionally tried these strategies also. Forum-shifting is a field that is politically quite relevant though, until now, hardly systematically explored. The focus of existing studies usually has been on the US or the European states (cf. esp. Braithwaite/Drahos 2000, cap. 24, Picciotto 1996). Nevertheless, Third World middle powers have played an increasingly prominent role in recent trade negotiations. Therefore, in our study, we intend to broaden the focus analysing the pro-active and reactive role of Third World middle powers in arena-shifting. We shall explore the dialectics of forum-shifting strategies of the dominant powers of the USA and the EU on the one hand, and of Third World middle powers on the other hand. Among the latter group, we have selected China, India, South Africa, Brazil and Turkey. These countries can be categorised in three sub-groups in regard to their regional alliances. China and India go it – more or less – alone. South Africa and Brazil are at the heart of regional groupings, while Turkey is associated with the EU and seeks full entry into the EU. These different positions are likely to have an influence on the respective trade negotiation strategies.

Theorising strategies of accumulation

International trade negotiations are a rather complex affair. There are state and non-state actors. There are complex lines of conflict, and these lines of conflict are to be explained. Some traditional theories of international relations are not well suited to dealing with these complexities. (Neo-)Realists only see state actors (e.g. Morgenthau 1993). They view states as "volitional entities" (hence often assume "unitary actors") (Palan 2000, 5). The relations between states are primarily analysed as power relations. This school can deal with conflicts between states. However, it is ill-equipped to deal with conflicts within the state. Other collective actors, i.e.

the whole civil society, are not present in their view. Theorists of international regimes like Krasner (1983) emphasise rules, norms and principles that enable a coherent behaviour of actors in the international arena and, thus, provide for stability in international relations. Thus, their theoretical approach is ill-suited to dealing with instability and conflict (Palan 1998). Besides, both strands of thinking display difficulties in dealing with the relationship between the economic and political sphere.

Approaches of critical international economy and of the theory of régulations are more suitable for these issues. They draw on Marxist, evolutionary institutionalist, and historical sociological traditions (Palan 2000, 7) as well, and in the case of the régulationist approach, to some extent on the Keynesian and post-Keynesian tradition (Boyer 1987, Orléan 1999). In their view, capitalist accumulation is not a smooth process. It is beset by instability and conflicting interests. These conflicting interests are processed by institutions. The mediation does not lead necessarily to a compromise. Thus, instability might persist. Though the concrete shape of these approaches differs, all of them pay attention to the particularities of historical time and social space.

The régulationist approach

International trade agreements have an impact on economic development. Positions on these issues taken by actors in civil society and by governments are shaped by their economic strategies and, in the case of wage workers, by the back side of accumulation, i.e. the reproduction and living conditions of the labour force. In order to deal with economic strategies, it is useful to have a framework that permits the identification of central traits of such strategies. The régulationist approach has developed such a conceptual framework. From a régulationist perspective, three typological axes of accumulation can be identified:

1. accumulation of productive or "ficticious" capital,
2. extensive or intensive accumulation,
3. intraverted or extraverted accumulation (Becker 2002, 76).

1. The first distinction is between a predominantly productive and a predominantly financial accumulation. From a Keynesian perspective, investors compare the rates of return of productive investments and different forms of financial investments. When the rate of return of financial investments is comparatively higher, a predominantly financial accumulation will prevail. Such investments are highly liquid, and changing perceptions rapidly exercise an influence on financial placements. Thus, they are inherently volatile (Orléan 1999). Keynes pointed out that high interest rates are an impediment to investment, and he was quite critical about the rentier's role in capitalism (Keynes 1997, 221, 376). Marx mainly analysed the productive circuit of capital. However, he pointed out that a second circuit of capital in the form of property titles (shares, bonds, real estate) does exist as well. He named this second

form of capital "ficticious capital" (Marx 1979, 482 seq., 510, cf. also Hilferding 1974, part II). The ficticious capital represents a claim on the surplus produced by productive capital. To this extent, the two circuits are linked. However, the financial investors might misjudge the profit prospects of their placements. For a certain time, they might be overly optimistic. The price of ficticious capital will rise. At one point, the euphoric mood will be sobered by the concrete realities of a lower than expected surplus made by the venture concerned. A fall of prices will ensue. The second circuit is extremely unstable from a Marxian perspective as well. Thus, both strands of régulationist thinking – the rather Keynesian one and the Marxist one – agree that a predominantly financial accumulation is inherently unstable (Orléan 1999, Plihon 2003, 41 et seq., Chesnais 1996, 253 ss, Chesnais 2004, 45 seq.). Authors like Harvey (1984, 304, 324 et seq.) and Arrighi (1994) see a relationship between a crisis of productive accumulation and the tendency towards financial accumulation. In such a situation, capital is faced with only reduced options for productive investments and increasing uncertainty. Thus, it looks for highly liquid forms of investment which allow for rapid reactions to changing conditions (Arrighi 1994, 221 et seq.). If there is a rush towards such forms of financial placements, prices of financial assets will rise – for some time. However, financial investments are unlikely to prove a way out of the malaise of productive accumulation in the long run. The financial sphere cannot totally emancipate itself from the productive sphere. Financial instability is likely to ensue. Stockhammer (2004, chap. 5) argues the other way round. In his view, there might and recently often did occur a "'shareholder revolution', that is the development of a market for corporate control and the reorientation of management priorities along the lines of creating shareholder value" leading "to a reduction in the growth rate desired by firms" (Stockhammer 2004, 164). Insofar as there is a trade-off between company growth and profits, this leads to a reduction of (productive) investment. Though there is a consensus on the relationship between slackening productive investment and financialisation, the views on causality diverge.

2.   The second analytic distinction is between predominantly intensive and predominantly extensive accumulation. It is based on how productivity growth is achieved and on how productivity growth and macro-economic development are linked. The conceptualisation of intensive and extensive accumulation was first developed by Aglietta (1987, 71 et seq.). He argued from a Marxist perspective. Therefore, his concept refers to the way relative surplus value is produced. In a predominantly extensive regime of accumulation, relative surplus value is achieved by the reorganisation of the labour process. The way of living of wage labour is not necessarily transformed in a predominantly extensive regime of accumulation. It might be that wage labourers' consumption is still partly based on goods produced in petty commodity production. There is not a strong link between the capital goods and consumer goods sector. In the predominantly intensive regime of accumulation, wage goods become cheaper. In such a regime of accumulation, workers consume goods almost exclusively produced in the capitalist sphere of production. The capital goods and consumer goods sector are strongly linked. According to Aglietta (1987,

72), growth is smoother and more rapid in the predominantly intensive regime of accumulation than in the predominantly extensive one.

Regulationists who argue from a post-Keynesian perspective have a slightly different conceptualisation though the same points are at the heart of their distinction. In the view of Mazier et al. (1993, 7), predominantly extensive accumulation is characterised by limited changes in the organisation of production and low productivity growth. Growth is based on the extension of wage labour. Consumption is only to a limited extent based on goods produced in a capitalist way. Therefore, insufficient demand is a recurrent limit to growth in this regime of accumulation. "In contrast to this, in a regime of intensive accumulation, conditions of production are systematically transformed with a view to increasing the productivity of labour. New investments primarily take the form of an increase in the capital stock per worker" (Juillard 2002, 154).

Thus, both currents stress the relationships between the development of productive forces, distribution, consumption and the links between the capital goods and consumer goods sector. This typology has been derived from the development trajectories of the industrialised states. However, the trajectory of today's peripheral and semi-peripheral states has differed from that of the industrialised states, inter alia, in so far as a capital goods sector usually has been lacking in phases of both extensive and intensive accumulation (Cartier Bresson/Kopp 1982, 326 et seq., Ominami 1986, 119 et seq., Mello 1998, 102 et seq). In their case, productivity growth has been dependent to a considerable extent on the import of machinery (and technology at large). Thus, their dynamics have had an important external imprint. There have been only a few exceptions where a significant capital goods sector has been developed. Amongst these exceptions are India, China and – for a while from the 1970s onwards – Brazil.

3.   This brings us to the third typological distinction, i.e. the distinction between extroverted and introverted accumulation. It deals with the relationship between the domestic and international markets, i.e. the share of exports and imports of goods, services and capital in relation to domestic activities.

First of all, we have to differentiate between different forms of activities, i.e. production of goods and services, productive and financial investment, and to some extent migration (cf. Beaud 1987, 71, Becker 2002, 70 et seq.). The role of activities focused on the domestic market and the role of exports and imports need not be necessarily of the same proportion in all of these spheres. The export quota might be high in the case of goods exports, but insignificant in the case of the export of productive or financial capital. Therefore, the issue of extroversion and introversion is to be tackled in a way differentiated enough to deal with an uneven degree of extraversion and introversion in a national or regional economy.

Secondly, it makes a difference whether international relations are predominantly based on exports or imports of goods and capital. An active extraversion relies on the export of goods and/or capital. Both forms of exports earn foreign exchange (at least when the exports are destined to a different monetary space). Thus, they lessen the foreign exchange constraint. A passive extraversion is characterised by the predominance of the import of goods and/or capital. A negative trade balance and the importation of capital (FDI or financial placements) are often linked to each other. A negative trade balance needs to be financed by the importation of capital. However, the import of capital will inevitably lead to foreign exchange payments of interest or profits at a later stage. In turn, this worsens the current account. Thus, the foreign exchange constraint is tightened. A passive introversion or import-based development is very vulnerable to changes in the international arena and prone to crisis. In its more pronounced varieties, passive introversion is often the long-term result of colonially inherited "dependent development" (Cardoso/Faletto 1976).

Michel Beaud (1987, 71 et seq.) links the type of extroversion to the issue of dominance in international economic relations. In his view, dominant national economies are characterised by significant foreign direct investment abroad. Investment and production decisions taken by companies with headquarters in a dominant economy shape the dynamics in other national (or regional) economies. They influence the goods trade which is to a considerable extent an intra-company trade. Dominated national economies are characterised by a considerable degree of foreign control over their production. Strategic investment (and disinvestment) decisions are taken abroad. To a considerable extent, the dynamics of the national economy are shaped by external actors. The export and import of financial capital produces similar relationships of domination and subordination.

However, elements of active and passive extroversion might co-exist. An interesting example is the present US economy. Export and import ratios are rather low, though imports have been consistently higher than exports over the last decade. There is a considerable US FDI abroad. However, the US economy is highly dependent on the import of financial capital in order to finance the highly negative trade balance and domestic consumption. In 2002, the US was the main importer of capital world wide accounting for 76 percent of all capital imports (Zeller 2004, 87, graph 2). It cannot be said that the US economy is a dominated economy. However, the reliance on capital imports indicates an increasing vulnerability.

The degree and character of extraversion has obvious consequences for strengths and vulnerabilities in international trade negotiations. In the case of a highly introverted development, low reliance on foreign capital and goods imports and a large domestic market, external vulnerability is very low. For decades, the US was in such a privileged position; however, lately its vulnerability has grown. Taken as a bloc, the EU would be in a similar position. There seem to be only very few candidates for a similar position in the future. China is among them (Frank/Manzenreiter 2005). India also might be a possible candidate. An active extroversion gives more leverage to negotiators. Highly import dependent states are in the weakest position.

Theorising arenas of norm making

The dominant economic strategies need adequate social, political and legal norms in order to be pursued with some measure of success. However, the demands of different factions of capital are likely to differ in some important respects. Thus, nation-states and international organisation have to deal with conflicting demands arising from accumulation strategies. National and international norm making cannot just be derived from dominant forms of accumulation. Furthermore, norm making is not just linked to accumulation. Other social demands are voiced as well. Accumulation strategies and norm making deeply affect social reproduction which is a sphere often neglected by liberal and critical economists alike (Moulaert/Swyngedouw 1989, 340, Peterson 2003, 79 et seq.). Demands concerning these two spheres might be highly conflicting. For example, service sector capital might be pressing for the privatisation of social services which might quite negatively affect social reproduction of large social groups and might thereby be leading to a deterioration or even informalisation of working conditions. In turn, this will affect the legitimacy of the governing parties, the state, and, possibly, the prevailing social order. Thus, struggles over national and international norm making are not just about accumulation, but they are about social reproduction as well. Therefore, the political actors are not confined to the capital/labour nexus, but might include peasant, feminist, ecological and other groups as well.

There is a strong link between the nation-states and international norm making. It is nation-states that are represented in the relevant international organisations. However, they are not alone in shaping international norms. At the international level, interest groups intervene in the process of norm making, liaising with the relevant parts of the bureaucracy of the nation-state and/or of the international organisation. In turn, international norms shape national norm and policy making. Thus, there is a dialectical relationship between the national and international level of norm making.

Since both nation-state governments and international organisations are involved in international trade negotiations, it is useful to tackle both of them conceptually. We shall begin with policy making at the nation-state level, and, then, proceed to discuss the international level. The capitalist state can be perceived as a specific social relation (Poulantzas 2002, 55 et seq.). "This implies that the exercise of state power (or, better, state powers in the plural) involves a form-determined condensation of the changing balance of forces. In other words, state power reflects the prevailing balance of forces as this is institutionally mediated through the state apparatus with its structurally inscribed strategic selectivity. Adopting this approach, the state can be defined as a relatively unified ensemble of socially embedded, socially regularised, and strategically selective institutions, organisations, social forces and activities organised around (or at least involved in) making collectively binding decisions for an imagined political community" (Jessop 2002, 40).

The state and international organisations are strategically selective. Following Jessop (2002, 40), "by strategic selectivity, (we) understand the ways by which the state considered as a social ensemble has a specific, differential impact on the ability of various political forces to pursue particular interests and strategies in specific spatio-temporal contexts through their access to and/or control over given state capacities". We shall highlight the main elements of strategic selectivity of states and international organisations. We shall deal with the strategic selectivity of states and international organisations separately since there are some noteworthy differences between the two.

The state's fiscal dependence on flourishing business is a first and very important element of strategic selectivity (Becker 2002, 131, Jessop 1990, 178 et seq., Hirsch 1990, 45 ss.). This endows business with a structural advantage over other social classes and interest groups. However, it is not possible to derive specific policies from the imperative of accumulation. In principle, these policies can take a variety of forms. The concrete outcome of state policies is influenced by several elements of strategic selectivity.

Gramsci (1971, 12) underlined that the state needs to be understood in relationship to civil society. Civil society is formed by numerous political and social "private" organisations. Interest groups with external roots, like transnational corporations, might be part, even an important part, of civil society. Thus, civil society is open to influences stemming from outside the national territory. Furthermore, civil society organisations might seek external allies (other NGOs, states or international organisations) in order to compensate for their domestic weaknesses (Cisař 2004). Civil society organisations are unequal in terms of resources, capacities to bring forward their demands, and ability to form external alliances etc. They strive to make the larger civil society accept their social norms and visions and to make the state adopt the policies and rules that they propose. Their ultimate purpose is to exercise "hegemony". In line with Gramsci, Jessop (2002, 6) defines "hegemony as the exercise of political, intellectual and moral leadership over a given political space in such a way as to bring social forces and institutions into conformity with the requirements of capitalist reproduction in a particular period". However, "hegemony" is not always reached. There might be a stalemate of contending groups.

Public debate is an essential vehicle in hegemonic strategies. Intellectuals play an important role in it. However, not all activities of civil society organisation are in the public limelight. There might as well be small lobby groups negotiating with agencies of the state behind closed doors in order to make them adopt their preferred rules or policies.

Political parties are a third strategic element of selectivity. They condense certain social demands and bring them to the parliamentary fora and, possibly, to the government.

The configuration of the state institutions is a fourth element of strategic selectivity. In order to influence policies, civil society groups need to approach specific agencies of the state, like the parliament, the bureaucracy of the ministries, autonomous authorities etc. (Bobbio 1988, 11 et seq., 86 et seq., Jessop 1990, 177 et seq., Becker 2002, 136 et seq.). The role of political parties in policy making depends to some extent on the legislative and control powers a parliament possesses. The distribution of power among the different branches of state is not a trivial issue, but decisively shapes the possible outcome of struggles over policies. For example, trade unions have relied (at least in Europe) on the parliamentary channel for a long time to get pro-union policies passed. A de-parliamentarisation of the state (or the loss of their long-term political party allies) would significantly affect their capacity to influence public policies. However, it is not just an issue of the relationship between parliament and government. For example, there has been a proliferation of autonomous authorities that, while formally being part of the state, hardly underlie any form of public accountability to parliament or ministries (Swyngedouw 2000, 447). Therefore, they enjoy considerable freedom from public scrutiny. On the one hand, they are less constrained by the demands made on the state in terms of popular legitimacy. On the other hand, they might be more permeable to the influence of small, but powerful social groups.

The recruitment rules for state personnel are a fifth element of strategic selectivity. The educational background and, more generally, the socialisation of state functionaries especially in the higher echelons, matters. This background endows them with certain social and political affinities which would not be without consequences for the policies they propose.

The concrete form of strategic elements of state selectivity are not fixed once and for all. Since their configuration impacts on the power relations, they are subject to endeavours to change them into this or that direction – as it suits the different social actors. The resulting pressures for constitutional or administrative reforms are likely to be particularly intense in times of profound socio-economic change.

The scale of the state institutions impacts as well on power relations. Social and political actors have different access to the diverse territorial layers of the state (municipality, region, national state, eventually supra-national state). Thus, the reconfiguration of spatial layers of the state might be an essential plank of state reform.

From spatial state reforms, entirely new layers of a state or even a new embryonic form of the state might eventually emerge. The emergence of the EU is an example of the latter. From modest beginnings, it has developed into a new hybrid form of a state. It has been equipped with some attributes of the state – like its own legislation, its own jurisdiction, its own money (though the European currency does not yet cover all EU states; cf. Ziltener 1999, 22 et seq.). However, the EU still lacks other attributes of a state, like its own forces of coercion. A European civil society is still weakly developed. EU state institutions are a mixture of supranational and international elements. The European Parliament and the European Commission are supranational institutions. The powers of the European Parliament are still relatively circumscribed. They stop far short of full legislative and budgetary powers. In contrast, the position of the European Commission is extremely strong covering legislative powers (a near monopoly on drafting legislation), executive powers and even some jurisdictional powers (supervising the implementation of EU legislation by member states). The Council of Ministers as an international institution has far-reaching legislative powers. Thus, EU institutions are extremely biased towards the executive branches of the state and lack a thorough separation of powers. Therefore, they are rather well insulated from popular pressures (Staniszkis 2004, 192, 198 et seq.).

With a few, though very significant exceptions, international norm making has not been in the public limelight. This implies that lobbying endeavours are often quite important. International norms are usually prepared by a specialised ministerial bureaucracy (or by the bureaucrats of autonomous bodies). The bureaucracy that deals with international issues usually has a specific esprit de corps. Parliaments are usually involved in the last stage of the process – i.e. ratification. Thus, there is a specific selectivity of the nation-state as far as its role in international norm making is concerned (cf. Halliday 2005, 50).

Both national governments and national and international civil society groups impact on the making of international norms and rules. International – more precisely inter-state – organisations are the fora where international norms and rules are forged. Insofar as they are norm-producing political bodies, international organisations are on a continuum with the state as a political form. However, their polity, their means of regulation, and their enforcement mechanisms are different from the (national) state. Their strategic selectivity is constructed in different ways from the national state's selective filters.

First of all, only an incipient international civil society exists. International campaigning does exist, but it is a rather exceptional occurrence. International debates have to be channelled through mainly national (or occasionally regional) media. The international public space is extremely fragmented (Roth 2001, 61, Aguiton 2002, 90). International lobbying efforts seem to be much more important than international campaigning. For international activities of civil society groups, requirements are high in terms of financial resources, language and educational abilities (e.g. the ability to use the "jargon" of international organisations). Therefore, the incipient international civil society is probably more unequal than the national ones. The challenges are enormous, particularly for NGOs and social movements originating in the Third World. They have to contend with norms of organisations standards, language, and topics that are by and large defined by the west (Wahl 1999, 43, Brand et al. 2000, 127). International organisations might grant access to (some) meetings to some NGOs or might provide consultative mechanisms to NGOs. On the one hand, this might increase the transparency of international negotiations. On the other hand, the inclusion into consultative fora might absorb a disproportional part of NGOs' working capacity while offering very little say in the decision-making process (Brand et al. 2000, 120 et seq., Wahl 2001, 134). The line between consultation and cooptation is a thin one, indeed.

Secondly international organisations are not dependent on direct fiscal revenue. Nevertheless, they depend on the contribution of member states. In extremis, key member states might invoke the financial power that they yield by threatening their withdrawal and eventually implementing it. This has direct consequences for the international organisation in question and it has indirect consequences for its international standing and legitimacy (Braithwaite/Drahos 2000, 564).

Thirdly, the institutional set-up of international organisations is crucially important yet different from the national state. It is usually governments (and only governments) that are represented in international organisations and entitled to vote in their decision-making bodies. The weight members carry depends to some extent on the formal and informal decision-making mechanisms.

Voting rules might give an equal voting right to each member states, as it is the case with UN organisations or the WTO, or they might distribute voting power according to the economic weight of the contributors, as in the case of international financial organisations like IMF and World Bank. Aglietta and Moatti (2000, 28) describe the consequences of this formula in the following way: "Due to the preponderance of the Western industrialised countries, the Fund has always expressed a specific consensus on economic diagnosis and prescriptions while becoming an almost universal institution." The prescriptions are specifically pro-western in outlook. Even within the group of Western countries, the US has enjoyed an exceptional status in the IMF because US voting rights surpass by far the second strongest member state and it has preserved a veto right on some crucial issues (ibid., 28). In the IMF and World Bank, openly biased voting procedures have preserved Western control over these organisations. However, they have exposed these organisations to criticism based on their lack of internal democracy and equality among the members.

It is not just the voting rights that matter. It is also of crucial importance which type of majority needs to be achieved in order to make a decision. There might be a simple majority, a qualified majority or unanimity. As a general rule, a broad consensus might be deemed necessary. Consensus-based decision-making implies avoiding formal voting as much as possible. In GATT/WTO, a decision of consensus is deemed to have been taken on a matter if no signatory, present at the meeting, formally objects to the proposed decision (Steinberg 2002, 345). A broad consensus gives broad legitimacy to a decision. This is one of the reasons why it is adopted although decision-making might be rather cumbersome (ibid., 345). In addition, it provides an incentive to the participants in the decision-making process to reveal their priorities. Acquiring this knowledge is valuable to key players because it enables them to deal with the respective priorities in an appropriate way (ibid., 363). At first glance, consensus-based decision-making favours relatively weak states. Formally, they might block decisions that are fundamentally contrary to their interests. De facto, they might be subject to informal coercion, like cutting of development aid in case of "unruly" behaviour (cf. Jawara/Kwa 2004, 150 et seq., Kapoor 2004, 553). Majority voting is less consensual; its outcome largely depends on formal voting rules (majority requirements, pondering of votes).

Before votes are taken, decisions need to be prepared. This process usually consists of formal and informal elements. Even a formally inclusive process of agenda- and decision-making might de facto be exclusive. In the WTO multiple agendas are debated at the same time. Small states lacking a resourceful foreign service cannot cope with these multiple demands. At best, they are able to deal with most the pressing issues. A lack of resources leads to their de facto marginalisation (Jawara/Kwa 2004, 21 et seq.). Furthermore, agenda-setting is often done in informal and much more restrictive meetings. In that case, the negotiation process is predetermined de facto by a restricted number of key players. Usually, this has been the case with international trade negotiations (Steinberg 2002, 354 et seq.).

Fourthly, the bureaucracy of international organisations plays an essential role in drafting documents and steering negotiations that goes beyond a merely "technical" support. It is the bureaucracy that prepares documents, makes some of the proposals or tables packages. In doing so, it might give a certain direction to negotiations.

Recruitments rules and staffing policies shape the composition of the bureaucracy. In turn, this affects the ways in which the bureaucracy pursues its (or adopts others') agenda (Steinberg 2002, 356, Jawara/Kwa 2004, chapter 7).

Fifthly, the enforcement of rules always has an element of interpretation. Hoping for an interpretation favourable to their interests, members of a convention might deliberately opt for litigation to achieve in this way what they could not achieve explicitly in negotiations (Smith 2004, 551).

It is useful to distinguish quasi-legal forms of enforcement and other forms of sanctioning unruly behaviour. In the case of quasi-legal enforcement rules, the contracting parties might submit to "private" arbitration tribunals or to dispute settlement units of the organisations. Technical and financial requirements to file a suit might be quite high – or even be prohibitively high for Third World states (Smith 2004, 548). Furthermore, there is the question of how decisions will be enforced. The international trade system relies heavily on trade sanctions in order to make members comply with findings in a litigious case. This "tends to favour larger markets" (ibid., 548). States with large markets can effectively punish offenders by restricting access to their market and they can more easily absorb the effects of sanctions imposed by another litigious party with the approval by the dispute settlement unit. In contrast, sanctions imposed by small states have little effect.

The IMF makes individual agreements with debtor states. Non-compliance is not sanctioned by a quasi-legal mechanism, but by withholding the disbursement of IMF funds. The direct effects of that measure usually are not high. However, such an IMF decision prompts other financial institutions to follow suit. They will also cut off the "offending" state from credit. This is an informal, but extremely effective form of enforcement.

Thus, enforcement rules have their in-built biases, as well.

Sixthly, spatial configuration matters. International organisations, rules and norms might be global in character or they might be regionally circumscribed. In negotiations, the power balance is directly affected by the question of who actually participates in the negotiation process and who does not and what is the relationship between the eventually contracting parties.

Furthermore, the space of norms depends on the spatial arena of negotiations. In the case of regionalised treaties, a globally fragmented space of norms and rules will emerge. Such a space enables economic actors (or at least some of them) to select from among different regulatory sets. Regionalised treaties and norms might create a zone of some exclusivity in terms of market access for goods or service exporters and investors. Such regional, bilateral or plurilateral agreements might fit particularly well with (neo-)mercantilist strategies (cf. Heckscher 1934, 325 et seq.) since they create specific advantages for economic actors that have specific national roots.

The norms evolving from the multiplicity of international organisations are not necessarily in harmony. Divergent social and state interests might prevail in different fora. International rules and norms are most likely to be rather coherent when one state representing a specific social bloc is in a "hegemonic" position. This implies that this "hegemonic" state takes into account the interest of other states in order to facilitate their acceptance of the norms proposed by the "hegemon". A state cannot play a hegemonic role without being a leading economic power having a competitive edge in the productive sphere and playing an outstanding role in international finance (cf. Cox 1987, 147 et seq., 265 et seq.).

Theorising switching of arenas of negotiation

The role of existing international organisations is redefined or new venues for rule and norm making are opened up in times of crisis (Gerbier 2001, 116 et seq.). Likewise, it is in these times that forum switching is most likely to occur. Though it is governments that finally decide which negotiation arenas to favour, civil society organisations – both national and international – seek to influence the process of arena selection, too.

Criteria for selection

The first factor to be taken into account is the strategies of civil society organisations in regard to international organisations and their role in international norm making. The demands originating from civil society groups are related either to accumulation or questions of social reproduction. Civil society organisations might even object to making certain norms at an international level at all. They might prefer to confine norm making in a given field to the national (or local) level (cf. Barša/Císař 2004, 183 et seq.).

Civil society groups favour arenas where governments who are rather close to their demands are particularly strong. Furthermore, they have to take into account the issue of transparency. Groups with broad popular support and a capacity for political mobilisation are likely to favour fora where the negotiation process is transparent and, thus, offers chances for public intervention. On the contrary, narrow interest groups with excellent access to key government officials have a preference for fora where negotiations are close to the chest of a few officials and where little information leaks to a broader public.

Secondly, the institutional set-up and enforcement rules are a criterion for selecting specific fora. Different institutional settings for negotiations, norm making and rule enforcement offer different opportunities for state actors (and social interest groups which they represent; cf. Braithwaite/Drahos 2000, 565).

Thirdly, the spatial realm – global or regionally circumscribed – is important. It has an impact on power relations in the negotiations. It results either in globally universal norms or in a diversity of rules and norms. The latter opens the way to picking the most suitable norms at least to some economic actors and creates privileged economic relationships among a specific group of states.

Modes of selection

Forum-shifting can be pursued in a number of ways. Key players in international negotiations can threaten to withdraw from certain fora and eventually take such a step. This damages the organisation in question both in terms of finances and prestige. Such a strategy has been pursued in particular by the USA. "Part of its thinking behind abandonment is that the abandoned international organisation will be shocked into a more compliant mode of behaviour, endeavouring to woo back the world's most powerful state (and its financial contributions) with more favourable policies and attitudes" (Braithwaite/Drahos 2000, 564). This strategy can be individually pursued by a few key states only.

Alternatively, a state or a group of like-minded states might shift an agenda from one global forum to another in order to increase the likelihood of success. A certain agenda might be pursued in a couple of different global fora in order to see where to impose it best.

Finally, an agenda might be pursued not just at the global level, but in regional, plurilateral or bilateral negotiations as well. To some extent, the latter might prejudice the outcome of global negotiations by creating regulatory "faits accomplis" in incipiently geographically more circumscribed areas. Alternatively, bilateral or plurilateral negotiations might create at least some regional fall-back options. From a perspective of national neo-mercantilism, the geographically limited character of a norm or rule might even be an advantage over a global one since it gives "national operators" a particular edge over third parties.

In the realm of forum switching, key players are at an obvious advantage. They can blackmail the organisation in question and other players by credibly threatening their withdrawal. They are more likely to be able to define agendas in different types of international organisations. In terms of resources, they are better equipped to negotiate in various fora in parallel. It is mainly a few Western states (US and EU) and, to some extent, some regional Third World powers that have such means at their disposal. "Clearly, very few actors in the context of global regulation have the capacity to run strategies of forum-shifting. In fact, as we shall see, only the US has used this strategy with any frequency", conclude Braithwaite and Drahos (2000, 565). In exceptional circumstances, however, weaker states can form large alliances which through numerical strength and pooled resources might attempt to shift fora too. This was the case when the Non-Aligned Movement and G-77 attempted to highlight UNCTAD to the detriment of GATT in the 1970s.

In the following, we shall outline some basic traits of forum shifting in international trade negotiations. We shall confine ourselves to the post-World-War II era because forum-shifting has evolved into a significant phenomenon only after 1945 (Braithwaite/Drahos 2000, 564).

Forum-shifting in international trade negotiations: A short history

Before 1945, international trade negotiations were located usually at a bilateral or plurilateral level. In the North-South dimension, colonial powers imposed trade policies on their colonies. The few remaining independent states, like China or the Ottoman Empire, usually had to accept highly inequitable treaties (e.g. Owen 2002,

108 et seq.). In the interwar years, attempts at international rule-making failed. With the exacerbation of the 1929 crisis, national states searched for individual ways out of the crisis often adopting beggar-thy-neighbour policies.

Towards the end of the Second World War, the major powers were looking for ways of international norm-making that would preclude a repetition of the experience of the interwar years. New international organisations dealing with international trade, international finance and reconstruction were to be founded. One of these initiatives aimed at founding an International Trade Organisation (ITO). The ITO proved to be a still-born child. The international trade agenda was moved to GATT which had come into being as part of the ITO endeavour. Thus, forum shifting was adopted as a strategic device already at the very beginning of systematic rule and norm making for international trade. The US was the prime mover in this shift.

The second significant attempt at forum-shifting in international trade negotiations was made during the crisis of the 1970s. At that time, it was not the US or any of the other major western governments that tried to shift the forum, but a large group of Third World governments. They tried to empower UNCTAD to the detriment of GATT. In the UNCTAD arena, they hoped to push through a formula that would stabilise the prices of raw materials, commonly their main export product. In the end, they failed in this endeavour. However, they were able to strike a more advantageous deal in the GATT negotiations than otherwise would have been the case. Former colonies of the European powers were able to negotiate a highly favourable agreement with the European Economic Community.

The third significant attempt of forum-shifting occurred after the demise of state socialism in the 1990s. It witnessed the end of GATT and the formation of the WTO with a much larger agenda and a treaty that was much more constraining for Third World states. However, negotiations in the WTO have been conflict-ridden and there has emerged a tendency towards bilaterism and plurilateralism.

We shall look at these three historic examples in more detail in order to contextualise the recent attempts at forum-shifting.

From aborted ITO to GATT

Planning for the post-war international order began already before the end of the war. The Anglo-American perspective on a new international order was first formulated in the Atlantic Charter in 1941. On the one hand, the Charter stressed the desire to reduce tariffs and to eliminate discriminatory treatment in international trade relations; on the other hand, it highlighted the concern for full employment and social welfare (cf. Graz 1999, 82 et seq.). These two priorities were not in perfect harmony. On the contrary, there was a tension between them, and they were defended by different social actors. In the USA, internationalised capital and one group of trade unionists came strongly out in favour of restoring an unequivocally international trade regime. Policies of economic stabilisation and welfare were to be subordinated to this. They had a very sympathetic ear in some branches of the state administration. It was especially sections of the trade unions that favoured a rather strong element of macro-economic planning and would have liked to make the liberalisation of international trade contingent on that. Another group of trade unions viewed trade liberalisation and social welfare for the majorities of the population as being at least in a tense relationship. Similar debates occurred in Britain, the second key state for shaping the new international economic order. Business interests and the corresponding current among the Tories favoured the option of international liberalism, whereas the Labour Party and Trade Unions stressed the need for macro-economic stability and social welfare (Graz 1999, Chapter 4 and 5). The British debate had a special taint, as imperial interests clustered around the City wanted to preserve preferential relations with British (ex-) colonies (Cain/Hopkins 1993, 269 et seq.). The balance was tilted closer to the liberalising position in the US government than in the British government. However, the tension was to persist through the negotiations. It reflected the contradictory relationship between two different key demands on both national and international regulation: on the one hand, demands linked to internationalised accumulation strategies voiced by sections of business and demands linked to the reproduction of the wage workers and social welfare on the other hand. The latter was crucial for the legitimisation of the social order and the state. Restoring or consolidating legitimacy was not a minor concern for the ruling circles in the Western states for the post-war era. Due to crisis and war, capitalism had lost a lot of legitimacy, and capitalist states were to face the political (and later military) competition of the Soviet Union, which was to emerge economically weakened but politically strengthened from World War II (Hobsbawm 1994, 271 et seq.).

The US and British governments envisaged three key international economic organisations: the IMF, World Bank, and ITO to be supplemented by the UN Economic and Social Council (ECOSOC). Though the IMF was to deal with international financial relations, some trade related issues were debated in the founding phase of the IMF, too. The British Treasury adopted the plan developed by John Maynard Keynes. Keynes proposed a multilateral payment system. Both deficit and excedentary countries should be obliged to make adjustments in order to reduce the disequilibria in the balance of payments. An international accounting unit, Bancor, was to be introduced and the conversion of Bancor into gold was to be ruled out (cf. Aglietta/Moatti 2000, 12 et seq.). From Keynes' point of view, the international monetary system should be freed from the rigidities of the gold standard. Neo-mercantilist strategies, which had been predominant in the search for a way out of the 1929 crisis, should be precluded by penalising countries with a permanent surplus of the current account. The US position shared the vision of a multilateral system. However, the US position diverged from the British one in crucial aspects. Since the US was likely to run a positive balance of trade and to export capital, the US government objected to the idea that excedentary countries need to take measures of adjustment, too. Furthermore, they wanted to establish the dollar as the key anchor of the international financial system, and they were in favour of maintaining convertibility between the dollar and gold. Due to the balance of forces of the time, it was basically the US position that prevailed (cf. Aglietta/Moatti 2000, 14 et seq.).

The US government was also the key player in establishing a post-war international trading system. The US government pursued a two-pronged strategy. On the one hand, it launched the initiative for the creation of an International Trade Organisation (ITO) in the realm of the United Nations. This endeavour culminated in the formulation of the Havana Charter in March 1948. On the other hand, it proposed international negotiations on the reduction of obstacles to international trade. Such a conference was held from April to October 1947 in Geneva. The 23 participating countries prepared a General Agreement on Tariffs and Trade (Rainelli 1996, 17). Thus, the *US government created the option of forum-switching from the very beginning of post-war institution making.*

The negotiations leading to the GATT were more focused both in terms of the number of participants and the contents of the eventual treaty. They related mainly to trade in goods, esp. the principle of most favoured nation, differentiated approaches to different kind of goods (e.g. industrial and agricultural goods), the position of regional trade blocs and derogations from free trade principles (Graz 1999, chap. 7). In spite of considerable conflicts in the negotiations and tensions even between key US ministries charged with the negotiations, the GATT debates were successfully concluded.

Negotiations for the Havana Charter were more broadly based – with 53 states eventually signing it, and the Soviet Union refraining. The issues debated in Havana went beyond the narrow concerns of trade encompassing inter alia the question of the protection of foreign investments. The compromise found on the latter issue was "unacceptable" to US industrial and financial groups since it gave states ample powers to regulate existing and new foreign investments (Graz 1999, 261). The various parties concerned did not want to cause failure of the negotiations. However, the US government was not willing and due to the domestic constellation of forces not able to offer a considerable reduction of US tariffs to other negotiation partners in order to make its propositions more acceptable to them. Thus, other negotiators pushed for their own propositions often emphasising the necessity to provide for derogations from free trade in order to foster national development and to deal with emergency situations. "The Charter enshrined a not negligible number of initiatives originating from representatives of countries, which had hitherto been marginalised in the negotiations, like France, Australia, India or Mexico" (Graz 1999, 275). The Charter was based much less on liberal principles of international economic relations than the US government had originally envisaged.

Though the US government did not rock the negotiations themselves, it decided not to submit the Charter for ratification to the Congress, where strong opposition to the Charter was to be expected. The international context was different from the immediate post-war years insofar as the cold war was in full swing in 1950. According to Graz (1999, 292 et seq.), the withdrawal of support by US business groups for the Charter was decisive in killing the project. US business groups objected to quite a number of derogations to free trade and protection of foreign investment in the name of national development. In particular, they complained about the level of protection for foreign investments, which was insufficient from their point of view. In addition, they were annoyed by the possibility to introduce derogations to free trade like quantitative restrictions in order to protect the balance of payments. They viewed other dispositives already negotiated at that time, like GATT or OEEC, as being closer to their interests. The domestic balance of forces within the USA had swung into a more free trade orientated direction. *The use of multiple fora in the negotiations enabled US business interests and a US government sensible to the change in the balance of forces to pick the treaty most favourable to their interests.* At the supra-regional level, this was GATT. In contrast to the stillborn ITO, "there was little reference to the social contract upon which the post-Second World War global institutional structure was to be built" (Wilkinson 2005, 17).

ITO was stillborn, GATT prevailed. It had a much weaker organisational structure than that envisaged originally for ITO. Not all states decided to sign the GATT. State socialist countries and a number of Third World states refrained from signing GATT – at least for many years. Some key Third World governments perceived GATT provisions as a constraint on development. Thus, GATT was not a truly global treaty. Over the next decades a number of negotiation rounds on reducing barriers to trade were commenced and concluded in GATT. Only in the 1970s, the first serious challenge to the liberal order of GATT was to emerge.

UNCTAD versus GATT

In the immediate post-war years, international trade negotiations were dominated by the western states. Third World states were in a marginal position in the international fora. This changed with the decolonisation of the 1950s and early 1960s. The numerical strength of Third World states in international organisations grew considerably. Where the principle of one state–one vote prevailed, as was the case with UN organisations, Third World states potentially yielded considerable voting power. This contrasted with the IMF and World Bank, where Western states preserved their uncontested dominance. Collective organisation of the Third World started with the Bandoeng Conference in 1955. Gradually, the Non-Aligned Movement (NAM) and the G-77 evolved. The latter was to play a co-ordinating role in international negotiations.

A chance to make their voice better heard emerged for Third World governments in the 1970s. It was the conjuncture when Fordism entered into crisis and the role of the US declined. Already during the 1960s, the US visibly lost some of its competitive edge over the Federal Republic of Germany and Japan. The war in Indochina became an increasing economic burden for the US. In the mid-1970s, the US defeat in Vietnam and the revolution in Portugal with the ensuing de-colonisation in the Portuguese colonies marked a low point of international US influence. The crisis of Fordism and US hegemony (the latter was, however, confined to the capitalist part of the World) translated into international economic turbulence. Exchange rates between the main currencies had to be adjusted. In 1973, the fixed exchange rate system was abandoned. These processes created uncertainty in international economic relations.

Accumulation in Third World states was usually characterised by a considerable degree of extraversion, especially of the passive type. Import dependence was high, and, accordingly, there was an urgent necessity to export. Therefore, Third

World economies were highly vulnerable to international turbulence. Third World governments strived to reduce the effects of international uncertainty on their economies which threatened to compromise their legitimacy. Whereas the economic effects of the crisis were threatening for the Third World, the political effects seemed to be promising. The US position was weakened; the roles among the western states were redefined. This produced new openings for Third World governments. OPEC was one of the first organisations to take advantage of the new situation (Raffer/ Singer 2001, chap. 8). It pushed through a considerable increase of the oil price. This represented an economic burden for other Third World states, but offered a political encouragement as well.

In their attempt to achieve a new international trade order, Third World governments chose UNCTAD as an alternative arena to GATT. UNCTAD was founded in 1964, with Raúl Prebisch as its first secretary-general. Together with Hans Singer, Prebisch had formulated the thesis of declining Third World terms of trade. This implied a scathing critique of free trade doctrines. In terms of a development strategy, import substitution involving some degree of trade protection was the consequence. This thinking was developed by CEPAL (Comisión económica para América Latina y el Caribe) of which Prebisch was also the first secretary general (cf. Kay 1989, 31 et seq.). UNCTAD was able to build upon this intellectual legacy of CEPAL. UNCTAD had a leadership and a staff that were sympathetic to the ideas and concepts originating from the Third World.

The debates about a new trade regime in UNCTAD were part of a wider debate on a New International Economic Order (NIEO). It was initiated by Third World governments and got a decisive impulse at the Non-Aligned Movement summit in Algiers in 1973. It included the following key demands:

- full legal and political sovereignty over raw materials;
- the right to form producer cartels and buffer stocks in order to stabilise commodity prices;
- a non-reciprocal trade regime giving Third World importers easier access to technology and access to consumer markets in industrialised countries;
- full participatory rights in international organisations, especially the IMF and World Bank;
- improved access to international finance, especially for the poorest countries (Tetzlaff 1982, 273 et seq.).

The programme enjoyed a broad social support in Third World countries. They pushed for a charter on the economic rights and duties of states in the UN general assembly. Western governments objected to three points in the proposal:

- the issue of nationalisation of foreign investments;
- the right to form producer cartels for raw materials;
- the issue of most-favoured nation arrangements and the issue of non-discrimination in international trade.

Six states – Belgium, Denmark, the Federal Republic of Germany, Great Britain, Luxembourg and the USA – voted against the charter (Tetzlaff 1982, 277). Most of these countries displayed a strong export orientation. Their leading circles defended free trade doctrines. The Federal Republic of Germany has had a very weak Keynesian tradition. Instead, German development strategies have had a strong neo-mercantilist imprint for many decades (Beck 2005, 50 et seq). In this tradition, the German government – of social-liberal colouring in the 1970s – rejected initiatives that bore an imprint of internationalised Keynesianism and infringed on neo-mercantilist strategies of industrial states. There was a debate on the NIEO in the Federal Republic of Germany, but the defenders of a NIEO – mainly solidarity groups – remained a small minority. There was no international campaigning on the issue, though there were parallel national debates.

Trade-related issues were debated at the UNCTAD. An integrated commodity programme proposed by the then UNCTAD Secretary-General, Germani Corea, in 1976 was at the heart of the debate. The proposal included the creation of a number of international commodity agreements aiming at the stabilisation of raw material prices. A common fund was to finance buffer stocks enabling a price stabilisation and programmes financing research, development, diversification and marketing. Western countries were fiercely opposed to the proposal. The Federal German government was one of the most vocal opponents. In 1979, "Western governments pushed through their point of view in all essential matters" (Tetzlaff 1982, 283). The project of the common fund was completely watered down. Its powers and financial resources were to be minimal. It was never to assume any real relevance.

Nevertheless, the UNCTAD debates had consequences for other arenas as well. This is most obvious in the case of the 1975 Lomé Agreement between the EEC and its former colonies in Africa, the Caribbean and the Pacific, which were called the ACP countries. "Blocking the demand for a New International Economic Order, the EEC made far-reaching concessions, granting ACP (African, Caribbean, Pacific) states an unprecedented strong position, including a contractual right to aid. Lomé 1 was the best arrangement SCs (Southern Countries, J.B/W.B) ever got from any group of donors. Its great innovation was Stabex, the STABilisation of EXport revenues" (Raffer/Singer 2001, 99 et seq.). Stabex partially compensated strong shortfalls in export earnings of selected agricultural products. However, it was not to interfere with marketing and price formation of commodities. Insofar as it did not interfere with the power of transnational corporations and their price fixing powers, it was much more acceptable to European governments. In the Lomé II convention, a similar device for mineral raw materials (SYSMIN) was introduced. The 1980s witnessed the decline of Third World influence. This was reflected in the subsequent Lomé conventions, which were characterised by a gradual shift towards the interests of business in the Western countries.

UNCTAD debates had a consequence for GATT negotiations also. In the final debates of the Tokyo round, Third World countries' point of view on a number of contentious points (i.a., subsidies, anti-dumping) were supported by a legal analysis of the legal department of the UNCTAD secretariat. Argentina, Brazil, Egypt,

India and Yugoslavia were the main protagonists of the Third World voicing the key demands. US officials voiced concern about the "UNCTADisation" of GATT (Steinberg 2002, 358). Some of the US negotiators contemplated the idea to shift all or part of the negotiations to the OECD. In that case, Western countries would have established a trade regime among themselves tailored to the desires of their dominant groups. Third World states would have had the possibility to enter such a trade agreement established by the West. However, narrow economic considerations were only part of the US government's political calculus. In the context of bloc confrontation and competition, the U.S. State Department did not want to alienate the Third World. Therefore, it argued successfully for concluding the negotiations in the GATT arena. This constellation enabled Third World states to make their interests prevail on a number of key points: "the developing countries received all of the rights to the subsidies code and the anti-dumping code, but they were not obliged to sign or otherwise abide by the obligations contained in these agreements" (Steinberg 2002, 357).

It can be concluded that *Third World states were able to open a significant new arena of international trade negotiations in the 1970s. This arena was UNCTAD.* They were able to set an agenda favourable to their position in UNCTAD. *However, they were not able to conclude the negotiations successfully.* Western governments were relatively united in their stand against the proposed mechanisms of commodity price stabilisation. Business groups and most media supported the governments' liberal stand. Dissenting views were in a rather weak position. Though western states were in a numerical minority, their strong economic position strengthened their political hand. Nevertheless, UNCTAD debates had an effect on other fora. Third World positions were strengthened in these negotiation arenas.

From GATT to WTO

In the 1980s, business sought to open up new areas for private investment or to enlarge existing ones. These endeavours centred around services, especially finance. Services were particularly important in the US where they accounted for 79 percent of employment and for around 60 percent of GDP in the late 1980s. US trade in services accounted for US$110 billion foreign exchange earnings in 1981. The trade surplus in services of US$ 38.9 billion was more than just a compensation of the US trade deficit in goods amounting to US$ 27.8 billion (Wiener 2005, 148). Likewise, British accumulation was finance-centred and highly internationalised. In many industrialised countries, there was a tendency to seek a way out of the structural crisis that had begun in the early 1970s by expanding externally. Increasing extraversion often has gone hand in hand with an increasingly extensive character of accumulation.

Business pressed for changes of régulation at various territorial levels. Changes in the US regulation were of particular importance. In the late 1970s, the US Federal Reserve raised the interest rates in a dramatic manner. This had a number of effects. High interest rates and deregulation of the financial sector stimulated financialised accumulation. High interest rates re-affirmed the international position of the US (Tavares 1997) and limited the policy choices of other states – both in the North and in the South. It became extremely difficult to sustain Keynesian policies because the financial burden linked to budget deficits grew rapidly due to the high interest rates (cf. Plihon 1996, 98 et seq., Matzner 2000, 63 et seq., Grahl 2004, 288). Many Third World states had to face the reality of not being able to service their foreign debt which had grown rapidly in the 1970s. In the process of re-negotiating their debts, they were coerced to accept a change of direction in their economic and social policies. They opened up their economies to foreign investors, refrained from industrial policies, cut social welfare payments and returned to the "liberal non-interventionist state" of the 19th century (Fiori 1999, 79). Their position in international fora was considerably weakened. The end of state socialism implied a second decisive shift in social and inter-state relations. Third World states lost the opportunity to play West against East which narrowed down their policy choices. Western countries lost their systemic antagonist, loosening the cohesion in the Western camp. Furthermore, Western governments saw less necessity to seek broadly based legitimacy for the existing social order after the demise of state socialism (cf. Brie/Klein 1993, 124 et seq.).

All these changes have left their imprint on the international trade negotiations of the 1980s and 1990s. In the Uruguay round of GATT (1986-1994), the US government sought a much broader agenda than just issues of goods trade. In view of their strong position of exports in services, it wanted to include services. In view of the advanced degree of internationalisation of US corporate business, it urged for an agreement on trade-related investment measures (TRIMs). Aiming at strengthening the position of US business in technologically advanced sub-sectors, it pushed for an agreement on trade-related aspects of intellectual property rights (TRIPs) (Wiener 2005, 146 et seq., Rainelli 1996, chap. 5). *The latter implied a shift in the negotiation arena since there were existing international arrangements on the issue of TRIPs* (Braithwaite/Drahos 2000, 67 et seq., May 2005, 164). At the beginning, the European Community was not enthusiastic about the new round. Third World states, led by India and Brazil, had serious objections, especially to the negotiations on services. They feared their economic marginalisation as a consequence of an agreement that would give TNCs a free reign in the service sector. They demanded that GATS should be optional, but not mandatory. "The US and Europe agreed to the formula 'distinct, but parallel'" (Wiener 2005, 150) in the negotiations. Likewise, Third World states were uncomfortable about the disempowerment of the World Intellectual Property Organisation (WIPO), and the switching of the agenda to the GATT forum (cf. Chorev, in this volume).

The organisational structure of GATT was not well suited to the broadening of its agenda. In 1990, the Canadian government proposed the creation of a World Trade Organisation (WTO). To some extent, this was a revival of the ITO project. As it had been planned for the ITO, WTO was conceived as a fully fledged international organisation complementing the global economic governance of the IMF and World Bank. In contrast to the ITO, however, an organic link with the International Labour Organisation (ILO) was not intended (Wilkinson 2005, 23). This was a crucial change showing that the moving forces for the WTO were unwilling to establish a link between trade and labour issues though – mainly Western trade unions – later tried to put the issue of labour standards on the WTO agenda (Haworth/Hughes 2005). This positioning in regard to labour rights was in line with predominant strategies of extensive and extraverted strategies of accumulation which were to be built on stagnating or decreasing real wages and/or longer working hours. The mandate of the WTO was to go far beyond the original role of GATT that had consisted of reducing tariff and non-tariff barriers to goods trade. The WTO was conceived as an international organisation that was to produce international norms that would coerce national norms into line with liberal doctrines. Western governments were unwilling to make any significant derogations to the principle of free international trade and investment to allow for national development strategies and the improvement of the living conditions of labour (cf. Graz 1999, chap. 8.2, Wilkinson 2005, 21 ss.). After the end of the Cold War, winning a broadly based social consensus has not been one of their preoccupations. However, they wanted to give the WTO much stronger enforcement mechanisms than those that had been at the disposal of GATT.

At first, the US Congress had reservations about the WTO's potential implication for US sovereignty. These fears were dispelled (Wilkinson 2005, 20), and both the US government and the European Community used the switch from GATT to WTO to impose their trade, service and investment agenda on reluctant Third World governments. The results of the various GATT negotiation groups were bundled into a single undertaking. Though the negotiations on GATS were "distinct, but parallel", GATS had to be accepted as part of the whole package. "After joining the WTO (including the GATT 1994), the EC and the United States withdrew from GATT 1947 and thereby terminated their GATT 1947 obligations (including its most favourite nation guarantee) to countries that did not accept the Final Act and join the WTO. The combined legal/political effect of the Final Act and transatlantic withdrawal from the GATT 1947 would be to ensure that most of the Uruguay Round agreements had mass membership rather than a limited membership" (Steinberg 2002, 360). The agreements of the Uruguay Round have been much more constraining for Third World states than previous GATT agreements (Steinberg 2002, 366). *The switching of arenas and founding of WTO paid off to the dominant forces in the US and Western Europe.*

Due to its central and extremely liberal role in global norm making, the WTO has been a highly controversial organisation almost from the beginning. Anti-globalist groups have been mobilising against it demanding at least the radical pruning of its powers. Another current demands the democratisation of the WTO and changes in its policies. "These critics have persistently challenged the liberalisation project at the heart of the WTO, and its democratic credentials" (Williams 2005, 45). Liberal think-tanks have come out in its defence (Williams 2005, 38 s.). The WTO has responded to the mobilisations by trying to assuage the criticism. It has offered limited access to ministerial meetings while, after the strong protest of anti-globalists and trade unions in Seattle in 1999, seeking venues for its meetings, like Doha, where mass protests are rather unlikely to occur. In addition, the WTO provided for liaison between its Secretariat and civil society groups (ibid., 37).

The strategic selectivity of GATT is continued in the WTO. Formally, the consensus principle has been maintained. However, it has proved almost impossible for most Third Worlds states to cope with the multiplicity of the WTO agendas. Only a few Third World states have a sizeable professional staff at Geneva (e.g. South Korea, Egypt, Nigeria or India). Some small or middle-sized states are not represented at all by permanent staff – as it used to be the case with Namibia, Mali or Mozambique (Jawara/Kwa 2004, 20 s., table 1.2). At important meetings, an adequate translation into the other officially recognised languages other than English (i.e. French and Spanish) was not provided for, which put delegations from Francophone countries and Latin America at an obvious disadvantage (Jawara/Kwa 2004, 97 s.). Key decisions for agenda setting have been made at restricted informal meetings (Steinberg 2002, 354 ss., Kwa/Jawara 2004, 17 s.). Unruly Third World governments have been pressurised to fall into line by Western governments (Kwa/Jawara 2004, 150 ss.). The WTO Secretariat has been close to the group of Western countries. Around 80 percent of staff originate from these countries sharing a common social, cultural and conceptual background with the staff of Western WTO missions. Therefore, it is not surprising that the Secretariat has been consistently biased in favour of Western demands (Steinberg 2002, 356, Kwa/Jawara 2004, chap. 7). For Third World states, the hurdles to Dispute Settlement mechanisms are high in terms of manpower and also financially. Enforcement of WTO rule is based on permitting the aggrieved party to impose sanctions on the offender. This way of sanctioning privileges states with large markets. On the one hand, the restriction of access to large markets penalises the offender in an effective way. On the other hand, they withstand sanctions imposed by other states more easily (Smith 2004). Thus, the WTO has been strategically selective in favour of Western state or quasi-states, mainly the US and the EU, and the interests they represent (usually strongly biased in favour of business interests).

This strategic selectivity has been questioned by a broad range of social groups – trade unions, ecological groups, anti-globalist movements etc. For the past few years, it has not been passively accepted by some of the Third World governments either. They have challenged Western positions a number of times. Both Western states and some Southern states have used tactics of forum-shifting and forum-blocking in international trade negotiations.

It was in the Seattle Ministerial Meeting in 1999 that controversies first came to a head. Outside the venue, an exceptionally broad alliance of social movements – ranging from trade unions to anti-globalists – challenged the neo-liberal WTO policies. Inside, major players had diverging priorities. The EU had "always been keen" on the launch of a comprehensive new round that includes negotiations on all "new issues' (competition, investment, trade facilitation and transparency in government procurement" (Jawara/Kwa 2004, 53). This reflected the neo-mercantilist bias in the dominant accumulation strategies and economic policies in EU. The EU was not keen on negotiating the reduction of agricultural subsidies. EU agriculture relies on such subsidies and the complex support system for (large-scale) agriculture has been part of the basic social compromises in EU. Due to NGO pressures, the EU was not unwilling to discuss the relationship between trade and environment, and trade and labour standards. The US government was especially keen to discuss services and industrial tariffs. It was subject to diverging pressures in regard to agriculture. Thus, its position on that issue was ambiguous. "Among the 'new issues', they (the USA, JB/WB) were especially keen advocates of transparency in government procurement and trade facilitation, as US-based multinational corporations were eager to ensure the existence of rule in these two areas, but they could do without competition and investment policy" (ibid, 53). Many Third World governments were still grappling with the consequences of the Uruguay round and were not keen on a new negotiation round. Those Third World governments that were not unwilling to see a new round usually had priorities that differed from both US and EU positions. A crucial area of concern to many Third World states was access to the agricultural markets in the North and agricultural subsidies (ibid., 54 et seq.). Key differences did subsist at the Seattle meeting which subsequently failed. "(T)hough the Seattle protesters were not the main reason for the failure of the conference their activities brought to public prominence objections to further trade liberalisation" (Williams 2005, 43).

Up to the next Ministerial Meeting in Doha in 2001, both the WTO Secretariat and key governments made considerable efforts to make the Doha meeting succeed. Consultations were a bit broader based than before. Western governments actively sought the support of key players from the Third World in order to start a new negotiation round. India emerged as the head of an oppositional camp in Doha. Western governments were willing to make a few discursive concessions, like the discourse of a "Development Round", and a few, quite limited substantial concessions (like the one on drugs in the TRIPs framework). However, the final outcome reflected the priorities of the US government and the European Commission (cf. Jawara/Kwa 2004, Chapter 4 and 5).

Third World governments drew their own conclusions from Doha. They hardened their stance at the next Ministerial Meeting in Cancún in 2003. They highlighted the issue of agricultural protection in a way that was welcome neither to the US government nor to the European Commission. The oppositional core was clustered around the G-20+ in which key Third World states were represented. A number of African cotton-producing states formulated a strong position on the issue of cotton-trade. Their intransigent position was a novelty. These developments were an unpleasant surprise to the US government and the European negotiators. They were unwilling to cede sufficient ground in order to enable a compromise. It seems that particularly the US government was not all too eager to find common ground with other parties (Jawara/Kwa 2004, xlix et seq.). In July 2004, a shaky compromise on relaunching the trade negotiations was finally struck (Evia/Gudynas 2004). The US government sought to break the unity of the G-20+group – with limited success. Both the USA and the EU have engaged in parallel plurilateral and bilateral trade negotiations with Third World states and groupings. Key Third World governments have developed their own strategies of arena selection and arena blocking. A web of interlocking negotiation arenas has been unfolded. The strategies of key players in regard to arena selection and switching will be scrutinised in this book.

The structure of the book

The book consists of nine chapters altogether, i.e. an introduction and a concluding chapter and seven country chapters. Since the USA and the EU have been the main protagonists both in setting the negotiation agenda and in switching negotiation fora, we start with the analysis of these two cases. In a sense, the first two country chapters constitute a first part of the book, while the analyses of the Third World Middle Powers make up the second part.

It has been argued above that for the purposes of our study it seems appropriate to choose (1) China and India on account of their size and therefore their capacity to single-handedly influence negotiation procedures; (2) South Africa and Brazil on account of their possible impact in the respective regional context and (3) Turkey on account of her specific position as member of the WTO and as EU-accession candidate.

The introductory chapter and the concluding chapter have been authored by the editors, *Joachim Becker* and *Wolfgang Blaas*, while the other chapters were written by experts of the respective country. The chapter on the USA was prepared by *Nitsan Chorev*, *Werner Raza* has written on the European Union. China was dealt with by *Weiyu Gao and Xiaoling Ji*, and *Muchkund Dubey* wrote the chapter on India. The case of Brazil was analysed by *Luiz Estrella Faria*, and South Africa has been examined by *Gottfried Wellmer*. Finally, *Gaye Yılmaz* took care of the Turkish case.

References

Acosta, A. (2004), El TLC o la voracidad sin limites. In: *La insignia*, 22 de septiembre (www.lainsignia.org/2004/septiembre/econ_021.htm).

Aglietta, M. (1987, 2nd ed.), *A Theory of Capitalist Regulation. The US Experience,* (London: Verso).

Aglietta, M., Moatti, S. (2000), *Le FMI. De l'ordre monétaire aux désordres financiers*, (Paris: Economica).

Aguiton, Ch. (2002), *Was bewegt die Kritiker der Globalisierung? Von Attac zu Via Campesina*, (Köln: Neuer ISP Verlag).

Arrighi, G. (1994), *The Long Twentieth Century. Money, Power, and the Origins of Our Times*, (London: Verso).

Barša, P., Císař, O. (2004), *Levice v postrevoluční době. Občanská společnost a nova sociální hnutí v radikální politické teorii,* (Brno: CDK).

Beaud, M. (1987), *Le système national/mondial hiérarchisé. Une nouvelle lecture du capitalisme mondial*, (Paris: La découverte).

Beck, St. (2005), After the Miracle: The Exhaustion of the German Model? In: Beck, St., Klobes, F., Scherrer, Ch. (eds.): *Surviving Globalization? Perspectives for the German Economic Model*, (Dordrecht: Springer), pp. 33-67.

Becker, J. (2002), *Akkumulation, Regulation, Territorium. Zur kritischen Rekonstruktion der französischen Regulationstheorie,* (Marburg: Metropolis).

Bobbio, N. (1988), *Die Zukunft der Demokratie,* (Berlin: Rotbuch).

Boyer, R. (1987, 2nd ed.), *La théorie de la régulation: une analyse critique,* (Paris: La découverte).

Braithwaite, J., Drahos, P. (2000), *Global Business Regulation,* (Cambridge: Cambridge University Press).

Brand, U., Brunnengräber, A., Schrader, L., Stock, Ch., Wahl, P. (2000), *Global Governance. Alternative zur neoliberalen Globalisierung?* (Münster: Westfälisches Dampfboot).

Brie, M., Klein, D. (1993), *Der Engel der Geschichte. Befreiende Erfahrungen einer Niederlage,* (Berlin: Dietz).

Cardoso, F. H., Faletto, E. (1976), *Abhängigkeit und Entwicklung in Lateinamerika,* (Frankfurt a.M.: Suhrkamp).

Cain, P.J., Hopkins, A.G. (1993), *British Imperialism. Vol 2. Crisis and Deconstruction, 1914-1990,* (London/New York: Longman).

Cartier Bresson, J., Kopp, P. (1982), *L'analyse sectorielle. Approche du système productif en Amérique Latine.* Thèse de doctorat, Université de Picardie, Amiens.

Chesnais, F. (1996), Mondialisation financière et instabilité systémique. In: Chesnais, F. (ed.): *Mondialisation financière. Genèse, coût et enjeux,* (Paris: Syros), pp. 251-307.

Chesnais, F. (2004), Le capital de placement: accumulation, internationalisation, effets économiques et politiques. In: Chesnais, F. (ed.), *La finance mondialisée. Racines sociales et politiques, configuation, conséquences,* (Paris: La découverte), pp. 15-50.

Císař, O. (2004), *Transnacionální politické sítě. Jak mezinárodní instituce ovlivňuje činnost nevládních organizací,* (Brno: IIPS).

Cox, R. W. (1987), *Production, Power, and World Order. Social Forces in the Making of History,* (New York: Columbia University Press).

Evia, G., Gudynas, E. (2004), Nuevo acuerdo de la OMC: muchos festejos, mucha ambigüedad, poca substancia. In: *La insignia,* 17 de agosto (www.lainsignia.org/2004/agosto/econ_017.htm).

Fiori, J. Luis (1999), Estados, moedas e desenvolvimento. In: Fiori, J. L. (ed.), *Estados e moedas no desenvolvimento das nações,* (Petrópolis: Vozes), pp. 49-85.

Frank, R., Manzenreiter, W. (2005), Mit oder gegen China? Japan, Südkorea und die Zukunft der regionalen Sicherheit in Nordostasien. In: Becker, J., Hödl, G., Steyrer, P. (eds.), *Der Krieg an den Rändern. Von Sarajewo nach Kuito,* (Wien: Promedia) (in print).

Gerbier, B. (2001), L'OMC et la théorie de l'économie internationale. In: Damian, Michel/Graz, Jean-Christophe (eds.), *Commerce internationale et développment soutenable,* (Paris: Economica), pp. 109-132.

Grahl, J. (2004), The European Union and American Power. In: Panitch, Leo/Leys, Colin (eds.), *Socialist Register 2005: The Empire Reloaded,* (London: Merlin Press), pp. 284-300.

Gramsci, A. (1971), *Selections from Prison Notebooks,* (London: Lawrence and Wishart).

Graz, J. Ch. (1999), *Aux source de l'OMC: La Charte de Havane, 1941-1959/ Precursor of the WTO: The Stillborn Havana Charta,1941-1959,* (Genève: Librairie Droz).

Gudynas, E. (2003a), El fracaso de la OMC y la sociedad civil. In: Claes/d3e (ed.), *OMC, poder y democracia. La sociedad civil en la cumbre ministerial de Cancún,* Montevideo, pp. 37-39.

Gudynas, E. (2003b), ALCA flexible, mínima y „a la carta". In: Claes/d3e (ed.), *Las sombras del ALCA. Promesas y realidades en las negociaciones de libre comercio en las Américas,* Montevideo, pp. 59-62.

Gudynas, E. (2004), Países de desarrollo relanzan un acuerdo comercial. In: *La insignia,* 18 de junio (www.lainsignia.org/2004/junio/econ_040.htm).

Halliday, F. (2005), *The Middle East in International Relations. Power, Politics and Ideology,* (Cambridge: Cambridge University Press).

Harvey, D. (1984, 2nd ed.), *Limits to Capital,* (Oxford: Blackwell Publishers).

Haworth, N., Hughes, St. (2005), From Marrakech to Doha and Beyond: The Tortuous Progress of the Contemporary Trade and Labour Standards Debate. In: Kelly, D., Grant, W. (eds.), *The Politics of International Trade in the Twenty-First Century. Actors, Issues and Regional Dynamics,* (Basingstoke: Palgrave Macmillan), pp. 130-143.

Heckscher, E. (1934), *Mercantilism. Volume 2,* (London: George Allen & Unwin).

Hilferding, R. (1974, 3rd ed.), Das Finanzkapital, (Frankfurt a.M.: EVA).

Hirsch,J.(1990),*KapitalismusohneAlternative? MaterialistischeGesellschaftstheorie und Möglichkeiten einer sozialistischen Politik heute,* (Hamburg: VSA).

Hobsbawm, E. J. (1994), *Age of Extremes. The Short Twentieth Century, 1914-1991,* (London: Michael Joseph).

Jawara, F., Kwa, A. (2004, updated ed.), *Behind the Scenes at the WTO: The Real World of International Trade Negotiations/The Lessons of Cancun,* (London: Zed Press).

Jessop, B. (1990), *State Theory. Putting the Capitalist State in its Place,* University Park.

Jessop, B. (2002), *The Future of the Capitalist State,* (Cambridge: Polity Press).

Juillard, M. (2002), Accumulation regimes. In: Boyer, R., Saillard, Y. (eds.), *Régulation Theory. The State of the Art,* (London: Routledge), pp. 153-160.

Kapoor, I. (2004), Deliberative Democracy and the WTO. In: *Review of International Political Economy,* 11(3), pp. 522-541

Kay, C. (1989), *Latin American Theories of Development and Underdevelopment,* (London: Routledge).

Keynes, J. M. (1997), *The General Theory of Employment, Interest, and Money,* (Amherst, N.Y.: Prometheus Books).

Krasner, St. D., ed. (1983), *International Regimes,* (Ithaca/New York: Cornell University Press).

Marx, K. (1979), *Das Kapital. Kritik der politischen* Ökonomie. Dritter Band. MEW 25, (Berlin: Dietz).

Matzner, E. (2000, 2nd revised ed.), *Monopolare Weltordnung. Zur Sozioökonomie der US-Dominanz,* (Marburg: Metropolis).

May, Ch. (2005), International Property Rights. In: Kelly, D., Grant, W. (eds.), *The Politics of International Trade in the Twenty-First Century. Actors, Issues and Regional Dynamics*, (Basingstoke: Palgrave Macmillan), pp. 164-182.

Mazier, J., Basle, M., Vidal, J.-F. (1993, 2nd ed.), *Quand les crises durent...,* (Paris: Economica).

Mello, J. M. Cardoso de (1998, 10th ed.), *O capitalismo tardio. Contribução a revisão crítica da formação e do desenvolvimento da economia brasileira,* (Campinas: Unicamp).

Morgenthau, H. J. (1993), *Politics Among Nations: the Struggle for Power and Peace,* (New York: McGraw Hill).

Moulaert, F., Swyngedouw, E. (1989), Survey 15. A Regulationist Approach to the Geography of Flexible Production Systems. In: *Enviroment and Planning D: Society and Space,* 7, pp. 327-345.

Ominami, C. (1986), *Le tiers monde dans la crise,* (Paris: La découverte).

Orléan, A. (1999), *Le pouvoir de la finance*, (Paris: Éditions Odile Jacob).

Owen, R. (2002), *The Middle East and the World Economy, 1800-1914*, (London: I.B. Tauris).

Palan, R. (1998), Les fantômes du capitalisme mondial: L'économie politique internationale et l'école française de la régulation. In: *L'Année de régulation,* 2, pp. 63-86.

Palan, R. (2000), New Trends in Global Political Economy. In: Palan, R. (ed.), *Global Political Economy. Contemporary Theories,* (London: Routledge), pp. 1-18.

Peterson, V. S. (2003), *A Critical Rewriting of Global Political Economy. Integrating Reproductive, Productive and Virtual Economies,* (London: Routledge).

Picciotto, S. (1996), The Regulatory Criss-Cross: Interaction between Jurisdictions and the Construction of Global Regulatory Networks. In: W. Bratton, J. McCahery, S. Picciotto, C. Scott (eds.), *International Regulatory Competition and Coordination. Perspectives on Economic Regulation in Europe and the United States,* (Oxford: Clarendon Press), pp. 89-123.

Plihon, D. (1996), Déséquilibres mondiaux et instabilité financière: la responsabilités des politiques liberales. In: Chesnais, François (ed.), *La mondialisation financière. Genèse, coût et enjeux,* (Paris: La découverte), pp. 97-141.

Plihon, D. (2003), *Le nouveau capitalisme,* (Paris: La découverte).

Poulantzas, N. (2002, reed.), *Staatstheorie. Politischer Überbau, Ideologie, Autoritärer Etatismus,* (Hamburg: VSA).

Raffer, K., Singer, H.W. (2001), *The Economic North-South Divide. Six Decades of Unequal Development,* (Cheltenham: Edward Elgar).

Rainelli, M. (1996), *L'Organisation mondiale du commerce,* (Paris: La découverte).

Raza, W. (2004), *Verhandlungen über ein Assoziationsabkommen EU – MERCOSUR – Stand der Dinge* (unpublished manuscript).

Roth, R. (2001), NGO und transnationale soziale Bewegungen: Akteure einer

"Weltzivilgesellschaft"? In: Brand, U., Demirovic, A., Görg, Ch., Hirsch, J. (eds.), *Nichtregierungsorganisationen in der Transformation des Staates,* (Münster: Westfälisches Dampfboot), pp. 43-63.

Ruiz Caro, A. (2004), Los limites de la Comunidad Sudamericana de Naciones. In: *La insignia,* 25 de noviembre (www.lainsignia.org/2004/noviembre/ibe_079.htm).

Smith, J. (2004), Inequality in International Trade? Developing Countries and Institutional Change in WTO Dispute Settlement. In: *Review of International Political Economy,* 11 (3), pp. 542-573.

Staniszkis, J. (2004), Początek i kres metafiziki państwa. In: Staniszkis, J., Kutz, K. *(w rozmowie z Jerzym S. Macem), to nie to...nie tak miało być,* (Warszawa: ego Dom Wydawniczy), pp. 172-200.

Steinberg, R. H. (2002), In the Shadow of Law or Power? Consensus-Based Bargaigning and Outcomes in the GATT/WTO. In: *International Organization,* 56(2), pp. 339-374.

Stockhammer, E. (2004), *The Rise of Unemployment in Europe. A Keynesian Approach,* (Cheltenham: Edward Elgar).

Swyngedouw, E. (2000), La reconversion du bassin minier belge et la restrucutration de l'État: la démocratie postfordiste déficitaire. In: Benko, G., Lipietz, A. (eds.), *La richesse des régions. La nouvelle géographie socio-économique,* (Paris: PUF), pp. 423-449.

Tavares, Maria da Conceição (1997, 3rd ed.), A retomada da hegemonia norteamericana. In: Tavares, Maria da Conceição, Fiori, J. L. (eds.), *Poder e dinheiro. Uma economia política da globalização,* (Petrópolis: Vozes), pp. 27-53.

Tetzlaff, R. (1982, 2nd improved ed.), Perspektiven und Grenzen der Neuen Weltwirtschaftsordnung. In: Nohlen, D., Nuscheler, F. (eds.), *Handbuch der Dritten Welt. Band 1. Unterentwicklung und Entwicklung: Theorien – Strategien – Indikatoren,* (Hamburg: Hoffmann und Campe), pp. 273-291.

Wahl, P. (1999), Auf der Suche nach dem gesellschaftsveränderndem Subjekt. Nichtregierungsorganisationen – übeschätzte Akteure. In: *Kurswechsel,* 1, pp. 38-46.

Wahl, P. (2001), „Sie küssten und sie schlugen sich" – Zum Verhältnis von NGO und internationalen Regierungsorganisationen. In: Brand, U., Demirovic, A., Görg, Ch., Hirsch, J. (eds.), *Nichtregierungsorganisationen in der Transformation des Staates,* (Münster: Westfälisches Dampfboot), pp. 121-139.

Wiener, J. (2005), GATS and The Politics of "Trade in Services". In: Kelly, D., Grant, W. (eds.), *The Politics of International Trade in the Twenty-First Century. Actors, Issues and Regional Dynamics,* (Basingstoke: Palgrave Macmillan), pp. 144-163.

Wilkinson, R. (2005), The World Trade Organization and the Regulation of International Trade. In: Kelly, D., Grant, W. (eds.), *The Politics of International Trade in the Twenty-First Century. Actors, Issues and Regional Dynamics,* (Basingstoke: Palgrave Macmillan), pp. 13-29.

Williams, M. (2005), Civil Society and the World Trading System. In: Kelly, D., Grant, W. (eds.), *The Politics of International Trade in the Twenty-First Century.*

Actors, Issues and Regional Dynamics, (Basingstoke: Palgrave Macmillan), pp. 30-46.

Zeller, Ch. (2004), Ein neuer Kapitalismus und ein neuer Imperialismus? In: Zeller, Ch. (ed.), *Die globale Enteignungsökonomie,* (Münster: Westfälisches Dampfboot), pp. 61-125.

Ziltener, P. (1999), *Strukturwandel der europäischen Integration. Die Europäische Union und die Veränderung der Staatlichkeit,* (Münster: Westfälisches Dampfboot).

Chapter 2

Political and Institutional Manoeuvres in International Trade Negotiations: The United States and the Doha Development Round

Nitsan Chorev

Introduction

The prospects of a new round of multilateral trade negotiations, following the establishment of the World Trade Organisation (WTO) in 1995, have been grim, especially with the collapse of the Seattle Ministerial Meeting in December 1999. Talks revived in the Doha Meeting, in November 2001, where the "Doha Development Agenda" provided the mandate for negotiations, but broke down again in the Ministerial Meeting in Cancun, in September 2003. Nevertheless, based on the experience of previous rounds, it seems safe to predict that in spite of recurrent crises, oblique predictions, and many missed deadlines, the Doha Development Round would result in a multilateral agreement. It is beyond the scope of this paper to envisage the content of such a future agreement. The focus, instead, is on current political strategies and those decisions that have been reached so far. In particular, the paper focuses on the institutional strategies that have been used by the United States in order to assure that the multilateral negotiations proceed, but also assure that the US meets its goals even if the multilateral negotiations fail to proceed or if they fail to reach favourable outcomes.

This chapter analyses the strategies that the US have employed in a set of "Doha-related" negotiations, which include negotiations under the auspices of the WTO and negotiations that are not, with "negotiations" encompassing talks over new rules as well as disputes over the implementation or interpretation of existing rules. The chapter focuses, in particular, on the three most contentious issues at the initial stages of the Doha Round: intellectual property rights, agricultural subsidies, and investment rules. The empirical analysis reveals several inter-related points: First, I show the central role of institutional manoeuvres, attempts to select a favourable institutional setting for the negotiations, among the various political strategies employed by the United States in the negotiations. Second, I argue that the choice of venue and its impact on the substantive outcomes can be more adequately analysed if we consider not the institutional arrangements of each forum separately, but the combined effect of the utilized and potential institutional options. Finally, I show that in the Doha-related negotiations, the institutional context had an important impact on the substantive outcomes of the negotiations. In particular, I show that the United States had the capacity to select the institutional venues and could generally achieve Doha-plus concessions by utilizing institutional settings outside of the WTO, but I also identify the compromises the United States had to make and identify the conditions under which institutional strategies failed.

Venue shopping: Potentialities and limits

The United States supported the launch of a new round of multilateral trade negotiations in expectation to gain better access into foreign markets for its manufacturing and service industries. For that to happen, however, the United States had first to overcome developing countries' demands to negotiate agricultural subsidies, not to negotiate the "Singapore issues" (including investment), and to re-negotiate those rules governing intellectual property rights that inhibit access to affordable medicine. These demands have put the United States on the defensive, if not as much as the EU. The US, in spite of its call for liberalization of the agricultural sector, has been reluctant to roll back its own domestic subsidies, which the Farm Act of 2002 increased in 80 percent. The US was also interested, even if not as enthusiastically as the EU or Japan, in advancing agreements on investment. Finally, the US was the principal target in regard to intellectual property rights, due to its zealous protection of the interests of pharmaceutical companies. Unexpectedly, developing countries have been quite effective, not only in blocking negotiations – the debates over agriculture and over the Singapore issues contributed to the failures of the Seattle and Cancun meetings, respectively – but also in gaining substantive commitments. In Doha, the United States accepted a re-interpretation of the Trade-Related Aspects of Intellectual Property Rights Agreement (TRIPS) that would enable easier access to drugs; three of the four Singapore issues were taken off the agenda of the round; and cuts of agricultural tariffs and subsidies are expected be included in the final multilateral agreement.

The literature on the Doha Round has so far analysed the Doha negotiations either by looking at the resources available to the negotiating parties and the political strategies employed in the course of the negotiations (Jawara and Kwa 2003) or by analyzing the institutional arrangements of the WTO negotiations (Narlikar 2004, Narlikar and Wilkinson 2004). Victory and defeat have been announced based on the outcomes in those particular settings. In such analyses, relations of power, strategic alternatives, and substantive outcomes are considered only within the options offered by WTO multilateral trade negotiations themselves.

To adequately analyse the negotiation outcomes, however, the larger institutional context has to be considered. In particular, careful attention should be paid to US Trade Representative (USTR) Robert Zoellick's repeated warnings that the US would seek institutional alternatives to the multilateral one to achieve those aims not achieved at the WTO. Zoellick usually refers to regional and bilateral alternatives, but there are also other options, less often mentioned, such as negotiations in other international organisations or dispute settlement procedures. In addition, Zoellick usually refers to such options as alternatives in case the Doha Round fails to materialize, but the US has often employed these options to complement the round – by counter-balancing or adding to outcomes achieved at the WTO against its perceived interests – and to lure countries back into the multilateral negotiation table. Indeed, the United States employed an impressive variety of institutional venues in attempt to impose its will. The United States engaged in alternative multilateral negotiations (OECD), regional negotiations (FTAA, CAFTA, SACU), bilateral negotiations (Chile, Singapore, Australia, Morocco), legalized unilateral options (Section 301), and legalized multilateral ones (DSU).

Scholars who study bilateral and regional trade agreements are mostly interested in the economic rationale for, and impacts of, such agreements in comparison to multilateral ones (Bhagwati 1993, Krugman 1991, cf. Mansfield and Milner 1999:592–595). By comparing the economic impacts of different forums of negotiations these studies implicitly recognize that institutions matter. However, the theoretical potential of considering the implications of institutional manoeuvreings is constrained by the tendency in the literature to assess the institutional options from the point of view of economic efficiency, rather than analyzing the conflict embodied in the process of deciding on the institutional location as well as in the negotiations themselves. Only recently have scholars, mainly of international relations, analysed the political dimensions of regionalism (cf. Mansfield and Milner 1999), including the strategic interplay between bilateral and multilateral negotiations (Mansfield and Reinhardt 2003).

It is in the literature on public policy that we can find the helpful notion of venue shopping, defined as the activities of strategic actors (both policymakers and interest groups) who attempt to locate or shift policy processes to those settings most hospitable to their interests (Sell and Prakash 2004:154, see Baumgartner and Jones 1993, Pralle 2003, Levy and Prakash 2003, Davis 2003, 2004). This literature draws on the following assumptions: there are alternative institutional settings in which the process of policy-making may take place; the institutional venue matters to the outcome of the negotiations, as venues may be more or less favourable to certain claims; finally, because the institutional location matters, it becomes an aspect of actors' political strategies: actors choose those institutions that would be favourable for their interests.

While this literature offers a fruitful starting point for the current analysis, it is limited in certain ways. In particular, the literature underplays the fact that institutional shopping itself is a matter of negotiations and political debates (Pralle 2003, but see Davis 2003). A more adequate analysis of venue shopping has to consider the conditions under which venues are selected, as well as what implications this has on the subsequent negotiations. Concretely, we have to find how the United States could force or convince other countries into its preferred alternatives, and how this affected the subsequent agreements. In addition, the literature on venue shopping tends to regard the possible venues as mutually exclusive. This limits our understanding not only of the ultimate outcomes, but also the initial institutional preferences. Instead, the institutional context to be considered in explaining outcomes needs to include the institutional environment at large, including potential institutional venues (e.g., the possibility of bilateral negotiations if the multilateral fails), those venues that are already utilized (e.g., when countries participate simultaneously in regional and multilateral negotiations), and those that are no longer available (e.g., after the exhaustion of the legal channels).

How do institutions matter?

International regimes[1] differ greatly in their forms, including the number of states participating, the decision-making rules and procedures, the range of issues covered, the degree of centralized control, and the extent of flexibility within them (Rosendorff and Milner 2001: 829, Davis 2004). Mainstream theories of international relations, however, maintain a concept of state power that provides little room for such differences to affect substantive outcomes. For neo-realists, political outcomes at the international level reflect the relative power of the participating states, power which is itself determined by the unequal distribution of economic and military resources and does not depend on the institutional arrangements in place (Waltz 1979). Institutionalist analyses of the international level, in turn, are dominated by rationalist approaches, which concentrate on the ability of international institutions to facilitate cooperation among states (Keohane 1984, 2002, Baldwin 1993). While neo-liberal institutionalists do suggest ways in which international organisations can act as independent intervening variables in world politics, therefore, their focus on the *efficacy* of institutional arrangements in maximizing the interests of participating nation-states has the outcome of downplaying power relations, conflicts and struggles. As discussed above, the literature on venue shopping reflects a similar bias.

My analysis of institutional arrangements draws instead on the historical institutionalist approach (Thelen and Steinmo 1992, Hall and Taylor 1996, Immergut 1998), which I apply to the international realm.[2] This approach contributes to our understanding of policy formation by showing that the relative influence of the political forces that struggle over policy outcomes is not determined exogenously or independently of the institutional context in which they struggle. Clearly, negotiation outcomes depend on conditions external to the negotiations themselves, including the distribution of resources between the parties, which determine what a party *could* offer to or deny from the other, or the parties' economic position, which determine whether the parties' interests are mutual or conflicted. Negotiation outcomes also depend on the political strategies employed by the parties, e.g., the amount of resources devoted (of those available), the prioritization of interests, or coalition building. Yet, historical institutionalists rightly argue that those political strategies (as well as other conditions usually considered external) are shaped by the institutional arrangements in place. It is by offering unequal opportunities and shaping the political strategies of the competing actors,[3] that institutional arrangements shape those actors' relative political influence and therefore the substantive outcomes. In other words, institutional arrangements matter because they have a *differential* impact on the ability of the competing political forces to pursue their interests and strategies.

The institutional arrangements in place shape the political strategies of the competing interests by making strategies more or less available and more or less effective. For example, institutional venues are different in the issues that parties can ask to cover and the issues that parties can require to exclude; in the number of participants and hence in the coalition possibilities; in the resources needed for available strategies to be effective; in the available concessions one could offer and threats one could use (for example, whether non-trade issues can be also negotiated); in the access participants have to core negotiations (e.g., whether all the parties participate, or whether some parties get to have "green rooms"); in the access non-participants have to negotiations; and in the role of mediating parties (e.g., the Secretariat in multilateral negotiations or panelists in judicial proceedings). These and other differences determine the bias of the different institutions settings.

Struggles over venues

The outcome of negotiations is the result of a constant interplay between the political strategies and the institutional arrangements of the venue(s) selected. We talk about an interplay, because political strategies and institutional arrangements affect each other. I described above how institutional arrangements affect political strategies, but political strategies also affect institutional arrangements because the latter may themselves be an outcome of previous political strategies (Chorev 2005b), and because political strategies of the participants determine what venue is selected. In particular, locations are not decided by consensus, nor are they unilaterally decided by one of the parties. Instead, the location of negotiations is an issue of struggle, with each party utilizes political strategies to ensure a favourable setting.

How should the negotiations *over* the institutional venue be analysed? Following an institutionalist approach, we need to ask whether there are institutional arrangements that govern venue shopping. For if power relations (in the neo-realist sense, as directly reflecting the unequal distribution of resources) determine the location, then it can be claimed that the analysis of institutional arrangements is redundant, merely a step in the way of those with power in getting what they want.

One critical difference between alternate institutional paths is the question of voluntary participation. There is an important distinction between those venues in which one party needs to convince the other to participate in and unilateral venues in which a party can force participation on the other. Examples of voluntary participation include bilateral, regional or multilateral agreements, with differences among the options: membership in a multilateral organisation forces a party into continuous engagement whereas bilateral agreements are often ad-hoc and are therefore more voluntary in nature. Non-voluntary examples are dispute settlement venues. In relative terms, the more voluntary the venue is, the more the initiating party has to lure the other to participate, at times by promising a more equalized forum. Hence, the inability to unilaterally force another party into negotiation puts the initiator in a more fragile position, for it needs to convince the other that it is in its interests to participate. This affects the relations between the parties independently of other conditions of inequality among them: whether participation is compulsory or voluntary would affect how the United States, when it is the initiating party, balances between coercive means and concessions. In the more voluntary venues, the United States would find itself, even if it gets what it wants, paying more dearly.

Alternative versus complementary venues

The literature on venue shopping, not unlike Zoellick's public statements, presents institutional venues as mutually exclusive strategies. However, we have to look at the institutional complex in its entirety. The political game is not only about choosing one venue over another, but playing one venue off *against* another, or one simultaneously with another. The outcomes of negotiations under one venue (e.g., bilateral negotiations) also depend on the institutional arrangements of other venues (e.g., multilateral negotiations or legal disputes). If we examine political strategies *across* institutions we find that bilateral and regional negotiations are, in fact, complementary to the Doha negotiations rather than interchangeable to or competing with them. The institutional venues, in effect, *rely* on each other, in various ways: First, the United States uses regional and bilateral negotiations in order to *force back into the WTO* and/or to weaken member-states' position at the WTO by undermining their collective initiations (e.g., require countries to leave the G-21 coalition if they want a bilateral arrangement with the US) or by altering their interests (making concessions at the bilateral level shifts the attitude towards similar concessions at the multilateral level). Second, at the same time the US uses bilateral in order to get *more* than it can in the WTO (e.g., TRIPS-plus conditions), without undermining the WTO as such. Finally, in some cases bilateral and multilateral negotiations depend on each other for success and complement each other. For example, in many regional negotiations, the path for success was the ability of the United States to negotiate some issues at the bilateral level, and other issues, such as agricultural subsidies, at the multilateral one.

It is the complementary aspect that also complicates the analysis and shows that the United States cannot simply replace multilateral negotiations with alternative venues. The attempt to reach a Free Trade Agreement in the western hemisphere is particularly revealing: once the Doha negotiations collapsed, Brazil was no longer willing to accept an agreement in which they make concessions on intellectual property rights or investment, without reciprocal concessions from the US on agricultural subsidies.

Venue shopping and US power

A major part of the empirical analysis below is a description of the means by which the United States over-compensated its concessions at the Doha round by other means. It shows that the US has utilized alternative institutional venues to maximize its ability to pursue its interests. It is due to such institutional manoeuvres that the United States could balance-out WTO compromises, that the Doha negotiations could proceed, and that they proceeded in terms that reflect US interests. In short, the Doha-related negotiations demonstrate that if the United States cannot achieve its interests in one venue (for example, the multilateral) is can often shift to another venue in which it can prevail (for example, regional/bilateral or judicial).

But the Doha-related negotiations also reveal that there are certain obstacles to the ability of the US to achieve what it wants. First, there is a significant difference in the balance between coercion and concession that the US can utilize in each venue (especially in diplomatic settings compared to judicial ones), that is, in the price that the US needs to pay for getting what it wants. Second, the US does not *always* get what it wants. The US had to give up not only in the Doha negotiations, but also in some of its legal initiations (Section 301 against South Africa), and in few of the regional negotiations (FTAA, SACU). Importantly, the main explanation to the failure of the regional negotiations is the failure of the multilateral ones, as I show and analyse below.

In conclusion, an analysis of the Doha Round of multilateral trade negotiations that does not consider institutional alternatives would provide only a partial understanding of recent developments. In what follows I offer an institutionally contextualized analysis of the Doha negotiations by describing the competing-yet-complementary options available to the United States and showing how the institutional arrangements in different venues affected the political influence of the competing parties and the negotiation outcomes.

Review of interests and disputes

After a period of strong growth between 1996 and 2000, the US economy experienced periods of recession and slow GDP growth: while real GDP increased 3,8 percent in 2000, it increased only 0,3 percent in 2001, and 2,4 percent in 2002.[4] The slowdown in the economy has had a strong impact on merchandise imports, which declined in 2001, before recovering some ground in 2002, when imports reached a c.i.f. value of $1,2 trillion. Exports declined even more sharply than imports, from $780 billion in 2000 to $694 billion in 2002. Largely as a result of lower imports, the deficit in the account of the balance-of-payments actually declined somewhat in 2001, from $411 billion in 2000 to $394 billion (3,9 percent of GDP), but increased again in 2002 to a record $481 billion (4,6 percent of GDP).[5] In contrast to a US merchandise trade deficit, the surplus in cross-border services trade amounted, in 2002, to $74,3 billion.[6] Important exporting sub-sectors are education, financial, and business services. Yet, the largest surplus in services trade has continuously been in royalties and license fees, which represent receipts and payments for intellectual property rights. The main trading partners for US exports in services in 2001 were: Japan (11,6 percent of the total); the United Kingdom (10,9 percent); Canada (9,1 percent); Germany (5,5 percent); and Mexico (5,5 percent). Despite recent economic difficulties, the

US economy has remained among the world's most competitive, and the United States has remained the world's largest import market, a key supplier of goods and services, a major magnet of global savings, and an international source of capital and technology. In 2004, exports constituted 10,39 percent of the GDP and imports constituted 15,98 percent of GDP.[7] The US trade patterns are also amongst the most geographically diversified all of all major WTO Members, which makes most other countries affected by its trade trends and policies.[8]

The United States supported a new round of multilateral trade negotiations in expectation for substantial cuts in tariffs, in particular of key developing countries like India and Brazil (GAO 2004,18), and better access into foreign markets for its service industries. Before it could begin shaping the negotiations in the direction it favoured, however, the United States was forced to deal with grievances voiced by developing countries. Major issues of contestation included intellectual property rights, agricultural subsidies and the Singapore issues.

Intellectual property

At the Uruguay Round of multilateral trade negotiations, which was concluded in 1994, the United States succeeded to introduce rules governing trade in services and intellectual property rights. The Agreement on Trade-Related Aspects of Intellectual Property Rights (TRIPS) has itself been the outcome of institutional manoeuvreing. Over the objections of developing countries, developed countries shifted the administration of intellectual property issues out of the weak World Intellectual Property Organisation (WIPO) and into the newly established WTO (Sell and Prakash 2004, 159–160). The United States also succeeded in strengthening the already superior enforcement capacities of the WTO.

The TRIPS Agreement regulated the manufacturing and trade in products such as films, music recordings, books, computer software, and medicines. As for medicines, key requirements included: patent protection for a minimum of 20 years, from the filing date of a patent application; protection of any invention, including of a product *and* process; protection of undisclosed information (including test data); and protection of trademarks (relevant for generic substitution and combating counterfeit drugs). While the TRIPS was an unequivocal victory of IP-reliant companies,[9] it did allow, against the strong resistance of US-based pharmaceutical companies (Sell and Prakash 2004, 160), "compulsory licensing", which authorizes a government, under specified conditions, to permit the manufacturing of patented drugs to a third party without the consent of the patent-holder. TRIPS also allowed "parallel importation", that is, importation of a patented product marketed in another country without the consent of the patent-holder.[10]

In light of the AIDS crisis and other pandemics, the provisions of TRIPS that had restricted access to medicines have soon become highly contested. Attempts by developing countries to amend TRIPS – a group of developing countries led by South Africa, Brazil and India, demanded a blanket exemption to TRIPS obligations in the interest of public health – have turned into one of the major challenges to the Doha negotiations. These developing countries received technical and moral support from a range of national and international non-governmental organisations, including Health Action International (an Amsterdam-based international network devoted to increasing access and improve rational use of essential medicines), Medicins sans Frontieres (a humanitarian medical aid agency), and Oxfam (an international development and relief agency). They also had the support of the World Bank, the United Nations Development Programme (UNDP), and the World Health Organisation (WHO) (Sell and Prakash 2004). Mobilized against them were brand-name pharmaceutical companies, represented by bodies such as the Pharmaceutical Research and Manufacturers of America (PhRMA). Their position was vigorously promoted by the US negotiators.[11]

The negotiations during the Doha round were mostly confined to the question of compulsory licensing. The TRIPS Agreement allowed compulsory licensing only as long as the medicines were intended for predominantly domestic consumption. This meant that the world's poorest countries, with no home-grown drug industry, could not turn to drug manufacturers in other countries to supply them with cheaper versions of patented drugs, and developing countries demanded to change that (E 6/9/2003, 13).

Agriculture

Agriculture has been a source of conflict at the GATT/WTO since its very inception. In order to protect the interests of non-competitive US-based agriculture, the General Agreement on Tariffs and Trade of 1948 practically excluded agricultural products from negotiations. The Uruguay Round produced the first Agreement on Agriculture, and included a commitment for further negotiations. These were launched in 2000. The Cairns group of agricultural exporting countries, including Canada, Australia and Brazil, wanted the new negotiations to bring the elimination of export subsidies, and significant cuts in trade-distorting domestic subsidies and in developed countries' tariffs. The United States also made allegedly far-reaching offers, although they came with conditions that were clearly intended to minimize the effect on US farmers. US negotiators, for example, were ready to dismantle subsidies only if the playing-field was levelled, which implied that countries with higher tariffs and subsidies must cut them by more than those with less support. Vigorously opposing such demands were countries that provide great support to their farmers: the EU, in particular, but also Switzerland, Norway, Japan and South Korea. The EU rejected the idea that export subsidies should be abolished, and it adamantly opposed the idea that those with higher tariffs and bigger subsidies should cut more (E 29/3/2003, 76).

Singapore issues

In the First Ministerial meeting, which took place in December 1996 in Singapore, the EU requested the introduction of four new issues to the negotiation table. Later referred to as the "Singapore issues", these included transparency in government procurement, investment policy, competition (antitrust) policy, and trade facilitation. Most developing countries objected the introduction of all four topics (Br March 2004, 3, 5).[12] The United States supported the initiation of negotiations over transparency in government procurement, but was less enthusiastic about investment and competition policy. On investment, the United States was concerned that it would undermine negotiations underway in the OECD on a multilateral investment agreement (MAI), which was scheduled for completion in May 1997 (GAO Feb 1997, 11, and see below). In regard to competition policy, the United States was concerned that this would open the door to negotiation on its antidumping rules, which the USTR was under great political pressure not to allow (GAO Feb 1997, 11). The United States therefore agreed to support the establishment of working groups in both areas only after securing agreement that no negotiation would move forward in either area absent an affirmative action by all the parties (GAO Feb 1997, 9–10).

US political strategies and institutional manoeuvres

Members of the WTO had several venues in which they could negotiate new agreements or dispute the interpretation of or compliance with existing rules. Those options included multilateral negotiations under the auspices of the WTO, multilateral negotiations under the auspices of other international organisations (such as OECD or WIPO), or regional or bilateral negotiations. Countries could also use the WTO dispute settlement mechanisms, or other regional/bilateral dispute resolution proceedings. Finally, countries could decide to act unilaterally, by using domestic administrative or judicial proceedings. America's resources permitted it a relatively free hand in choosing the venue in which to proceed, and US negotiators engaged with all of those options.

Option 1: Multilateral negotiations

The "Doha Development Agenda" was launched in the Fourth Ministerial Conference in Qatar, Doha, in November 2001. Negotiations soon focused on the three most contentious issues: intellectual property rights, agricultural subsidies, and the Singapore issues. The results have not reflected US's preferences: it was forced into concessions in the area of intellectual property rights, and it failed to play a conciliatory role between the EU and others on agriculture and the Singapore issues. Moreover, those disputes seriously threatened the possible continuity of the negotiations.

TRIPS: The Doha Declaration and the 30 August Decision

Intensive talks before the Meeting in Doha had failed to bridge differences between the countries that demanded a "pro-public health" interpretation of TRIPS and the

United States. Backed by Switzerland, Canada, Japan and Australia, US negotiators strongly opposed Brazil and India's demands for a declaration that nothing in the TRIPS Agreement should prevent governments from taking measures to protect public health (FT 24/10/2001). The United States nevertheless offered some concessions to developing countries that could not afford patented AIDS drugs. A week or so before the Doha meeting, USTR Zoellick announced that the least developed countries should have until 2016 to implement patent laws, instead of the 2006 deadline required under TRIPS, and pledged not to legally challenge moves by sub-Saharan African countries to obtain cheap AIDS and other life-saving drugs (WP 2/11/2001).

At the Doha Ministerial Conference, moreover, US negotiators agreed to adopt a Declaration on the TRIPS Agreement and Public Health (the "Doha Deceleration"). The Declaration stated, in Paragraph 4, that Member states "agree that the TRIPS Agreement does not and should not prevent Members from taking measures to protect public health", and that the TRIPS Agreement "can and should be interpreted and implemented in a manner supportive of WTO Members' right to protect public health and, in particular, to promote access to medicines for all". Paragraph 5, more specifically, confirmed that the TRIPS Agreement has room for flexibility at the national level, namely with regard to the determination of the grounds for compulsory licensing and the admission of parallel imports. Paragraph 6 instructed the WTO Council for TRIPS to offer a report, no later than the end of 2002, of how Members lacking or with insufficient manufacturing capacities can make effective use of compulsory licensing (Br Jan 2004, 1, 21).

Following the instructions in paragraph 6, WTO Members spent close to two years in negotiations over which countries should be eligible importers of generic versions of patented drugs. A significant breakthrough came in December 2002, when all WTO members agreed on a compromise offered by the Chairman of the TRIPS Council, but the proposal was rejected by the US (NYT 17/3/2003, A8). Only towards the end of 2003, an agreement was finally reached. The Decision on Implementation of Paragraph 6 (the "30 August Decision"), which partly reiterates the December 2002 compromise, spells out the circumstances and conditions under which countries without pharmaceutical capacity can make use of compulsory licensing to import generic versions of patented drugs (Br Jan 2004, 1, 21). The United States succeeded in inserting the demand that such generic medicines could be imported only to cure life-threatening disease, and as long as it was a public health emergency (NYT 31/8/2003). The US agreed to the accord only after it also won a statement from the Chair of the General Council, attached to the Declaration, assuring that the Declaration "should be used in good faith to protect public health ... not be an instrument to pursue industrial or commercial policy objectives". The statement also called for special measures to prevent drugs being smuggled back to rich country markets, including special packaging or different-coloured tablets. The Decision took the form of an *interim* waiver of Members' obligations under TRIPS, which would last until the TRIPS Agreement was permanently amended (WP 31/8/2003, Br 8 Dec 2004, 8, 42).

The two agreements should not be seen as a complete defeat for the US government, and for the US-based pharmaceutical companies whose interests it represents. Access to drugs was encased with such cumbersome bureaucratic procedures to discourage poor nations from using their rights (Br Jan 2004, 1, 21).[13] Probably for this reason, PhRMA praised the agreement (NYT 31/8/2003). Nevertheless, the symbolic as well as the legal victories of developing countries, in spite of the US explicit objection, should not be discarded.

Agriculture

In the Doha Ministerial Declaration, member governments committed themselves to negotiations aimed at substantial reductions in tariffs on agricultural products; reductions of, with a view to phasing out, all forms of export subsidies; and substantial reductions in domestic support. It soon became apparent, however, that the Declaration was open to disturbingly competing interpretations. While some Cairns group members read the Declaration as a commitment to the elimination of export subsidies, EU officials stressed that Members were only committed to 'working in the direction of' such elimination (Br Nov/Dec 2001, 9, 1). As for the substantial reductions in domestic subsidies, some Cairns and Like-Minded Group (a coalition of developing countries) members regarded this mandate as a potential gate for negotiations for all types of domestic subsidies, whether or not they distorted trade, whereas the EU stated that this would only refer to those subsidies that distorted trade and were not tied to programmes that limited production (Br Nov/Dec 2001, 9, 2). The US, in turn, rejected EU's interpretation that "all forms of export subsidies" applied to export subsidy in other export competition regimes, such as export credits, food aid or state-trading enterprises.

US's alleged support for substantial reductions in trade-distorting domestic subsidies came under great scrutiny when the US Congress passed, in May 2002, the *Farm Security and Rural Investment Act of 2002* that would increase government spending on agriculture by 80 percent – an additional $82 billion over ten years to the already promised $100 billion. The US government argued that the law was in no way in conflict with its support of agricultural liberalization during the Doha Round (E 11/5/2002, 92).[14] In July 2002, two months after Bush signed the bill into law, the administration unveiled an ambitious proposal to liberalize agricultural trade that included eliminating export subsidies for farm products over five years, removing $100 billion in global trade-distorting subsidies, and cutting the average global tariff on farm products from 62 percent to 15 percent. The plan had, however, a problematic self-serving appearance. For example, it focused on eliminating export subsidies, which are used far more by the Europeans than by the United States (E 3/8/2003, 12, E 27/72002, 75).

Attempts by US and EU negotiators to agree on a starting point for negotiation led to a 13 August 2003 joint proposal. On cutting agricultural tariffs, the parties suggested a mixture of the American demand that countries with higher tariffs should cut them more and the European demand that all countries cut their tariffs by an equal percentage. On export subsidies, the US gave up its goal of eliminating export subsidies altogether and the Europeans agreed to get rid of subsidies in certain products that matter to poor countries (without naming what those products might be). On trade-distorting payments, the proposal offered to cap a share of total agricultural production at 5 percent. The proposal was silence in regard to other distorting payments and those farm subsidy programmes not considered to be distorting (E 16/8/2003, 65, E 6/9/2003, 73).

In reaction to the proposed EU/US framework, a new block of developing countries emerged, and denounced it as far too timid (NYT 14/9/2004, A1). Led by Brazil, China, India, and South Africa, this Group - initially called G-20, and later G-21 or G-20-Plus – became a powerful voice in the subsequent Fifth Ministerial Meeting in Cancun, in 10–14 September 2003. The Group rejected the US/EU proposal and required instead more subsidy cuts and tariff reductions from rich countries (E 20/9/2003, 30).

Singapore issues

The ultimate cause of the failure of the Cancun meeting, however, was not the dispute over agricultural subsidies, but over the Singapore issues.

The Doha Ministerial Declaration contained, at the insistence of the EU and Japan, an agreement that negotiations on investment, competition policy, transparency in government procurement, and trade-facilitation "will take place after the Fifth Session of the Ministerial Conference on the basis of a decision to be taken, by explicit consensus, at that session on modalities of negotiations". The EU considered this a mandate to launch negotiations at the Cancun meeting or shortly thereafter. Most developing countries, in contrast, interpreted the provision to mean that a decision to launch such negotiations had to be taken by explicit consensus (E 6/9/2003, 73, Br Nov–Dec 2001, 9, 6).

Two days into the Cancun conference over 90 countries signed a letter saying that they were not willing to open negotiations on the Singapore issues. The EU initially refused to compromise. Only in the final morning of the meeting the EU chief negotiator, Pascal Lamy, finally offered to give up the two most controversial issues: investment and competition policy. The offer, however, was rejected by a coalition between three groups of the poorer, largely African, WTO Members, who refused to negotiate on any of the issues (Br Sept–Oct 2003, 7, 1). At that point, the Conference Chair said he saw no basis for compromise and declared the meeting over (E 20/9/2003, 30).

On WTO negotiations

Multilateral negotiations under the auspices of the WTO are rightly considered to be most beneficial to US interests. They are more efficient than bilateral or regional options, for rather than having to reach agreements via negotiations with each state separately, multilateral negotiations allow for decisions that apply to all member-states. They also allow the United States, when confronted with developing countries' demands, to share the burden of compromises with other developed countries, especially the EU. Furthermore, the institutional arrangements of the WTO granted a bargaining advantage to countries with large economies.[15] A widely used example is the practice of "green room" negotiations, where only a small number of countries, but always the United States, participate. The large number of participants also traditionally provided an advantage to the United States, for it made it more difficult for one or few "dissenting" voices to insist on their point. In short, US's political and economic position, given the institutional arrangements in place, allowed the US to prevail in the negotiations, so GATT and WTO agreements commonly reflected US interests.

However, the recent increase in the number of member states that are developing countries, combined with greater public attention to the negative impacts of trade liberalization on poor countries' economic growth and public health, resulted in an important shift in the bargaining position of the negotiating countries. The compromise on access to drugs should be seen in light of US failed political manoeuvres in other venues (see below), and not merely as an outcome of a different negotiating balance. Still, the willingness and ability of developing countries to block progress in the negotiations, both in Seattle and in Cancun, have put the EU and the US in an unprecedented defensive position.

Option 2: Regional and bilateral agreements

Zoellick's reaction to the collapse of the Cancun meeting was far from conciliatory. He targeted in particular G-21 members, blaming them for the collapse and for the "missed opportunity … to achieve global farm reform", and denouncing their approach as springing from a "culture of protest that defined victory in terms of political acts rather than economic results" (NYT 26/9/2003, 1). "The hard rhetoric of the 'won't do' overwhelmed the concerted efforts of the 'can do'", Zoellick stated (NYT 14/9/2003, A1). He emphasized, however, that the Cancun fiasco did not spell the end of his efforts to get freer trade. The US plan, said Zoellick, involved "advances on multiple fronts". If "won't do" countries held up the global talks, the Bush administration would proceed with "can do" countries on a bilateral and regional basis (E 18/10/2003, 56, Br Sept–Oct 2003, 7, 3). As the spokeswoman for EU Trade Commissioner Pascal Lamy put it: "What comes after Cancun was the crude reality of statements by the United States, saying to countries, 'If you don't want to deal in the WTO, we will deal elsewhere'" (WP 3/8/2004, A14).

Of course, simultaneous negotiations were initiated also before Cancun. The Free Trade Agreements of the Americas (FTAA), for example, was launched in 1994. Still, the sense of urgency after Cancun was clearly felt, both in more earnest attempts to conclude negotiations, and in launching new ones, including with Andean countries and with Panama, as well as with Bahrain, the United Arab Emirates, and Oman (the last three undoubtedly motivated more by geopolitical concerns than economic ones).

These initiatives followed a general pattern of concessions and demands: the US would offer (slightly) better access to textile or agricultural products to its market, and would demand investment and/or TRIPS concessions (Abbott 2004a, 7). The US successfully concluded, under such conditions, free trade agreements (FTAs) with Chile, Singapore, Morocco and Australia, and a US-Central America Free Trade Agreement with El Salvador, Guatemala, Honduras, and Nicaragua, to which Costa Rica and the Dominican Republic later joined. Less successful were attempts to conclude the FTAA and to reach a free trade agreement with the Southern African Customs Union (SACU).

TRIPS-plus

Following the Doha Declaration and the August 30 Decision, the United States made efforts to undermine the flexibilities recognized by those multilateral statements by negotiating bilateral and regional FTAs that included provisions contradictory to the letter and spirit of TRIPS and the subsequent decisions (Abbott 2004b, 2). While the intellectual property provisions of these agreements vary in their specific terms, the common objectives of the United States, achieved to different degrees, were to limit potential exclusions from patentability (e.g., preclude the exclusion of plants and animals), require the grant of patents for "new uses" of known compounds, require patent term extension under certain conditions (e.g., unreasonable delays in granting patents), prevent parallel importation, limit the grounds under which compulsory licenses may be granted (e.g., to national emergencies and circumstances of extreme urgency), and allow for the prosecution of non-violation nullification of impairment claims. The United States also negotiated for data exclusivity provisions that provide five to ten years of "non-reliance" on originator test data.[16] In the case of Australia, the United States has negotiated an entry point into the national pharmaceutical price control system (see below). In the case of SACU, the United States has negotiated compliance with non-WTO international standards (various WIPO treaties), and obtained commitments to strengthen domestic enforcement procedures (Br Nov 2004, 10, 17). In short, the US followed an explicit policy of including "TRIPS-plus" provisions in its free trade agreements (Br July–Aug 2004, 7, 17).[17]

Australia: The price of medicines

When the American public began to protest that they have to pay more for brand-name prescription drugs than consumers in other industrial nations, pharmaceutical companies argued that Americans bear too much of the cost of research and suggested that the solution lied in raising the prices abroad, rather than reduce prices in the United States (NYT 17/11/2004). These sentiments were echoed in Congress. Jon Kyl (R–AZ), in a joint hearing of the international trade subcommittee and the health care subcommittee of the Senate Finance Committee, stated:

I've long thought that the prescription drug price controls employed by foreign countries amount to an unfair trade practice … because they block the access of US product to foreign markets. But worse is that the price controls impose unacceptable burdens on the United States as our consumers end up paying the bulk of the cost for research and development …. And I think the answer in the United States is not that we should adopt price controls … but rather that we should continue to work with other countries to reduce or eliminate their price controls.[18]

In the negotiations of the Australia-US Free Trade Agreement (AUSFTA), US negotiators targeted the Pharmaceutical Benefits Scheme (PBS), which was established under the Australian *National Health Act of 1953*. Due to amendments to the Act that intended to ensure universal access to affordable medicines, prices for new drugs in Australia are among the lowest in the developed world (NYT 17/11/2004). The AUSFTA attempts to limit the ability of the PBS to ensure low prices of medicine in various ways. The interpretive principles of the Agreement, for example, focus on enhancing the rights of manufacturers of "innovative" pharmaceuticals and contain no unqualified assertion of consumers' rights to equitable and affordable access to necessary drugs; transparency provisions allow US pharmaceutical applicants (but not consumer or public health organisations) to ask for an independent review of decisions by the Pharmaceutical Benefits Advisory Committee (PBAC); the agreement permits a pharmaceutical manufacturer to disseminate pharmaceutical information via the Internet, which may eventually facilitate direct-to-consumer advertising (DTCA) which is currently illegal in Australia; and the agreement allows a damages claim if a "benefit" the United States could reasonably have expected to accrue under AUSFTA is not realized, even though no specific provision has been breached.

Singapore-plus/NAFTA-minus: Investment

FTA provisions on investment were initiated in reaction to the collapse of the MAI negotiations under the auspices of OECD in 1998 (see below). Rather than pursuing similar agenda at the WTO, which the negative reaction to the Singapore issues made improbable, the US decided to move to the regional/bilateral level. In these initiations, of great importance was the extent to which the US would pursue an investment liberalization agenda similar to the highly criticized provisions of the North American Free Trade Agreement (NAFTA).

Chapter 11 of NAFTA allows an investor to lodge a complaint against the host government with an arbitral tribunal. This was vehemently criticized for granting compensation for investors when countries pass laws, such as environmental regulations, that serve the public good, and for having the effect of dictating domestic policies by imposing compensation when foreign corporations are hurt.[19] In response to a series of challenges to environmental laws by private investors under this Chapter,[20] Congress adopted a mandate in the Trade Act of 2002 that required investment provisions of future trade agreements to ensure that foreign investors are not accorded "greater substantive rights" than US investors enjoy under US law.

While in subsequent agreements US negotiators did generally adopt a NAFTA-*minus* agenda, many of the investment rules reflect a strong commitment to liberalization and do reiterate, with modifying provisions, the rights of investors under NAFTA.

The investment chapter in CAFTA, for example, provides a high level of protection for foreign investors, including national treatment and most-favored nation treatment, as well as an investor-state dispute settlement mechanism. Moreover, the chapter retains from NAFTA the controversial concept of direct or indirect expropriation "through measures equivalent to expropriation or nationalization". On the other hand, the CAFTA Agreement does try to forestall abuse through explicitly stating that expropriation-type measures can be taken "for a public purpose". An annex specifies that: "except in rare circumstances, non-discriminatory regulatory actions by a Party that are designed and applied to protect legitimate public welfare objectives, such as public health, safety and the environment, do not constitute indirect expropriations" (Br Feb 2004, 2, 14). The investment sections in the bilateral free trade agreements with Chile and Singapore similarly include strict financial conditions curbing the use of capital controls, as well as aggressive safeguards for intellectual property rights. At the same time they make some improvements to the NAFTA Chapter 11 model by providing more transparency, public input in the dispute, and mechanisms to improve the investor state process by eliminating frivolous claims.

Agriculture

While the average tariff of agricultural imports into the United States was 12 percent, some sectors were protected by extremely high tariffs and/or by global quotas. The United States was expected to provide parties to regional or bilateral trade agreements with better access for agricultural imports. While the United States did reduce some of its agricultural tariffs, it generally provided only minor concessions on its most sensitive products. In the US-CAFTA, for example, tariffs imposed by the US on peanuts and cotton, as well as the 26 percent out-of-quota tariff (TRQ) on beef, will be phased out over a 15-year period; US tariffs on dairy, which are as high as 60 percent on import-sensitive products, will be phased out over a 20-year period, with tariffs backloaded and safeguards applied; the approximately 100 percent TRQ on sugar will not be cut and the sugar allowed to the United States will amount to about 1,1 percent of US sugar consumption in the first year, which will grow very slowly over fifteen years to about 1,6 percent of consumption by year 15. The negotiations with Australia yielded similar results. Increases in quotas on dairy amount to about 2 percent of the current value of total US dairy imports. US above-quota duties on beef will be phased out over an 18-year period, and initial increased imports from Australia under the TRQ quota will amount to about 1,6 percent of US beef imports. Sugar was excluded altogether (E 14/2/2004, 85).

While the United States could reach agreements regarding agricultural tariff cuts, it refused to negotiate domestic subsidies. This refusal was at the core of the difficulties of the negotiations of FTAA and the negotiations with SACU.

The Free Trade Area of the Americas (FTAA)

Negotiations for creating a Free Trade Area of the Americas (FTAA) were launched by the leaders of 34 countries of the western hemisphere (Cuba was excluded at the US's insistence and French Guiana, since it is officially part of France) in 1994. The Latin American countries had two major issues it expected to resolve through the negotiations. First was the issue of agricultural tariffs and subsidies. Brazil, the second largest market after the United States, was hurt by high tariffs on its beef, soybeans, and orange juice, as well as by tariff quotas on sugar. Second was the issue of antidumping actions against Latin American manufacturing exports (Carranza 2004, 321, E 21/4/2001, 19). The US, in turn, wanted the FTAA to avert discrimination against US exporters when other countries, especially Brazil but possibly the EU, enter into FTAs with South and Central American countries without US participation (Hufbauer et al. 1999, 67, GAO July 1997, 17, GAO March 2001, 4). Less defensively, the US was interested in a 'deep integration' agenda, which intended to include international investment rules, the revision of national regulations that have discriminatory effects on trade and investment (including intellectual property, national standards, and financial, industrial, technology, competition and environmental policies), as well as the revision of national corporate, industrial, and even political structures that impose restraints on trade and investment (Haggard 1995, 203, Carranza 2004, 320).

After the collapse of the Cancun meeting in September 2003, the US had strong incentives to revive the FTAA negotiations (Carranza 2004, 330). However, the results of this seemingly obvious strategic shift illustrates the fallacy of seeing these options as insulated and therefore interchangeable, rather than inter-dependent and complementary.

The first difficulty was political. The diplomatic relations between the United States and other members of the FTAA soured when many Latin American countries joined the G-21. Brazil's pivotal role in the G-21, in particular, infuriated American trade negotiators. Following the Cancun meeting, the two parties spent weeks publicly bad-mouthing each other. Zoellick cast Brazil as leader of the "won't-do" countries and blamed it for the collapse of the negotiations; Brazil's foreign minister, Celso Amorim, accused the United States of "making threats" against its partners (E 18/10/2003, 56, NYT 20/10/2003, Br Sept–Oct 2003, 7, 16).

A more fundamental difficulty was the fact that the success of FTAA was dependent on concessions that the United States was expected to make at the Doha round. As mentioned above, Latin American countries demanded that the United States cut its agricultural subsidies. Yet the United States insisted that agricultural subsidy reductions must be negotiated in the WTO, for it could not compromise its subsidy levels without obtaining corresponding concessions from the EU and other countries (Br Sept–Oct 2003, 7, 16). As Deputy USTR, Peter Allgeier, remarked: "[T]he place to negotiate [on agricultural subsidies] is the global negotiations. We cannot negotiate disciplines on domestic supports in a regional context and leave the

European Union and Japan and others to continue their subsidy practices without any restraint."[21]

The collapse of Cancun in September 2003 has therefore shaken the regional negotiations as well. Once the expectation that what the United States could not provide regionally it would provide multilaterally was frustrated, Brazil reversed its strategy. First, the presidents of Argentina and Brazil signed a statement of intent in which they declared that South American countries would resist efforts by the US to undermine their unity in regional and global trade talks, would maintain the G-22 alliance, and would continue pressing for more equitable trade for farmers in developing countries (NYT 20/10/2003). Second, Brazil announced its preference for an "FTAA-light", that is, a regional agreement that would *not* include disciplines on intellectual property protection, services, investment, or government procurement.

The United States was compelled to accept the new conditions, and in the Eighth FTAA Ministerial Meeting that took place in Miami, in 20–21 November 2003, the parties agreed on the narrower agenda (NYT 20/11/2003). US officials, frustrated with the prospect of a watered-down hemispheric trade agreement, focused on free trade agreements with the Andes, Central American countries and the Caribbean (E 7/2/2004, 51, E 20/11/2004, 63).

SACU-US FTA

The attempt of the US, initiated in November 2002, to have a regional agreement with five member countries of the Southern African Customs Union (SACU) – Botswana, Lesotho, Namibia, South Africa, and Swaziland – had a similar trajectory.

A SACU-US FTA stemmed from intentions expressed in the Africa Growth and Opportunities Act (AGOA) of 2000 to initiate negotiations with beneficiary countries to increase free trade between the US and sub-Saharan Africa. Possibly, the primary motive of the US government was to equal the Trade, Development and Cooperation Agreement (TDCA) that entered into force between the EU and South Africa in 1999 (Br Nov 2004, 10, 17). SACU countries, in turn, were interested in locking in the benefits of AGOA and extending the range of products that qualify for preferential tariffs. Yet, SACU negotiators felt overstretched by the ambitious demands of the US, who had pushed for a significantly more comprehensive deal than the one South Africa had with the EU, so negotiations stalled even before Cancun (Br July–Aug 2004, 7, 16). After Cancun, the disagreement widened. As described by South Africa's chief trade negotiator Zavier Carim, "[s]ome difficulties have emerged from the fallout from Cancun in the sense that the US had always proposed to deal with antidumping and subsidy issues at the WTO level rather than bilaterally. With the WTO negotiations having no clear direction at the moment, and the possibility that the [Doha] Round will be extended, we are in limbo at the multilateral level" (Br Sep–Oct 2003, 7, 19). SACU therefore requested the United States to broaden the free trade area agreement under negotiation to cover agricultural subsidies and antidumping rules, a request that the United States refused to fulfil.

The opportunities and constraints of Doha-plus initiatives

The initiation and conclusion of free trade agreements after Cancun had important material and political implications that served US interests, but only to an extent. First, bilateral and regional agreements helped to force countries back into multilateral negotiations, at times while undermining their strategic options. Second, some bilateral and regional agreements were used to gain concessions beyond those possible at the WTO negotiations. At the same time, however, FTAA and SACU demonstrate that it was easier to the United States to gain Doha-plus concessions in bilateral and regional agreements when these were in tandem with multilateral negotiations, not as a replacement to them.

Bilateral and regional negotiations affect the strategic position of WTO members in the multilateral negotiations   First, FTAs weaken the opposition for multilateral agreements for those agreeing to make concessions to the United States have less reason to oppose similar concessions at the multilateral level. As Deputy USTR, Peter Allgeier, remarked: "[T]here is a linkage between these two negotiations and we are trying to use the agricultural negotiations in the FTAA to build support for our proposals for agricultural reform in the WTO."[22] Second, bilateral or regional agreements create incentives for countries *excluded from the agreements* to make concessions in the multilateral negotiations to eliminate the discrimination to which they would be subjected (Carranze 2004, 330).[23] Third, as the case of G-21 illustrates, the United States used its leverage at the bilateral level to pressure countries to abandon previous positions and strategies. After Charles Grassley, the chair of the Senate Finance Committee, suggested that no country in the G-21 could get a bilateral deal with the United States, several Latin American countries desperate for a deal with the United States – including Colombia, Costa Rica, Ecuador, Guatemala and Peru – gave in to American pressure and pulled out of the G-21 (E 18/10/2003, 56, NYT 20/10/2003). In short, as summarized by Zoellick himself: "By pursuing multiple free trade initiatives, we are creating a 'competition for liberalization' that provides leverage for openness in all negotiations, establishes models of success that can be used on many fronts, and develops a fresh dynamic that puts America in a leadership role."[24]

The United States gets in regional and bilateral agreements concessions it could not have gotten in the WTO negotiations   Because US's most desired concessions are those providing access into its protected sectors, such as agriculture, the US currently has greater leverage in bilateral rather than multilateral negotiations. First, it is easier to persuade US agricultural producers to give minor concessions to particular countries (in the case of some agricultural products, very minor concessions), rather than to surrender their exceptional treatment as a whole. This means that US negotiators can offer bilaterally what they cannot offer at the multilateral level or, to put it differently, that bilateral concessions are less "expensive" than multilateral ones. Moreover, since such concessions are more significant when they are discriminatory (e.g., opening US agricultural market *only* to Chile rather than to all agricultural exporters) the US government can make greater demands in return to its concessions. In short, it is by providing discriminatory concessions that the United States could convince other countries to prefer bilateral rather than multilateral forums and to ask for Doha-plus provisions regarding intellectual property and investment. The details of the bilateral agreements should make it obvious that US's "sacrifice" was minute compared to the concessions made by its trading partner, but it is still the case that the US had to offer a preferential treatment. This stems, as I suggested in the introduction, also from the fact that the partners of regional or bilateral agreements have to be more actively convinced into the agreement.

The paradox of bilateralism   In spite of the concessions the US could achieve from its partners, there were also clear disadvantages to the bilateral or regional options. First, although bilateral or regional agreements might give the US preferential access to specific markets which might be an attractive achievement in its own right, the United States was interested in market access on a global scale, and such goal was better achieved through multilateral agreements, rather than through bilateral or regional ones. The lack of systemic logic behind the choice of bilateral partners reveals the symbolic rather the material benefits of bilateral agreements. Second, and most importantly, it is often impossible to separate the regional/bilateral negotiations from the multilateral. If agricultural subsidies are impossible to negotiate at the bilateral/regional level, then the fate of the regional negotiations is tightly linked to the fate of the multilateral negotiations and a multilateral crisis would either weaken US bargaining leverage or make an agreement impossible.

In short, while bilateral and regional negotiations enable the United States to force countries back into multilateral negotiations, and to gain significant concessions from the parties to the agreement, such negotiations can only partially replace the multilateral negotiations and many would fail to materialize without leaning on the multilateral base. Regional and bilateral negotiations cannot, and are not intended to, replace multilateral negotiations. Instead, negotiations are aimed to complement each other as a web of institutional alternatives in which one political option requires the other. It is a set of concessions *across* agreements that is most beneficial for the United States.

Option 3: Judicial proceedings

The notion of "venue shopping" should cover not only diplomatic venues but also legal ones, at both the national and international levels. Judicial mechanisms for resolving disputes are generally less effective as venues for imposing new rules (although legal venues could create new obligations by imposing a particular interpretation of disputed provisions of agreements), but can be found quite useful in enforcing implementation of existing rules. Possible legal venues include litigation in the country of the respondent (with the complainant being a private actor and the defendant the state), in the country of the plaintiff (e.g., Section 301, with the complainant being the state and the defendant a private actor or another state), or at the international level (both parties are states). While legal venues are generally effective, I argue that failed legal initiatives in the case of TRIPS served as a turning point in the international perception on the issue of access to drugs, which then allowed, against the will of the United States, the Doha Declaration and the 30 August Decision.

Section 301

Section 301 of the Trade Act of 1974 gives the US president authority to take unilateral retaliatory actions against foreign countries that violate trade agreements or otherwise maintain laws or practices that restrict US commerce. Special 301, which was added in 1988, authorizes the USTR to identify countries that do not provide adequate protection to intellectual property and to impose sanctions against them.

With the conclusion of the TRIPS Agreement, IP-reliant businesses, represented by bodies like the International Intellectual Property Alliance (IIPA), began to aggressively lobby USTR and pursue litigation to block practices of other countries that were allegedly violating the Agreement. USTR used Special 301 "Watch List" to effectively combat targeted TRIPS violations, for example, the production of unauthorized copies of "optical media" products or insufficient protection of test data submitted by drug companies to health authorities. USTR has also used Special 301 to force implementation of TRIPS-plus provisions on signatories of bilateral agreements such as Chile. Many such 301 investigations culminated in bilateral agreements in which the target state succumbed to US's demands. The US also, if rarely, imposed unilateral trade sanctions. More often, unresolved cases were referred to the dispute settlement mechanisms of the WTO (see below).

The USTR, prompted by a strong lobby of PhRMA, also targeted South Africa. In reaction to South Africa's *Medicines and Related Substances Control Amendment Act of 1997*, that pharmaceutical companies vehemently attacked for being inconsistent with South Africa's TRIPS obligations,[25] he placed it on the 1998 Special 301 "Watch List" (Sell and Prakash 2004, 161). The Amendment Act permitted the health minister to revoke pharmaceutical patent rights if he deemed the associated medicines to be too expensive. It further empowered the minister to order compulsory licensing if the patentee engaged in abusive practices, defined as a failure to sell a drug in adequate amounts to meet demand, or a refusal to license the product on reasonable terms so that domestic firms might meet demand. It also permitted parallel importation of drugs. The law required pharmacists to employ generic substitution unless the doctor or patient forbade it, set limits on pharmacy markup rates, and banned in-kind inducements from drug manufacturers to physicians (Shamir 2005).

Eighteen months after putting it on its "Watch List", the two countries reached a bilateral understanding under which South Africa pledged to abide by WTO rules and the US pledged to drop its demands that South Africa ease parts of the law that had prompted the Special 301 challenge (NYT 18/9/1999). In May 2000, the Clinton administration issued an Executive Order that extended the agreement with

South Africa to other sub-Saharan African governments. The order declared that the United States would not seek any revision of intellectual property policy in sub-Saharan African countries if that policy promoted access to HIV/AIDS medications and remained consistent with the TRIPS Agreement (WP 11/5/2000). After taking office in 2001, the Bush administration indicated that it would not rescind Clinton's Executive Order.

WTO's Dispute Settlement Understanding

The Dispute Settlement Understanding (DSU), which was part of the Uruguay Round Agreements, strengthened the dispute settlement procedures of the WTO by eliminating the veto power of parties over the formation of a panel and the adoption of panels' reports, and strengthening the WTO's enforcement mechanisms (Chorev 2005a). The DSU led to a dramatic increase in the number of complaints, including a significant high number of filings based on the TRIPS Agreements. Initially, the United States was particularly active. Between 1995 and 2000 the United States filed 16 cases (consolidated into 12 cases). Respondents included developed countries (such as Japan, EC, and Canada), but also Pakistan, India, Argentina and Brazil. Of the 12 consolidated cases initiated by the United States the US won in 2 cases, the US reached a "mutually agreed solution" without a ruling in 9 cases, and 1 case is still pending. The US won in a case regarding India's Patent Law (DS50, DS79) and a case regarding Canada's term of patent protection (DS170). The mutually agreed solutions are most commonly possible when the respondent is willing to change its practices or policies without disputing the complaint. In those 9 cases, therefore, the United States effectively transformed IP domestic practices in the direction of further compliance with US's perception of TRIPS obligations.[26] The United States has not filed a TRIPS-related case since 2000.

The rise and fall of adversary challenges

Importantly, the legal initiations described above preceded the Doha round of multilateral negotiations, and not only did the US government pledge to stop its unilateral legal challenges at the domestic level, it also, at least for the time being, stopped initiating DSU cases. This was not due to the inefficiency of the measures. On the contrary, Section 301 and the WTO dispute settlement mechanisms provided effective ways for the United States to enforce compliance on others. Instead, it was probably a political decision, also practiced during previous multilateral negotiations, in order not to create diplomatic tensions and upset partners through adversary means and try, instead, to resolve issues as part of the negotiations as a whole.[27] More significantly, the recent lack of activity should be interpreted as a consequence of US's failed attempts to use legal channels to block developing countries' access to drugs. Having withdrawn its Special 301 case against South Africa, the US administration - backed by the US Congress – seemed ready to avoid future public embarrassments. The Doha Declaration can itself be seen as another instant in this trajectory. That is, the Declaration as well as the 30 August Decision were possible only due to the earlier decision of the United States not to *force* compliance on South Africa and other countries.

Yet, the decision not to pursue "crude" or visible adversary venues, as well as the Doha Declaration and the 30 August Decision, did *not* stop the United States from trying to alter other countries' laws. As we saw, the United States merely shifted its strategic focus, trying to make governments to agree to such changes voluntarily, in return to US concessions, rather than via judicial coercion.

Another important consequence of the DSU was that it offered institutional manoeuvreings for other countries. In a case initiated in 2002, Brazil filed a case against US cotton subsidies (DS267). The issue of cotton became central to the Doha negotiations when in Cancun a group of four West African countries – Benin, Burkina Faso, Chad and Mali – called on the US and others to agree then (as opposed to waiting to the end of the round) to abolish their cotton subsidies within the following three years. They also asked for $300 million in immediate compensation for losses they have been suffering in the world market (NYT 13/9/2003, A12). The US government provides a $3 billion-plus a year to cotton farmers (compared to the EU that gives $1 billion, mostly in Greece and Spain), and the US negotiators were fiercely opposed. Their position was reflected in the draft text that emerged halfway through the Cancun meeting, where the promises on cotton were vague, pledging a WTO review of the textiles sector, but with no mention of eliminating subsidies or of compensation. Worse, it suggested that the West African countries should be encouraged to diversify out of cotton altogether (E 20/9/2003, 30). Yet, in a ruling dated from August 2004, the WTO panel confirmed that US cotton subsidies exceeded the caps the US had agreed to and were therefore illegal. The United States appealed the decision. Possibly, the decision has already affected US negotiators, who since shifted their position on cotton (see below).

Option 4: Other international organisations?

In a hearing before the House Committee of International Relations, a member of the Heritage Foundation announced:

> [G]iven the great disparities in world opinion over the efficacy, and even the definition, of free trade, the United States must be prepared to enact free-trading coalitions of the willing if the Doha round stalls.... [T]he Bush administration needs to embrace the idea of Global Free Trade Association – a coalition of the willing determined to maximize trade liberalization throughout its member states. States around the globe that meet certain, predetermined, numerical criteria relating to trade policy, capital flows and foreign investment, property rights, and regulation would automatically qualify for the grouping .... [A]gain a coalition of the willing, this time in trade, is the way forward.[28]

While the United States has never seriously considered the replacement of the GATT/WTO with another *trade* organisation, US negotiators have always been "venue shopping" for other multilateral options. Often it was determined that the GATT/WTO would be the most favorable venue to follow, as the decision to channel intellectual property negotiations from WIPO to the GATT in the early 1990s illustrates. At other times, as in the case of investment, US negotiators did attempt to utilize a different venue.

US business believed that negotiations over investment liberalization under the auspices of the OECD would lead to an investment pact of the "tightest standards" which would be impossible to achieve under the WTO (FT 29/10/1996). Following such sentiments, OECD Ministers launched in 1995, just after the conclusion of the Agreement on Trade-Related Investment Measures (TRIM), negotiations on a multilateral agreement on investment (MAI). The expectation was that non-OECD members, in particular upwardly-mobile Asian and Latin American nations, would join the treaty (NYT 27/12/1995). OECD members, however, could not overcome disagreements, such as French and Canadian demands that the agreement should exclude cultural activities, EU insistence that its members be allowed to continue giving preferential treatment to one another's investors, and US unwillingness to reconsider the use of sanctions designed to penalize foreign investors in Cuba, Iran and Libya (FT 25/3/1998). The MAI negotiations finally collapsed when France refused to renew negotiations in October 1998. With the collapse of the negotiations, the Working Group on Trade and Investment at the WTO remained the only multilateral forum where investment issues were under discussion. As we saw, at the point the United States preferred the bilateral channel.

Back to Option 1: The revival of the Doha negotiations

On February 11, 2004, Zoellick embarked on a whistle-stop tour of key capitals in three continents in order to engage in "strategic dialogue" with WTO members on how to move the Doha Round forward. In his tour, Zoellick made two central points. The first was that without a commitment to the elimination of agricultural export subsidies by a specific date, the Doha Round would continue to languish. The second was that agreement could be found on addressing trade facilitation as part of the Round, but that all other Singapore issues should be dropped (Br Feb 2004, 2, 1). Zoellick also reiterated that the US would be ready to substantially reduce domestic agricultural subsidies, provided that the EU, Japan and other heavy subsidizers did the same, and that both developed *and* developing countries agreed to increase market access through substantial tariff cuts (Br March 2004, 3, 5).

Agricultural subsidies   In July 27–30, 2004, in Geneva, some 25 trade ministers agreed on a "framework" for the rest of the Doha trade round. The biggest achievement was a seven-page "framework for establishing modalities in agriculture". This framework included a commitment to eliminate export subsidies (against EU's initial objection), as well as promises to rein in other forms of export support, such as export credits (used by the US) and state trading organisations (used by Canada). Rich countries also agreed to deeper cuts in trade-distorting domestic subsidies. The plan is to make "substantial" cuts, with the biggest subsidiaries slashing most, a formula that benefits the United States and was a top priority for Zoellick (E 7/8/2004, 67). The subsidy cuts could include some of the $19 billion given annually to American farmers who raise cotton, rice, corn, wheat and soybeans. But developing countries questioned whether there would be an overall reduction in American subsidies or simply shifting subsidies from one category to another (NYT 2/8/2004). Countries without subsidies (including Japan, Norway and Switzerland) agreed to make changes as well, e.g., the highest agricultural tariffs will be cut more deeply than the lowest ones (NYT 1/8/2004).

Cotton   The 31 July decision also commits Members to addressing the issue of cotton "ambitiously, expeditiously, and specifically, within the agriculture negotiations". Although the US was previously opposed to singling out cotton in the negotiations, and possibly as a result of the WTO negative decision, the July decision declares that negotiations must ensure "appropriate prioritization of the cotton issue independently from other sectoral initiatives" (Br July–Aug 2004, 7,1).

Singapore issues   The EU has given up on its ambitions to expand the Doha agenda to new areas, such as investment. Echoing this concession, The Geneva decision established modalities for negotiations on trade facilitation only (Br July-Aug 2004, 7, 1).

TRIPS   It is important to avoid the impression that negotiations will go smoothly from now on, as the negotiations over intellectual property rights illustrate. In the final meeting of the WTO Council for TRIPS on 1–2 December 2004, the African Group – which includes all African WTO Members – submitted a proposal for converting the waiver provided for in the 30 August 2003 Decision into a formal amendment of the TRIPS agreement. Many developed countries criticized the proposal, arguing that it sought to re-open the debate on the substance of the Decision and would only complicate current discussions. The supporters of the proposal countered that the suggested text was only an attempt to simplify the complex nature of the waiver (Br 8 Dec 2004, 8, 42).

Conclusions

Considered chronologically, it is possible to identify a chain of strategies used by the US government in its attempts to impose a particular perception of intellectual property rights on other countries. First, and before realizing the political sensitivity of the issues at hand, the US government willingly adhered to the demands of the pharmaceutical companies and, quite heavy-handedly, used judicial proceedings to enforce compliance. While judicial venues such as Special 301 and the DSU were generally successful, in the particular case of access to drugs – thanks to the counter-political strategies of developing countries and NGOs – it turned into a public relations disaster. These had far-reaching impacts, including US's acceptance of the pro-health Doha Declaration and the 30 August Decision.

But the United States did not genuinely alter its position. At the same time that US negotiators made concessions at the multilateral level, they searched for other venues to counter-balance them. This applied to issues of intellectual property, but also to investment. As *The Economist* described this strategic logic: "if WTO negotiations are going too slowly, then concentrate on the FTAA; if the FTAA bogs down, sign bilateral deals with enthusiastic parties such as Chile" (E 21/4/2001, 19).

Indeed, in some cases the United States got in regional and bilateral agreements concessions it could not have gotten in the WTO negotiations. Some bilateral and regional FTAs did not only reiterate TRIPS conditions, but made them even more stringent. As for investment rules, at the same time that United States agreed to the exclusion of the issue from the WTO negotiations, it negotiated bilateral and regional provisions that reproduced the highly-criticized conditions of NAFTA. The US also took advantage of the stalled talks on agriculture in the multilateral level to provide discriminatory concessions, by way of tariff reduction, in its bilateral and regional agreements. Commonly, however, bilateral and regional agreements depended on and were tightly linked to the multilateral negotiations. First, bilateral agreements were used to persuade or force countries back to the multilateral negotiations. Second, because some concessions, such as cuts in agricultural tariffs, could have been made only multilaterally, the possibility of a regional or bilateral agreement often depended on parallel multilateral negotiations. Bilateral and regional agreements therefore could function as a complement but could not replace the multilateral negotiations.

This web of institutional inter-dependence usually allowed US negotiators to maximize their benefits from negotiations. However, other countries showed their ability to use institutional manoeuvres to weaken US's position. This chapter presented three such examples: developing countries effectively blocked the multilateral negotiations until their demands were appreciated, this had a secondary impact of weakening US's leverage in bilateral and regional negotiations for US negotiators could not offer concessions at the multilateral level in turn for concessions at the bilateral one, and, finally, the DSU enabled developing countries to undermine US's position and claims in the negotiations.

In short, an institutionally-contextualized analysis of the complex web of Doha-related negotiations reveals the analytical importance of considering the complete set of venues of negotiations for understanding the strategies of the participants as well as the resulting outcomes.

References

Abbott, F. M. (2004a), "The Cycle of Action and Reaction: Latest Developments and Trends in IP and Health." ICTSD-UNCATD Dialogue on Ensuring Policy Options for Affordable Access to Essential Medicines. Published in: P. Roffe,

G. Tansey and D. Vivas-Eugui (eds.), *Negotiationg Health: Intellectual Property and Access to Medicines,* (Earthscan, 2005).

Abbott, F. M. (2004b), "The Doha Declaration on the TRIPS Agreement and Public Health and the Contradictory Trend in Bilateral and Regional Free Trade Agreements." Occasional Paper 14, (Quaker United Nations Office).

Baldwin, D., ed. (1993), *Neorealism and Neoliberalism,* (New York: Columbia University Press).

Baumgartner, F. R. and Bryan D. J. (1993), *Agendas and Instability in American Politics,* (Chicago: University of Chicago Press).

Bhagwati, J. (1993), "Regionalism and Multilateralism: An Overview." In *New Dimensions in Regional Integration,* edited by Jaime de Melo and Arvind Panagariya, 22-51, (New York: Cambridge University Press).

Carranza, M. E. (2004), "Mercosur and the End Game of the FTAA Negotiations: Challenges and Prospects after the Argentine Crisis." *Third World Quarterly* 25(2):319-337.

Chorev, N. (2005a), "The Institutional Project of Neo-Liberal Globalism: The Case of the WTO." *Theory and Society* 34(3): 317-355.

Chorev, N. (2005b), "Making and Remaking State Institutional Arrangements: The Case of U.S. Trade Policy in the 1970s." *Journal of Historical Sociology* 18(1-2): 3-36.

Correa, C. M. (2001), "TRIPS Disputes: Implications for the Pharmaceutical Sector." Occasional Paper 5, (Quaker United Nations Office – Geneva).

Curzon, G. and V. Curzon (1973), *Hidden Barriers to International Trade,* (London: Trade Policy Research Centre).

Davis, Ch. L. (2003), "Setting the Negotiation Table: The Choice of Institutions for Trade Disputes." Paper presented at the 2003 Annual Meeting of the American Political Science Association, (Philadelphia), www.princeton.edu/~cldavis/files/fora.pdf.

Davis, Ch. L. (2004), "International Institutions and Issue Linkage: Building Support for Agricultural Trade Liberalization." *American Political Science Review* 98(1): 153-169.

Finlayson, J. and M. Zacher (1981), "The GATT and the Regulation of Trade Barriers: Regime Dynamics and Functions." *International Organisation* 35 (4): 561-602.

GAO - General Accounting Office (1997), "World Trade Organisation: Observations on the Ministerial Meeting in Singapore." Testimony Before the Subcommittee on Trade, Committee on Ways and Means, House of Representatives. GAO/NSIAD-97-92.

GAO - General Accounting Office (1997), "Trade Liberalization: Western Hemisphere Trade Issues Confronting the United States." Report to the Chairman, Subcommittee on Trade, Committee on Ways and Means, House of Representatives. GAO/NSIAD-97-119.

GAO - General Accounting Office (2001), "Free Trade Area of the Americas: Negotiations at Key Juncture on Eve of April Meetings." Report to the Chairman, Committee on Finance, U.S. Senate. GAO-01-552.

GAO - General Accounting Office (2004), "World Trade Organisation: Cancun Ministerial Fails to Move Global Trade Negotiations Forward; Next Steps Uncertain." Report to the Chairman, Committee on Finance, U.S. Senate and Chairman, Committee on Ways and Means, House of Representatives. GAO-04-250.

Geuze, M. and H. Wager (1999), "WTO Dispute Settlement Practice Relating to the TRIPS Agreement." *Journal of International Economic Law,* 347-384.

Haggard, St. (1995), *Developing Nations and the Politics of Global Integration,* (Washington D.C.: Brookings Institution).

Hall, P. A. and R. C. R. Taylor (1996), "Political Science and the Three New Institutionalisms." *Political Studies* 44: 936-957.

Hufbauer, G., J. Scott and B. Kotschwar (1999), "US Interests in Free Trade in the Americas." In *The United States and the Americas: A Twenty-First Century View*, edited by A. Fishlow and J. Jones, (New York: W. W. Norton).

Immergut, E. M. (1998), "The Theoretical Core of the New Institutionalism." *Politics & Society* 26 (1): 5-34.

Jawara, F. and A. Kwa (2003), *Behind the Scenes at the WTO,.* (London: Zed).

Ikenberry, G. J. (2001), *After Victory: Institutions, Strategic Restraint, and the Rebuilding of Order after Major Wars,* (Princeton: Princeton University Press).

Keohane, R. (1984), *After Hegemony,* (Princeton: Princeton University Press).

Keohane, R. (2002), *Power and Governance in a Partially Globalized World*, (London: Routledge).

Krugman, P. (1993), "Regionalism Versus Multilateralism: Analytical Notes." In *New Dimensions in Regional Integration*, edited by Jaime de Melo and Arvind Panagariya, 58-79, (New York: Cambridge University Press).

Levy, D. and A. Prakash (2003), "Bargains Old and New: Multinational Corporations in Global Governance." *Business and Politics* 5(2):131-150.

Mansfield, E. D. and H. V. Milner (1999),. "The New Wave of Regionalism." *International Organisation* 53(3): 589-627.

Mansfield, E. D. and E. Reinhardt (2003), "Multilateral Determinants of Regionalism: The Effects of GATT/WTO on the Formation of Preferential Trading Arrangements." *International Organisation* 57: 829-862.

McGillivray, F. (2000), Democratizing the World Trade Organisation, (Hoover Institute).

Narlikar, A. (2004), "The Ministerial Process and Power Dynamics in the World Trade Organisation: Understanding Failure from Seattle to Cancun." *New Political Economy* 9(3): 413-428.

Narlikar, A. and R. Wilkinson (2004), "Collapse at the WTO: A Cancun Post-Mortem." *Third World Quarterly* 25(3): 447-460.

Oxfam (2004), "Undermining access to medicines: Comparison of five US FTAs." Oxfam Briefing Note www.oxfamamerica.org/pdfs/fta_comparison.pdf.

Pierson, P. and T. Skocpol (2002), "Historical Institutionalism in Contemporary Political Science," in *Political Science: The State of the Discipline,* edited by I. Katznelson and H. V. Milner, (New York: W. W. Norton).

Pralle, S. B. (2003), "Venue Shopping, Political Strategy, and Policy Change: The Internationalization of Canadian Forest Advocacy." *Journal of Public Policy* 23(3): 233-260.

Rosendorff, P. B. and H. V. Milner (2001), "The Optimal Design of International Trade Institutions: Uncertainty and Escape." *International Organisation* 55(4): 829-857.

Sell, S. K. and A. Prakash (2004), "Using Ideas Strategically: The Contest Between Business and NGO Networks in Intellectual Property Rights." *International Studies Quarterly* 48: 143-175.

Shamir, R. (2005), "Corporate Responsibility and the South African Drug Wars: Outline of a New Frontier for Cause Lawyers." In *The World Cause Lawyers Make: Structure and Agency in Legal Practice*, edited by A. Sarat and St. Scheingold, (Stanford University Press).

Steinberg, R. H. (2002), "In the Shadow of Law or Power? Consensus-Based Bargaining and Outcomes in the GATT/WTO." *International Organisation* 56 (2): 339-374.

Thelen, K. and S. Steinmo (1992), "Historical Institutionalism in Comparative Politics" in *Structuring Politics: Historical Institutionalism in Comparative Analysis*, edited by S. Steinmo, K. Thelen and F. Longstreth, (Cambridge: Cambridge University Press).

Waltz, K. N. (1979), *Theory of International Politics*, (New York: McGraw-Hill).

Wilkinson, R. (2001), *Multilateralism and the World Trade Organisation: The Architecture and Extension of International Trade Regulation*, (London: Routledge).

World Bank, (2002), "Intellectual Property: Balancing Incentives with Comparative Access." Global Economic Prospects and the Developing Countries.

World Health Organisation (2001), "Globalization, TRIPS and access to pharmaceuticals." WHO Policy Perspectives on Medicines. No. 3, (Geneva: World Health Organisation).

World Trade Organisation (2001), Doha Ministerial Declaration. WT/MIN(01)/ DEC/1.www.wto.org/english/thewto_e/minist_e/min01_e/mindecl_ e.htm#implementation

World Trade Organisation (2004), Trade Policy Review: United States. Secretariat Report. WT/TPR/S/126. www.wto.org/english/tratop_e/tpr_e/tp226_e.htm

Newspapers

Br = Bridges
E   = The Economist
FT = Financial Times
NYT = New York Times
WP = Washington Post

Notes

1   I use the notion of "regime" to refer to both formal and informal means of organisation at the international realm.

2   Historical institutionalists commonly confine their arguments to the domestic level, and hence to institutional arrangements of the national-state (Pierson and Skocpol 2002, but see Ikenberry 2001). I rely on current formulations of the historical institutional approach to the state but offer a modified formulation, which is attentive to the capacity of institutions to affect political strategies and influence of both state and non-state actors. For more detailed elaborations see Chorev 2005a, 2005b.

3   In the international political realm competing interested actors include member-states, global and domestic economic actors and other non-governmental organisations, as well as, at times, officials of international organisations or panelists in judicial proceedings.

4   The data in this section is based on WTO (2004).

5   The numbers do not fully match due to the WTO report's reliance on different sources.

6   Since 1999, the US surplus in trade in services has been shrinking, especially in 2001, mainly due to a steep decline in travel, passenger fares, and other transportation, affected by a weak economy and September 11th.

7   Compare to 1970, when exports constituted only 4,27 percent of the GDP and imports constituted only 5,65 percent of GDP, and 1990, when exports constituted 7,76 percent of the GDP and imports constituted 8,53 percent. U.S. Department of Commerce, Bureau of Economic Analysis, National Income and Product Accounts Tables, Table 1.1.6. <http://bea.gov/bea/dn/nipaweb/index.asp>.

8   US's major export destinations are still neighboring countries or other developed countries. In 2002, these included Canada (23 percent of total exports), the EU (15) members (21 percent), Mexico (14 percent), and Japan (7 percent). US's larger suppliers are Canada (18 percent of total imports), the EU (15) (19 percent, of which the UK supplies 3,5 percent and Germany 5 percent), Mexico (11 percent), China (11 percent), and Japan (10,4 percent).

9   See Sell and Prakash 2004, 160, World Bank 2002. For a reading that emphasizes the flexibilities inscribed in the text see Abbott 2004b.

10   Parallel importation enables competition and hence lowered prices for the patented product. Moreover, patent-holders cannot use their patent rights in the importing country to prevent parallel importation if the patent-holder's right has been "exhausted" in the exporting country (WHO March 2001).

11   The support of the US government was not free. In the fiscal year July 2003 – June 2004, for example, PhRMA spent US$150 million on influencing public policy, of which US$17,5 million was spent to fight price controls and protect patent rights in trade negotiations (E 3/11/2001, 90).

12   Bridges (Br) is a newsletter published by the International Centre for Trade and Sustainable Development (ICTSD). See www.ictsd.org/monthly/index.htm

13   The requirements included: (1) the country seeking to import generic copies under compulsory license must be a WTO Member. (2) It must have "made a notification to the Council for TRIPS of its intention to use the system as an importer". (3) Most importantly, the country must also notify to the TRIPS Council the name and expected quantity of the product needed, as well as confirm (unless it is a least-developed country) that it lacks the domestic capacity to manufacture the product. The compulsory license will only cover the production and exports of the specific quantity of the product

notified to the WTO. As of November 2004, not a single eligible country has notified to the WTO either its intention to use the system as an importer, or a specific shortfall of a particular drug (Br Nov 2004, 10:21).

14   The US government also argued that the plan was consistent with its existing WTO commitments - in the Uruguay Round it agreed to set ceilings on its trade-distorting agricultural subsidies in the amount of $19,1 billion (compared to the EU, which has a ceiling of €69 billion) - though some doubted it (E 11/5/2002, 92, E 2/11/2002, 14).

15   On the biased procedures of the GATT, and later the WTO, see Curzon and Curzon 1973, Finlayson and Zacher 1981, 591-92, McGillivray 2000, Wilkinson 2001, Steinberg 2002, Jawara and Kwa 2003, Chorev 2005a.

16   This means that for the first five to ten years following registration of a drug, government regulatory authorities cannot rely on originator test data to approve a bio-equivalent generic product (with clear implications for use of compulsory licensing). Some FTAs link data exclusivity with patent protection so as to protect producers from obtaining marketing approval at any time during the patent period, even in preparation to enter the market upon patent expiry.

17   CAFTA and the FTA with Morocco were accompanied by "side letters" on public health which state that the FTAs should not prevent the Parties from taking measures to promote access to medicines or to implement WTO decisions regarding the TRIPS Agreement. These side letters have an important interpretive value, but they do not change the binding TRIPS-plus provisions in the text (Oxfam 2004:5, Abbott 2004b, 3).

18   Jon Kyl, a joint hearing of the international trade subcommittee and the health care subcommittee of the Senate Finance Committee. International Trade and Pharmaceuticals. 108th Congress. 27 April 2004.

19   An additional point of criticism was that arbitration, more than judicial proceedings in courts, are biased in favor of business: arbitrations take place in secret and there is no room in the process to hear non-parties who might be hurt; there is no appeal; when companies seek to recover damages, arbitration panels tend to focus narrowly on the issue of whether a company's profits were affected by a government action and they don't need to consider whether the action or law in question was necessary to protect the environment or public health, or even to stop a corporation's harmful behavior.

20   For example, when Mexico barred Metalclad, an American company, from building a toxic-waste treatment plant without a permit on a site authorities considered dangerous, the company won a $167 million judgment.

21   Peter Allgeier, Deputy USTR, hearing before the International Trade Subcommittee of the Senate Finance Committee. Free Trade Area of the Americas. 108th Congress. May 13, 2003.

22   Peter Allgeier, Deputy USTR, hearing before the International Trade Subcommittee of the Senate Finance Committee. Free Trade Area of the Americas. 108th Congress. May 13, 2003.

23   The same logic works also in the relations between bilateral and regional agreements. For example, one of the incentives for CAFTA was to increase the pressure on Brazil to sign up to the proposed FTAA (E 15/2/2003:54).

24   Robert Zoellick. Hearing before the House Committee on Ways and Means. President Bush Trade Agenda. 108th Congress. 11 March 2004.

25   In addition to lobbying for the intervention of the US government, multinational pharmaceutical companies orchestrated with the South African Pharmaceutical Manufacturers Association (PMA) a legal challenge to the Act in South Africa. In 1998,

the PMA challenged the constitutionality of the Act at the High Court of South Africa. The issue of constitutionality was intended to detach the dispute from the questions of public health and access to medicines. As soon as the issue of health as a greater public good has become a dominant part of the debate, the pharmaceutical companies found themselves forced to withdraw their case, which they did in March 2001 (for an extensive analysis of the case see Shamir 2005).

26   For a review of some of these cases see Geuze and Wager 1999, Correa 2001.

27   During the Tokyo Round, for example, the Secretary of Treasury had the authority to waive negative countervailing duty decisions.

28   Statement of John C. Hulsman, PhD Research Fellow for European Affairs, the Davis Institute for International Studies, The Heritage Foundation. Future of Transatlantic Relations. House Committee of International Relations. 11 July 2003.

Chapter 3

European Union Trade Politics: Pursuit of Neo-Mercantilism in Different Fora?

Werner Raza*

Introduction

Trade has always been an important field of European Union politics. Indeed, it can be listed among the earliest fields of competence of the European Communities (Smith 1999). Though not the core of the European integration process itself, from an economic point of view, much of what was materialising in terms of economic integration – in particular the creation of the Single Market – was motivated by the idea that the removal of barriers to trade through the creation of a common market would be beneficial to welfare and growth. The latter is of course also the essence of trade liberalisation in the multilateral trading regime. Economic integration within the EU and trade liberalisation on an international level are therefore compatible projects. From this explicitly liberal perspective, trade liberalisation and economic integration in Europe have not only been considered as enhancing economic welfare, but as important vehicles to bypass protectionist pressures at the national level (cf. Schäfer 2006).

Not surprisingly then, the Common Commercial Policy of the EU was seen as an outward-oriented complement to the central economic dimension of European integration. With the implementation of the European Single Market, the liberalisation of network industries and the evolution of big European corporations with an explicitly international outreach in the 1990s, both the internal structure of economic and political interests and the distribution of competences between the Member States and the European Union, upon which external trade policy rests, have however undergone a profound transformation. As a consequence the economic significance of trade policy has increased, and the political importance attached to trade policy by major political actors has expanded considerably.

This is indeed well reflected in the empirical importance, external trade has assumed over the 1990s for the European economy. Extra-EU trade has expanded considerably both in merchandise and service trade. From 1991 to 2004 the share of external merchandise trade (export plus imports) to EU-15 GDP rose from 14.92 to 21.86 percent (cf. Annex Table 3.1). For services, the share of external trade to EU-15 GDP rose from 5.51 to 7.12 percent from 1990–2004 (cf. Annex Table 3.2). Measured against world exports, the EU was able to expand its market share in merchandise trade from 16 percent in 1991 to 20 percent in 2004. A similar trend holds true for services: Though the EU's share of world exports in services decreased from a high of 24.52 percent in 1990 to 20.71 percent in 1992, it was able to maintain this level over the period to 2004, when it reached 20.81 percent. On the other hand, over roughly the same period the share of US exports in world merchandise exports exhibited a decline of 3 percent-points to less than 15 percent, and of 1.7 percent-points to 15.3 percent for services (cf. UNCTAD 2004, 2005). Thus, compared to its main rival in international trade, the EU's performance turns out to be quite favourable. The EU has become the world's largest and most important trading bloc. Against the spectacular emergence of Asian countries, in particular China and India, on the global scene, it was able to increase its market share in merchandise trade and it has maintained its leading role in services trade.

In this article, we will endeavour to explain the politico-economic factors that contributed to the increasing extraversion of the EU and the central role that trade policy has played in that process. Therein, the specific role of forum shifting as a strategy deliberately applied by EU policy-makers to pursue their interests in international fora will be investigated. For our purposes, the analysis of strategies of forum-shifting provides a heuristic device that enables us to better understand the dynamics of trade policy. Thus we hope to make a contribution to the systematic explanation of the transformation, which the economies of the EU have undergone during the last two decades.

However, it should be clearly borne in mind that when discussing the issue of EU trade policy and the shifting arenas through which it tries to accomplish its goals, we must pay specific attention to the particular institutional nature of EU politics. Any articulated EU trade policy is the result of a complex internal institutional process, where different political and social actors intervene. Thus, before we can endeavour to analyse the different trade policy arenas, which the EU utilises for the pursuit of its interests, we firstly need to explain the conceptual framework and the institutional structure of the Common Commercial Policy (CCP). Through this analysis we will not only gain a deeper understanding of the institutional dynamics of EU trade politics, but we will see that forum shifting is already an integral part of EU politics itself; for the EU is a hybrid political organisation consisting of different levels, in particular the supra-national and national levels. Thus, political actors in the EU choose their level for political action out of strategic considerations.

Neo-Mercantilism as the conceptual basis of EU Trade Politics

As is codified in Article 131 of the Treaty of the European Communities, it seems to be generally accepted among EU trade policy makers that liberal trade theory and the economic benefits it promises should form the legitimate conceptual framework for EU trade politics. Indeed, it would be very hard to find an EU trade-policy maker who would openly be in favour of protectionism. Most of all, the EU Commissioners in charge of external trade to date have all been very outspoken about their liberal trade convictions. Otherwise, one might suppose, they would not be considered as qualified for the position.[1]

Table 3.1 Development of International Merchandise Trade EU-15, selected indicators 1990–2004 (at current prices)

	1990	1991	1992	1993	1994	1995	1996	1997	1998	1999	2000	2001	2002	2003	2004
Value of Extra-EU Exports[1]	395,91	403,43	415,30	468,12	523,77	573,28	626,29	721,13	733,43	760,19	942,04	985,75	997,24	979,62	1068,45
Value of Extra-EU Imports[1]	442,51	471,62	465,39	464,71	514,33	545,25	581,01	672,57	710,54	779,82	1033,44	1028,40	989,24	992,72	1094,30
Net Extra-EU Exports[1]	-46,60	-68,19	-50,09	3,41	9,44	28,03	45,28	48,56	22,89	-19,63	-91,40	-42,65	8,00	-13,10	-25,85
Net Extra-EU Exports as % of GDP	n/a	-1,16	-0,82	0,06	0,15	0,42	0,64	0,66	0,30	-0,24	-1,05	-0,47	0,09	-0,14	-0,26
Extra-EU Export/Import-Ratio	0,89	0,86	0,89	1,01	1,02	1,05	1,08	1,07	1,03	0,97	0,91	0,96	1,01	0,99	0,98
Share of Extra-EU Exports to GDP-EU-15	n/a	6,88	6,79	7,63	8,14	8,56	8,91	9,75	9,48	9,35	10,85	10,96	10,70	10,36	10,80
Share of Extra-EU Imports to GDP-EU-15	n/a	8,04	7,61	7,57	7,99	8,14	8,27	9,10	9,18	9,59	11,90	11,43	10,62	10,49	11,06
Share of Extra-EU Exports to World Exp.	n/a	16,00	15,60	15,98	15,35	15,88	15,84	16,00	16,70	16,22	14,90	15,94	15,92	16,22	20,09
Share of Extra-EU Imports to World Imp.	n/a	17,64	16,78	14,83	14,50	14,73	14,40	14,64	15,26	16,12	15,66	15,37	15,07	15,40	19,90
Share of Extra-EU Ex- & Imports to World Trade	n/a	16,82	16,20	15,29	15,06	15,39	15,12	15,48	16,10	16,10	15,20	15,55	15,55	15,65	19,90

[1] ... Billion Euro from 1.1.1999/ECU until 31.12.1998

Source: Eurostat, New Cronos Database; European Commission/DG ECFIN Ameco Database; author's calculations.

Table 3.2   Development of International Services Trade EU-12/15*, selected indicators 1990–2004 (at current values)

	1990	1991	1992	1993	1994	1995	1996	1997	1998	1999	2000	2001	2002	2003	2004
Total Extra-EU Exports**	203.749	204.552	206.074	196.079	208.374	233.035	251.996	264.869	264.315	281.490	286.231	292.967	316.477	379.209	456.273
Total Extra-EU Imports**	179.204	181.724	188.620	180.260	193.236	216.322	234.404	242.147	250.205	273.593	279.399	283.979	293.561	345.650	413.168
Net Extra-EU Exports**	24.545	22.828	17.454	15.819	15.138	16.713	17.592	22.722	14.110	7.897	6.832	8.988	22.917	33.559	43.106
Exports as % of GDP EU-15	2,93	2,83	2,61	2,74	2,74	2,67	2,83	3,17	3,06	3,26	3,59	3,65	3,62	3,57	3,74
Imports as % of GDP EU-15	2,58	2,51	2,39	2,52	2,54	2,48	2,64	2,90	2,90	3,17	3,51	3,54	3,36	3,25	3,38
Net Exports %-GDP EU-15	0,35	0,32	0,22	0,22	0,20	0,19	0,20	0,27	0,16	0,09	0,09	0,11	0,26	0,32	0,35
Exports as % of World Exports	24,52	23,47	20,71	19,55	19,14	18,81	18,98	19,22	18,83	19,42	18,73	19,06	19,42	20,36	20,81
Imports as % of World Imports	20,82	20,07	18,60	17,85	17,88	17,43	17,88	17,95	18,26	19,17	18,42	18,60	18,12	18,73	19,08

*…until 1991 data refer to EU-12, from 1992 onwards to EU-15; **… Million USD at nominal exchange rates,
Source: OECD Statistics on International Trade in Services; OECD National Accounts; Eurostat; UNCTAD Yearbook of Statistics Online Database; author's calculations

The strategic approach taken in practical trade policy work by EU trade officials seems however to be inspired to a greater extent by another important theoretical tradition in economic thinking, i.e. Mercantilism (for an introduction see Schumpeter 1954, chapter 7; the classic study is Heckscher 1934, see also Stapelfeldt 2001 for a politico-economic analysis). This doctrine prescribes as a general rule for policy the maximisation of the proceeds from external trade, which entails fostering exports while restricting imports.

Under this doctrine, whether we refer to it historically or in order to characterise present-day trade politics, the State is seen as the principal agent for safeguarding the international interests of a national economy and its prime stake holders. The intervention of the State in external trade policies is motivated by a variety of reasons, both political and economic. While the absolutist State first and foremost wanted to maximise the inflow of gold and currency, modern capitalist states aim at fostering business opportunities for domestic enterprises abroad, while at the same token they shield particular businesses from economic pressure that might arise from international competition. Apart from the interests of capital, states, in particular democratically legitimised ones, have to accommodate other interests and so called non-trade concerns with their trade policy objectives. These relate to geo-strategic and defence interests, but also to social, environmental, or developmental motivations as expressed by political agents or civil-society. Thus, trade policy makers need to take into account a variety of aspects into their strategies. It is thus hardly surprising that modern capitalist states have extensively used a variety of economic instruments in trade politics in order to foster their specific ends. Indeed, it could be argued that quite paradoxically the importance of trade politics increased with the establishment and consolidation of a world-market. States have thus always been active agents. What has changed is the particular forms and degrees of freedom states have at their disposal when applying instruments of trade politics. While in the second half of the twentieth century, the application of classical or primary instruments of trade, like tariffs, quotas, or export subsidisation became increasingly circumscribed as a consequence of the multilateral rules of GATT and processes of regional integration, states shifted to using a wide array of secondary economic policies to foster their external commercial interests. These include virtually every field of economic policy, in particular exchange rate policy, fiscal policy, industrial and technology policy, but increasingly also labour market and wage policy, education policy and even health policy (cf. Jones 1986). Indeed, during the era of neo-liberal globalisation, i.e. since the late 1970s, the majority of industrialised and developing states have re-configured the ensemble of their economic policy instruments so as to foster external competitiveness. As a consequence of new currents in mainstream economic thinking, in particular endogenous growth theory, also EU policy makers have started to stress the importance of aligning the mentioned secondary economic policy fields to the presumptive necessities of the much acclaimed information and knowledge society. This becomes particularly clear with regard to the EU's Lisbon Strategy, which was adopted by the Heads of States and Governments in March 2000 at the European Council in Lisbon. The Lisbon Strategy (or Agenda) strives to transform the European

Union into the most competitive and dynamic economic region by 2010 through a re-alignment of the totality of economic policies as described above.[2] Thus societies and their many institutions like universities, schools, hospitals, kindergartens, their infrastructure and even the state apparatus itself are seen as an important source of an economy's competitiveness. Curiously, this strategy resembles many notions that were already advocated by developmentalist economic thinkers of the late eighteenth–early nineteenth century like Alexander Hamilton (1791) and Friedrich List (1844).

While EU trade policy certainly aims at increasing its net exports, its policies on import protection are certainly not fully in line with classical mercantilism. This would be hardly possible in an increasingly internationalised economy, where EU-based companies operate large production networks across a wide range of countries. Thus, import restrictions are applied more selectively. The sector which has been protected the most is agriculture with a mean tariff of 30 percent.[3] Interestingly, since the median tariff rate is only 13 percent, the difference to the mean tariff of 30 percent is explained by the relatively high number of peak tariffs in the EU. That means protection has been focussed on particular products. Here, protection has traditionally been high with regard to agricultural inputs, where due to historic reasons the EU wanted to stimulate local production. These products include both unprocessed goods like meat, and agricultural commodities designated for further processing within the EU, like sugar (average duty 350 percent), milk and milk products (average duty 87 percent), or grains (average duty 53 percent). Other agricultural products, which count in total for 27 percent of all agricultural imports, in particular inputs like skins and hides, certain fibres (cotton, wool, flax) or oils, where intra-EU supply is not abundant, have however been subject to zero or very low tariffs. Though levels of protection in agriculture are thus in general higher in the EU than in the US and Japan, the EU is nevertheless the world's largest importer of agricultural goods (see European Commission 2005, 18).

Tariff protection for the industrial sector in the EU has however been subject to a very substantial decrease in the period after World War II. Since raw materials with a weighted average of 0,1 percent and intermediate goods with a weighted average of 3,0 percent as inputs for EU industry typically are not subject to notable tariffs, the remaining tariff protection in industrial goods is mainly concentrated on finished manufactured products. Though with a weighted average of 3,5 percent, import tariffs for finished products are in general at a very moderate level, some 12 percent of all finished products – mainly consumer goods – still have tariffs of 10 percent or more (see European Commission 2005, 11). In contrast, intermediate goods do not have peak tariffs exceeding 10 percent. Trade defence instruments such as anti-dumping or anti-subsidies measures, however, are still applied on a broad basis. Similar applies to the services sector. Since the 1980s, EU or Member States' services regulations that discriminate against third-country suppliers have been dismantled through processes of deliberate liberalisation and deregulation within the EU itself. Discriminatory regulatory measures are mainly upheld for a small number of mostly public services, though a process of gradual regulatory erosion is taking place even in the most sensitive sectors like water provision or health and social services.

Hence, though central elements of mercantilism can still be found in EU trade politics, it seems to be more appropriate to use the term neo-mercantilism when depicting the conceptual foundation of current EU trade policy. There still exist elements of classical mercantilism like the active promotion of exports and the pro-active role played by the state bureaucracy (i.e. the EU-Commission) in dismantling trade barriers of third countries and in actively intervening abroad in the interest of European based companies. Yet other elements of today's trade politics deviate from the classical mercantilist dogma. In particular, the importance of import protection has changed, while trade policy has lately become more integrated with other economic policy fields. Thus, the term *neo*-mercantilism seems to be more appropriate to circumscribe the conceptual foundation of EU trade politics.

In practical EU-trade policies this doctrine has been translated into the concept of offensive versus defensive interests. The overall objective then consists in achieving through trade negotiations a final balance that is considered to be generally advantageous by the main political actors in the EU. Offensive interests include those sectors where European companies are actively seeking improved market access and thus contribute towards increasing trade surpluses. Here the exports of certain agricultural products, most manufactured goods, and most services sectors are usually subsumed. Similarly, the EU is actively pursuing a regulatory agenda that aims at firstly deregulating discriminatory national regimes relating to investment, government procurement, and intellectual property rights. Secondly, the EU is pushing for the establishment of harmonised multilateral regulatory arrangements in those fields that secure non-discriminatory treatment for EU companies. Particularly in bilateral trade negotiations, these objectives are intended to provide better market access and a reduction of regulatory requirements for EU companies.

Defensive interests, on the other hand, include those sectors, where domestic economic interests call for protection against competition from third countries – most notably in agriculture, or where certain economic activities are supplied on a not-for-profit basis, i.e. a range of public services like education, health and social services, etc. Notwithstanding the aforementioned examples, the question if a certain economic activity is qualified as an offensive or defensive interest is not pre-given, but often subject to heated political debate. In these debates, the particular interests of the political actors, i.e. the Commission, Member States, Parliament, business and civil society organisations may diverge and result in sometimes contradictory outcomes. For instance, economic sectors which the Commission, a majority of Member States and business organisations consider to be of offensive interest, might as a result of political debate become later re-classified as a defensive interest. If neither side is able to push through its position entirely, a compromise might be struck which tries to advance certain offensive interests while safeguarding particular interests for protection. A case in point are public services where some actors stress the export potential of, say, EU water, postal, or telecom service providers, while others stress the importance of these sectors for social well-being in the EU and argue against any (further) liberalisation moves. Thus, if neither side is able to fully push through its position, a seemingly schizophrenic outcome might be that the EU, while requesting that other countries open up the respective sectors, refuses to do the same in its own territory, with reference to some normative concerns – in WTO parlance "legitimate policy objectives".[4] In other words, while the refusal to apply liberal economic logic is justified on political or ethical grounds, it is demanded that the other party act according to the very same economic logic they themselves have refused to apply.

While this way of conducting trade politics in practical terms is certainly not unique to the EU, but seems to underlie the trade policy approach of many trading nations, in particular that of the US, the EU does not dispose exactly of the same mechanisms to execute the strategy. While the US as the dominant political and military power has very few, if any, inclinations to compromise in order to achieve its goals, and instead draws upon a wide arsenal of political, economic and increasingly military means of coercing other nations into agreements, the EU typically has to apply a combination of carrots and sticks, specifically suited to the particular case. Thus, for example, in the EU's bilateral trade negotiations, the trade agreements are usually supplemented by political, cultural and scientific/technological cooperation. For developing countries and LDCs, some sort of development assistance programmes and funds typically will be offered, or preferential market access is granted for products of special export interest to developing countries, such as with the recent Everything but Arms (EBA) – initiative of the EU for LDCs. The latter was launched in February 2001, when after the failure of the third WTO Ministerial Conference in Seattle in 1999 the Commission had realised that the launch of a new round of multilateral trade negotiations was only to be achieved after overcoming the reluctance of LDCs (European Commission 2004). Something similar applies to the multilateral level, where the propensity of the EU to compromise on some issues which are not at the heart of its own agenda and thus entail only a minor economic burden to the EU, but could trigger trading partners into a compromise which on balance is still attractive to the EU, is comparatively higher than the propensity of the US to do the same. A recent case in point provides the provisional agreement on TRIPS and public health that was reached in August 2003, shortly before the fifth WTO Ministerial Conference in Cancún. The issue of providing drugs for the combating of epidemic diseases – in particular HIV/AIDS – at affordable cost was of particular relevance to many developing countries, and with the active support of the EU formed part of the Doha Development Agenda. However unsatisfactorily the compromise reached in the run-up to Cancún on compulsory licenses and parallel imports of drugs still might have been from the perspective of many developing countries, it was intended to demonstrate to developing countries that the EU was engaged in brokering a deal that the US had for months stiffly resisted. A final solution was only reached after protracted negotiations with the US in December 2005.

Although, as we have tried to show, the EU has to apply somewhat more subtle strategies in trade policy making than the dominant global power, the willingness to engage in costly compromises is of course circumscribed. A particularly attractive way to avoid trade deals that are considered unacceptable to EU trade policy makers is forum-shifting (cf. Braithwaite/Drahos 2000). Forum-shifting is applied both between different multilateral organisations and between the multilateral and the bilateral levels. We will provide examples of this in subsequent chapters.

The institutional structure of EU trade policy

The institutional architecture of EU trade policy is characterised by a peculiar and rather complex net of competences and relations between the principal political organisations of the EU (EU Commission, Council, European Parliament), the Member States and business as well as civil society organisations. Trade policy was already established as a competence of the European Communities in the Treaty of Rome in 1957. Together with internal market, competition and agriculture policies, trade policy formed the core of the economic dimension of European integration right from its start. In the Treaty of Rome, the CCP rested on three principles: a common external tariff, common trade agreements with third countries, and the uniform application of trade instruments across Member States. Thus, the CCP is divided into two areas: the Conventional Commercial Policy and the Autonomous Commercial Policy. The latter consists of anti-dumping measures, countervailing duties and other unilateral measures by the EC. The former relates to bi- and multilateral trade policy, in particular the negotiation of the 600 trade deals the EU has already entered into (Elsig 2002, p. 42). The Conventional Commercial Policy will be discussed below.

Though it did not come about without resistance, the transfer of trade policy to the supra-national level by the EC founding Members was clearly motivated by the desire to insulate the policy-making process from domestic influences and protectionist pressures (cf. Hanson 1998). Thus a more liberal international trading order should be fostered. Secondly, a single voice in trade policy was expected to strengthen the political influence of the EC at the international level and make the negotiations of trade agreements function more effective. Interestingly, until the Amsterdam summit, the legal norm of the Treaty of Rome governing the CCP (ex Art 113 TEC) remained almost unchanged (Meunier, Nicolaïdis 1999). Only with the Treaty of Amsterdam was a further qualitative shift of competences to the EU level to commence.

In historical perspective, i.e. when one observes the evolution of the trade chapter from the Rome Treaty to the Maastricht, Amsterdam and Nice Treaties, respectively, a long-term shift of competences in trade matters to the community level becomes evident. But that shift did not occur gradually. During the 1960s and 1970s EC Member States still enjoyed some leeway in conducting unilateral trade measures. Only with the Single European Act and the coming into existence of the Single Market in 1992, did a substantial harmonising shift to the Community become level evident.

Article 113 of the Treaty of Rome (later Art 133 in the consolidated TEC of 1997 and thereafter) already conferred an exclusive competence to the Community in trade matters. The provision was however lacking in legal clarity as to which issues were covered under the CCP. The European Commission was given the competence to conduct trade negotiations, albeit upon a mandate given to it by the Council of Ministers (General Affairs). In practice, however, the mandate was drafted by the Commission. Trade decisions are taken by the Council of Ministers with a qualified majority. A major problem came up with the so-called new issues in trade policy, in particular services and intellectual property rights. These "new issues" appeared in trade politics at the end of the Tokyo round of GATT, but became central to trade negotiations only with the Uruguay Round (1986–1994). Since services and intellectual property rights touch upon sensitive issues of domestic regulation, the Member States were increasingly reluctant to delegate authority on these issues to the community level. In 1992, the Blair House Accords on the question of liberalising agriculture between the EU and the US led to a major crisis between the Commission and the Member States, in particular France. In combination with the difficult ratification processes of the Treaty of Maastricht in France, Denmark and Ireland during this period, all of this contributed to increasing Member States' reluctance to cede power to the EU-level. The conflict finally culminated in the wake of the conclusion of the Uruguay round of GATT. Here two questions were at stake: firstly, who should sign the final agreement of the round; and secondly, who should become a member of the new World Trade Organisation (WTO). These questions were finally submitted to the European Court of Justice, which issued a legal opinion on 15 November 1994.[5] While confirming that the Community had exclusive competence on trade in goods, much to the annoyance of the Commission, the Court held that with regard to services and intellectual property a mixed competence between the Community and the Member States prevailed, giving Member States de-jure the power to veto trade negotiations in these fields. Thus, it may be inferred that the judges refused to decide on a political issue of that order under the prevailing political circumstances. The ECJ thus continued its practice of striking a balance between fostering integration and respecting Member States vital domestic political interests. Besides, amongst criticism voiced by some Member States against it during the debates on the Treaties of Maastricht and Amsterdam, it seemingly wanted to consolidate its institutional position (Meunier, Nicolaïdis 1999, Alter 1998). The changed political climate prevented the Intergovernmental Conference that led to the Treaty of Amsterdam from altering the distribution of competences significantly. In Art 113, which became renumbered as Art 133, a paragraph (5) was amended which allowed for future expansion of exclusive competence to the new issues of services and intellectual property through unanimous vote, preserving for the Member States the right to veto any shifts in competences.

A new though only partially successful initiative to shift the distribution of competences in favour of the Union happened with the Treaty of Nice. The new issues of services and intellectual property rights became exclusive competences of the Union, except for certain exceptions, where the rule of unanimous decision and a mixed competence continued to apply. These included matters where the adoption of internal rules requires unanimity and the Community has not yet exercised the powers conferred upon it. The same applies to certain essential services (education, culture, health and social services). The latter in effect secured Member States' parliaments a stake in trade politics, since national ratification of trade treaties was still required. With the Draft Constitutional Treaty of 2004 (in the version adopted by the European Council Conference in November 2004) the field of Foreign Direct Investment was designated to become an element of the Common Commercial Policy, while competences with regard to services and intellectual property rights were further shifted to the Community level. Though as a consequence of pressure in particular from France, limited exemptions for sensitive services sectors were upheld; services (as well as intellectual property rights) generally fall within the exclusive competence of the Union. Any remaining competences of national parliaments in trade politics, in particular the ratification of trade treaties, would thus be eliminated (cf. Herrmann 2006, see also Krenzler/Pitschas 2006 for a detailed discussion). Thus, the democratic control of the Member States through their national constituencies has been weakened.

On the other hand, the stake of the European Parliament (EP) was somewhat upgraded. While before Maastricht the role of the EP was marginal, with the Treaty of Maastricht the EP has gained in influence with the assent procedure for certain agreements (Art 300, ex Art 228.3), e.g. trade agreements with important budgetary implications or agreements entailing amendments to community acts where the EP had the right to co-decide (cf. Elsig 2002). But in practice the European Parliament has not been an active agent in the CCP until recently, confining itself to its rights of consultation and the issuance of resolutions ahead of major trade events. In the draft European Constitutional Treaty the EP will however acquire co-decision rights in trade politics. From a legal perspective, it seems clear that the right to co-decision applies in cases where trade agreements will require implementation through EU legislation. In cases where this will not be necessary, it currently remains disputed whether the EP has to give its assent or not. Since most trade agreements, in particular those of the WTO, require at least in part legislative implementation, it is nevertheless to be expected that the Draft Constitutional Treaty will considerably strengthen the role of the EP (see Krajewski 2006, pp. 247–8).

Though formally rather circumscribed, in terms of practical politics the role of the EP in trade politics has only gained in significance over the last 10 years. The Commission by way of Pascal Lamy, Commissioner for trade from 1999–2004, intensified its involvement with the EP's Committee on Industry, External Trade, Research and Energy. Lamy conducted regular information sessions with the Committee. Selected Committee Members were given access to confidential documents, e.g. the requests and offers in the GATS 2000 negotiations. The Parliament issued statements and communications on trade issues and before important trade negotiations. All of these activities served as an additional legitimation of EC trade politics, and helped, as the Commission itself has claimed, to "make the criticisms of civil society more constructive" (European Commission 2004, 26). In 2004, after the constitution of the new Parliament for the legislative period 2004–2009, a new Committee on International Trade was installed in the Parliament, thus signalling that trade policy was given a higher weight by the new legislature.

Besides the European Commission, the Council of Ministers still remains the most important actor in EU trade policy. The Council adopts the mandate drafted by the Commission with a qualified majority, upon which the Commission conducts the negotiations for the European Union in consultation with the Member States. The final trade agreement has to be adopted by the Council (General Affairs and External Relations, GAERC), in general with a qualified majority, though practically by consensus. Institutionally, this is mediated through an ad-hoc forum, the 133 Committee, named after the respective article in the TEU. The 133 committee has been described as one of the most powerful in European Union Politics, both by academic experts (Elsig 2002, Christiansen and Kirchner 2000) and civil society (WWF 2003). In this committee (and its sub-committees), the Member States and the Commission discuss all trade issues and define the respective EU positions. Typically this is done by way of consensus. Only in cases of disagreement will issues be transferred to higher-level fora, in particular COREPER (Committee of Permanent Representatives) and the GAERC. The 133 committee in its various formats (Members, Deputies, and Services etc.) is formed by Commission staff from DG Trade and representatives of the Member States' trade ministries. These delegates have in turn to consult internally: the former with other Commission agencies (inter-Directorate General consultations), the latter with other government agencies and ministries and to a – from country to country varying – extent with civil society stakeholders (business, trade unions, NGOs etc). Thus, day-to-day trade policy is to a very large extent shaped and executed by bureaucrats, with detailed information on the 133 meetings not accessible to the general public. Democratic transparency and accountability of this institutional architecture is therefore limited, and indeed has provoked repeated criticisms (cf. WWF 2003, Murphy 2000).

In sum, it should have become evident that the initiative, agenda-setting and execution of EU Trade Policy reside predominantly with the European Commission. Member States dispose of important decision-making powers via the Council, with the 133-Committee serving as the central institutional forum for day-to-day policy-making. The influence of national parliaments is continually eroding, while the European Parliament has slightly gained in importance. It has, however, not acquired any significant decision powers in trade matters so far. The full implications of the trade provisions of the Draft Constitutional Treaty, in case the treaty were to enter into force, which after the failed referendums in France und the Netherlands in May/June 2005 seems to be quite unlikely, remain to be seen. Lately, it was argued that with the new constitution trade politics could be increasingly subsumed under the general principles and interests of the EU's common external and security policies (Monar 2005). That might weaken the EU-Commission and revaluate the Council and the future Minister for External Affairs, who will simultaneously be Vice-President of the Commission. Thus, EU trade politics might eventually become more stringently subsumed under the EU's geopolitical and strategic interests, hence mimicking the prevalent US approach to trade politics.

Transparency and accountability in EU trade politics

The institutional architecture of EU trade politics has major implications for the possible forms of participation of stakeholders and their influence upon the political process. The first implication is that the current institutional setup constrains the participation of those actors that have traditionally focussed their activities upon the national or local levels. These actors include in particular trade unions, social movements, civic and neighbourhood organisations, as well as petty commodity production (local trade and craftsmen) and small-scale farmers. On the other hand, large-scale businesses and service enterprises are comparatively at advantage, since their financial resources as well as their international orientation facilitate political representation at a supra-national level (van Appeldorn 2002). Not surprisingly then, EU trade politics is primarily shaped and influenced by the agendas of corporate lobbying groups. The most important among them in the field of trade are the *Union des Industries de la Communauté européenne* (UNICE), the LOTIS Committee and Group, respectively, of International Financial Services, London, and the European Services Forum (ESF).[6] Communication is however not a one way street, since the EU-Commission and in particular DG Trade actively consults business organisations, in particular at the early stages of policy formation. A case in point is the formation of the ESF. ESF was formed in 1998 by major European service corporations at the explicit request of the Commission. The latter complained about the lack of an identifiable organisation *vis-à-vis*, and proposed to the European service industry the formation of a lobbying organisation specifically devoted to services, which the Commission reckoned on becoming an increasingly important area of trade politics. A second case in point occurred in the context of the GATS 2000 negotiations, when DG Trade was consulting large European water companies about their particular needs and interests before drafting requests and offers in the GATS negotiations.[7] Thus it need not always be the case that business drives politics, but due to a pro-active and strategically thinking bureaucracy like DG Trade the opposite might happen as well.

The public discourse on globalisation that began to intensify in the second half of the 1990s in general, and the failures of both the OECD negotiations on a Multilateral Agreement on Investment (MAI) in 1998 and of the third Ministerial Conference of the WTO in November 1999 in Seattle in particular, did not remain without repercussions on trade politics in the EU. It contributed significantly to a shift in the discourse on trade politics. Criticism could be voiced more easily and it was received by political opinion leaders and the media with more openness, if not sympathy, than before. Thus, trade policy-makers at EU level as well as in the Member States became increasingly exposed to public scrutiny and in particular the many criticisms put forward by civil society organisations. Also other political organisations like the European Parliament became more active on trade issues and demanded from the EU-Commission to be informed and consulted on a regular basis. Under these circumstances, the trade Commissioner in office since 1999, Pascal Lamy, a liberal French socialist, made an initiative to introduce a consultation mechanism with civil society on all trade-related issues. Numerous meetings of DG Trade officials have taken place over the course of the last years. It is generally perceived that the informational content and news value of these meetings are limited. Nor could it be observed that via these consultations the influence of civil society on the direction and content of trade policies has significantly increased (Woolcock 2005). In fact, it arguably provided trade officials with a platform to legitimise positions that had already been taken beforehand. Nonetheless, at least to some extent it provided NGO representatives an opportunity to establish personal contacts with trade officials and thus eventually extract some extra information on particular issues. By installing a facility to refund travel expenses for NGO participants not resident in Brussels, the Commission coincidentally might even have contributed to fostering the process of civil society networking and cooperation on EU political affairs.

Furthermore, also by way of responding to demands from civil society organisations, the EU-Commission decided in 1999 to start a programme to conduct impact assessments of all its legislative and political acts. This extended also into trade politics, where DG Trade in 1999 commissioned a study from the University of Manchester to develop a methodology for the conduct of Sustainability Impact Assessments (SIA) for all trade agreements, the EC was negotiating bi- and multilaterally. During the last years a series of SIA studies were commissioned by DG Trade with the aim of assessing the likely economic, social and environmental impacts of major trade agreements with e.g. Chile, MERCOSUR, the Gulf Cooperation Council, the ACP countries, as well as the Doha Round negotiations in the WTO.[8] Though a considerable amount of financial and staff resources were devoted to these studies, their impact upon DG Trade's actual conduct of these negotiations seemed to be rather circumscribed. The results of the SIA studies were in no way binding for EU trade negotiators. By using standard economic methodology in its assessment of trade liberalisation impacts, e.g. CGE-models, in the majority of cases the findings highlighted positive effects of trade liberalisation. Only in a few cases negative impacts were identified, e.g. in environmental services, calling for a more cautious approach in the negotiations. It was considered a success when thanks to a revision of the methodology trade negotiators in DG Trade recently became obliged to issue a written statement on how – or how not – they have integrated the findings of the studies into their negotiating strategies. In those few cases with likely negative impacts, trade officials criticised or rejected the validity of the studies' findings. Thus it became evident that to a large degree the SIA studies remained an academic exercise, which more than anything else just served a legitimising purpose for the general direction of EU trade policies as defined by the Commission.

Thus, by way of summarising, we can state that the shift in the discursive field in the aftermaths of Seattle, Genoa and other major events at international level, translated into some efforts of the major political player in EU trade politics, the EU-Commission, to open up a limited space for interaction with civil society. Though that should be considered an achievement, its impact upon the strategic direction of European trade politics must be so far considered as limited. Of much greater importance, then, were grassroots campaigns and Europe-wide political mobilisations against particular trade issues, such as against the EU-Commission's conduct of the GATS negotiations in the year 2003. These campaigns were able to at least partially prevent further liberalisation in certain areas, for instance in essential public services (water, education, health, audiovisual services) in the GATS 2000 negotiations. Nonetheless, it must be concluded that neither discursive politics nor practical activism has achieved a principal change in direction away from prevailing pro-liberalisation EU trade politics.

Forum shifting in European Union trade policy-making – The case of services

GATS as an evolving regulatory regime for services and the erosion of existing international regulatory frameworks

Interestingly, most public debates depict GATS as a central vehicle for the breaking up of domestic services markets and a major tool for pushing-through market liberalisation in the services industry. While this is certainly not off the point, the particular mechanisms which are deployed to establish a more integrated services market internationally are not sufficiently differentiated in most public debates. While market access negotiations receive the thrust of public attention, arguably the so-called "rules negotiations" are – at least in the long run – of the same, if not of a higher importance for the effective liberalisation of services. That term describes a wide array of domestic regulatory instruments which include *inter alia* subsidies, government procurement, safeguard clauses, with these issues at the centre of the current negotiations, but also extending well into all sorts of qualification requirements, licensing procedures, technical standards etc. As opposed to trade in goods, where tariff-barriers have for a long time been considered the main impediment to trade, in services the existing diversity of the regulatory framework for a particular service sector between countries is commonly considered the major impediment to increasing international trade in that sector. Companies which want to supply a service in another country will have to bear the cost of complying to the rules that govern the provision of that services in the host country. These rules may vary widely between countries, but in addition they could not even be uniform within a particular country, given that many countries have federal systems, which delegate to certain competences sub-national political entities (federal states, provinces, Länder, municipalities). Thus, foreign service suppliers may face distinct legal norms pertaining to, say, zoning laws, construction codes etc. even within a singly country. Of course, these particular legal architectures are the outcome of specific historical and political developments, and enshrine to a certain extent commonly held values and norms of a society. Nevertheless, from the perspective of liberal trade theory and their proponents they are in principle seen as non-tariff trade barriers. Notwithstanding the existing diversity of legal norms between countries, political and economic integration has long preceded the current debate on globalisation. Thus, many regulatory bodies and organisations have been established, partly as international associations of professional bodies, partly as organisations under the auspices of the United Nations, partly as independent international organisations, the aim of which was to develop regulatory frameworks for particular economic activities at international level. In certain sectors these efforts went further than in others, depending upon economic necessities and political will. Nonetheless, in certain sectors, particularly in network services like postal and telecommunication services, well-established organisations have long been engaged in setting up international norms to facilitate the exchange of information or products across borders. However, from the perspective of liberal trade theory, this institutional framework had perhaps two serious shortcomings: firstly, it did not significantly reduce regulatory heterogeneity among countries, since typically the international norms would only establish the interfaces between distinct national regulatory systems; and secondly, these regulatory frameworks and the associated international organisations, respectively, would not dispose of effective means to enforce the implementation of internationally agreed standards.

Thus, very much like in the case of intellectual property rights, the establishment of an agreement for the liberalisation of services' trade in the WTO was from its very beginnings a grand project for the re-regulation of service activities at international level (cf. the seminal study of Krajewski 2003). In contrast to the prevailing international framework, the GATS does not only define the interfaces between regulatory systems, but aims at least in the long-term at institutional isomorphism, the over-arching template being what was termed "pro-competitive regulation" by critical commentators (Grieshaber-Otto/Sinclair 2004). Thus the GATS does include in its framework agreement provisions on major regulatory issues such as transparency, domestic regulation (qualification requirements, licensing, technical standards), subsidies, government procurement, mutual recognition of professional qualifications etc., the regulatory parameters of which are generally inscribed in liberal trade theory. For instance, all of these are as a matter of principle seen as an impediment to trade, as trade-distorting, as burdens to economic activity etc, which therefore should be subjected to controls abolishing them or securing that they not be more burdensome than necessary. Thus the framework agreement, though not abolishing most of these measures outright, defines the normative framework of a long-term working agenda to be executed within the WTO. Furthermore, in the context of sectoral market access negotiations, the harmonisation of rules of the particular sector under scrutiny will be negotiated in parallel. This was the case with financial services, where in addition to sectoral liberalisation commitments contained in Member States' lists of specific commitments, annexes and protocols to the GATS negotiated after the conclusion of the Uruguay Round in 1996–1997 contain a host of regulatory standards. Perhaps this parallelism of market access and rules negotiations became even more evident in the negotiations on basic telecommunication services, also concluded after the end of the Uruguay Round in 1997. Here again, the common regulatory principles were laid down in detail in an Annex and a so-called Reference Paper on Telecommunication Services. Thus, institutional dynamics with regard to regulation have been gradually shifted to the WTO to the detriment of existing institutional fora like the International Telecommunication Union.

Forum shifting and pro-competitive regulation – The case of postal services

In the current GATS 2000 negotiations, regulatory rivalry appeared in other sectors as well. One sector of particular export interest to the EU is postal and courier services. Here as a consequence of the process of liberalising postal services in the EU, which was started in the second half of the 1990s and is projected to be fully implemented by 2009, big corporations with international outreach have developed, the most important of these being *Deutsche Post AG.* These companies have been pressing the Commission and the Member States to support their expansion strategies via the GATS negotiations. To this effect the Commission has followed three avenues: firstly, it has requested comprehensive market access for postal services to its WTO partner in the GATS negotiations since 2000; secondly, it has done so on the basis of a new classification scheme for postal and courier services, which was tailored to the interests of European postal services providers; and thirdly, together with like-minded WTO Members it has developed a new reference paper for postal services (WTO Document TN/S/W/26) in an attempt to establish a common regulatory framework for the sector. The reference paper contains standards for licensing, universal service obligations, independent regulatory authorities, and transparency, which basically mimic the prevailing regulatory framework in the liberalised postal services sector in the EU. By actively promoting a regulatory framework for postal and courier services, the scope and importance of the regulatory work conducted in the Universal Postal Union (UPU) will be significantly reduced (cf. Grieshaber-Otto/Sinclair 2004). UPU, like the ITU, was already founded in the second half of the nineteenth century (1874). After World War II it became a special agency of the UN. UPU has traditionally been in charge of setting the rules for international mail exchange. In 1999 a report to the UPU Convention written by the Secretary-General highlighted possible conflicts between GATS and a number of UPU regulations, concerning in particular re-mailing, terminal dues, and the issue of postage stamps. Though these issues have not been resolved in detail, it is clear that pressure is increasing to align UPU regulations to binding WTO and GATS principles. Thus, in the EU Reference Paper on Postal and Courier Services, chapter III.D. questions the conformity of the UPU terminals' dues system with GATS and notably its Most-Favoured Nation obligation.[9] The paper concludes by calling upon WTO Members to support ongoing efforts within the UPU to establish a more cost-oriented terminal dues system. Thus a process typical for forum-shifting will possibly be reinforced that, drawing upon two strategies described by Drahos & Braithwaite (2000: 564f.), could be characterised as pursuing the same agenda in more than one organisation while threatening the organisation less advantageous to one's objectives with abandonment. As Grieshaber-Otto/Sinclair (2004) assert, since the 1980s pressure by transnational courier operators and other lobbying groups upon UPU to reform its regulatory system and assist in converting postal services provision into a "competitive, costumer-oriented business"[10] has continually increased. In an effort to maintain its role and position, the organisation itself started in the early 1990s to already re-orient its function and agenda by establishing a Postal Development

Action Group. The work programme for the period 2004–2008 explicitly stresses the need for "public Posts to transform themselves into viable, active businesses able to compete in the communications market and provide the universal postal services to the entire population throughout the territory".[11] Thus, although reform activities in UPU well pre-date the entry into force of the GATS, and should thus be seen as related to the emergence of sectoral liberalisation/privatisation trends that were initiated either at national level or through other international organisations, in particular the World Bank and the IMF, it seems feasible to conclude that the coming into existence of GATS in 1994 and subsequent liberalisation work on postal services within GATS were a decisive impetus in dynamising the institutionalisation of "pro-competitive regulation" also in the activities of UPU. By drafting a reference paper and pushing other WTO Members to adopt it in the current round of GATS negotiations, the EU is actively advancing this particular strategy of forum shifting for the sake of its big postal corporations.

The GATS 2000 negotiations and EU water liberalisation policies

The service sector has in recent trade negotiations been one, if not the pre-eminent issue for European Union trade politics. This applies both to the multilateral trade negotiations at WTO level and to bilateral trade policies. With the start of the GATS 2000 negotiations in January 2000, the EU has been the main thriving force (*démandeur* in WTO parlance) of further liberalisation of trade in services. During the first phase of the GATS negotiations which culminated in the submission of liberalisation requests in June 2002, the EC has been intensively engaged in submitting negotiating proposals both for the market access pillar of the GATS negotiations and the "rules-negotiations", the latter being concerned with extending the regulatory framework of the GATS to disciplines for domestic regulation, transparency, subsidies, government procurement and safeguard clauses. With regard to the internal preparatory process in the EU, the EC extensively consulted with services industries in order to gain a deeper understanding of major demands of business in particular service sectors (cf. Schilder et al. 2005). That refers to most of the major sectors of export interest for large European service companies, but is particularly well-documented for the water industry (Gould 2000). In a series of communications between DG Trade and major European water multinationals, the EC actively engaged the companies to participate in the GATS negotiations and asked for detailed information on the particular problems, demands and wishes of the companies in terms of improved market access in third-countries as well as regulatory obstacles the companies encountered during their business operations abroad. The latter, for instance, explicitly referring to universal service obligations, companies might consider too burdensome.[12] Following the intense contacts with business organisations and Member States, the Commission on 30 June 2002 tabled initial requests for market access to 109 WTO Member States. 72 of these contained requests to provide market access for water provision and waste water services for European companies, thus actively promoting the business interests of the French, and to a lesser extent the German and English water multinationals. Interestingly, a number of EU Member States, most notably Germany, were not particularly pleased with these offers, since they rightly feared that these requests would in turn step up pressure to open up the water sector in the EU. Hence, these Member States explicitly stated in the 133 Committee (Services) that they would not accept any offer of the EU on water services. This in turn, was seemingly against the interests of France, which promoted an EU offer on water provision, obviously in the interest of the French water companies, which consider the prevailing system of public water provision in countries like Germany or Austria an obstacle to their business interests. The pressure exercised by the EU on water liberalisation in the framework of the GATS negotiations is particularly interesting since it came at a time, when the liberalisation of the water sector within the European Union had not been accomplished, but became a prominent goal of the Commission in its internal market strategy 2003–2006.[13] Then Internal-Market Commissioner Frits Bolkestein repeatedly declared that the Commission wanted to open public sector water services to competition. Since liberalisation of water traditionally has been – besides pensions, health and social services – a most sensitive political issue, the plans of the Commission met with stiff opposition from towns and municipalities as well as a wide variety of civil society organisations. Against this background of strong resistance within the EU, the GATS negotiations became a second strategic forum for the proponents of water liberalisation (cf. Scherrer et al. 2004). If a direct liberalisation in the EU were not to be achieved, the drive to liberalise water provision internationally would arguably increase the medium and long-term prospects of liberalisation also in the EU. For, a state that aggressively pursues the liberalisation and privatisation of water services on a global scale will sooner or later erode the legitimacy of its case for liberalisation, if it refuses to surrender its own water services to private companies for the sake of a rather dubious "European social model", as the EU has done in the GATS negotiations. Thus the rationale for pushing water liberalisation in the GATS negotiations was at least to a considerable degree motivated by domestic interests to break up public sector water services also in those EU Member States that had not done so yet. Furthermore, the decision to subject water services to the logic of trade negotiations made it a "tradable commodity", which under specific tactical or strategic constellations could be bargained against some other concession from trading partners. Thus by maintaining the full range of requests of other WTO Member States, while at the same time withholding any market access offers on water services, in such a system the opportunity costs in terms of foregone bargaining concessions from other countries tend to rise. Overtime, this makes it increasingly difficult to maintain opposition to water liberalisation in its own territory.

Nevertheless, for the time being, three major reasons can be identified, which have prevented any commitment from the EU Member States on liberalising water services since 2003. Firstly, under the terms of the Treaty of Nice, for such a decision unanimity would be required in the Council. Secondly, public protests all over Europe were strongly opposing any liberalisation move. Thirdly, as was to be seen shortly thereafter, requests for reciprocity in water liberalisation from other WTO

Members in response to the EU requests were largely absent. This is for a number of reasons, which include inter alia: a widespread unpopularity of water liberalisation/privatisation in most parts of the world, a negative record of already implemented liberalisation/privatisation of water services, and thirdly the lack of competitive water utility companies outside Europe, since nearly all major international players in water utilities are European.

Thus, although the Commission had to exclude any offer on water liberalisation from the initial EU offer it submitted to WTO Members on 29 April 2003, it succeeded in stepping up political pressure upon a wide range of mainly developing countries to surrender their water sectors to private companies. Also in the revised requests to WTO Members in January 2005, the EU maintained its requests for improved market access for European water multinationals. It was however clarified that the EU did not aim at dismantling public sector provision or provision through exclusive rights. That meant, in effect, that the EU requested that European water companies be allowed to participate on a non-discriminatory basis in public tendering procedures. Thanks to massive protests from civil society and trade unions, the EU also had to scale down the requests to LDCs, as these were given the "option" either to open-up water provision or, alternatively, refuse-disposal services. An attempt of a few EU Member States at the initiative of Belgium to withdraw the requests on water liberalisation from the EU list of requests was however not successful, due to the resistance from the Commission, France and other Member States (in particular the UK and the Netherlands).

Besides the multilateral level and its interplay with domestic EU politics, we have also to consider the interplay with bilateral trade negotiations. As it is an explicit goal of the EU that bilaterals should be by definition so-called "WTO-plus" agreements, the EU as a matter of principle in bilateral negotiations intends to extend the level of liberalisation commitments beyond that already achieved in the WTO, or in this case, the GATS level of commitments. Liberalisation of water provision came into play, in this respect, in the trade negotiations with MERCOSUR about the conclusion of an association agreement. These negotiations started in 1999, but were only gaining momentum in 2003 after a phase of stagnation caused in particular by the severe economic crisis in Argentina in 2001–2002. The negotiations were planned to be finalised in October 2004. The main interest of MERCOSUR in the negotiations was directed towards agricultural market access, while the EU wanted further liberalisation in industrial goods, services, investment and government procurement. After the initial EU offer in the GATS negotiations was submitted by the end of April 2003, the Commission intensified its preparatory work in the EU-MERCOSUR negotiations. In particular, it prepared a services offer, which in its first draft did contain a market access commitment for water services. This, of course, completely contradicted the official position of the Commission, in particular of Trade Commissioner Pascal Lamy, who shortly before in the context of heated public debates about the EU's GATS offer had declared that the EU did not intend to open up public services via trade negotiations. Obviously after various protests the offer on water services was withdrawn in subsequent drafts of the EC offer on services to MERCOSUR.

The political project of liberalising the public provision of water extends however beyond the domain of trade policies. It is well-known that the EU actively promotes the participation of private companies in the water sectors in the transition economies through public-private-partnership-projects funded by the European Investment Bank and the European Bank for Reconstruction and Development, respectively, and other financing facilities. Furthermore, the EC and the governments of Member States actively intervene on behalf of European water companies when it is considered that their interests are negatively affected by host country governments in- and outside Europe.[14]

Forum shifting in European Union trade policy-making – The case of investment

Besides services, the EU has over the last decade been one of the most active proponents of extending the domain of both multi-and bilateral trade politics to include the issue of investment, the latter being the most important among the so-called Singapore issues of investment, competition, government procurement and trade facilitation.[15] Though by the year 2002 almost 2200 investment treaties existed at bilateral level (UNCTAD 2003), these treaties typically cover issues related to investments already in place (liberalisation of current payments and capital movements, guarantees of investor's property rights, settlement of investment disputes), and thus do typically not regulate the so-called pre-investment phase, i.e. the terms under which foreign investors may enter a country (market access) and the treatment they are given by that country (preferably non-discrimination, i.e. national treatment). Only since the late 1990s can a tendency to extend the scope of the bilateral investment agreements be observed.

In the 1990s a multilateral agreement on investment was one of the central issues of the trade policy debate. It was one of the major concerns of the US business community in the Uruguay Round, which considered the abolishment of a wide array of host country regulations on foreign equity participation, performance requirements, local content requirements, residence requirements for staff etc. as a major impediment to the free movement of capital, the latter being perceived as equally if not more important than the free movement of goods. Due to its limited coverage of barriers to investment – basically only local performance requirements – and exceptions for developing countries, the TRIMs agreement as an outcome of the Uruguay Round was however judged a disappointment by the business community (Trebilcock/Howse 1999). Therefore, activities were moved towards the OECD in the second half of the 1990s, an organisation with a long record in regulating international investment dating back to the 1970s.[16] It was perceived that in the OECD as the main organisation of the industrialised countries a consensus on a global investment agreement could be reached more easily since the spectre of interests of its constituency – the economically advanced countries – should supposedly be easier to align. Once an agreement would be reached, other countries could join, or alternatively, OECD countries could focus their efforts upon coercing other nations – in particular those seeking to attract foreign direct investment – into accepting the OECD agreement as a blueprint for multilateral investment regulation (cf. Braithwaite, Drahos 2000, Trebilcock, Howse 1999). As is well-known, after the draft MAI was leaked to the public in 1997, massive public protests let to a total breakdown of the negotiations in April 1998.[17]

Notwithstanding a general climate marked by reluctance, if not outright refusal to deal with the issue of an international investment agreement by most developing countries, efforts in particular of the EU were re-directed towards including investment in the negotiating agenda of the Millennium Round of trade negotiations, which was supposed to be started with the WTO Ministerial Conference in Seattle in November 1999. The negotiating mandate given to the Commission by the Council in October 1999 expressly endorsed investment as a priority for the WTO negotiations.[18]

After the failure of the Seattle conference, only with the fourth Ministerial Conference in November 2001 in Doha, Qatar did it become possible to commence a new round of multilateral trade negotiations. In the Doha Declaration, it was foreseen that negotiations on investment would start at the fifth WTO Ministerial Conference to be held in Cáncun, Mexico in September 2003. The Declaration stipulated however that such a decision on the modalities of the negotiations was to be taken by explicit consensus. However, such a consensus could not be reached by September 2003. The failure to initiate negotiations on the Singapore issues (with the exception of trade facilitation) led WTO Members to drop investment, competition and government procurement from the agenda of the Doha Round. This was very much against the intentions of the EU, which had become the prime *démandeur* with regard to the Singapore issues and hence had fought hard to keep them on the negotiating agenda. For the EU officials in charge of the negotiations in Cáncun, abandoning them was a major concession to its trading partners.

Interestingly, while the US was the leading advocate of concluding an investment agreement during the Uruguay round of trade negotiations, it seemingly became less active on the issue at the multilateral level thereafter. Supposedly, this is related to the successful conclusion of the NAFTA treaty, which came into force in January 1994. With chapter 11 NAFTA contains arguably the most far-reaching and detailed investment provisions of any bilateral or regional trade agreement. Later it should become a model for the MAI negotiations in the OECD (Szepesi 2004a). Seemingly, the NAFTA experience had shown to US trade policy makers that regional and bilateral negotiations provided a venue more opportune to US interests. After the failure of the MAI, the US as a matter of fact was not taking the lead in pushing for negotiations in the WTO. Instead, the US opted for pushing far-reaching commitments on investment in its bilateral negotiations. That being the case the question arises why the EU – apart from also very active Japan – did not follow the US example but stepped in as the central promoter of a multilateral agreement on investment in the WTO? A possible explanation relates to institutional factors, i.e. the fact that the EU at Community level lacked an exclusive competence for investment. Member States retained the right to conclude bilateral investment treaties, even with the Treaty of

Nice. Since in multilateral negotiations the Commission had the lead, it was in the institutional self-interest of EU trade officials to push for multilateral negotiations on investment, thus de-facto expanding their competences at the expense of EU Member States.

The active role at the multilateral level notwithstanding, the EU started to progressively include investment provisions in the bilateral agreements it negotiated since the second half of the 1990s. While the association agreements which were concluded with the Euro-Mediterranean partners[19] between 1995 and 1997, and the Trade, Development and Cooperation Agreement with South Africa in 1999 contain only rather shallow provisions on investment, the level of commitments pushed for by the EU rises considerably thereafter. The bilateral agreements with Mexico, which entered into force in 2000, and the agreement with Chile (concluded in 2002, provisionally in force since 1 February 2003) go beyond the investment promotion commitments to be found in the MED agreements. They include provisions on (i) the progressive liberalisation of current payments and capital movements, (ii) national treatment obligations for services, and in the case of Chile also for other economic activities, (iii) performance, i.e. full GATS art. XVI market access requirements. Though both the EU and Mexico as well as Chile[20] retain exceptions to this general commitments, the agreement with Mexico, and even to a higher degree, the EU-Chile agreement contain to date the most far-reaching investment provisions of the EU's bilateral trade agreements (Szepesi 2004a). However, all of the EU's bilateral agreements fall short of the far-reaching provisions contained in Chapter 11 of NAFTA, since specifically investment protection provisions are not included. These are left to the bilateral investment agreements of the EU Member States. Nevertheless, in the absence of a multilateral treaty on investment, the EU obviously has also entered the bilateral venue for advancing its economic interests on investment liberalisation and the other Singapore Issues, respectively. Consequently, it has intended to step up the pace and extent of this bilateral investment agenda in the latest negotiations with MERCOSUR. In addition to the agreement with Chile, in the case of MERCOSUR the Commission has pressed for the inclusion of the pre-investment phase, i.e. market access. Against the background of a particularly strong engagement of European corporations in the MERCOSUR countries – the EU accounts for roughly 60 percent of total FDI inflow to MERCOSUR countries, especially in transport, communication and financial services, a straightforward motivation for the EU resides in securing a more advantageous legal framework for the sizable stock of EU FDI in the Southern Cone countries.

A similar thing applies to government procurement, where the EU has pressed hard for opening up MERCOSUR's market for government purchases. In particular, the EU wants Brazil to extend its commitments to the sub-central level, and to state enterprises in utilities (water, energy, transport). The latter account for most public purchases, which are estimated by the OECD at 7 percent of Brazilian GDP.[21]

Another case in point is the negotiations of an investment chapter following the review of the EU-Mexico trade agreement, which started in 2004. The agreement which came into force in 2000 foresaw negotiations on sectoral commitments in services, to be commenced by a decision by the joint council to be taken no later than three years after the entry into force of the agreement. In 2005 Mexico made a proposal to start new negotiations on liberalising investments, which *inter alia* were to include investment protection and thus exceeded the competences of the Commission. The Commission consequently proposed to the EU Member States to extend the negotiations towards these issues and include them into a future investment agreement with Mexico. This, of course, would ultimately render the existing bilateral investment treaties with Mexico obsolete. In a similar vein, the EC tried to use expand its competencies with regard to investment when proposing a negotiating mandate to the EU Member States in late 2005 for the initiation of negotiations with the EUROMED countries on services and investment. Here too, while Member States are very supportive of negotiations on the issues, they are reluctant to cede additional powers to the community level. However, it is increasingly difficult for Member States to argue against expanding the scope of the investment negotiations, when trading partners like Mexico voice such demands. Thus, pressure to give more competencies to the Community level are mounting over time.

Concluding remarks

Judged against the mercantile logic described in this chapter, EU trade policy has been a success, with the external trade balance of the EU-15 improving in overall terms during the period from 1990 – 2004. Until 1992 the EU-15 taken together had constantly run trade deficits. For the years from 1993 to 1998 the EU-15 accumulated sizable trade surpluses both in merchandise and in services trade. During the years from 1999 until 2004 the picture is somewhat mixed, with the EU running minor trade deficits in goods trade, while increasing its surplus in services trade. In sum, the trade balance has, however, turned positive in 2002 and remained so in 2003 und 2004 (cf. Figure 3.1). In overall terms, the EU's position in international trade has thus consistently improved since the beginning of the 1990s. This might be considered somewhat surprising, since one could have expected that the implementation of the Single Market and monetary unification during the very same period would have increased the economic integration within the EU to the detriment of its integration with the global economy. But what happened was, quite to the contrary, a parallelism of inward and outward integration. Both intra- and extra-EU trade flows have increased relative to EU-GDP in the 1990s (cf. Koopmann 2006).

Hence, the implementation of the Single Market in the 1990s, monetary unification in the late 1990s and the Stability and Growth Pact notwithstanding, the EU's position in world trade provides a picture that might be categorised as an extraverted regime of accumulation, where internationalisation of the economy both via trade and investment is privileged compared to the stagnant evolution of the domestic market and in particular aggregate demand (cf. Becker/Blaas in this volume). Quite interestingly, GDP growth in the EU – and in particular in the EURO-zone – has been disappointing during the very same period of time, with persistent high levels of unemployment and a major re-distribution of income and wealth taking place largely to the detriment of wage earners and lower strata of the population. Apparently one could argue that without the advantageous evolution of the external account the economic situation in the EU would have been even worse. This indeed appears to be the opinion propagated by a mainstream of economic experts. Contrary to that, another explanation which is more inspired by a Keynesian/Kaleckian theoretical framework would stress the systemic link between the orientation upon raising the external competitiveness of an economy and the contractionary effect thereof on the domestic market. Tight monetary and fiscal policies, real-wage increases that remain below the growth of inflation and productivity, flexibilisation of labour markets: all these policies are legitimated with the need to raise the relative competitive position of the European economy vis-à-vis its main global competitors.

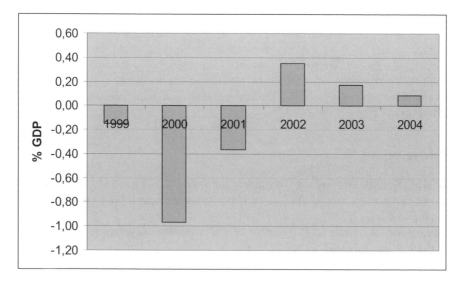

**Figure 3.1   Trade Balance Goods and Services EU-15, 1999–2004
(percent GDP EU-15)**
Source: EUROSTAT, OECD

Thus, from the perspective of this macro-economic shift that has taken place over the course of the last 15 years, the economic effects of EU trade policy appear to be much more ambivalent, at least when the benchmark for evaluation applied is the overall development of the economy, and thus, ultimately, the well-being of the people. Against the current mainstream of active extraversion in EU trade policy-making, one could instead argue that the rising outward-orientation of the EU's economic strategy, as enshrined in the Lisbon Strategy, is aggravating economic problems not only within the EU, but is also detrimental to the development of the world economy. If according to Global Keynesianism (cf. Sauer 2004, Köhler 1999) it is correct that the world economy should be considered a demand-led regime of accumulation, then it would be straightforward for the EU as the largest trading block in the world to assume a larger share of the responsibility for the stability and prosperity of the world economy. Instead, currently the EU profits immensely from the debt and import-driven economic growth of the USA and the economic boom in China. If current growth trends in these countries, in particular in the US, would eventually prove unsustainable, the global economy and thus international trade would be hit hard. Continuing with the current strategy of active extraversion, as Becker and Blaas have put it in their introductory essay to this volume, would thus exacerbate the EU's exposure to the vagaries of the globalising world economy. Consequently, the EU would be well-advised to re-orient its regime of accumulation towards more introverted, socially cohesive and environmentally sustainable growth strategies. That would be beneficial both for the EU itself and the world economy alike, since the EU would thus be able to eventually accept current account deficits in order to stabilise global demand.

Prevailing EU neo-mercantilism and aggressive strategies to advance global market liberalisation by way of *inter alia* forum-shifting would thus gradually be substituted by a more cooperative approach to international economy policy-making. Admittedly this does not seem very realistic at the moment, but the economic rationale for advocating a different world economic regime seems more plausible than ever.

References

Alter, K. (1998), Who are the "Masters of the Treaty"? *European Governments and the European Court of Justice, in: International Organisation*, Vol.52, No. 1, pp.121-47.

Braithwaite, J., Drahos, P. (2000), *Global Business Regulation*, (Cambridge: Cambridge University Press).

Christiansen, T., Kirchner, E. (eds.) (2000), C*ommittee Governance in the European Union*, (Manchester: Manchester Univ. Press).

Elsig, M. (2002), *The EU's Common Commercial Policy. Institutions, Interests and Ideas*, (Aldershot: Ashgate).

European Commission (2004), *Trade Policy in the Prodi Commission 1999-2004 – An Assessment, European Commission, Brussels*, 19 November 2004.

European Commission (2005), *Trade and Competitiveness Issues Paper*, Directorate General for Trade, Brussels, 01/09/2005.

Grieshaber-Otto, J., Sinclair, S. (2004), *Return to Sender. The Impact of GATS "Pro-Competitive Regulation" on Postal and Other Public Services*. Canadian Centre for Policy Alternatives, Ottawa, http://www.policyalternatives.ca/index.cfm?act=news&do=Article&call=111&pA=A2286B2A&type=5.

Hamilton, A. (1791), *Report on Manufactures* (zit.n. der Gesamtausgabe von Lodge, 2nd edition, 12 vol., (New York and London 1903, vol. IV).

Hanson, B.T. (1998): What happened to Fortress Europe? External Trade Policy Liberalization in the European Union, In: *International Organization*, Vol.52/1, pp. 55-85.

Heckscher, E. F. (1934), *Mercantilism*, 2 volumes, (London: Allen & Unwin).

Herrmann, C. (2006), Die Rolle der erweiterten Union in der WTO: Das Integrationsmodell der Union als geeignetes Leitbild für die Mitwirkung? In: Bruha, T., Nowak, C. (Hg.), *Die Europäische Union: Innere Verfasstheit und globale Handlungsfähigkeit*, (Baden-Baden, Nomos), pp. 229-236.

Jones, R.J. B. (1986), *Conflict and Control in the World Economy: Contemporary Economic Realism and Neo-Mercantilism*, (Brighton: Harvester Press).

Koopmann, G. (2006), Institutionelle Aspekte der Handelspolitik in der Europäischen Gemeinschaft und ihre Rolle in der Weltwirtschaft, In: *Bruha, T., Nowak, C. (eds.), Die Europäische Union: Innere Verfasstheit und globale Handlungsfähigkeit*, (Baden-Baden, Nomos), pp. 265-289.

Köhler, G. (1999), Global Keynesianism and Beyond, in: *Journal of World Systems Research*, Vol V, 2, 1999, pp 253-274.

Krajewski, M. (2003), *National Regulation and Trade Liberalization in Services. The legal impact of the General Agreement on Trade in Services (GATS) on National Regulatory Autonomy*, (The Hague: Kluwer).

Krajewski, M.(2006), Demokratische Kontrolle der Gemeinsamen Handelspolitik. In: Bruha, T., Nowak, C. (eds.), *Die Europäische Union: Innere Verfasstheit und globale Handlungsfähigkeit*, (Baden-Baden: Nomos), pp. 237-252.

Krenzler, H.G., Pitschas, C. (2006), Die Gemeinsame Handelspolitik im Verfassungsvertrag – ein Schritt in die richtige Richtung. In: Herrmann, C., Krenzler, H.G., Streinz, R. (eds.), *Die Außenwirtschaftspolitik der Europäischen Union nach dem Verfassungsvertrag*, (Baden-Baden: Nomos), pp.11-42.

List, F. (1844), *The National System of Political Economy*, (Longmans, Green and Co., English Edition 1922).

Monar, J. (2005), Die Gemeinsame Handelspolitik der Europäischen Union im EU-Verfassungsvertrag: Fortschritte mit einigen neuen Fragezeichen, In: *Aussenwirtschaft, 60. Jahrgang* (2005), Heft 1, Zürich, pp.99-117.

Meunier, S., Nicolaïdis, K. (1999), Who speaks for Europe? The Delegation of Trade Authority in the EU, in: *Journal of Common Market Studies*, Vol. 37, No. 3, September 1999, pp.477-501.

Murphy, A. (2000), In the maelstrom of change: the Article 113 Committee in the Governance of External Trade Policy, in: Christiansen, T., Kirchner, E. (eds.): *Committee Governance in the European Union*, (Manchester: Manchester Univ. Press), pp. 98-114.

Sauer, Th. (2004), Globaler Keynesianismus versus Deglobalisierung? Makroökonomische und normative Grundlagen alternativer Weltwirtschaftsordnungen, in: Biesecker, A., Büscher, M., Sauer, Th., Stratmann-Mertens, E. (eds.), *Alternative Weltwirtschaftsordnung. Perspektiven nach Cancún*, (Hamburg: VSA), pp.53-69.

Schäfer, W. (2006), Europa, Exit-Option und Steuern. In: Bruha, T., Nowak, C. (eds.), *Die Europäische Union: Innere Verfasstheit und globale Handlungsfähigkeit*, (Baden-Baden, Nomos), pp. 255-263.

Scherrer, Ch., Beilecke, F., Fritz, T., Kohlmorgen, L. (2004), *Liberalisierung öffentlicher Dienstleistungen durch das GATS. Gemeinwirstchaftliche Auswirkungen in den Sektoren Wasserversorgung und Verkehr (Schiene, ÖPNV), Schriftenreihe "Zur Zukunft öffentlicher Dienstleistungen"*, Nr. 4, (Kammer für Arbeiter und Angestellte für Wien: Wien), http://wien.arbeiterkammer.at/pictures/d22/LieberalisierungBd.4.pdf.

Schilder, K., Fuchs, P., Deckwirth, C., Frein, M. (2005), *Freie Fahrt für freien Handel? Die EU-Handelspolitik zwischen Bilateralismus und Multilateralismus, Herausgeber: Weltwirtschaft, Ökologie und Entwicklung – WEED*, (Berlin: Evangelischer Entwicklungsdienst).

Schumpeter, J.A. (1954), *History of Economic Analysis*, (New York: Oxford University Press).

Smith, M. (1999), The European Union, in: Hocking,B., McGuire, St. (eds.), *Trade Politics. International, Domestic and Regional Perspectives*, (London: Routledge), pp.275-289.

Szepesi, St. (2004a), Comparing EU free trade agreements – Investment, *InBrief* No. 6D, July 2004, European Centre for Development Policy Management, Maastricht, www.ecdpm.org.

Szepesi, St. (2004b), Comparing EU free trade agreements. Competition Policy and State Aid, *InBrief* No. 6E, July 2004, European Centre for Development Policy Management, Maastricht, www.ecdpm.org.

Stapelfeldt, G. (2001), *Der Merkantilismus. Die Genese der Weltgesellschaft vom 16. bis zum 18. Jahrhundert*, (Freiburg: ça ira-Verlag).

Trebilcock, M.J., Howse, R. (1999), *The regulation of international trade*, 2nd ed., (London: Routledge).

UNCTAD (2003), *World Investment Report 2003*, Geneva.

UNCTAD (2004), *UNCTAD Handbook of Statistics 2004*, United Nations, New York and Geneva.

UNCTAD (2005), *UNCTAD Handbook of Statistics 2005*, United Nations, New York and Geneva.

Van Appeldorn, B. (2002), *Transnational Capitalism and the Struggle over Europe*, (London: Routledge).

Woolcock, S. (2005), European Union Trade Policy: Domestic Institutions and Systemic Factors, in: Kelly, D., Grant, W. (eds.), *The Politics of International Trade in the Twenty-First Century. Actors, Issues and Regional Dynamics*, (Houndsmill: Palgrave Macmillan), pp.234-251.

WWF (2003), *A League of Gentlemen. Who really runs EU Trade Decision-Making, World Wide Fund for Nature-UK*, November 2003.

Notes

*   Valuable comments from Alice Wagner and Joachim Becker are appreciated. Responsibility for any remaining errors is exclusively with the author.

1   That might have been particularly true with respect to the liberal credentials of the two Trade Commissioners from the UK, Leon Brittan (1994–1999) and presently, Peter Mandelson. Even Pascal Lamy, a French Socialist, who served as EU Trade Commissioner from 1999 to 2004 and recently was appointed Secretary-General of the WTO, was quite clear on this. He was however the first commissioner who during the last year of his mandate made an attempt to initiate a debate on "collective preferences", i.e. general beliefs and values a polity held with regard to e.g. environmental or social standards, and the ramifications this would entail to trade politics. Lamy was, however, at pains to differentiate the safeguarding of these legitimate objectives in trade politics from "protectionism" (See e.g. Lamy's speech "The emergence of collective preferences in international trade: implications for regulating globalisation" delivered at the Conference on "Collective preferences and global governance: what future for the multilateral trading system", Brussels, 15 September 2004; http://europa.eu.int/comm/ archives/commission_1999_2004/lamy/speeches_articles/spla242_en.htm). In the end, the debate turned out to be short-lived, as Lamy's successor Peter Mandelson has not shown any inclination to continue on it.

2   For an overview of major documents and reports see http://europa.eu.int/ growthandjobs/.

3   All cited tariffs are bound MFN rates based on final URAA implementations.

4   For an illustration see the chapter below on the EU's strategy with regard to water provision in the current GATS negotiations.

5   Court of Justice of the European Communities, Opinion 1/94, 15 November 1994.

6   See www.unice.be, www.ifsl.org.uk/, and www.esf.be for details on these organisations.

7   See www.corporateeurope.org for a list of the documents.

8   For an overview see http://europa.eu.int/comm/trade/issues/global/sia/studies.htm.

9   Terminal dues are tariffs received by postal operators for the delivery of international mail. However, the UPU terminal dues regulations grant operators from developing countries differential treatment, thus possibly violating the GATS Art II MFN-obligation.

10   UPU Resolution C 25/1999, cited in Grieshaber-Otto/Sinclair 2004.

11   UPU Resolution C 7/2004, Universal Postal Union policy and action on postal reform and development for 2005- 2008, www.upu.int/postal_dev_reform/en/pdag/resolution_ c7-2004_en.pdf, acessed at 04.06.2005.

12   See Gould (2003) and www.corporateeurope.org.

13   Internal Market Strategy - Priorities 2003–2006 [COM(2003) 238 final].

14   One of the latest examples being the conflict between water multinational Suéz and the government of Argentina on the results of private water provision in Buenos Aires in 2004–05, where the Commission but also individual EU Member States have repeatedly intervened in favour of the French based company and reminded the Argentine authorities to comply with their contractual obligations.

15   The name Singapore Issues refers to the 1st Ministerial Conference of the WTO, which took place in Singapore in 1996. There, a decision was made to establish a Working Group with the aim of discussing the interaction between trade and investment.

16   See the 1976 OECD Declaration on International Investment and Multinational Enterprises. Also the OECD Guidelines for Multinational Companies date back to 1976.

17   Trebilcock & Howse (1999), however, are of the opinion that the MAI might have failed anyway due to disagreements between the contracting parties on culture, labour rights

and the extraterritoriality effects of US legislation, in particular the Helms-Burton Act, which had already surfaced before the public debate on the MAI began.

18   Preparation of the Third WTO Ministerial Conference – Draft Council Conclusions, Doc.No. 12092/99, Brussels 22. Octobre 1999.

19   MED-Agreements with Israel (1995), Tunisia (1995), Morocco (1996), Jordan (1997), Palestinian Authority (1997).

20   Chile made two reservations with regard to capital market liberalisation. Firstly, EU investors benefiting from voluntary investment programmes are obliged to retain the proceeds of such investment in the host country for a period of time between one and five years (Annex XIV, Art. 1). Secondly, Art 3 of Annex XIV authorises the Central Bank of Chile to enact measures to restrict or limit current payments and transfers of capital from or to Chile. These measures include in particular reserve requirements (cf. Szepesi 2004a).

21   European Commission "Commission Expectations for the Next Round of EU-MERCOSUR Negotiations", internal document, DG Trade, 2003.

Chapter 4

India and the WTO

Muchkund Dubey

In this Chapter, the role of India in the trade negotiations in GATT/WTO will be analysed in the backdrop of the evolving development strategy and trade policy of India since its independence. In the first section of the Chapter, after giving a brief sketch of the structure of and the trends in the Indian economy, an attempt has been made to trace the evolution of the export and import policies of India. The second section traces the history of India's role in the international trading system, starting from the GATT, covering the Uruguay Round of Trade Negotiations and going through the negotiations in the various Ministerial Meetings of the WTO, culminating in the July, 2004 Consensus for carrying forward the ongoing Doha Round of Trade Negotiations. In the third section, India's position on selected negotiating sectors/ issues has been analysed in the context of the importance and implications of these issues for India's development. The sectors/issues concerned are agriculture, services, non-agricultural market access, the Implementation Issues, Special and Differential Treatment for Developing Countries, TRIPS Agreement, regional trade agreements, and the Singapore Issues. In the next section, the positions on the main negotiating issues of interest groups like the business community, the state governments, the Parliament, the trade unions, and civil society organisations have been analysed and their extent and nature of influence on the governments policies on these issues has been brought out. The last section contains a brief analysis of the consequences for the Indian economy, of the agreements reached and regimes put in place as a result of the WTO negotiations. It is obviously not possible to establish a direct co-relation between the WTO agreements and the outcomes in the Indian economy during the last 10 years or so. Therefore, all that one can do – and has been done in this section – is to trace the major changes in those economic variables which are likely to be influenced by the implementation of commitments under these agreements.

The Indian economy and India's evolving development strategy and trade policy

The GDP growth of the Indian economy during 1950–1951 to 1979–1980 was 3,5 percent and during 1980–2002 was 5,2 percent (Virmani 2004). If we take into account the population growth rate of 2,15 percent per annum between 1950–1951 to 1980–1981, the increase in per capita income was only 1,37 percent (Dandekar 1992).

Throughout the period 1950–1951 to 1979–1980, the development strategy was predicated on the assumption of market failure, lack of trust in the private sector and the belief that the State alone can deliver the desired economic and social outcomes. There was, therefore, a rapid expansion in the State's role in the economy and proliferation of rules, regulations and mechanisms to exercise control over private sector activities. The major achievements during this phase was laying the foundations of a fairly diversified economy and building a whole chain of first rate research institutions. However the vast expansion of the public sector and the proliferation of controls which earned India the sobriquet of "licence-permit raj", resulted not only in a relatively slow rate of growth but also in an all round inefficiency in the economy.

The situation started changing from the beginning of the 1980s. Throughout this decade, measures were taken to remove restrictions and controls and open up the economy. Even though these measures were half-hearted and ad hoc, they already set the trend towards liberalisation. After the economic crisis of 1990–1991, India commenced a full-fledged policy of liberalisation which is continuing till today. With this, the Indian economy has reached a new phase of growth.

Over the last 40 years or so, there has been a major transformation in the structure of the Indian economy. The share of agriculture value added to GDP has gone down from 46,54 percent in 1960 to 22,67 percent in 2002. The share of industry value added has increased from 19,40 percent to 26,61 percent during the same period; whereas the share of service value added has jumped from 34,06 percent to 50,72 percent.[1] However, in spite of the reduced contribution of agriculture to the country's GDP, agriculture continues to remain the most important sector of the Indian economy. Agricultural and allied activities are the source of the livelihood for 65-70 percent of the Indian population i.e. for over 650 million people.

Throughout the post-independence period, India has shown remarkable success in keeping inflation under reasonable control. The average inflation rates were 6,7 percent during 1956–1957 to 1975–1976, 7,5 percent during 1976–77 to 1979–80 and 8,5 percent during 1980–81 to 1990–91 (Jalan 1992).

From the late 1970s, India's gross domestic savings as a percentage of GDP has been maintained above 20 percent. It went up from an average of 16 percent during the period 1956–1957 to 1975–1976 to 21,2 percent during 1976–1977 to 1979–1980. In the last 30 years or so, the average savings ratio seems to have reached a plateau ranging between 22 percent to 26 percent.

India's trade policy

Trends in exports

India's export earnings remained stagnant during the first decade and a half after independence. Exports as a percentage of world exports declined sharply from 2,5 in 1947 to 0,9 in 1966. This lack of performance on the export front was policy induced and not due to independent external factors beyond India's control (Bhagwati 1970).

The average export performance during the Third Five Year Plan (1962–1966) improved significantly over the average for the Second Five Year Plan. While still relying heavily on the export of traditional items like oil cakes and meal, iron ore, cashew kernel, coffee and jute manufactures, the Indian economy emerged during this period as an exporter of engineering goods, and chemical & allied products.

The devaluation of 1966, together with import liberalisation was expected to usher in a new era of export-oriented growth. But this did not come about because the devaluation and the accompanying policy measures proved abortive due to a variety of reasons. The stagnation in India's exports continued till the early 1970s, followed by significant growth in the rest of the decade. The growth was not sustained in the early 1980s. But from 1985–1986, export growth picked up significantly and continued till 1989–1990, until it collapsed during the economic crisis of 1991–1993. The growth revived in 1993–1994 under the impact of the policy of liberalisation. In the decade 1986–1996, the value of India's exports grew by over 9 percent a year in every year but two i.e. 1991–1992 and 1992–1993. During 1993–1996, the growth was nearly 20 percent per year on average (Srinivasan 1998). India's share of world exports declined from 0,9 in 1966 to 0,42 in 1980. The share has since been creeping up, reaching 0,77 percent in 2002; but it is yet to reach the level of 1,02 percent in 1960, let alone the pre-war level of 2,5 percent (Jalan 1992).

There has been a significant change in India's exports structure of goods. For example, the share of food items has come down from 28,10 percent in 1980 to 12,31 percent in 2002, that of agricultural raw material from 4,99 percent to 1,05 percent, and of ores and metals from 7,50 percent to 4,33 percent. On the other hand, the share of manufactured goods has gone up from 56,64 percent to 74,80 percent, of chemical products, from 4,18 percent to 11,15 percent, and of other manufactured goods from 46,20 percent to 55,22 percent.[2]

In the immediate post-independence period, the United Kingdom claimed an overwhelming share of India's trade. In 1950–1952, 25,9 percent of India's exports went to the United Kingdom. The share came down drastically to 6,5 percent in 1992–1993. India's exports to USA have maintained a steady trend. They were 18,1 percent of the total in 1951–1952, 14,1 percent in 1972–1973 and 18,8 percent in 1992–93. Starting from an insignificant position, the USSR emerged as a major destination of India's exports in the mid-1960s and remained so until a couple of years before the disintegration of the Soviet Union in 1990. USSR's share of India's exports went up from 0,9 percent in 1951–1952 to 15,5 percent in 1972–1973. In the latter year, the USSR emerged as the largest trading partner of India, with USA following closely with a share of 14,1 percent of India's exports. Both Japan and Germany emerged as significant export destinations for India, increasing their shares of India's exports respectively from 2,0 percent in 1951–52 to 11,1 percent in 1972–1973 and from 1,3 percent in 1951–1952 to 7,7 percent in 1992–1993. After the disintegration of the Soviet Union, Russia's share of India's exports has gone down sharply, declining to only 3,2 percent in 1992–1993. It went down further to only 1,2 percent in 2000–2001.

Today Europe is the most important destination for India's exports, accounting for 24,46 percent, followed by USA (21,96 percent). The share of the developing economies in India's exports has gone up from 35,23 percent in 1950 to 42,87 percent in 2003.[3] India's exports to its neighbouring countries have increased dramatically since these countries set upon the path of liberalisation. India is now the biggest source of imports for both Bangladesh and Sri Lanka.

Thus India's export destinations are well diversified. India, therefore, has to make special effort to nurture its trade relations with all major trading nations and in all the regions.

Balance-of-payment position   With a few brief interregnums of favourable balance-of-payment positions, throughout the post-independent period until the launching towards the end of 1991 of the policy of full-fledged liberalisation (Jalan 1992), India suffered from persistent balance-of-payment problems. India faced an acute balance of payment crisis in 1990–1991. During this period, the reserves came down to as low a level as being just enough to finance two weeks' imports. The slide in the reserve position was halted mainly by the restoration of confidence in the Indian economy as a result of the launching of the policy of full-fledged liberalisation. Soon thereafter, India started accumulating reserves, both due to increased inflow of foreign capital and trend of buoyancy in export earnings. The reserves have gone up steadily since then and for the last few years they have reached an embarrassingly high level of over $100 billion.

Export-import policy

Export Policy   The First Five Year Plan was indifferent to export performance. From the Second Plan onwards, India followed a policy of import-substitution industrialisation, which turned out to be an important reason for India's failure to achieve an adequate growth in exports. The policy of import-substitution industrialisation was very much influenced by the export pessimism that prevailed at that time. Subsequent events did not bear out the hypothesis of export pessimism. In spite of the protectionist policies of industrialised countries, particularly in the field of agriculture and textiles and clothings, world trade in the post-war period grew faster than world output and several developing countries, particularly in East and South-East Asia, used exports as one of the most effective means of accelerating growth and substantially reducing poverty. India, on the other hand, remained mired in its inward-looking development strategy, which largely accounted for its being one of the slowest growing economies in the developing world and resulted in the creation of a highly inefficient and incompetitive economic structure.

Even while world market conditions are constrained by protectionist and other restrictive measures, this still leaves plenty of scope for individual countries to increase their shares of the world market by adopting appropriate export promotion measures. India showed awareness of this possibility from the beginning of the Third Five Year Plan and adopted a wide variety of export promotion measures.

Exports acquired much greater salience in India's economic policy in the mid-1970s. However, the real shift in India's export policy started in the late 1970s and early 1980s. Earlier, export policy was pursued in isolation of import policy. Export promotion measures went side by side with rigid import control. Moreover, there was only a feeble effort to embed exports in the structure of the economy. From the 1980s, exports were increasingly seen as an integral part of development activities.

Import policy   Import control in India dates back to the Second World War. Subsequently, periods of liberalisation alternated with periods of restriction depending upon the balance of payment position. Between 1951-55, there was progressive liberalisation of imports and a move away from import controls towards a greater reliance on the tariff mechanism. This trend was undermined by the foreign exchange crisis of 1956–57. The import control policy fashioned during the period 1956–1966 aimed at exercising comprehensive and direct control over foreign exchange utilisation. There came to develop an almost complete reliance on an elaborate and a very complex allocative mechanism (Bhagwati 1970). In the 1980s, a direct link was sought to be established between export and import policy. Liberalisation of imports took the form of delicensing as well as tariff reduction. However, liberalisation resulted in a surge in imports without commensurate rise in exports.

Import liberalisation is linked to export because it can help in lowering the cost of the machinery used for export production and that of raw materials, spare parts etc., that go into such a production. However, import liberalisation itself may not bring about an expansion in exports in the absence of such pre-conditions for making exports competitive, as improvement in skills, adequate infrastructure, lower transport cost, market management etc.

The spurt in the imports in the 1980s in the absence of commensurate increase in exports laid the foundation for the dramatic decline in the reserve position and hence the balance of payment crisis of 1990–1991. During the crisis, import control was tightened by a variety of measures. These were all withdrawn during the liberalisation period. Moreover, tariffs were gradually brought down and full convertibility was introduced on current account.

Peak tariffs were reduced to 35 percent in 2000–2001, to 30 percent in 2002–2003 and 20 percent in January 2004. The government has announced its intention to bring down the peak tariff to the level of 10 percent prevailing among South-East Asian countries.[4]

In compliance with its obligation under WTO, the Government abolished all Q.Rs imposed on balance-of-payment grounds with effect from the end of March 2001. This led to certain alignments in the peak tariffs levied on agricultural products. Applied tariffs were raised for some agricultural and dairy products. In some cases, very low applied tariffs were raised through a process of renegotiations.

India's role in the international trading system

India in GATT

India has a record of an active interaction with the multilateral trading system ever since its inception. An Indian delegation participated in the UN-Conference on Trade and Employment held in Havana in 1948. India had earlier participated in the tariff negotiations which were held prior to the Havana Conference and which were incorporated in the General Agreement on Tariffs and Trade (GATT).

From the perspective of developing countries like India, GATT's achievements can at best be regarded as mixed. The successive rounds of trade negotiation held under GATT no doubt resulted in a substantial lowering of tariff barriers from which developing countries also benefited. But because of the application in these negotiations of the principles of reciprocity and the principal suppliers rule, duties were reduced mainly on products of export interest to industrialised countries.

Moreover, Article XXIII of GATT on dispute settlement was not of much importance to developing countries. The penultimate remedy under this Article is to permit retaliatory measures by slapping higher tariffs having an effect equivalent to the impairment or nullification caused, and the ultimate remedy is to be permitted to withdraw from GATT. Developing countries cannot afford to resort to either of these remedies.

Developed countries misused the GATT rules to virtually close their markets for agricultural exports from developing countries. This they did by taking a waiver from the application of GATT rules to trade in agricultural products. They also transgressed Article XIX of GATT to impose on developing countries regimes like the Short Term Agreement on Textiles (STA), the Long-Term Agreement on Textiles (LTA) and the Multi-Fibre Agreement (MFA) for semi-permanently subjecting exports of their textile products to quantitative restrictions (Q.Rs.). India was one of the worst sufferers from these regimes, as textiles remained its most important export item until the end of the 1980s and the second most important export product for a long time thereafter. Developed countries transgressed GATT also to subject other competitive imports, like iron and steel, footwear, electronic products, semi-conductors etc., from developing countries to restriction by resorting to such devices as voluntary export restriction (V.E.Rs), Grey Area Measures etc.

India, along with other developing countries, played a major role in bringing about changes in GATT rules, designed to meet the special needs of developing countries. In the process of the review of GATT Articles in 1954–1955, India was strongly behind the move which culminated in the insertion in GATT of Article XVIII permitting imposition of import restrictions by developing countries in order to promote the establishment of a particular industry or to safeguard their external financial position and ensure a level of reserves adequate for the implementation of their programmes of economic development.

The Haberler Commission was appointed in 1957 and it submitted its report in 1958 when India was the Chairman of the Contracting Parties. As a follow-up of the Haberler Commission's recommendations, the GATT institutional structure was streamlined and among others, a separate committee, i.e. the Third Committee, was set up to deal with the problems of developing countries. India remained very active in this Committee until it was substituted by the Committee on Trade and Development in 1965 following the adoption of Part IV of GATT. It was in these committees that the demand of developing countries for duty free access of tropical products to the market of the developed countries was agitated. As a result, India secured suspension of duties on tea by developed countries in 1965.

India was one of the principal negotiators of STA, LTA and MFA. Having got reconciled to the asymmetrical treatment for textiles in GATT, India in these negotiations tried to and succeeded in securing a better base period for fixing quotas, reasonable rates of growth in the quotas and flexibility in switching from one item to the other for the purpose of fulfilling the quotas.

In 1962, at the Cairo Summit of the Non-aligned Countries, India was in the forefront of countries which took the initiative for a decision by the Summit, to call for the convening of a UN-Conference on Trade and Development. UNCTAD profoundly influenced the institutional and legal structures and the philosophy of GATT. It was largely in response to the convening of the UN Conference on Trade and Development that GATT expedited the work in its Working Party of Preferences and set up a Committee on Legal and Structural Framework from which emerged the Part IV of GATT.

Some of the most convincing arguments in favour of preferences to developing countries were advanced by India in the GATT Working Party on Preference which met from 1962-1967 until the deliberations were transferred to the newly established UNCTAD. Finally, a consensus on the essential features of the Generalised System of Preferences (GSP) emerged at the Second UNCTAD, held in Delhi in February 1968. The United States in 1971 became the first developed country to grant preference under GSP. This was done through a GATT waiver valid for 10 years. From 1979 onwards the GSP was legalised under the Enabling Clause included in the Framework Agreement of the Tokyo Round of Trade Negotiation.

India made one of most important contributions in the Committee on Legal and Structural Framework to the formulation of Part IV of GATT. The Indian Representative was the Chairman of the Contracting Party in 1965 when at its main session, the last-minute differences on the new Part IV were ironed out and the final text was adopted.

A commonly expressed view is that developing countries like India have been free riders in the GATT and they did not actively participate in the various rounds of trade negotiations under GATT. This contention is far from the truth. India could not have participated in the GATT trade negotiations as actively as developed countries did because the negotiations were held on the basis of the principal suppliers rule. In spite of this, India prepared itself for every round of the negotiations. It took pains to identify products of export interest to it and negotiated hard, including offering concessions of its own, to get tariff concessions on these products.

Besides, India made a strenuous effort for building into the GATT system, the necessary flexibility for applying rules, specially for imposing trade restrictions, in order to pursue its development objectives, to safeguard its trade interests and to obtain enhanced access in the markets of developed countries.

In configuring its position in GATT, India was no doubt influenced by the development strategy it was following at that time. In the first decade and a half after the establishment of GATT, barriers that member countries maintained on the import of manufactured goods were generally high. The level of protection for manufactured products was high before successive rounds of negotiations under GATT brought them down substantially. It is also a fact that though commodity prices have always fluctuated, the fluctuations during the first decade and a half of the post-war period, were particularly sharp. As a result, it frequently ran into severe balance-of-payment problems. Besides, it lacked physical and institutional infrastructures for development and the technological level of its economy was very low. In such a situation, it naturally decided to industrialise and build infrastructure and other production structures, and ensure its food security on a self-reliant basis. This necessitated its seeking all the flexibilities needed to pursue these goals. Its mistake did not lie in seeking these policy flexibilities in GATT, but sticking to them for too long, even after the achievement of an impressive success in industrialisation and building economic and institutional structures, even after export opportunities started beckoning from external markets following the substantial dismantling of barriers to trade, and even after foreign capital started moving freely to seek avenues for investment.

India in the Uruguay round

The United States, supported by other major developed countries, made a determined bid from the early 1980s onwards, to seek agreement on launching a new round of trade negotiations under GATT, with services included on the agenda. India and most other developing countries opposed this move, because they did not want to get involved in another round of trade negotiations so soon after the last round in Tokyo from which their gains were limited and yet to be implemented. They believed that GATT should concentrate on accomplishing the task remaining after the Tokyo Round, of redressing the asymmetry of their position in the world trading system.

India and other developing countries were not in favour of bringing in services on the GATT agenda because of their perception that on account of the incipient stage of the growth of their services industries, they had nothing to gain from the liberalisation of trade in services and that their own liberalisation of services imports would frustrate their effort to develop service industries. The other arguments advanced by India against the inclusion of services on the GATT agenda was that it militated against the basic mandate of GATT which was confined to trade in goods, and that the opening up the service market would, by obliging developing countries to concede 'right to establish', amount to an intrusion into their sovereign space for macro-economic policy-making.

In the Programme of Action that emerged at the end of the 1982 GATT Ministerial Meeting, the developing countries succeeded in preventing the launch of a new round, in keeping the services out of the GATT negotiating agenda and keeping the limelight focussed on the issues pending from the Tokyo Round. Nevertheless, the United States scored a major point in getting services included in the 1982 Programme of Action, as a subject to be studied by individual member countries under the overall GATT umbrella.

After the Ministerial Meeting, developed countries, while paying lip service to the ongoing work programme, fully used the GATT forum for putting relentless pressure on the developing countries for launching a new round of trade negotiations. India and other developing countries kept on resisting it as long as they could. And when they were ultimately obliged to yield in Punta del Este Ministerial Meeting of GATT in September 1986, they tried to safeguard their interests as much as possible in the Punta del Este Declaration launching the new round.

India played a leading role in resisting the move to launch a new round. In the beginning, it had the support of all developing countries in this endeavour. However, by June 1985, the number of those resisting the new round got reduced to 24. By the time of the Punta del Este Meeting, the number got reduced to 10 consisting of Argentina, Brazil, Cuba, Egypt, India, Nicaragua, Nigeria, Peru, Tanzania and Yugoslavia.

India fielded a strong delegation in Punta del Este. The uppermost concern of the Indian delegation was services. When it became clear that it would not be possible to exclude services from the negotiating agenda, India's goal got focussed on preventing cross retaliation in services. To prevent the possibility of retaliation, India succeeded in obtaining a legal separation of the negotiating processes in goods and services. However, the device of the two separate tracks of negotiation and keeping open the possibility of a different framework, perhaps outside GATT, for the implementation of the results of the negotiations on services, was only a fig leaf to cover the firm intention of developed countries and the GATT Secretariat to bring services under the dispute settlement mechanism under GATT. If there was still any illusion regarding the separateness of the two streams of negotiations, it was dispelled in the Dunket Draft Text which brought all the agreements resulting from the Uruguay Round Negotiations under the single umbrella of the proposed Multilateral Trade Organisation (MTO) (later renamed WTO) and provided for a single dispute settlement mechanism for all WTO agreements.

The Indian delegation did not pay much attention to the implications of the formulations agreed on other new items on the agenda, like Trade Related Investment Measures (TRIMS) or Trade Related Aspects of Intellectual Property Rights (TRIPS). The delegation justified its acceptance of the formulation on TRIMS on the ground that it only sought the full implementation of Article III and Article XI of GATT in relation to investment measures. However, the agreed formulation on TRIMS in the Punta del Este Declaration had wider implications. The Indian delegation was also not worried about the formulation on TRIPS, because it thought that the subject was to be considered strictly within the confines of the relevant GATT Articles. Little did the Indian delegation realise at that time that the agreed formulation on TRIPS would become the basis for the WTO TRIPS Agreement.

The Punta del Este Declaration was a triumph for developed countries in that they at long last succeeded in getting a new round of trade negotiation launched, with all the new items in. For developing countries like India, it was essentially a defensive exercise to minimise damages with, of course, one exception. And that was the formulation on textiles where the mandate was the "eventual integration of this sector into GATT on the basis of strengthened GATT rules and disciplines".[5]

India at Montreal

A mid-term review of the Uruguay Round Negotiations was held in Montreal at a Ministerial Meeting of GATT in December 1988. One of the highlights of the Meeting was the determined bid of developed countries to stretch the mandate on IPRs by writing into trade laws norms and standards of IPRs, and the attempt of developing countries led by India to prevent this from happening.

There was a near agreement on the basis of a draft circulated by the Chairperson of the working group on this subject, on bringing norms and standards of IPRs within GATT's ambit, until India with the support of a few members of the Group of 10 circulated an alternative draft, essentially proposing the transmittal of this subject to WIPO. The Indian move effectively prevented an agreement on this contentious subject by stretching out the discussion until the dying hours of the Meeting.

There was a near agreement in Montreal on services. The Indian representative in the group which carried out negotiations on this item, played a very important role in paving the way for making the eventual General Agreement on Services (GATS) as flexible for developing countries as possible.

The negotiations on textiles remained deadlocked as developed countries did not accept the demand of textile-exporting countries like India to set a deadline for the integration of MFA with GATT, and for keeping the safeguards mechanism non-discriminatory.

The Montreal Meeting collapsed on the issue of agriculture. No legal account was taken of the various proposals made in Montreal or of the progress made in the negotiations based on these proposals.

The fragmented unity of the developing countries in the form of the Group of 10 was sustained until the Montreal Meeting. Up to that time, these countries, with the help of other developing countries successfully carried out a damage limitation job in the new areas of the negotiations and valiantly sought to achieve positive results in the traditional areas, particularly market access.

India at the Geneva meeting

The GATT Contracting Parties made an attempt to pick up the threads left behind in Montreal in their meeting in Geneva in April 1989. The hallmark of the Geneva meeting was the surrender on TRIPS following the final collapse of the Group of

10. What ultimately led to the surrender in Geneva was the collapse of the India-Brazil solidarity, each blaming the other for chickening out. Several African countries publicly gave vent to their disappointment at India's surrender because they had pinned their hope on India standing firm. In Geneva, the Chairperson's text on IPR on which India almost single-handedly prevented consensus in Montreal, was accepted virtually without any important change. This paved the way for the eventual Agreement on TRIPS.

Dunkel draft text

At the end of 1991, the then Director General of GATT, Mr. Arthur Dunkel, presented a Draft Final Act (DFA) embodying what he thought could be the agreed outcome of the Uruguay Round. In the Dunkel Draft, the text on the TRIPS Agreement was included without affording to developing countries a chance to negotiate its clauses. All proposals made by the developing countries to balance the text were set aside. In the Agreement on TRIMS, a provision on the review of the Agreement was included at the last moment, which provided to developed countries the opening to press for rule making in the areas of investment and competition policy.

During the best part of the period after the release of the Dunkel Draft and before the Brussels Ministerial Meeting, the Government of India did not take any step known to the public, to renegotiate on issues posing problems for India. On the contrary, it went all out to sell the Uruguay Round package to the Parliament and the public. The Government prepared a note justifying how the provisions in different agreements served India's interests and how they did not call for any change in the country's laws. The agreements which were played up most prominently as conferring benefits to India were those on Textiles and Clothing and Agriculture. The subsequent events falsified these presumptions. Many independent scholars, researchers and civil society organisations had in their studies and comments brought out the inequities and imbalances in the agreements (Dubey 1996). Besides, ironically it was India which later took the lead in bringing out these inequities and imbalances in the form of the "Implementation Issues" identified by developing countries following the Seattle Ministerial Meeting.

India at Singapore

The Singapore Ministerial Meeting of WTO was held in December 1996. India went to Singapore with the negative mission of preventing the inclusion of certain items on the agenda of WTO rather than with a pro-active agenda of its own to serve its trade interest. India had not presented a single paper during the preparatory phase of the Meeting except the one on textiles presented jointly with other textile exporting countries.

The main brief carried by India to Singapore was to prevent the inclusion on WTO's agenda of new issues like trade and investment, trade and competition policy, transparency in government procurement and trade facilitation. India failed in its effort. These issues were included on the agenda and have since then come to be known as the Singapore Issues.

In the agreement reached in Singapore there was a recognition of a link between these issues and trade. It was agreed to establish working groups to examine the various aspects of the relationship. A decision would be taken after two years on how to proceed further with this matter.

India and like-minded developing countries did succeed in not allowing the issue of relationship between trade and labour standards to be put on the WTO agenda. In fact, in the Singapore Ministerial Declaration, the developing countries scored several points on this issue. The Ministers "rejected the use of labour standards for protectionist purposes" and agreed that "the comparative advantage of countries, particularly low-wage developing countries, must in no way be put into question". Moreover, the ILO's competence to set standards for and deal with labour standards was clearly recognised.

The rejection of the 'link' in Singapore[6] does not mean that developing countries got the problem out of their way once and for all. There was every indication that several developed countries were under tremendous domestic pressure and, hence, determined to bring this issue on the WTO agenda. These countries had got observance of core labour standards included in some of the multilateral (like NAFTA) and bilateral agreements they had concluded with developing countries; and they were mandated by their legislators to continue to pursue this issue actively at bilateral, regional and multilateral levels.

India at Seattle

By the end of the Singapore Ministerial Meeting, a set of issues clearly emerged as the main focus of the future endeavour of India and other developing countries in WTO. These were to:

- prevent the further widening of the WTO agenda;
- oppose the launching of any new round of negotiations; and
- seek to remove the inequities and imbalances in the Uruguay Round agreements.

These, in a sense, became the permanent brief for these countries for the WTO Ministerial Meetings that followed as well as in the WTO deliberations between these Meetings.

India and other developing countries wanted the Seattle Ministerial Meeting of WTO which was held in December 1999 to be confined to mandated negotiations, mandated reviews and the Implementation Issues. Their main objective was to seek an improvement in market access for their export products and a review of the existing agreements with a view to introducing changes in them which would take care of their concerns.

Major developed countries, particularly the EU, Japan, Canada and Switzerland wanted the Ministerial Meeting to launch a new round of trade negotiations, called the Millennium Round, with the inclusion of new items like labour standards, environment protection, investment, competition policy etc.

The failure of the Meeting to adopt any declaration or decision came as a great relief to developing countries. These countries and the vast majority of some 50,000 representatives of civil society organisation which had assembled at Seattle, were jubilant that there would be no new round.

The real reason for the failure of the Meeting was the sheer inability of the governments represented at Seattle to bridge, during the time available to them, the distances separating them on major issues. This crisis in the WTO system, of which the Seattle collapse was a dramatic manifestation, came about mainly because of the insistence of major developed countries to pack the WTO agenda with an expanding set of non-trade related issues in order to take advantage of the unique enforcement mechanism of the WTO. Domestic political compulsions on the eve of the US-Presidential election compounded this basic dilemma facing the international trading system. This led to an exaggerated emphasis on the US position on labour standards.[7]

Some progress was made on some issues of importance to India in the discussions in Seattle, though they could not acquire the status of legal decisions because of the failure of the Meeting. These are reflected in the abortive draft Ministerial declaration. For example, the importance of the Implementation Issues was recognised and an assurance was given that they would be tackled on a best endeavour basis. But developed countries did not concede anything in substance on this point. They continued to insist that they would not acquiesce to any basic change in WTO agreements.

The Singapore issues were by no means buried under the debris of the Seattle Meeting. They remained alive and very much on the agenda of developed countries. All that developing countries achieved was a temporary breathing space during which they could recharge their batteries and be ready to confront the issues again. The chaos and confusion prevailing in Seattle did not allow these issues to be joined seriously. This was left for later occasions, particularly for the Doha Ministerial Meeting.

India was able to forge against very heavy odds, and a substantial degree of unity among about a dozen developing countries on a common platform of these countries in Seattle was helpful. However, the success in thwarting the efforts of major developed countries to impose their agenda was shared more widely among developing countries in general. Seattle thus created an environment of a wider unity among them.[8] It was, therefore important to strengthen the bridge that got spontaneously built across developing countries in Seattle.

India at Doha

The starting position of India at the Doha Ministerial Meeting of WTO held from 9-12 November 2001 was not very much different from that at Seattle. In short, India wanted no new round and the agenda to be confined to mandated negotiations and reviews and the Implementation Issues. As in the past, India's position in the beginning was shared by most other developing countries. The EU was insistent on what it called further deepening and broadening of multilateral cooperation, negotiation and rule-making. The EU justified the introduction of investment and competition policy both on economic and systemic grounds.

By far the most important outcome of the Doha Meeting was the launching of a new round of trade negotiations, popularly known as "the Doha Round". As a concession to the position of countries like India, officially it was not called the Doha Round, but the "Doha Work Programme". But *de facto*, it was a new round, because it had a beginning and an end, the entire exercise was taken up as a single undertaking and a trade negotiating committee was set up to co-ordinate the negotiations.

India saw the twin pillars of its negotiating platform i.e. no new round and no Singapore issues – collapse at Doha. A new round was launched and all the Singapore issues were put squarely on the agenda. In addition, the linkage between trade and environment was conceded beyond any shred of doubt.

On the Singapore issues, a major advance from the point of view of developed countries was the recognition of "the case for a multilateral framework" or "agreement" with regard to all these issues.[9] It was also agreed that negotiations on such frameworks "will take place after the Fifth Session of the Ministerial Meeting". The objectives of the multilateral framework were agreed upon. It was also agreed that the working groups on these subjects will, in their work during the next two years, focus on the core elements to go into the framework. These elements precisely are the stuff a multilateral trade regime is made of. This meant that negotiations would *de facto* commence in the working groups themselves and the text would be finalized *de jure* two years later after some hard bargaining following further negotiations.

Mainly on the insistence of India it was, however, stipulated that the negotiations would commence after the Fifth Session only "on the basis of a decision to be taken, by explicit consensus --- on modalities of negotiations".[10] This qualification might not in the ultimate analysis, make much of a difference. If a consensus could not be blocked on the substantive issue of negotiating regimes on these items, then how could it be expected to be blocked on the narrower issue of the modalities of negotiations?

The Indian delegation negotiated very hard in Doha and was able to carry most of the developing countries along with it on most of the issues. As a result, some important gains were made and losses minimised in some critical areas. On the Singapore issues, India had the support of other developing countries until almost the last leg of the journey when India was left almost alone to defend the position espoused by developing countries until that moment.

By far the biggest gain for India and other developing countries from the Doha Meeting was the flexibility provided to them in the Declaration on the TRIPS Agreement and Public Health, adopted at the Meeting. Though the Declaration was only in the nature of a clarification of the TRIPS Agreement and not an amendment to it, it was still very important because it makes for clarity as to what the developing countries can provide in their own legislations on patents and what action can be taken on the ground, based on such a provision.

The Declaration would not prevent developed countries to go to the WTO's dispute settlement mechanism or to courts to get their rights under the Agreement enforced. However, having agreed to the Declaration, they would be on a weaker legal and moral ground if they challenge the exercise by any developing country of the flexibility provided in the Declaration.

The Declaration would enable India's pharmaceutical industry to re-acquire a part of the space it would have lost in a few years time when India would be fully implementing the TRIPS Agreement. India failed in its efforts to get included in the Declaration a provision on discretion on the part of developing countries facing such crises, to make parallel imports of drugs from other developing countries. This would have given to the Indian pharmaceutical industry expanded space in foreign markets also. The compromise reached was to recognise "the problem that those having none or insufficient manufacturing capacities would face difficulties in making effective use of compulsory licensing" and to instruct the TRIPS Council to find an expeditious solution to this problem, and report to the WTO General Council before the end of 2002" (paragraph 6 of the Declaration).

The Doha Ministerial Meeting extensively dealt with the Implementation Issues. The Doha Declaration contains a separate section on these issues; in addition, a separate 8-page Decision has been taken on the subject.

The effect of the decision in Doha was to make the negotiations on outstanding Implementation Issues an integral part of the new round of trade negotiations. With this, developing countries gave up their earlier stand that these issues should be resolved on their own merits without being linked to any new round of trade negotiations which necessarily involved providing *quid pro quo* in other areas, for obtaining satisfactory solution to the outstanding Implementation Issues. As these issues arose because of the imbalances and inequities inherent in the existing agreements, the developing countries had all along taken the view that they should not be asked to pay any price for getting them resolved. But in Doha, they agreed to negotiate on these issues in the new round which is conceived as a single undertaking.

The Decision gives the present status of the progress made in addressing the Implementation Issues. The developing countries could not get any of the early harvest that they expected from the consideration of these issues.

The Doha Declaration contains some interesting provisions on Special and Differential Treatment (S&DT) for developing countries. The Committee on Trade and Development was instructed to identify those S&DT measures which are non-binding and consider the legal and practical implications of converting them into mandatory provisions. The Committee was to report to the General Council by July

2002. The Committee was also asked to consider how S&DT "may be incorporated into the architecture of WTO rules". No deadline was fixed for reporting on it. In addition, S&DT provisions have been built into the mandates of negotiations in specific sectors. This is most explicit in the formulation on agriculture.

The formulation on negotiations in the agriculture sector has some seemingly positive elements for developing countries like India. The objective of the negotiations includes "reduction of, with a view to phasing out, all forms of export subsidies; and substantial reduction in trade-distorting domestic support". The formulation also provides flexibility to meet special needs of the developing countries. It states that their special needs, including food security and rural development, shall be taken into account.

India has no reasons to derive much comfort from the above formulation. For, the real obstacle to the prospects of India's agriculture export in the world market is not so much the export subsidies of developed countries as their domestic support. And on domestic support, the agreement is only to reduce "trade distorting" support, a concept which over the years has enabled developed countries to retain most of their domestic subsidies. There can be strong economic justification to argue that all subsidies are trade-distorting in the sense that any payment to farmers can provide a cushion to them for producing more and thereby distorting trade.

India's initiative on Implementation Issues proved to be the rallying point for the unity of the developing countries in the preparatory process of the Doha Meeting. At Doha, developing countries were able to maintain a greater degree of unity and cohesion than in the Uruguay Round or at the Seattle Conference. This unity was not forged overnight. It started almost a year and a half ago, mainly centered round the Implementation Issues.

The Doha Work Programme subsequently came to be known as the Doha Development Round. This was a spin put on it by interested parties, particularly by the top echelon of the WTO Secretariat and some of the high-level EU negotiators, to mislead the developing countries into believing that the negotiating round that was launched in Doha was primarily intended to serve their interest. The subsequent events demonstrated that this was not at all the case.

India at Cancun

The Cancun Ministerial Meeting held in September 2003 went the same way as the Seattle Meeting. It ended in failure, without being able to adopt any declaration or substantive decision. It was expected that the Meeting would take some long-pending decisions to impart impetus to the Doha Round negotiations. But this did not happen.

The Doha Round was euphemistically called the Development Round. What made it look like a Development Round were: (a) the provisions in the Doha Declaration on S&DT measures for developing countries; (b) the Decision on the Implementation Issues; (c) Declaration on the TRIPS Agreement and Public Health; (d) on-going review of the TRIPS Agreement; and (e) liberalisation of trade in agriculture. But in the run-up to the Cancun Meeting no progress was made on any of these issues.

On the other hand, developed countries were pressing hard on progress in areas where they were the *demandeurs,* i.e. the Singapore issues, liberalisation of trade in services and elimination or substantial lowering of industrial tariffs. It was thus an irony that the new round in which developing countries were being asked to assume additional responsibilities but which was designed primarily to benefit the rich countries and to further limit developing countries choice of macro-economic policy instruments, in return for no progress on issues of interest to them, was being dubbed as a Development Round.

Liberalisation of trade in agriculture had been a matter of great interest to developing countries because of the enormous promise for market access that these countries had seen from the implementation of the Agreement on Agriculture. In the Doha Round of negotiations on agriculture, developing countries, in an attempt to bring down the domestic support level of developed countries, presented a very ambitious proposal, providing for the elimination of the Blue Box subsidies (minimum trade-distorting) and a substantial reduction of Amber Box subsidies (trade distorting). Besides, they called for a capping of support in all the Boxes, including the Green Box (non trade-distorting), at 10 percent of the value of agricultural production. They also proposed that special agricultural safeguards should be available only to developing countries.

The CAIRNS group of countries also started with the goal of bringing down substantially the level of domestic subsidies in major importing countries. However, after the indication that the EU and the USA had no intention to reduce their domestic support in any significant measure in the foreseeable future, the CAIRNS group followed the United States by shifting their emphasis in the negotiations from domestic subsidies reduction to enlarging market access mainly by seeking far-reaching reductions in agricultural tariffs, substantial reductions in export subsidies, and regulating export credits and food aid. This became a cause of great concern to countries like India. If India is obliged to bring down its current tariff levels by big margins and bind them, this would cause large scale distress to the millions of farmers engaged in agricultural production. Besides, this would be highly asymmetrical because countries like India would be required to take commitments for drastic tariff cuts, while major developed countries would maintain their domestic subsidies more or less at the current level, and may even increase them. Developing countries like India, because of paucity of resources, do not have this means of protection available to them. Therefore, tariff is their only protection.

The position of countries like India became even more difficult when the EU and the USA decided to present a common position which did not hold out any promise for a substantial reduction in their subsidies and which almost totally ignored the special situation prevailing in developing countries. Because of these differences, there was no agreement on the modalities for the negotiations on agriculture before the Cancun Meeting.

Further liberalisation of trade in services is a principal objective of the Doha Round but here the developed countries are the *demandeurs* and the developing countries are the ones under pressure to open up their service markets. This is mainly because the service sector in developing countries is still in an incipient stage of development. India is in a somewhat different position in this regard in that its service sector has come to occupy a very important position in the national economy. Close to 50 percent of India's GDP is now derived from services. Moreover, liberalisation in the service sector can help in making this sector more competitive by way of the infusion of additional investment, technology induction and access to the marketing network of multinational companies.

India's main competitive advantage in the service sector, however, remains in Mode-4 of service supply i.e. the movement of natural persons.[11] India knows that its ability to get access under Mode-4 service supply will depend a great deal on its offering concessions to foreign service providers in these and other sectors and in other modes of supply, particularly Mode-3.

Therefore, India's brief at the Cancun Meeting was not to adopt a closed-door or negative attitude in the services negotiations but to participate fully in them. The Government of India had endorsed a negotiating strategy according to which offers of liberalisation in varying degrees could be made in a wide range of services. But the Indian delegation was authorised to make offers for liberalisation in these sectors only after making a judgment regarding the prospects for liberalisation for supply of services under Mode-4. And the prospects did not look at all bright on the eve of the Cancun Meeting. India and other developing countries had gained very little from the liberalisation offered in the first round of the negotiation on the movement of natural persons. The announcement by the United States of a ceiling of 65,000 persons for the issue of H-I visa had further dampened prospects in this regard. Besides, the rigorous restrictions imposed on travel to the United States following the 9/11 event was not a good augury for meaningful negotiations for the liberalisation of services supplied under Mode-4.

As regards Non Agricultural Market Access (NAMA), because of its competitive advantage in several industrial sectors, particularly textile and steel products, India had important interest in the negotiation for removal of barriers in these sectors. On the other hand, India's option for further lowering industrial tariffs had become extremely limited because of the removal by it of all Q.Rs by March 2001. Thereafter, India had been left with the existing industrial tariffs as the only means of protecting its industry, which was very important to prevent deindustrialisation in some sectors, particularly the small scale sectors.

Besides, after the tariff liberalisation under the Uruguay Round, the number of non-tariff barriers imposed by developed countries had proliferated. India was, therefore, very much interested in securing substantial reductions in these non-tariff barriers and finding a means somehow to control the proliferation of such barriers.

India, therefore, had problems in accepting the US proposal for eliminating all tariffs on non-agricultural products by the year 2015. It had, initially, shown preference for the EU proposal which called for compressing all tariffs into a flatter range, mainly by eliminating tariff peaks, and significantly reducing tariff escalations. India was also seeking the application of the special dispensation in favour of the developing countries provided for in the various Articles of GATT. In spite of these precautionary moves and legitimate claims for special treatment, the brief given to the Indian delegation for negotiations for NAMA was quite positive.

The seed of the failure of the Cancun Meeting had been sown earlier through the missed deadlines, lack of seriousness in the treatment of development issues, particularly of the Implementation Issues, and fading out of hope for any meaningful reform of the agriculture sector by major developed countries. Another reason for the failure was the aggressive pursuit by developed countries of the Singapore issues in total disregard of the views of the developing countries. In the face of such a strong unified opposition by developing countries, developed countries, particularly the EU, were inclined to compromise, keeping Investment and Competition Policy out and confining their ambition to seeing negotiations commence on Government Procurement and Trade Facilitation.

It was developing countries' frustration on agriculture that turned out to be the last straw on the camel's back. These countries were driven to desperation when the US and EU cemented their differences and submitted their joint proposal in which the interest of developing countries was totally ignored. This compelled developing countries to make agriculture the breaking point at the Meeting. They did so because this issue intimately affected the life of vast multitudes of their peoples. Besides, their position on it appeared fair to all impartial observers.

The initial reaction of the United States and the EU to the failure of the Cancun Meeting was harsh and somewhat intemperate. They singled out a few countries, particularly India, and squarely blamed them for the collapse of the Meeting.

India had not undertaken as intensive an exercise for coalition-building among developing countries before the Cancun Meeting, as it did before the Seattle and Doha Meetings. It did not take any initiative to call a meeting of either the SAARC[12] Commerce Ministers or those of the G-15 developing countries, to formulate a common position on the issues before the Meeting. This could have been due to the fact that the same issues that were raised at Doha remained valid for Cancun and there seemed to be a view that not much preparatory work was required for the Cancun Ministerial Meeting.[13] However, as it turned out, India emerged as one of the leaders of the two most important groupings of developing countries that emerged during the course of the Cancun Meeting i.e. G-20 on agriculture and the Group on Singapore issues.

The emergence of G-20 was almost universally regarded as one of the most important political developments in the process of WTO negotiations. This Group effectively blocked the consensus demonstrating that there could be no decision in the WTO on any significant issue without reflecting the voice and interest of the developing countries. The emergence of G-20 also compelled those questioning the validity of the coalition of developing countries in groups like G-77 and the Nonaligned Movement, and instead suggesting, for negotiating purposes in forums like WTO, the formation of issue-based groups including both developed and developing countries, to go back to the drawing board and seriously rethink their position.

The survival of a single issue based group like the Group-20 cannot be taken for granted. The unity of the Group is likely to come under intense pressure as the specifics relating to agriculture are negotiated. This is because of the sharp differences in the interests of the leading members of the Group on various issues relating to these negotiations.

It is, therefore, extremely important for G-20 to look for ways and means and take timely initiatives for keeping itself relevant and united. One of the means to be adopted for this purpose is to reach out to and have intensive dialogue with the other groups of developing countries in WTO like the G-33, G-90, the African Group, the ACP countries etc. Secondly, though the group's focus is agriculture, it should become a part of the process of forging wider solidarity among developing countries. This can be achieved by initiatives by member countries of the Group in other forums for South-South cooperation. The successful conclusion of the on-going round of the General System of Trade Preferences (GSTP) among Developing Countries can play a very important role in this regard. The framework of GSTP can enable members of G-20 to do for other members and for developing countries outside the Group what they cannot do within the multilateral forum of the WTO.

India and the July 2004 Decision

On July 31 2004, the WTO Council agreed on a framework package to keep the Doha Round going. The package was negotiated essentially among India, Brazil, Australia, EU and USA and was later on adopted by consensus. The most important achievement of this consensus was that it restored to the multilateral system the confidence that had been severely eroded after the collapse of the Cancun Meeting. The July 2004 Decision essentially lays down the framework for the modalities for negotiations on agriculture and NAMA and provides the modalities for negotiations on Trade Facilitation. There are definitely some plus points for India in the package but they considerably fall short of India's known positions on the relevant issues.

On agriculture, the Decision provides that there will be a 20 percent reduction in domestic subsidies "in the first year and throughout the implementation period" (paragraph 7). It has been further provided that the Green Box will be reviewed to ensure that it has no or at least minimum trade distorting effect. Another important element of the Decision is that the Blue Box support will not exceed 5 percent of a member's total value of agricultural production during a historical period. The importance of this agreement should not be exaggerated because a subsidy at the level of 5 percent of total production can be a huge amount. Besides, the base period from which the 5 percent will be calculated will be agreed through negotiation. There could be a great deal of variation depending upon the base period selected. A real setback for developing countries is that the July 2004 Decision legitimises the Blue Box. In the Decision "members recognised the role of the Blue Box in promoting agricultural reforms" (paragraph 13).

There is a provision for negotiating criteria for recourse to direct payment for production limiting programmes. This could open the way for the United States shifting some of its subsidies under the Green Box to the Blue Box.

Besides, the European Union has extracted a concession for retaining a degree of flexibility in complying with the 5 percent target. Thus, the 5 percent ceiling at the moment appears to be full of uncertainties. In any case, it is a big retreat from the position that the developing countries had taken preparatory to the Cancun Meeting, i.e. to get rid of the Blue Box category altogether.

In the Decision, there is an agreement to eliminate export subsidies. However, the deadline by which export subsidies are to be eliminated is subject to negotiation. So far as India is concerned, export subsidies by developed countries do not constitute an important barrier to the access of its agricultural products to third country markets. Besides, export subsidies are a very small percentage of total subsidies given by developed countries.

There is not much for India in the text on the reduction of the *di minimis*[14] level of 10 percent of subsidies that can be given by developing countries. The language used is that the members will negotiate to bring down the *di minimis* level and only those developing countries will be exempted which allocate their *di minimis* subsidies to resource poor farmers. The Indian subsidies are available to all farmers; therefore, India is not exempted and will have to join the negotiation for bringing down the *di minimis* level.

On agricultural tariffs, the reduction will be on the basis of a tiered formula, which means that, first, there will be a harmonisation of tariffs i.e. those applying higher rates will have to effect deeper cuts. Since India's agricultural tariffs are on the higher side, this formula will not work to its advantage. India's preference was for the linear approach with average and minimum cuts.

There is a provision in the text for agreeing on a list of "sensitive products" on which tariffs may be reduced to a lesser extent. This provision is applicable to both developed and developing countries.

The concept of "special products" based on the criteria of food security, livelihood security and rural development needs, has been recognised in the text. The flexibility under this category would be available only to developing countries. Developing country Members will have the flexibility to designate an appropriate number of such products. However, the criteria for choosing these products will be subject to negotiation. This will inevitably put limitations on the flexibility granted to developing countries for designating such products.

On the Singapore issues, the developing countries have gained decisively in the consensus Decision. The first three of the Singapore issues will not form part of the Work Programme of the Doha Round and hence no work will be undertaken towards commencing negotiations on them during the Round. Even the on-going studies on them could be postponed for the time being. There was already an informal agreement in Cancun on keeping these items out. In the Decision, this has been formalised. The members have decided by explicit consensus to start negotiations on Trade Facilitation and agreed on the modalities for that, which are spelt out in the text.

Important negotiating issues for India

Agriculture

The agricultural scene in India is dotted with small farms and landholdings. The average landholding in India is a little more than 1,5 acres. Therefore any sudden turn of agricultural fortune affects a vast number of small farmers and thousands of households. It is, therefore, a political necessity for any government in India to protect Indian farmers from the vicissitudes of agricultural fortunes and ensure a minimum level of security and income stability for them.

Agriculture was not given the priority it deserved in the early years of India's planned development effort. Neglect of agriculture made the country heavily dependent on food imports and became a major factor contributing to India's chronic balance-of-payment problem. A realisation of the imprudence of this policy and the lesson learnt from the severe drought of 1965–1966, resulted in the government attaching higher priority to agriculture and investing much larger resources in terms of inputs, credits, technology and infrastructure building in this sector. This triggered the Green Revolution of the 1970s and much higher rates of agriculture growth in the 1980s.

Agriculture suffered neglect again with the commencement of the period of full-fledged liberalisation in the early 1990s. There was a marked decline in investment in agricultural infrastructure starting from the mid-1990s and continuing up to the present time.

India faces many problems in agriculture, including low productivity, poor market development, inadequacy of infrastructure like irrigation, research facilities, rural connectivity, godowns, refrigeration facilities, inadequate and poor extension services, poor farming techniques and post harvest technology, and limited purchasing power of the vast majority of the population. Unless these obstacles to agricultural growth are overcome, no amount of improvement in access to foreign markets is going to make Indian agricultural products competitive in these markets.

Though full-fledged economic reforms, commencing from 1991–1992, have continued uninterrupted, reform of the agricultural sector is yet to happen. The long reforms agenda includes higher level of investment in irrigation, R&D, extension services, credit, insurance and rural infra-structure, and reforms in the policies of procurement, subsidies and public distribution. Indian agricultural products are unlikely to be competitive in the world market unless these reforms are carried out.

India's total export of agricultural products in 2002 was only $ 4 billion which is a very low figure for a country of India's size. India's aggregate levels of support (AMS) are around 7 percent of the value of agricultural production, which is well below the *di minimis* of 10 percent for developing countries. While acceding to the Agreement on Agriculture, India did not go in for tariffication and relied on the Agreement's provision for applying restrictions on balance-of-payment ground. However, when India failed to justify Q.Rs on this ground and was obliged to eliminate all Q.Rs, including those on agricultural products by the end of March 2001, tariffs remained the only instrument of protection for India's agriculture.

India's tariff bindings, on the whole, are sufficiently high. Average binding rate is 117 percent, and the highest 350 percent for some varieties of edible oils. For some items like foodgrains and milk powder the bindings in March 2001 were zero. But these have since been renegotiated and bindings have been increased, with tariff quotas also in place.

The high hopes of developing countries from the Agreement on Agriculture, for increasing their agricultural exports to developed countries did not come true as a result of both the modest measure of liberalisation agreed to be undertaken under the Agreement on Agriculture and the manner in which the Agreement was implemented. Taking advantage of the flexibility provided in the Agreement, developed countries, rather perversely, managed not only to maintain but also to substantially increase their domestic subsidies. Besides, several of these countries resorted to what has come to be known as "dirty" tariffication, increasing their bound tariffs to dizzying heights, going as high as 700 percent in the case of Japan.

The mandated negotiation on agriculture according to Article 20 of the Agreement on Agriculture began on January 1 2000. India submitted a written proposal on 15 January, 2001. The Indian proposal can be broadly classified into two categories: (a) those designed to increase the flexibility available to developing countries for providing domestic support to the agricultural sector with a view to ensuring food and livelihood security; and (b) those intended to seek opening up of the markets of developed countries by meaningful reductions in tariffs, substantial reduction in domestic support and elimination of export subsidies by developed countries.

The mandatory negotiation has been at a standstill for the last 5 years because countries like EU and Japan which are not inclined to undertake any meaningful commitment to reduce their domestic subsidies have taken the position that progress in the mandatory negotiation must be related to progress in other areas in the Doha Round. In the Doha Round, there has not been an agreement on even the modalities of negotiation in this sector. However, in the July 2004 Consensus, some of the important elements of the modalities were agreed upon.

Services

Both the output of the service sector and export of services have grown phenomenally in the last two decades. What has made the real change in services is their much enhanced tradability due to the technological revolution. It was, therefore, natural that there would be pressure for making rules to govern trade in services and bringing them within the framework of the international trading system. In spite of this, India opposed the move spearheaded by the United States in the early 1980s to include services on the GATT agenda. There were legitimate grounds for taking such a position at that time, some of which still remain valid. In a meeting of the captains of service industries convened by the Government in Delhi in the early 80s, almost all the participants were of the view that their service sector industries were at a very early stage of development and not at all capable of withstanding competition from the powerful multinational corporations of developed countries which dominated global service trade and output.

The situation changed substantially during the course of the next decade or so. The service sector has since come to occupy a very important place in the Indian economy. In some areas of services India has come to acquire competitive advantage. This is particularly true of services supplied under Mode-4, i.e. movement of natural persons. The share of services in India's total trade increased from 20 percent in 1995 to 28 percent in 2000. Recently the availability of highly skilled persons at competitive costs had enabled the country to establish a presence in cross-border supply of IT-enabled services, like back office activities, processing, billing, call centres, medical and legal transcriptions, tele-medicines and tele-education. Thus, while India's main competitive advantage remains in Mode-4 supply, recently it has come to acquire such an advantage in Mode-I supply also.

In the first round of the GATS negotiations, the progress achieved was quite modest. In most cases the *status quo* prevailing was brought under binding. The commitments made in the Mode-4 supply of services were highly limited and circumscribed by numerous conditionalities. These included severe limitation on duration, rigorous requirements of qualifications and works experience, equally rigorous licensing, residency and citizenship requirements, work related permit barriers, quantitative limits on the number of persons who can enter, nature and terms of employment, economic needs tests, local market need tests and other qualification requirements.

During these negotiations, India undertook commitments in 6 out of 12 major sectors. India made no commitment in Mode 1 and 2 supply of services except in telecommunication and insurance. In Mode-3, commitment was made to permit foreign equity in service sectors up to a maximum of 51 percent, except in telecommunication where the maximum was 25 percent. Under Mode-4, horizontal commitments were made permitting intra-corporate transfers and entry of professionals and business persons and only to a limited extent to those providing services under a service contract.

The commitments made by India did not reflect the autonomous liberalisation process that started from the early 1990s. For example, India bound foreign equity participation to 51 percent under Mode-3 in the communications sector, though in reality up to 74 percent of foreign equity in this sector is permitted. In computer and related services India permits 100 percent equity participation, though it left the sector unbound under GATS.

Soon after the beginning of the current negotiations on services India submitted its proposal for the liberalisation of movement of professionals. The suggestions made in the proposal include the following:

- Need for establishment of multilateral norms to reduce the scope for discriminatory practices in use of Economic Needs Tests;
- Social Security contributions need not be required to be made for temporary movement of professionals, as they are not eligible for receiving benefits of such contributions;
- Administration of visa regimes may be made more transparent. The notion of a separate GATS Visa for personnel covered by horizontal and sectoral commitments scheduled by a Member, different and less onerous from the

normal emigration visa may be considered. The idea is that this would allow service providers to move in and out of the market without time-consuming visa requirement;

- The work relating to the establishment of multilateral norms to facilitate Mutual Recognition Agreements (MRAs) among developing countries should be expedited. This is because the non-recognition of qualifications by developed countries often acts as a serious barrier to market entry;
- Developed countries should, in their offer, include specific categories of natural persons, including lower and middle level skilled workers, delinked from Mode-3, for periods of stay longer than one year.

India has received requests from some 25 countries in a large number of sectors. For each of these sectors most countries have asked for full commitment under Mode 1, 2 and 3 and have sought relaxation of restrictions like limits of equity participation, forms of legal entity etc. The basic negotiating strategy of developed countries in the services sector is to increase the number of service sectors that can be opened up and deepen the commitment for liberalisation in sectors where negotiations have already been held. These countries are trying to achieve these objectives by deploying their superior bargaining strength. In the sectors not yet covered by negotiations under GATS, the objective of these countries is to restrict or remove the ability of the developing countries to maintain regulatory measures designed to protect public interest by such devices as limiting the size and number of service operations and making service providers responsible for the protection of the environment etc. The requests of USA and EU include removal of regulation subjecting foreign take-over to government approval, laws requiring foreign investors to form joint ventures in some sectors, and regulation of land ownership.

It is true that GATS permits member countries to choose the sectors they will liberalise and the extent of liberalisation. Article XIV of GATS can be invoked to protect the public interest or for maintaining moral or public order. The precise purpose of the demands of the developed countries seems to be to whittle down the flexibility provided in the GATS and limit, if not eliminate, the policy choices the developing countries have managed to retain in GATS.

Several economists have suggested unilateral liberalisation by developing countries of their service industries. There is no doubt a case for unilateral liberalisation and the Government of India has undertaken some significant measures in this regard. However, the case of unilateral liberalisation must be qualified by a whole set of very pertinent considerations. By far the most important among them is the displacement of local firms, and the consequent job loss that it can cause if pursued indiscriminately. In an economy where service industries are mostly in the informal sector which is a major source of employment, indiscriminate liberalisation can cause widespread suffering with grave political consequences.

Moreover, until now foreign capital inflows into India in the service sectors, particularly tourism, health and education have been very limited in spite of the partial liberalisation undertaken in these sectors, particularly in tourism. In the areas of public services, multinational corporations have little incentive to invest. In particular, they are less likely to go to urban slums and rural areas where incomes are very low. The liberalisation of public utility services pose special problems, such as uncertainty in the supply of the services concerned, adverse effects on the supplies to disadvantaged groups and regions, and reduction in government funding and engagement due to the entry of foreign service providers.

In spite of the above considerations, India has adopted quite a positive approach towards the services negotiations. India has identified a large number of service sectors across which it is prepared to strike give-and-take bargains. In lieu of getting further access for its services particularly in Mode-4, it is prepared to consider binding the liberalisation done under its economic reforms programme and offer future liberalisation. India has already submitted an offer list improving upon its past bindings and there are reports that another offer list incorporating further improvements is under consideration.

Non-Agricultural Market Access (NAMA)

Because of India's relatively advanced and diversified manufacturing sector, it has an important interest in seeking a larger access to foreign markets for products of this sector. India's main interests are in textiles, steel products, leather goods, chemicals and pharmaceuticals, ancillaries for automobile industry, machinery, and transport and other equipment. In several of these products, India faces peak tariffs, tariff escalation and a plethora of non-tariff barriers in the markets of developed countries. India is also interested in opening up its own markets for foreign products in certain sectors in order to attract private foreign capital and technology and to make these sectors more competitive. However, following the elimination of non-tariff barriers by March 2001, tariffs remain the only means of protection for Indian industries.

Textile products have been one of the leading export earners for India. The textile industry in India contributes 4 percent of GDP and 33 percent of foreign exchange earnings and is the largest employer, employing 40 million workers.[15] India has the largest number of spindles next to China. The industry was delicensed in 1991 and has since then gone through significant rationalization and further measures of liberalisation. The Government anticipates a 15 percent growth in the industry and significantly higher growth in exports during the coming years.

From the beginning of 2005 when the MFA regime came to an end, a real opportunity for developing countries like India of expanding exports in textiles and clothing has opened up. However, in its bid to avail itself of this opportunity, India faces formidable competition from China. Trade data for the first few months of the year 2005 already indicate that it is China which has registered the largest gains from the elimination of quotas after the disappearance of MFA. The governments of the importing countries in which there has been a surge of imports of Chinese textiles, have threatened to take measures in accordance with the terms and conditions accepted by China in its negotiations with them for accession to WTO. In response to the protest of the importing countries, particularly EU and USA, China has already taken unilateral measures, including imposition of an export levy, to restrict its textiles export to these major countries.

This provides an opening for India, even though it may be for a short period. The Indian textile industry is now better poised and organised to take advantage of this opportunity. The data for the first few months of 2005 show that India has also improved its position in the US market after 1 January 2005, though not to the extent China has. The Indian industry is aware that reductions in tariff peaks and escalation and NTBs would help but the real task is on the supply side i.e. to compete in terms of quality, delivery schedule etc.

India in general can be expected to adopt a positive approach to the negotiations on NAMA, subject of course to the need for protecting some industries, particularly those in the tiny and small scale sectors which provide employment to millions of people. In the last two budgets, the Government of India has announced its plan to bring down tariffs to the level prevailing in East and South East Asia. Recently a committee on the rationalization of tariffs has suggested a road map according to which by the end of 2006-2007 India would have 5 percent tariffs on the import of basic raw material, 8 percent for intermediate goods, 10 percent for finished goods that are not consumer durables, 20 percent for consumer durables, 50 percent for motor vehicles and up to 150 percent for demerit goods. This recommendation has more or less been accepted by the Government and can be expected to be implemented.[16]

The implementation issues in the WTO

A large number of the agreements and understandings reached during the Uruguay Round were unequal and unbalanced from the point of view of developing countries like India. Half way through the ten year implementation period, several of the inherent inequalities and imbalances of the Uruguay Round agreements started coming to the surface. It was found that some of the agreements were not being implemented in their true spirit. Some of the agreements proved extremely injurious to the interest of the developing countries. Provisions of the WTO Agreement, relating to special and differential treatment in favour of the developing countries, were of a non-binding and non-contractual nature, couched in best endeavour terms. In the process of implementation, developed countries took advantage of such formulations and totally ignored these provisions.

Non-governmental research institutions, individual scholars, civil society organizations, and grass root movements in developing countries played a major role in bringing to public attention the imbalances and inequalities in Uruguay Round agreements and the sufferings to the people caused by the manner in which they, particularly those on TRIPS and Agriculture, were implemented. There was, therefore, a mounting public pressure on the governments of many developing countries, particularly so in India, either to renounce these agreements or to get them drastically modified. The policy-makers in India found it impossible to ignore the public pressure for reopening some of these Uruguay Round agreements.

India was, therefore, in the forefront of the countries raising the Implementation Issues in WTO. Developing countries identified and reached agreement among themselves to pursue a set of Implementation Issues during the preparatory process of and at the Third WTO Ministerial Meeting in Seattle. In the run up to the Seattle Meeting a group of like-minded developing countries, including India, submitted two documents containing lists of Implementation Issues, the total number of which came to be around 95.

At the Seattle Meeting a Ministerial Working Group on Implementation Issues was established. On 1 December 1999 the Chairman of the Group circulated a draft decision on Implementation Issues for inclusion in the Declaration to be adopted at the end of the Meeting. It was stated in the draft that the evaluation of the Implementation Issues had "revealed serious concerns among many members specially developing countries, about the implementation of the results of the Uruguay Round". The draft proposed the establishment of a special mechanism under the WTO General Council to pursue these issues. Since the Seattle Meeting collapsed without adopting any declaration the Chairman's draft text had no legal validity.

After the Seattle Meeting developing countries pursued the Implementation Issues in the WTO General Council. In a decision adopted on the subject on 3 May 2000, it was agreed that the Council, meeting in special sessions, would address these issues.

Thereafter, the Implementation Issues remained in the centre of attention in the WTO for two full years in special sessions of the General Council. In these sessions, developing countries took the view that all Implementation Issues needed to be addressed and resolved before the Doha Meeting. According to developed countries the main task under this clause was to assist the developing countries to implement the Uruguay Round agreements, and not to seek to redress the inequalities and imbalances inherent in them. The Doha Meeting comprehensively dealt with the Implementation Issues.

After the Doha Meeting, Implementation Issues no longer remained central to the deliberations in the WTO. The space vacated by them was usurped by issues and modalities which could impart momentum to the Doha Round. By the time of the Cancun Meeting the Implementation Issues had receded into the background.

Special & Differential Treatment (S&DT) for developing countries

Developing countries have all along been accorded some kind or the other of special treatment in the international trading system. In the beginning, their effort was to get greater flexibility in the application of trade rules in order to be able to pursue their development objectives. Some of the examples of earlier S&DT measures are Articles XVIII and XXVIII-bis, and Part-IV of GATT and the Enabling Clause of the Tokyo Round of Trade Negotiations.

The S&DT concept underwent a significant transformation after the Uruguay Round of Trade Negotiations. Earlier, S&DT measures were mainly in the nature of providing flexibilities and policy space in the realm of trade in order to enable the governments of developing countries to assist development. In the Uruguay Round agreements, the emphasis shifted to a variety of other measures, most of which were often of an *ad hoc* and once-for-all nature. These included fixing different thresholds for the application of rules (in taking countervailing measures, in determining permissible subsidies, *di minimis* levels), permitting the group of least developed countries to derogate from certain obligations altogether, establishing different time periods for implementing commitments, technical assistance and capacity building.

Developing countries have derived little benefit from S&DT measures even ten years after the WTO agreements went into operation. This is mainly because of their inherent character and limitations. It will not be an exaggeration to state that in most cases developing countries have been chasing a mirage in pursuing S&DT measures. This is because:

- These measures are couched in general hortatory terms and are agreed upon on a best endeavour basis. Since no contractual obligations have been taken, the dispute settlement mechanism of WTO cannot be invoked to enforce their implementation.
- Some of the S&DT measures are qualified by the stipulation that any measure a member country can take for exercising the flexibility under these provisions must be consistent with the objective and nature of the agreement concerned.
- In some agreements, S&DT measures have been made subject to negotiations. Given the weak bargaining position of developing countries in negotiations, it is unlikely that these countries would ever be able to get these S&DT provisions implemented.
- In the majority of the cases S&DT measures are in the form of technical assistance. The amount of technical assistance to be given is, in the very nature of things, left to the discretion of developed countries. There is no way in which, a developed country can be obliged by virtue of these provisions to part with a particular amount or a particular kind of technical assistance.

In the discussions that took place in the Committee on Trade & Development between the Doha and Cancun Ministerial Meetings, developed countries started questioning the very economic justification of S&DT measures. The rational for S&DT measures have been discussed ever since the negotiations for the formulation of the Havana Charter. These are:

- Equality between unequals is inequitable. There is disparity between developed and developing countries not only in terms of per capita incomes and export supply capacities but also in terms of market power, industrial base, R&D capability and capital & technological edge. It is, therefore, necessary to provide the developing countries level playing field;
- Development of developing countries is the primary responsibility of these countries themselves but the international community has the responsibility to assist in this process. There was a consensus on this concept for well over two decades between the mid 50s till the mid 70s;

- Development of developing countries will redound to the benefit of developed countries by way of enhancing the former's capacity to import and also by way of contributing to the stability of the global economy;
- A late comer among the justification for S&DT measures is the consensus on the principle of 'right to development'.

There is, therefore, no way developing countries can give up pursuing S&DT measures. At the same time, the pursuit of these measures in most cases has been in vain. Moreover, by pursuing these non-enforceable measures, developing countries are only dissipating their bargaining strength derived from the concessions they have already made through unilateral trade liberalisation. So far as India is concerned, many of the S&DT measures are simply not applicable to it and it does not need most others to which it may have a formal claim. Nevertheless, India is supporting these measures for the sake of solidarity with other developing countries. This position is not sustainable both in India's own interest and in the long-term interest of the developing countries. India should, therefore, take initiative for being selective in pursuing these measures.

The discussion on S&DT measures in the run up to the Cancun Meeting moved into esoteric directions. It has not been brought back to the track after the Cancun Meeting. But unlike the Implementation Issues of which they constitute the main body, the S&DT measures are unlikely to disappear from the WTO agenda or remain relegated to the background for too long.

Agreement on Trade Related Aspects of Intellectual Property Rights (TRIPS)

The TRIPS Agreement went against the 1970 Patent Act of India in most of its important aspects. Some of the examples of divergence were:

- In the Indian Patent Act only process patents could be granted for food, pharmaceutical and agro-chemical products;
- The duration of patents was 5 to 7 years for the above mentioned products and 14 years for those for which product patent could also be granted;
- The Indian Act excluded nuclear energy, methods of agriculture and horticulture;
- Biological processes and products not patentable;
- Effective provisions for compulsory licensing of patents, and a provision for the revocation of patent in public interest.

In India, which till the other day maintained the practice of processed patent only in the food, pharmaceutical and agro-chemical sectors, the introduction of product patent will lead to a substantial increase in the prices of life-saving drugs, most of which are covered by patents. Therefore, after the new regime becomes fully operational, it would be very difficult to make life-saving drugs available to the poor people in India at reasonable prices. In a country with a massive backlog of poverty, millions of people will suffer on this account.

Compatibility of the TRIPS Agreement with CBD The Convention on Bio-Diversity (CBD) was signed in Rio in 1992. The TRIPS Agreement which came into force three years later, is incompatible with CBD in several respects. The review of Article 27.3(b) of the TRIPS Agreement commenced in 1999 and that of the Agreement as a whole in 2000. India, in its submission to the TRIPS Council where the review exercise is going on, made extensive proposals for making the TRIPS Agreement compatible with CBD. India also submitted other proposals to remove the imbalances and inequalities in the TRIPS Agreement. Most of these proposals have also been pursued during the course of the discussion on the Implementation Issues. The following are some of the proposals made by India:

- Full disclosure of the sources of the biological material and traditional knowledge used for taking out patents;
- Prior consent of the country whose resources and knowledge are obtained for patenting;
- Provision of a mechanism of profit sharing on an equitable basis with those who possess such knowledge and material, including rural and indigenous communities;
- On the question of patentability, elimination of the distinction between the biological processes on the one hand and non-biological and micro-biological process on the other. All these processes should be non-patentable;
- Provision of protection to geographical indications other than wines and spirits. In the case of India, this would include *Darjeeling Tea, Kolhapuri Chappals, Kanchipuram Sarees, Basmati Rice* etc.

Neither in the discussion on the Implementation Issues in the special sessions of the WTO General Council nor in the TRIPS Council has it become possible to get any of these proposals accepted. The United States in particular has strongly opposed all these suggestions and has shown no interest in the revision of the TRIPS Agreement. Consequently, the whole process of the review of the Agreement was relegated to the background in the negotiations preparatory to the Cancun Conference and has remained so since then.

The only progress made was in the Declaration on the TRIPS Agreement and the Public Health at the Doha Ministerial Meeting. This became possible mainly because of the outcry of the civil society organisations, mostly from developed countries against the distress caused to the people in African countries because of their inability to source drugs at affordable prices to cope with the epidemic of HIV/AIDS. However, para 6 of the Declaration remained pending for almost two years until the Cancun Ministerial Meeting. A solution to this paragraph was found just before the Cancun Meeting. The solution like any other agreement of this nature was a compromise and not entirely satisfactory to developing countries.

Amendment to the 1970 Patent Act After India acceded to WTO, it became automatically a party to the TRIPS Agreement also. This made it necessary for India to align its legislations relating to IPRs, particularly the 1970 Patent Act, to the requirements of the Agreement. Indian IPR legislations relating to copyrights, trade marks, geographical indications have all been brought into conformity with the TRIPS Agreement. But serious problems arose when it came to aligning the 1970 Patent Act with the Agreement.

The amendments to the 1970 Act were carried out in three stages. The first set of amendments to this patent law was enacted in 1999, four years after it was due, to make a provision for a Mail Box and for the grant of Exclusive Marketing Rights (EMR). The second set of amendments was passed in 2002, two years after it was due, in which the relevant provisions of the TRIPS Agreement were extended to products for which India was already granting product patents under its law. This included provisions relating to duration, scope including extension of patent protection to micro-organism, compulsory licensing etc. The third set of amendments were enacted very recently, extending the grant of product patents to those products i.e. pharmaceutical, food and agro-chemicals for which only process patents were granted under the Indian law.

The whole issue of India's adherence to the TRIPS Agreement and amendments to the 1970 Act to give effect to it, have evoked a great deal of controversy and agitation in the country. The main criticism has been that in the sets of amendments proposed the government was not taking full advantage of the flexibility provided in the TRIPS Agreement in order to safeguard national interest. The public agitation on this issue has been one of the reasons why deadlines could not be met in moving the first two sets of amendments. In the third set of amendments, the government at the last stage introduced a number of very important amendments under the pressure of and based on the suggestions made by civil society organisations, independent experts and the domestic pharmaceutical industry, particularly Indian Drug Manufactures Association (IDMA), which incorporates mainly small and medium size pharmaceutical companies.

Plant Variety and Farmers Right   Article 27(3)(b) of the TRIPS Agreement provides that "members shall provide for the protection of plant varieties either by patents or by effective *sui generis* system or by any combination thereof". The Government of the day in India was inclined to follow the patent route but it opted for the *sui generis* alternative following a determined campaign launched by civil society organisations to stop patenting of seeds. The draft legislation for the *sui generis* system was under consideration for a long time when consultations were held with civil society organisations, academics and experts outside the government. As a result, the Indian Parliament adopted The Protection of Plant Varieties & Farmers' Rights Act 2001 (PPVFRA). The rules for giving effect to this Act were framed in 2003 but notification to bring this Act into force was issued only in mid-2005. The Act serves the dual purpose of having a *sui generis* protection of plant varieties as well as having provisions for protecting farmers' rights.

The International Union for the Protection of the New Variety of Plants (UPOV) has been held out as a model for a *sui generis* system. The Government of India applied for the membership of UPOV (1978) in May 2002. This was in spite of the enactment of the PPVFRA the main purpose of which was to go beyond UPOV for safeguarding India's interest in the protection of its genetic resources and to provide for farmers rights. The application is still pending.

The Bio-diversity Act   India has one of the richest sources of bio-diversity in the world. Because of the modern bio-technology revolution, bio-diversity has become one of the most important means of addressing poverty in the country and contributing to its growth and prosperity. It is also an extremely important source of export earning. A bio-diversity legislation was needed to protect India's bio-diversity and indigenous knowledge from corporate giants who could have taken advantage of the legal limbo prevailing in the country and transferred out genetic material without proper agreement or payment.

India, therefore, enacted a Bio-diversity Act in 2002. The purpose of the Act is to provide for conservation of bio-diversity, sustainable use of its components and equitable sharing of the benefits arising out of the use of biological resources and knowledge. The Act prohibits any person who is not a citizen of India or a non-resident citizen of India or a body corporate or association not incorporated in India, from obtaining any biological resources occurring in India or knowledge associated therewith, for research or for commercial utilization, without previous approval of the National Bio-diversity Authority to be set up under the Act.

Geographical Indications   There is no Indian geographical indication which is protected nationally or internationally. Nevertheless, the Indian Parliament adopted the Geographical Indications of Goods (Registration & Protection) Act, 1999, to strengthen its claim in future. The Act provides for the registration and better protection of geographical indications relating to goods.

Regional Trade Agreements (RTAs) and India

Article XXIV of GATT provides for a departure from the MFN principle enshrined in Article I, for the purpose of establishing free trade areas (FTAs) and customs unions (CUs). The way Article XXIV has been applied has been causing considerable concern to several WTO member countries and particularly to India which is not a member of any functioning FTA. There are several ways in which the proliferation of RTAs is adversely affecting the trade interests of countries remaining outside these agreements. Some of these countries, including India, have already lost a chunk of the share of their markets in major developed countries members of mega-groupings, for example the US market for textiles after the establishment of NAFTA. The recent trend of providing preferential access to investment resources and technologies coming from developed member countries of such groupings compounds the problem of discrimination suffered by outside countries.

RTAs are no longer motivated only by the consideration underlying Article XXIV nor are they confined to merely creating a preferential trading area. There are compulsions of a much wider and more important nature for entering into an RTA. Therefore, they have come to stay and are likely to proliferate further in future.

So the issue is not of stemming the tide of RTAs, but of applying to them rules and regulations and encouraging features which will make them compatible with the multilateral trading system and which will contribute to the achievement of the general objective of freeing trade globally. There is thus an urgent need to impose stronger discipline on the creation of RTAs. In the Doha Declaration, the Ministers agreed to negotiate for clarifying and improving WTO procedures under the existing WTO provisions applying to RTAs. Only preliminary and seminar-type of discussions have so far been held on this issue.

Recently, there has been a conscious shift in India's trade policy in favour of free trade agreements (FTA) on a regional and bilateral basis. This is essentially because of the perception of the gains from such arrangements. But, this is also due to the fear of being left out in the cold in the world trading order. The frustration arising out of the failure of the effort spread over a decade to create a regional grouping in South Asia has in no small measure been responsible for engendering this fear. India is a member of the South Asian Association for Regional Cooperation (SAARC). But SAARC took nearly 20 years to take a highly tentative step forward in the direction of establishing an FTA. A highly unfavourable political climate, particularly frequent tensions in the relations between India and Pakistan, the two largest countries of the region, has been the principal factor impeding the progress towards regional integration in South Asia. Another reason is the overwhelmingly large presence of India in the region which calls for a pivotal role of and much larger sacrifice by India in the short run in order to impart momentum to the process of regional integration. This is, however, not forthcoming because of a variety of reasons.

In an effort to diversify its choice of regional groupings, India took the lead in creating the Indian Ocean Rim Association for Regional Cooperation. It also joined the initiative for creating the BIMSTEC i.e. Bangladesh, India, Myanmar, Sri Lanka and Thailand Economic Cooperation. BIMSTEC has adopted a framework agreement to create a free trade area among the member countries, which, according to some analysts is simpler and more far-reaching than the framework agreement for establishing a South Asian Free Trade Area (SAFTA) adopted at the Islamabad SAARC Summit in January, 2004.

India has signed an FTA with Sri Lanka which, during the short period it has been in operation, has led to a dramatic increase in the two-way trade. This has encouraged both the countries to go in for a Comprehensive Trade Agreement which has reached an advanced stage of negotiation. India has also recently signed an FTA with Thailand and a Comprehensive Trade Agreement with Singapore. A proposal by India for entering into an FTA with Bangladesh is currently under consideration by the Bangladesh Government. Discussions are going on for creating an FTA between India, Brazil and South Africa. The Chinese Prime Minister, during his visit to India in April, 2005, showed an interest in exploring the possibility of an FTA between the two countries. India's reaction to it was cautiously positive.

In its 'Look East Policy' adopted more than 10 years ago, India has succeeded in forging various links of cooperation with ASEAN and has applied for the membership of the Asia and Pacific Economic Cooperation (APEC). India is also trying to link up, through different forms of cooperation, including where possible preferential trading arrangements, with the Gulf Co-operation Council, South African Customs Union, COMESA, MERCOSUR and the Andean Community. A framework agreement for a preferential trading arrangement was signed with MERCOSUR in June 2003.

Singapore issues

Developed countries, particularly the EU, have been trying very hard to engage WTO in negotiations for rule making in ever expanding areas of economic policy. Developing countries, on the other hand, have been strongly opposed to getting involved in this kind of negotiation. They regard the issues considered fit by developed countries for such rule making, as non-trade related and falling essentially in the domain of general development and industrialisation policies of developing countries.

Rule making at the international level in the areas like investment, competition policy etc., disregards the differences in the size, structure and the stage of development of the economies of developing countries. Different rules and ample flexibility in the application of rules are called for in different situations in order to optimise benefits from opportunities available in these areas. A one-size-fits-all recipe which is implicit in the harmonisation of rules in these areas at the global level cannot serve the interests of countries at different stages of development. It can only further squeeze the policy choices of these countries and make the present unequal international trading system even more inequitable.

Developed countries argue that rule making in these areas is designed mainly to serve the interest of the developing countries. For example, an investment regime at the global level would enable developing countries to attract larger flow of foreign private investment. Internationally agreed rules of competition would enhance the efficiency of their economies and give them competitive edge in the world market. An international trade facilitation regime would save transaction costs by huge margins. A figure of 150 billion dollars per year has been quoted in this context. There is, no doubt, some merit in these arguments, but the promised outcome is heavily dependent on the manner in which the market forces operate on the ground both at the national and international levels, and on a variety of factors which have nothing to do with rule making at the international level.

The real purpose of developed countries behind this pressure for rule making at the international level is not to serve the interest of the developing countries but their own interest. This is clear from the kind of proposals they have put forward for discussion in the working groups set up in the WTO to carry forward the work on the Singapore Issues. For example, in the working group on investment, they are pressing for agreement on measures and standards which will suit the interest of their multinationals seeking investment opportunities in developing countries, and have either ignored or rejected all proposals designed to ensure that foreign investors conform to social objectives like environmental protection, poverty alleviation, protection of human rights and reducing income disparities, both personal and regional. In competition policy, developed countries have laid emphasis on non-discrimination, limits on government's power and intervention designed to serve social objectives and a blanket ban on cartels. On the other hand, they have refused to discuss proposal made by developing countries for curtailing the restrictive business practices of multinational companies.

Among the new issues, the one that has attracted the maximum attention is investment. The arguments which India has advanced against rule making in WTO on investment, include the following:

- The argument that a regime for investment protection will lead to an increase in the amount and quality of private foreign investment is not borne out by empirical evidence. At the global level, even without an international investment regime, FDI flows increased from $ 200 billion in 1991 to $ 1trillion by the end of the 1990s. The flow of FDI depends upon a variety of factors other than investment rules, in particular the state of development of the physical and social infrastructure, the state of governance, political climate etc.

- If unregulated, liberalisation of foreign investment can have horrendous consequences in terms of adverse impact on balance of payment position, on the viability of local enterprises, on the balance between local and foreign participation and ownership, and on the political and economic stability of the host country. Also, FDI may crowd out domestic investment with all the other related adverse consequences rather than constituting a net addition to investment.

- Till recently, developed countries and successful developing countries have regulated foreign direct investment by treating different sources and kinds of FDIs differently, laying down conditions of entry, limitations on ownership and control and transfer of funds, and imposing performance requirements and conditions of technology transfer. There is no reason why the developing countries today should not have the same freedom of choice of policy instruments to regulate FDI.

One of the procedural arguments advanced by India against an international regime on investment is that there already exists an elaborate framework of investment protection and dispute settlement mechanisms at the bilateral and multilateral levels. Developing countries are competing with each other in concluding bilateral agreements with developed countries to facilitate the flow of foreign private capital. Some of the investment protection and dispute settlement mechanisms at the international level are MIGA under the World Bank, the International Convention on Settlement of Investment Disputes, and the UN Committee on International Trade Law. Besides, in the WTO itself, the GATS provides for liberalisation of rules for commercial presence, which includes foreign investment (Mode-3). Investment rules are also built into the Agreement on Trade Related Investment Measures (TRIMS). It seems that developed countries are unhappy with the flexibility provided in the

GATS and are therefore seeking a rigid and binding investment regime which, among others, can supercede the inherent constraint to Mode-3 liberalisation under GATS.

India has also drawn attention to the failure of more than three years of efforts within the OECD to conclude a Multilateral Agreement on Investment, in spite of the fact that all negotiating partners there were developed countries. How much more difficult it would be to reach an agreement in WTO which has a much larger membership than OECD's, and which includes both developed and developing countries?

Positions and roles of different interest groups

Till the end of the Uruguay Round, policy making on international trade issues was almost the sole preserve and privilege of the Central Government. There was hardly any transparency in such policy making. Consultations with interested groups were sporadic and entirely up to the discretion of the Government. The only interested group whom the Government used to consult occasionally was the business community.

Soon after the establishment of the WTO, the trade issues became of great public interest partly because of the far-reaching implications and consequences of some of the WTO agreements and partly because of the radical transformation in the strength, role and influence of civil society organisations (CSOs) all over the world, including India. The Government came to realise that some of the major WTO agreements whose ramifications went deeper down to the State and local levels, could not be implemented without the support of the people at different levels. At the same time, it also became clear that the Government needed the support of the people for effectively pursuing its position in international forums and for resisting moves in these forums, which in its judgement were not in India's interest. The situation got accentuated because of the adverse consequences of the implementation of the TRIPS Agreement and the pressure mounted by developed countries to bring new issues for rule making under WTO. This led to intensive consultations by the Government at different levels, preparatory to the Seattle Meeting. Since then there has been a much greater transparency in Government's WTO policy-making largely due to the unprecedented empowerment of the CSOs, the intellectual contribution and advocacy role of independent experts and think tanks and the beginning of an era of coalition governments at the Centre.

Among the various interests involved, there has been a long tradition of consulting trade and industry and associate them with international negotiations on economic issues. This is partly because India has throughout, including at the height of its socialistic policy, remained a mixed economy in which the private sector has played an important role. Thus, representatives of apex associations of trade and industry organisations formed a part of the Indian delegation to the first UNCTAD in February/March, 1964. The pattern was repeated in all Ministerial Meetings of WTO starting from Seattle.

Before the Seattle Meeting, the Government set up an Advisory Board on WTO Matters which included as members top-level executives of apex trade and industry bodies. They played a very active role and brought rich inputs based on research into the meetings of the Board. Almost all the apex trade and industry bodies have their research wings on WTO issues which produce extremely useful research and policy papers. They also regularly organise seminars, workshops and interaction with top policy makers of India's major trading partners, eminent international experts and WTO and UNCTAD officials.

The trade and industry in India generally shares the national positions on major WTO issues like TRIPS, Agriculture and Singapore Issues. On negotiations for access (i.e. NAMA, Services) to foreign markets, they would like the Government to be more pro-active. But on the question of the opening of the Indian market, while agreeing that there has to be inevitably a *quid pro quo* and that this should be pursued even on its own merits, their general inclination is protectionist.

The State governments in India should have a major say in formulating policies on WTO issues. Though negotiations on international issues is the prerogative of the Central Government, the sectors on which WTO rules have a major impact, i.e. agriculture, natural resources, education, health etc., are in the State List i.e. the States have the primary responsibility in these sectors. In spite of this, the States do not play much of a role in shaping the Government's policies on WTO issues. None of the States has developed expertise or institutional infra-structure to deal with such issues. There is no standing consultative machinery on this subject between the Centre and the State governments. States are seldom represented in the Indian delegations to WTO meetings. Since the Singapore Meeting, the Central Government has been going through the formality of consulting State Governments, but the consultation is perfunctory.

Even the Indian Parliament is not effective in influencing policies on WTO issues. There is no constitutional requirement to get policies on WTO matters approved by the Parliament or get treaties (in the present context, WTO agreements) ratified by it. In the Parliamentary system of government on the British model that India has, this is supposed to be the exclusive responsibility of the Executive, that is the Cabinet. There is recently a move initiated mainly by CSOs and supported by some important political leaders and parties, that the Constitution of India should be amended to oblige the Government to submit all treaties which vitally affect India's national interest and which impose on India obligations in perpetuity, for ratification by the Parliament.

Whatever little influence the Parliament is able to exercise is through debates on the budget and other subjects, adjournment motions and during the regular question hour. However, these procedures are of a limited value. The Government has a majority in the House, and it does not very much care for dissenting voices expressed during the debates or the question hour. The Parliament has not built any expertise or research capability on WTO issues, in spite of it having at its disposal one of the richest libraries in the country and ample resources for research purposes.

A recent innovation in the Indian Parliamentary practice has been the institution of standing committee for each Ministry. The effectiveness of these committees very much depends upon the dynamism of their Chairpersons. At one time, the Parliamentary Standing Committee for the Ministry of Commerce organised a series of hearings on the outcome of the Uruguay Round and produced one of the very few comprehensive and thoughtful reports on the subject. However, the report, though of great historical and academic importance, could not achieve much by way of influencing policies.

The Government of India usually consults political parties on important national issues. This was the practice even during the era of one-party government until 1996, with a couple of brief interregnums of coalition government. But Uruguay Round negotiations were not among these issues. From 1996 onwards, when the Indian polity entered the era of coalition government at the Centre, consultations with political parties both within the coalition as well as those outside became a necessity for the Government in order to ensure its political survival. So far as WTO issues are concerned, from the Singapore Meeting onwards, the Government has regularly started consulting political parties.

In the middle-of-the road majority parties like the Bhartiya Janata Party (BJP) and Congress, there are factions which are strongly opposed to liberalisation and have made self-reliance an important plank of their political platforms. The mainstreams of these parties are for economic reforms and liberalisation, but the parties in order to remain united, have to keep their radical factions also in the fold. This influences the party's and the government's stand on WTO issues. The present government depends critically on left parties for remaining in power. Therefore, these parties have come to exercise significant influence on government's policy on WTO issues, as on other important issues. Recently, the left parties played a decisive role in obliging the Government to accept further amendments of crucial importance to the nation and to the world, to the amendments of the 1970 Patent Act passed by the Indian Parliament.

The trade unions in India have generally been concerned with WTO issues. But the mainstream trade unions operating mainly in the organised labour sector, have not in general played much of a role in influencing government's policy on these issues. The only time when these trade unions were very active was when the link between trade and labour standards was a burning issue in the WTO forums. These Indian trade unions unanimously evolved and adopted the stance of opposing the link. This included even those trade unions which are affiliated to the IFTUC, the Western-dominated international trade union which has been in favour of the link. During this period, these mainstream Indian trade unions brought out pamphlets/ booklets, organised seminars and launched movements to protest against the link, in collaboration with CSOs and independent experts.

The farmers' unions and peasants' associations have been active on the aspects of WTO agreements which have implications for the Indian agriculture and for rural life. They have generally taken a strong stand against globalisation of agriculture, the elimination of Q.Rs on agricultural products and patenting of seeds. They have joined CSOs and independent research and advocacy organisations in the movements for preservation of the bio-resources of the country and for ensuring farmers' rights.

These trade unions and associations do not have research capability or regular programmes of activities of their own on WTO issues. They have been essentially mobilised by CSOs to agitate on these issues. This has gone some way towards influencing the Government's policy.

CSOs of India have exercised by far the most important influence on the Government's policy on subjects within WTO's realm. The modern information and communication revolution has knit them together as never before and has made them a part of the worldwide movements of CSOs. This has also been a critical enabling factor in the development of their research capabilities. Some of the CSOs active on WTO matters in India can boast of better research capabilities than the agencies of the Government dealing with WTO and even universities in India. In fact, they are co-opting university teachers and researchers in large numbers for getting their research work done. They are able to muster scientific and technical expertise not available with the Government. The CSOs have often brought out implications of WTO agreements and negotiating issues which the Government has either failed to grasp or anticipate or has deliberately suppressed. CSOs networks, including those with headquarters in Western countries like Medicines San Frontiers, Oxfam etc., have been instrumental in mobilising trade unions and peasants' movements for their advocacy work and for mounting mass movements and agitations to compel the Government to change its policies or adopt policies advocated by them. They have successfully co-opted for their task political parties and leaders and members of Parliament. Representatives of CSOs have been on Government's Advisory Board on WTO matters and on expert committees and groups to draft legislations designed to give effect to and derive maximum advantage from WTO regimes. They have had a decisive impact on the kind of legislations that came to be enacted. The more specialised the CSO, the greater its influence. Here two Indian CSOs can come in for special mention: the Gene Campaign for the preservation of bio-resources and indigenous knowledge, equitable benefit sharing with the communities, and farmers rights; and Equations which is active in the field of services, particular public utility services. Some of the methods that CSOs and independent experts and think tanks have come to deploy include establishing people's or citizens' commissions and public hearings.

The main thrust of CSOs ideology, and hence advocacy, is anti-globalisation and anti-liberalisation. This is partly a prior commitment and partly founded on solid research and empirical evidence. There are, however, a few CSO and some prominent independent research institutions which produce research work and undertake advocacy work in support of globalisation and liberalisation. Most of the CSOs are funded externally, but the latter variety is funded much more lavishly.

Consequences for the Indian economy

Unlike the East Asian and South-East Asian countries, India has not followed an export-led growth strategy or a strategy predicated on the flow of FDI. But in the last 25 years India has placed much greater emphasis than before on exports and FDI as key factors for accelerating growth. Since 1992-1993, India has been implementing a comprehensive programme for internal and external liberalisation.

India is committed to take full advantage of the opportunities offered by globalisation and, for this purpose, to integrate its economy with those of the major economic powers. But in doing so, India will not allow its problems of the backlog of massive poverty, of unemployment and inequality to get accentuated. Given its pluralistic society and the marginalisation of vast numbers and many groups of its population, India is also duty bound to follow a policy of inclusive development. Finally, it is India's national policy to pursue self-reliance in areas of frontier technology and for ensuring food and energy security. India's liberalisation policy will always be qualified by these basic considerations. India would also like to retain maximum autonomy for macro-economic policy making and in making judgments on policy choices. India's policy on and attitude towards issues on the agenda of WTO will essentially be shaped by these considerations.

It is very difficult to quantify the consequences of India's policy on issues for negotiation in WTO, for India's growth, trade and investment. This is mainly because of the contribution of factors other than those related to these policies, to growth, trade and investment outcomes. It is extremely difficult to isolate these factors and quantify the part of these outcomes which can be directly attributed to opening up of the economy in general and opening up in pursuance of commitments undertaken in WTO, in particular. In the trade field, unilateral liberalisation undertaken by India has pulled far ahead of liberalisation commitments under WTO agreements and negotiations. However, this unilateral liberalisation is related to and influences what is going on in WTO. At times, WTO disciplines can be a catalyst for domestic liberalisation. On the other hand, domestic liberalisation can generate the confidence and provide a basis for taking initiatives in WTO negotiations and shaping WTO disciplines.

The growing size of the Indian economy due to its recent much faster rate of growth, its expanding market and far-reaching unilateral liberalisation undertaken by India, have certainly enhanced its relative bargaining strength in WTO negotiations and should imbue the Indian negotiators with confidence to make bolder moves for give-and-take in WTO negotiations. Unlike China, India has not undertaken WTO commitments to lock in or provide a spur to its programme of domestic liberalisation. Quite often, India has got locked into WTO commitments under pressure or duress and without anticipating their consequences and has come to regret them subsequently.

China consciously accepted the commitments exacted by major powers as a price for the Chinese accession to WTO, in order to accelerate domestic reforms and adjustments, create an efficient market environment and transform China's inherent economic strength into practical competitive advantages (Long Guoqiang et al. 2004). India has not undertaken WTO commitments in such a spirit primarily because of its inability to carry out a thorough-going programme of domestic reforms and restructuring. But, the changes brought about by WTO have no doubt triggered important changes in the Indian economy, like rationalisation of certain industries, managerial reforms and strategic repositioning to gain competitive advantage in the world market. Besides, India has also put in place legal administrative and enforcement mechanisms to conform to and meet the challenges of WTO regimes. For example, India has revised existing laws, enacted new legislations, strengthened the institution for evaluating applications for patents, and is building the information base for utilising the WTO dispensation on anti-dumping and countervailing measures.

Some of India's economic indicators recently have been very encouraging. These cannot be attributed directly to the policy of liberalisation undertaken within and outside WTO. But one can say for what it is worth that these have coincided with the first ten years of the life of WTO.

India's GDP of late has been growing on an average at the rate of over 6 percent per annum. The Wholesale Price Index rose by only 4,55 percent per annum during 2000–2004.[17] India's exports went up from $18 billion in 1991–1992 to approximately $45 billion in 2000–2001. The growth in export was 28,6 percent in 1994–1995 to 1995–1996, 27,6 percent in 1999–2000 to 2000–2001 and 22,1 percent in 2001–2002 to 2002–2003. Software exports grew from about $ 2,7 billion in 1998–99 to nearly $ 14 billion in 2003–2004.[18]

India's trade as a percentage of GDP increased from 8,10 in 1970 to 30,82 in 2002; and its exports as a percentage of GDP from 3,61 percent in 1970 to 15,22 percent in 2002. This represents a dramatic change in the openness of the Indian economy.[19] India's share of global exports increased from 0,42 percent in 1980 to 0,60 percent in 1995. Since then it has been steadily moving upward, reaching the figure of 0,77 percent in 2002.[20]

The net inflows of FDI increased from only $ 240 million in 1990 to $ 3,03 billion in 2002. The total inflow is still very low in relation to the size of the Indian economy, but the rate of growth is very high, which is a good augury for the future.[21]

References

Bhagwati, J. and Desai, P. (1970), *India: Planning for Industrialisation 1970*, (OECD & Oxford University Press).

Dandekar, V.M (1992), Forty Years After Independence; in: Janal B. (ed.), *The Indian Economy: Problems and Prospects*, (New Delhi: Penguine Books).

Dubey, M. (1996), *An Unequal Treaty : World Trading Order After GATT*, (New Delhi: New Age International Limited).

Janal, B. (1992), Balance of Payments; in: Janal, B. (ed.), *The Indian Economy: Problems and Prospects*, (New Delhi: Penguine Books).

Long, G. et al. (2004), China After WTO: Adjustment, Reform and Promotion of Competitiveness; in: Debroy B. and M. Saqib (eds.), *Future Negotiation Issues at WTO: An India-China Perspective*, (New Delhi: Globus Books).

Srinivasan, T.N. (1998), India's Export Performance: A Comparative Analysis; in: Judge Ahluwalia and IMD Little (eds.), *India's Economic Reforms and Development: Essays for Manmohan Singh*, (New Delhi: Oxford University Press).

Virmani, A. (2004), *India's Economic Growth: From Socialist Rate of Growth to Bharatiya Rate of Growth: A Working Paper for the Indian Council for Research on International Economic Relations*, (ICRIER: New Delhi).

Notes

1   Source: World Bank, World Development Indicators (CD-ROM) and the relevant issues of the Economic Survey, Ministry of Finance, Government of India.
2   Source: UNCTAD Handbook of Statistics, CD-ROM, 2004.
3   Ibid.
4   Source: Budget Speeches during the last 5 years.
5   Ministerial Declaration on the Uruguay Round, Punta del Este, 20 September 1986.
6   The Chairperson of the Ministerial meeting in his concluding remarks stated: The declaration "does not inscribe the relationship between trade and core labour standards on the WTO agenda".
7   "Virtually everyone agrees that President Clinton's surrender to political pressure in election year from the unions was at the heart of the Seattle debacle". Jagdish Bhagwati in an interview to the Economic Times, Delhi, published in its issue of 25 January 2000.
8   The Chairperson of the African Group at the Seattle Meeting stated that it was wrong to assume that developing countries were as naïve in Seattle as they were at the time of the signing of the Uruguay Round texts. "Developing countries have shown that they are well prepared this time", he said.
9   Paragraphs 20, 23 and 26 of the Ministerial Declaration, Doha, 14 November 2001.
10   Ibid.
11   Article 1 of the General Agreement on Trade in Services defines services in terms of the following modes of supply: "(a) from the territory of one Member into the territory of any other Members; (b) in the territory of one Member to the service consumers of any other Member; (c) by a service supplier of one country, through commercial presence in the territory of any other Member; (d) by a service supplier of one Member, through presence of natural persons of a Member in the territory of any other Member". In brief, they are referred to as: Mode 1. through cross-border movement of services; Mode 2. through the movement of consumer to the source of supply; Mode 3. through commercial presence; and Mode 4. through the movement of natural persons.
12   South Asian Association for Regional Cooperation.
13   Saman Kalegama and Indra Nath Mookherji, "WTO & South Asia – From Doha to Cancun" in Economic & Political Weekly, Mumbai, 13 September 2003, at 3866.
14   Domestic support not exceeding 5 percent of a Member's total value of production of a basic agricultural product during a relevant year (product – specific) or of the value of that Member's total agricultural production (non-product-specific) shall not be included in the Aggregate Measurement of Support to which reduction commitments shall apply. For developing countries, this de minimis percentage is 10 percent. (Article 6 of the Agreement on Agriculture). But this Article does not preclude reduction in these di minimis percentages themselves through future negotiations.
15   Amir Ullah Khan: Indian Textiles and the WTO: Need for Value Addition and Competitiveness, in Future Negotiation Issues at WTO: An India-China Perspective; edited by Bibek Debroy et al.; Globus Books, New Delhi, 2004.

16 Report of the Task Force on Indirect Taxes, Chaired by Vijay Kelkar, December, 2002.
17 Sources: World Bank, World Development Indicators (CD-ROM); and the relevant issues of the Economic Surveys of the Government of India, Ministry of Finance.
18 Ibid.
19 Ibid.
20 Source: UNCTAD's Handbook of Statistics, CD-ROM, 2004.
21 Sources: World Bank, World Development Indicators (CD-ROM); and The relevant issues of the Economic Surveys of the Government of India, Ministry of Finance.

Chapter 5

China's Economic Development, Trade and Foreign Investment

Weiyu Gao and Xiaoling Ji

Introduction to China's economy

Before the implementation of the reform and opening up policy initiated by Deng Xiaoping, China was characterised by planned economy, by few if any private enterprises, little foreign investment,[1] and limited foreign trade. It took China 20 years to rise from being an agricultural country in the late 1970s to become the sixth largest economy, the largest recipient of foreign investment and the third largest trade country in the world.

Since China initiated the reform and opening up policy in the late 1970s, the national economy has experienced a sustained and steady development. From 1978 to 2005, China's real GDP growth averaged 9.4 percent per year. As of 2005, China's GDP totalled US$ 2.223 billion, which made China the seventh largest economy in the world. Meanwhile, GDP per capita amounts to over US$ 1.700 (at current exchange rates), taking China into the group of the mid-lower income countries. Compared to countries like Brazil and India, however, there is still a dominating manufacturing sector in China with a contribution to GDP of more than 50 percent (see Figure 5.1).

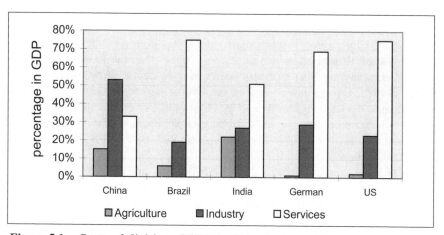

Figure 5.1   Sectoral division of GDP in China in comparison
Source: China Statistical Yearbook, 2004, PRC National Bureau of Statistics

Furthermore, it is the ownership structure which makes the Chinese economy peculiar. As a country with a socialist market economy, China's economic system features the domination of public ownership and the co-development of various forms of ownership. For the purpose of the current topic, it is important to note that private business has expanded impressively in the last decade. Between 1993 and 2003, the number of private companies surged from 90.500 to over 3 million with an increase of employment from under 4 million to about 43 million. Furthermore, from the early 1990s to 2004 the output value of private enterprises increased 47,6-fold. Perhaps even more importantly, many of the private enterprises have switched their attention from such traditional sectors as retail, catering, service and repair to those sectors with a high content of knowledge, science and technology.

Despite these impressive developments in China, a number of problems still exist including: increasing income disparities; high price rises for energy and raw materials; occasional occurrence of severe accidents in production; resource waste and environmental pollution; difficulties in raising grain output and farmers' income. However, as the government is fully aware of the existing problems with China's economic development and will continue to implement macro control policy,[2] there is reason to believe that China's economy will continue to grow at about the current pace.

If there is no severe random shock, China's GDP will reach above 20.000 billion RMB, or 4.000 billion US dollars (at current purchasing power parities) in 2020. With this GDP, China will be ranked the third largest economy in the world. Hence, China will play a more important role in international trade and investment, and will further strengthen its economic cooperation with other countries.

China's foreign trade

An overview of China's foreign trade

Since 1978, China's import and export volume has been growing at an average annual rate of 15 percent, which is not only higher than the growth rate of the national economy, but also 8 percent higher than the annual growth rate of world trade. In 1978, China's import and export volume ranked the 32nd in the world. According to the latest figure released by Ministry of Commerce, in 2004, China's import volume, export volume and the total trade volume ranked third in the world, compared with fourth in 2003. The total volume increased by US$ 300 billion to US$10.000 billion.

In 2005, the export volume totalled US$762 billion, an increase of 28,4 percent over the previous year. The rapid export growth can be attributed to the thriving market demand as a result of the robust growth of the world economy. It is worth noting that in 2004 the export of non-state-owned enterprises exceeded US$100 billion for the first time, reaching US$101 billion, thus accounting for 17 percent of the total export volume.

Table 5.1   China's trade volume and balance (unit: US$100 million)

Year	Trade Volume	Export	Import	Trade Balance
1981	440.2	220.1	220.2	-0.1
1982	416.1	223.2	192.9	30.4
1983	436.2	222.3	213.9	8.4
1984	535.5	261.4	274.1	-12.7
1985	696.0	273.5	422.5	-149.0
1986	738.5	309.4	429.0	-119.6
1987	826.5	394.4	432.2	-37.8
1988	1027.8	475.2	552.7	-77.5
1989	1116.8	525.4	591.4	-66.0
1990	1154.4	620.9	533.5	87.5
1991	1357.0	719.1	637.9	81.2
1992	1655.3	849.4	805.9	43.6
1993	1957.0	917.4	1039.6	-122.2
1994	2366.2	1210.1	1156.2	53.9
1995	2808.6	1487.8	1320.8	167.0
1996	2898.8	1510.5	1388.3	122.2
1997	3251.6	1827.9	1423.7	404.2
1998	3239.5	1837.1	1402.4	434.8
1999	3606.3	1949.3	1657.0	292.3
2000	4743.0	2492.0	2250.9	241.1
2001	5096.5	2661.0	2435.5	225.5
2002	6207.7	3256.0	2951.7	304.3
2003	8509.9	4382.3	4127.6	254.7
2004	11547.4	5933.6	5613.8	319.8
2005	14221.0	7620.0	6601.0	1019.0

Source: 1981–2003 data available at
www.gov.cn/test/2005-06/27/content_10116.htm, 2004 and 2005 data available at www.statis.gov.cn

2004 also witnessed an increase of 36 percent in import to US$ 561,4 billion. Several factors explained this increase. The main factor was the fast economic growth in 2003 and 2004, especially the increase in fixed assets investment, which resulted in a huge demand for energy, raw materials, and machinery. Meanwhile, the continuous increase in commodity price in the international market led to an increase in import volume, and the lowering of import duty also stimulated import demands. Starting from the latter half of 2004, as the government measures to strengthen and improve macroeconomic control measures started to take effect, import demand was gradually curbed and accordingly the import increase slowed down to 30,3 percent from 43 percent in the first half of the year.

The mix of importation and exportation was further optimised in 2004. The export volume of electrical machinery rose by 42,3 percent to US$323,4 billion, accounting for 54,5 percent of the total export. The export of new and high-tech products reached US$165,5 with an increase of 50,2 percent, and accounting for 27,9 percent of the total export. Electronic and information related products such as integrated circuits, laptop computers, cellular phones and liquid crystal monitors also had a rather rapid increase. In terms of imports, the importation of energy, raw materials and machinery equipment increased impressively, with the importation of cotton, coal, iron ore, crude oil, refined oil product, household appliances and electronic products, and machinery equipment by 120 percent, 73 percent, 40,5 percent, 34,8 percent, 34,1 percent and 28 percent respectively.

In the meantime, China's foreign trade services also maintained good development momentum. The total volume amounted to US$134,6 billion, with an increase of 32 percent, thus accounting for 8 percent of China's GDP and 10 percent of the foreign trade. International tourism was the biggest winner, with a volume of US$44,9 billion, or 33 percent of the service trade revenue.

From 1992–2003, Japan remained China's largest trading partner. In 2004 the European Union, after its eastern expansion, replaced Japan and became the first largest trading partner of China, with a bilateral trade volume of US$177,3 billion, an increase of 33,6 percent. The US and Japan came second and third, with a trade volume of US$169,6 billion and US$167,9 billion. The US remained the largest market for China's exports, and Japan the largest source country of China's imports. Table 5.2 lists China's leading trading partners in the past two years.

Table 5.2   Top 10 Trading Partners (Unit: US$ billion)

Rank	2003		2004	
	Economies	Total Trade	Economies	Total Trade
1	Japan	133.57	EU	177.29
2	US	126.33	US	169.63
3	EU	125.22	Japan	167.89
4	HK SAR	87.41	HK SAR	112.68
5	ASEAN	78.25	ASEAN	105.88
6	S. Korea	63.23	S. Korea	90.07
7	Taiwan Province	58.37	Taiwan Province	73.82
8	Russia	15.76	Russia	21.23
9	Australia	13.56	Australia	20.39
10	Canada	10.01	Canada	15.52

Source: China Statistical Yearbook, 2005, PRC National Bureau of Statistics

Foreign trade policy

Guiding principles of China's foreign trade   China practices a unified foreign trade management system. The legal system of foreign trade management centres around the Foreign Trade Law of the People's Republic of China, including laws and rules concerning customs, foreign exchanges, commodity inspection, anti-dumping and anti-subsidy, commodity importation and exportation, importation and exportation permission.

Taking effect on 1 July 1994, the Foreign Trade Law is the basic law in China's foreign trade. It stipulates China's basic foreign trade system and the rules of conducting foreign trade, and defines the basic principles of the importation and exportation of commodity and technology as well as international service trade. These basic systems of foreign trade management include the following:

- The system of foreign trade permit
- While setting up the principle of free importation and exportation of goods and technologies, the law also stipulates items whose importation and exportation are forbidden or restricted.
- The Foreign Trade Law makes relevant stipulations regarding most favoured nation status treatment, national treatment and the market access of international service trade.
- The system of anti-dumping and anti-subsidy investigation and protection measures is established to maintain a fair market order.
- The Foreign Trade Law also stipulates a number measures to promote foreign trade development, such as setting up an import and export bank, establishing a foreign trade development fund and risk fund, implementing the system of tax rebate for exports, and encouraging the development of the consulting service of foreign trade.

Foreign trade policy in recent years   Starting from 1 January 2004, China's rates of VAT rebate for exports have been lowered by an average of 3 percentage points. The new rates of rebates will comprise five levels, i.e., 5 percent, 8 percent, 11 percent, 13 percent and 17 percent. Products that were previously entitled to 17 percent rebates include clothing, electrical appliances and electronic products; transport vehicles, instruments and meters were lowered to 13 percent. Beginning November 2004, the rates of VAT rebate for certain information technology items, such as integrated circuits, were raised to 17 percent from 13 percent.

On 6 April 2004, the amended Foreign Trade Law[3] was approved at the 8th meeting of the 10th National People's Congress (NPC) Standing Committee after a two-year-long review of all laws concerning foreign trade. The new law, which went into effect on 1 July, contained three major changes. 1) Individuals are allowed to conduct foreign trade business. 2) Legally registered foreign trade operators, including naturalised persons, legal persons and other organisations, can now import and export goods and technology without obtaining administrative approval. 3) Foreign trade rights for a percentage of special products such as petroleum, grain, chemical fertilizer, cotton, sugar and edible oil, which were completely reserved for state-owned enterprises in the past, will be granted to formerly unauthorised companies.

The New Foreign Trade Law has been hailed by the EU Chamber of Commerce for its greater consistency with China's WTO commitment.

Problems with China's development of foreign trade

Between 1978 and 2005, import and export volume increased at an average annual growth rate of 17 percent, much higher than that of GDP. However, despite the continuous rapid growth of foreign trade in recent years, some problems still exist.

First, comprehensive returns need to be improved (Wang 2005). The changes in the mix of exports in recent years still leave much to be desired. China still relies on the exportation of consumption goods with low added value and low technology content. According to Li (2005), of all the industrial exports in 2004, new and high-tech products accounted for only 27 percent, most of which had to rely on foreign core parts for key technology. Zheng (2005) maintains that the exportation of energy-consuming products and products that cause pollution to the environment is increasing too fast.

Second, the guiding principle of "export to earn foreign exchange" has produced some negative effects, resulting in the problem of competing with each other by cutting prices.

Third, China has now entered a phase of an increasing number of trade disputes (Wang 2005). In 2002, China's exports accounted for 5,2 percent of the world volume, but anti-dumping cases against China constituted 16,5 percent of all the anti-dumping cases in the world. In 2003, 59 anti-dumping cases against China were put on file, involving US$2,2 billion.

Ran (2005) takes a look at developing countries' anti-dumping cases against China. The data indicate that the number of anti-dumping cases and the sectors involved continue to rise (see Table 5.3).

Table 5.3   Developing Countries' Anti-Dumping Cases against China

	1980-1989	1990-1994	1995-2003	total
India	0	4	69	73
Brazil	1	7	23	31
South Africa	0	12	33	45
Mexico	0	16	18	34
Argentina	0	7	70	79
Peru	0	0	15	15
Turkey	0	0	22	22
Venezuela	0	0	19	19
Other countries	1	0	19	19
Total	2	46	288	377

Source: Ran (2005), p.122

Last, as Tang and Hu (2005) point out, China's foreign trade system is far from perfect, with a huge disparity with the international conventions. The process of shifting government functions lags behind the reform of economic institutions and the requirements of international rules. A perfect, transparent and unified legal trade environment and a fair operation mechanism remain to be established.

China's Foreign Direct Investment

An overview of China's FDI

Since the inception of China's reform and opening-up policy, foreign direct investment in China has soared. Figure 5.2 indicates the growth of foreign direct investment in China.

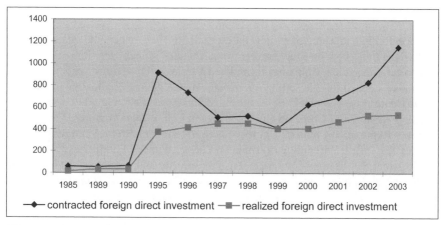

Figure 5.2   Foreign Direct Investment in China: 1985–2004
Source: PRC National Bureau of Statistics
www.stats.gov.cn/tjsj/ndsj/yb2004-c/indexch.htm, Unit: 100 million US dollars

China absorbed US$60,6 billion of direct foreign investment in 2004, 70 percent of which was by the manufacturing industry. Enterprises receiving foreign investment saw an export increase of 40,9 percent to US$338,6 billion accounting for 57,1 percent of the total exports, an increase of 2,3 percent over the previous year. The importation by enterprises receiving foreign investment increased by 40 percent and reached US$ 324,6 billion, accounting for 57,8 percent of the total imports, an increase of 1,6 percent over the previous year.

Since China's entry into the WTO, the environment for foreign investment has further improved, and foreign investment now takes on new features. Chong Quan, spokesman for Ministry of Commerce, explains three features of foreign direct investment in China in 2004. First, the structure of FDI has been further optimised. FDI grew rapidly in manufacturing, electric machinery and other high-tech areas, and it encouraged the setting up of research and development centres and regional headquarters in China, with nearly 700 R&D centres and over 30 regional headquarters established; meanwhile newly increased FDI in areas such as iron and steel, cement and aluminium were effectively curbed as a result of macro-economic control measures. Second, FDI witnessed rapid growth in north-east China's old industrial bases. The eastern region remained in its dominant position in attracting FDI, the central region witnessed robust growth, and the western area still lagged behind in this aspect. Third, major Asian investors and the old 15 member countries of the European Union all increased their investment to China last year.

The Commission of Global Economic Policies at Kearny, the leading American consulting firm, released its annual report on the Foreign Direct Investment Confidence Index for 2004. China again topped the list in attracting foreign direct investment for the third consecutive year after rising to the top in 2002.

China's foreign investment policy

China's foreign investment policy dates back to 1979, when the State Council drafted the first "Law on Sino-Foreign Joint Venture", which went into effect in the same year. Since then, China has formulated a series of laws, rules, regulations, and provisions concerning the setting up, management, end, and liquidation of foreign-funded enterprises. Among these, the most important ones include: Law of The People's Republic of China on Chinese-Foreign Equity Joint Ventures; Law of The People's Republic of China on Chinese-Foreign Contractual Joint Ventures; and The Law of The People's Republic of China on Foreign-Funded Enterprises.[4]

To strengthen foreign investors' sense of security and to protect the legitimate rights and interests of enterprises, the Chinese government has signed agreements with many countries with a view to encouraging and protecting investment as well as to avoid dual taxation.

China utilises foreign capital in the following three ways: direct foreign investment (which includes Sino-foreign joint ventures, Sino-foreign cooperation corporations, and solely foreign-funded enterprises, foreign-funded stockholding companies and Sino-foreign cooperative development companies), foreign loans (which includes loans from foreign governments, international monetary organisations, overseas banks as well as export credit and the issuing of bonds on overseas markets), and other foreign investment (which includes issuing shares in overseas markets, international leasing, compensation trade, and processing and assembling business).

In a bid to encourage overseas investment in the central and western regions, beginning from September 1996, local authorities from the central and western provinces were empowered to give approval to overseas-funded projects with total investment capital under US$30 million, up from the previous amount of US$10 million. Since the Chinese government started to implement a strategy of developing the western region in late 1999, more preferential treatments have been extended to foreign investment in inland provinces and regions. Upon expiration of the preferential tax polices, foreign-invested enterprises may enjoy 50 percent reduction of corporate income tax for another three years.

To gear foreign investment toward the country's industrial development, and to facilitate the protection of investors' legitimate interests, the Chinese government formulated and issued the "Provisions on Guiding Foreign Investment Direction" and the "Catalogue for the Guidance of Foreign Investment Industries".[5] After China's entry into the WTO, the above two rules were revised and took effect on 1 April 2002. According to the new catalogue, for some years to come, China will encourage foreign investment in the following fields:[6]

- The transformation of traditional agriculture, development of modern agriculture, and the industrialisation of agriculture;
- Infrastructure and basic sectors such as transportation, energy, raw materials;
- New and hi-tech industries such as electronic information, biological engineering, new materials and astronomy, as well as the establishment of R&D centres;
- The transformation of such traditional sectors as machinery, light industry, textiles with advanced and applicable technology, as well as the upgrading of the equipment industry;
- The comprehensive utilisation of resources and renewable resources, environmental protection projects as well as urban engineering projects;
- The favourable sectors in the western region with comparative advantages;
- Projects involving products exclusively for exports.

As of the day when the new catalogue takes effect, the foreign investment project in the fields listed in the new catalogue will enjoy preferential policies like exemption from imported equipment duties and import value-added duty.

A new version of the "Catalogue for the Guidance of Foreign Investment Industries" came into effect on 1 January, 2005. Projects receiving foreign investment under the categories of "encouraged" will enjoy tariff-free imports of machinery and equipment for their own use and the import value-added tax will also be exempted. The catalogue also reflected China's WTO commitment by specifying the liberalisation schedule of foreign ownership of different sectors.

Problems in FDI

25 years ago, Coca Cola entered the Chinese market, becoming the first joint venture in China. In 2003, the number of foreign-funded enterprises amounted to 226.373. Along with the rapid development, some problems have arisen in foreign investment, which are mainly reflected in the following aspects.

First, the distribution of foreign investment is far from optimal, as is illustrated in Table 5.4. Despite government policies to guide foreign investment (see the previous section), FDI has been concentrated in the labour-intensive manufacturing sector. Investment is rather limited in agriculture, infrastructure, and new and high-tech industries, whose development tops the government agenda.

Table 5.4   Sector Distribution of Foreign Investment in 2003

	US$10,000	%
Agriculture, forestry, husbandry, fishery	100084	1.9%
Mining	33635	0.6%
Manufacturing	3693570	69.0%
Utilities	129538	2.4%
construction	61176	1.1%
Geological prospecting, water conservancy	1777	0.0%
Transportation, storage, telecommunications	86737	1. 6%
Wholesale, retail, catering	111604	2. 1%
Finance, insurance	23199	0. 4%
Real estate	523560	9. 8%
Social services	316095	5.9%
Health, sports and social welfare	12737	0.2%
Education, culture, art, radio, movie, TV	5782	0.1%
Science, research, technology	25871	0.5%
others	225102	4.2%
Total	5350467	

Source: PRC National Bureau of Statistics, www.stats.gov.cn/tjsj/ndsj/yb2004-c/indexch.htm

Second, the regional distribution of FDI needs to be optimised. Table 5.5 presents provinces or municipalities that received the most and the least foreign investment in 2002 and 2003.

Table 5.5   The top 5 and bottom 5 provinces in FDI attraction

Regions	FDI 2002	Regions	FDI 2003
Guangdong Province	21.6%	Jiangsu Province	20%
Jiangsu Province	19.4%	Guangdong Province	14.8%
Shandong Province	9%	Shandong Province	11.4%
Shanghai	8.1%	Shanghai	10.3%
Fujian Province	7.3%	Zhejiang Province	9.4%
Qinghai Province	0.09%	Qinghai Province	0.048%
Guizhou Province	0.073%	Gansu Province	0.044%
Ningxia Autonomous Region	0.042%	Ningxia Autonomous Region	0.033%
Xinjiang	0.036%	Xinjiang	0.029%
Tibet	0	Tibet	0

Source: Converted from data from PRC National Bureau of Statistics
www.stats.gov.cn/tjsj/ndsj/yb2004-c/indexch.htm

The top five regions attracting FDI are all more developed coastal provinces or municipalities. And the five regions at the bottom are all western regions, areas where investment is most needed.

Problems are also present in the management of FDI in China. The following issues are discussed by Chen and Xiao (2004):

- The problem of government transparency has affected confidence in investment in China.
- Some local governments have attracted foreign investment in a haphazard manner, resulting in low-level redundant construction and the development of some highly polluting industries.
- In the efforts to attract foreign investment, some local governments have placed quantity above quality, and have neglected the management of the realisation of foreign investment, thus the discrepancy of contracted and realised foreign investment.
- While enjoying many preferential policies, foreign-funded enterprises are also subject to many different fees.
- The management of foreign-funded enterprises is unsatisfactory due to a lack of qualified management talents and the backward management technology and mode.

The consequences of trade and foreign investment

The significance of trade and foreign investment cannot be overemphasised. In the past 20 years, export and foreign direct investment have made a great contribution to China's economic growth and technological advances. In this section, we will examine the consequences of China's trade and investment policy.

The impacts of foreign trade

In 2004, China's foreign trade volume reached US$ 1.154,8 billion with a growth rate of 35,7 percent, among which exportation increased at a rate of 35,4 percent and importation increased 36,0 percent. The favourable balance of trade reached US$ 32 billion. In the meantime, China surpassed Japan and ranks number 3 in the world following Germany and the United States in terms of international trade volume.

The rapid growth of international trade has continuously played an important role in promoting China's economic growth, which is reflected in the following four aspects:

- Rapid growth of exportation has helped to balance the inadequate domestic consumption demand, and has hence played a role as an important engine driving the growth of the Chinese economy. For example, as pointed out by Yao Jingyuan, spokesman of the National Statistics Bureau, exports contributed 0,3 percent to the 8 percent economic growth rate in 2002. The exportation here refers to the net importation that serves as the driving force behind the national economy.

- Through international trade, Chinese enterprises learned more about management experience, new technology, and the international market, which certainly enhanced their international competitiveness.
- The fast growth of international trade also stimulated the development of private enterprises and township enterprises in the 1990s. In 2003, the ratio of industry value-added by non-SOE (State-owned enterprises) to the total industry added value reached 42,55 percent, which had increased almost 10 percentage points compared with that in 1999.
- International trade, mainly export, has created many opportunities and jobs in the China's coastal area, which has absorbed millions of peasants moving from rural areas to cities, and substantially increased their living standards.

In the meantime, the increase in China's import has also made a contribution to the recovery of the world economy, especially the economic growth in the East Asian area. 2004 witnessed faster growth in importation than exportation, with most of the import growth coming from Asian countries. In 1990, Asian countries' exports to China accounted for less than 7 percent of their total exports, and in 2003 the figure rose to over 50 percent. In 2004, the export growth in Japan, Korea, Malaysia, the Philippines, and Australia almost all came from trade with China. Korea's trade with China exceeded that with the US, which is generally believed to be an epoch-making event in East Asia.

The UN Trade and Development Report, 2004[7] has the following to say about China:

- The current acceleration of growth in world output and trade reflects the recovery in the United States and faster growth in a number of developing countries in Asia, especially China and India.
- In 2003 and the beginning of 2004, it (China) was a major engine of growth for most countries in the region (Asia). A large proportion of its imports, which have been growing even faster than its exports, are coming from the rest of Asia.
- China has been the lynchpin. Its particularly strong growth has, to a large extent, contributed to the acceleration of growth across Asia.

According to Li and Zhao (2005), Steve Roach, Chief Economist of Morgan Stanley also pointed out the promoting role of China's economy in world economic growth. According to him, in 2003, China's imports from the US accounted for 22 percent of its export growth, from Germany 28 percent and from Japan 32 percent. Moreover, China also contributed to 3–7 percentage points to the economic growth of Korea, Thailand, Singapore and Malaysia. As China increased the importation of high value-added products from these countries, the role played by China in promoting their industry and employment became even stronger.

However, some economists in China have expressed concern about China's over-reliance on foreign trade. Shen Jiru,[8] a research fellow with the Chinese Academy of

Social Sciences, claimed that the foreign dependency rates, referring to the volume of imports and exports in a nation's gross domestic product, stood at 14–20 per cent for the United States, Japan, India and Germany. But China's foreign dependency rate grew from 15 per cent in the early 1980s to almost 70 per cent last year. He maintains that the great dependence of China's economy on foreign trade could have certain negative impacts on the country's future development:

- Discount the country's ability to withstand global economic fluctuations and political instability;
- Result in more trade disputes and heavier pressure on the appreciation of RMB;
- Hinder China's ability to make independent economic decisions;
- Lead to a distortion of resource distribution and aggravate the government's financial burden due to various preferential policies to encourage exportation;
- Affect the profitability of companies engaged in foreign trade with the relegation of foreign trade power

The impacts of foreign investment

From 1979 to 2003, foreign direct investment in China totalled US$500 billion, which is a great driving force behind the 10-fold increase in GDP during this period. China's policies to attract foreign investment have no doubt been successful. The consequences of foreign investment can be understood from the following aspects.

First, foreign investment has been conducive to the accumulation of primary capital. The Chinese are famous for their propensity to save. For example, in 2003, Shanghai residents' average saving rate was 25,7 percent. However, due to an imperfect capital market, China's savings cannot be effectively transferred into investment. Hence, foreign direct investment serves as an important part of the capital, which promoted economic growth in China.

Second, foreign investment has induced institutional improvement (Shen 2005). In order to attract foreign investment to meet their requirements of the expansion of foreign businesses in China, governments at different levels make unremitting efforts to improve the investment environment, shift government functions, improve efficiency, speed up reform in economic and political institutions, and to standardise the market economy regime.

Third, the entry of foreign companies, especially multinational companies, broke the local monopolistic market structure, strengthened the competition in China's domestic market, and hence stimulated domestic companies to enhance their competitiveness.

Fourth, with foreign capital comes an advanced management concept – capital management, personnel management etc., which thus gives domestic enterprises opportunities to learn about management experience and new technologies through exchange and cooperation.

Fifth, along with the entry of foreign companies, new technology, new designs, and new products were transferred into China, which helped domestic enterprises enhance productivity and product quality.

As of December 2004, 500.479 foreign enterprises were approved to invest in China, with contracted foreign capital of US$ 1.062,13 billion, and the realised foreign investment of US$ 555,25 billion. Direct foreign investment contributed to the improvement of life and employment. Currently, 23,5 million people are employed by foreign invested enterprises, with each enterprise employing about 100 people.

However, some economists have expressed their concerns about China's over-reliance on foreign investment. For example, continuous expansion in the scale of accumulated foreign capital may threaten the surplus in the current account; the entry of highly competitive foreign company may pose a threat to the development of local enterprises, etc.

China as a WTO member

China's schedule of commitment under WTO

On 11 December 2001 China officially became a WTO member, an event hailed by the whole nation. China's negotiation lasted 15 years, but from the very beginning, the country was determined to become a WTO member. As is reviewed in a report of China's 15-year efforts to become a WTO member,[9] the late Chinese leader Deng Xiaoping said as early as 1984 that China cannot develop in isolation from the world. The former Chinese president Jiang Zemin, in guiding China's negotiation for accession to the WTO, put forward three principles:

- The WTO without China is incomplete.
- China must enter the WTO as a developing country.
- China should stick to a balance between rights and obligations.

China's WTO accession is believed to have a number of merits. It will further promote its economic reform and opening-up, and hence be conducive to attracting more foreign investment and enhancing the quality of economic performance. Above all, the most important benefit lies in that WTO membership will help China build a competitive market oriented economy. On the other hand, the minuses of WTO accession are also evident. Due to the fact that China's SOE reform has not been completed yet, WTO entry means that China's SOEs and certain industries will have to face heavy pressure from international competition, especially for the service sector and high-tech industry.

Under China's WTO accession agreement, China made substantial market access commitments. The following is a summary of China's commitments in key areas:[10]

- Phase-out of non-tariff barriers on imports – Import license requirements will be eliminated within five years of accession, and all quotas will be phased out within five years of accession.
- Tariff cuts – average import tariffs for industrial products will be lowered from 13 percent in 2001 to 9,3 percent by 2005, and further to 9,2 percent in 2008, and the average tariff for agricultural products will be cut to 15,5 percent in 2005 and to 15,1 percent in 2008.
- Conditions on foreign investment – The WTO Agreement on Trade-related Investment Measures will be implemented; requirements on trade and foreign-exchange balance, local content, and export performance will be ceased or eliminated.
- Trading rights – China agrees to provide trading rights to foreign companies, to be progressively phased in over three years. Majority ownership in wholesale joint ventures will be allowed within 2 years of accession with no geographic or quantitative restriction by then. There will be no geographic, quantitative, equity/form of establishment restriction in retailing within 3 years of accession.
- Opening-up of other services – China has also agreed to relax foreign investment restrictions on many important services industries, including distribution services, telecommunications, financial services, and professional services. For value-added services in telecommunications, foreign partners will be able to own up to 50 percent with no geographic restriction within 2 years after accession. For mobile voice and data services, foreign operators can own 25 percent upon accession, and rise to 35 percent one year after accession and then up to 49 percent after 3 years. Foreign banks will be able to conduct local currency business with Chinese enterprises 2 years after joining the WTO, and all geographic and client restrictions will be removed within 5 years after accession. For non-life insurance, branches or joint ventures with 51 percent foreign ownership will be allowed upon accession. Wholly-owned subsidiaries will be allowed in 2 years. For life insurance, JVs with 50 percent foreign ownership will be allowed upon accession.

Although the concessions China made for entering into the WTO are anything but small, especially compared with other developing countries, the benefits from WTO accession are understood to overshadow the potential losses. After weighing the pros and cons, the Chinese government decided to accept the conditions of WTO membership, and was ready to honour its commitments. Ever since China introduced the reform and opening-up policy in the late 1970s, trying to get integrated into the global market has always been a goal pursued by the Chinese government.

China's WTO negotiation and consequences

China's efforts to resume contracting party status in the GATT and later become a member of the WTO are generally divided into three phases. The first phase, from mid 1980s to July 1986, features China's consideration of and preparation for resumption of contracting party status in the GATT. The second phase, from February 1987 to October 1992, is a period when China's economic and trade institutions were reviewed, with the status of market economy or planned economy being the core issue. In the third phase, bilateral negotiations on market entry and multilateral talks on drafting legal documents of China's WTO entry began. In 1995, China officially applied to become a member of the WTO and thus began bilateral negotiations with 37 WTO members, among which the Sino-US negotiation is of no doubt the longest and toughest one. China's negotiation with the US was by all means the toughest. Both sides made concessions.

As was revealed in an interview[11] with Long Yongtu, the chief negotiator for China's accession to the WTO, China made concessions on the anti-dumping issue and the non-market-economy clause in negotiations with the US. This is corroborated by the testimony[12] made by Peter Davidson, the general counsel of the U.S. Trade Representative, to U.S.-China Security Review Commission on August 2nd, 2001.[13] Davison mentioned three mechanisms or three concessions made by China that would ensure protection against Chinese imports. These three mechanisms, which became multi-lateralised, involve the anti-dumping laws, the "product-specific" safeguard, and a textile product-related mechanism, the latter two both featuring "a market disruption injury standard" and allowing measures against imports from China only.

However, Long Yongtu also made it clear in the interview that China made concessions on the anti-dumping agreement in exchange for maintaining the position on more vital issues to China, like a rejection of commitment to opening capital market and the free convertibility of RMB and the liberation of foreign exchange rates within fives years of WTO accession.

Being a multi-lateral organisation, efforts for accession to the WTO entail both bilateral and multilateral negotiations. The problem with regard to the former lies in the confusion generated as bilateral negotiations are conducted one by one. Therefore, apart from the US, China also had to negotiate with other member countries, the toughest one being the EU, as the EU demanded more concession from China on issues like insurance, telecommunications, retail and tariff. Breslin (2003, 219) cited an USTRO negotiator as saying that when the EU negotiated "a bilateral side deal" with China on issues like insurance licenses they "inserted language … that would prevent some of our firms from equivalent treatment".

On top of bilateral negotiations, China was also involved in multilateral negotiations on its journey to the WTO. As is reported in Gong (2001), Shi Guangsheng, the then Minister of Foreign Trade and Economic Cooperation, revealed that the core issue in bilateral negotiations was to ensure that China could enter the WTO in the capacity of a developing country and that in multilateral negotiations was to ensure a balance between rights and obligations with issues ranging from tariff, non-tariff measures, agriculture, intellectual property rights, and the opening of service industry, with agriculture subsidy and the service industry being the hard core. As a country with a large agricultural sector, China must ensure the rights to fair and reasonable trade and income growth of its 900 million farmers. The service industry is the engine of modern economic development. While the service trade in developed countries represents 70-80 percent of their GDP, in China it occupies only 30 percent of GDP. It was therefore imperative that the sectors enjoyed a gradual and orderly transitional period after the WTO accession.

As China entered the WTO as a country of non-market economy, the post-WTO-accession years have witnessed a growing number of ant-dumping complaints against China. 2005 alone recorded 51 such cases, and marked the 11th year when China suffered the largest number of anti-dumping cases.

In the past several years, China has relied heavily on bilateral negotiations for its market economy status. As of the end of 2005, a total of 51 countries acknowledged China's market economy position, including Korea, a country with a trade volume of over $100 billion dollars with China. With more countries joining this group, Chinese enterprises will find themselves in a more favourable environment when it comes to anti-dumping cases against China.

China's progress in honouring the WTO commitments

2004 marked the third anniversary of China's WTO entry. Liu and Chen (2005) and Liang (2004)[14] present an overview of China's fulfilment of WTO commitment. Table 5.6 is a summary of their conclusions.

Table 5.6   Tariff change since China's WTO entry

	2003	2004	2005	2008
General Tariff	11.5%	10.6%	10.1%	10%
Tariff for Industrial Products	10.3%	9.5%	9.3%	
Tariff for Agricultural Produce	16.8%	15.6%		15.1%

Source: Liu and Chen (2005) and Liang (2004)

1. Tariff has been lowered steadily   It is worth mentioning that China's tariff for agricultural produce in 2003 was much lower than the world average of 62 percent. The US tariff stood at 12 percent, the EU at 20 percent, and Brazil and Argentina at 35 percent. So it is apparent that China has done a much better job than almost all WTO members in opening the agricultural produce market.

2. Non-tariff barriers have been slowly phased out   2004 witnessed the abolition of the import quota and import licensing administration for four categories of goods— petrol products, rubber products, automobiles and cranes and their parts as well as motorcycles and their parts. At the same time, China increased the import quota for automobiles, rice, vegetable oil, edible sugar, cotton, fleece, fertiliser, and at the same time lowered the proportion of state-operated trade in crude oil, refined oil product, soy-bean oil, palm oil, fertilizer, thus raising the proportion of non-state operated trade.

3. The trade right has been opened to foreign companies gradually   China's commitment to allow all enterprises, both domestic and foreign, and individuals to enjoy the right of foreign trade was honoured in the new Foreign Trade Law. Enterprises receiving foreign investment now occupy a dominant position in China's foreign trade (see Table 5.7), and the foreign trade of collective-owned and private enterprises have also witnessed rapid development.

Table 5.7   The ownership structure of international trade

	Foreign-invested enterprises		Private enterprises		State-owned Enterprises	
	Export	Import	Export	Import	Export	Import
2001	50.1%	51.6%	7.3%	5.8%	42.5%	42.5%
2002	52.2%	54.3%	10.1%	6.9%	37.7%	38.8%
2003	54.8%	56.2%	13.7%	9.8%	31.5%	34.5%

Source: compiled from Liang (2004):
www.ce.cn/ztpd/tszt/hgjj/2004/zgrssnh/snrslxc/200412/06/t20041206_2495758.shtml

4. The opening up of the service sector was accelerated   In 2003 China honoured its commitment in such fields as banking, insurance and tourism ahead of schedule. On June 1 2004, China put into practice New Administrative Measures for Foreign-Invested Commercial Enterprises, and thus honoured the commitment of distribution right. The new Foreign Trade Law, which came into effect on July 1st, honoured the commitment to open the foreign trade operation right six months ahead of the schedule. During the three years since China's WTO entry, China has issued 40-odd rules and regulations concerning the opening-up of services, covering the fields of finance, distribution, logistics, tourism and architecture.

5. The efforts to protect intellectual property rights have taken effect   On September 17th, the WTO Council for Trade-Related Aspects of Intellectual Property Rights reviewed China's progress in honouring its commitments in the "Trade-Related Intellectual Property Rights Agreement". The council gave a positive evaluation of the achievements China made in IPO, and especially the efforts to honour the WTO commitments. In the first half of 2004, a two-month anti-privacy and counterfeiting campaign was launched under the Industrial and Commercial Administration, the Press and Publications Administration, General Administration of Customs, and State Intellectual Property Rights. Industrial and Commercial Administrative departments investigated and prosecuted 4306 cases of trademark infringement, with a fine of nearly 30 million RMB, or US$ 3,6 million. Copyright administrative departments inspected over 8.000 CD and software dealers and seized 1,5 million pirated CDs. More importantly, last year, China established the Comprehensive Coordination Mechanism of the Enforcement of Intellectual Property Rights and the mechanism of regular communication with foreign-funded enterprises.

Challenges in the post-transition period

2005 marks the end of transition period for most sectors gained in China's WTO entry negotiation. According to China's commitment to the WTO, China will further open its market in the post-transition period and are now faced with the following challenges (Liang 2004):

- With the increasing integration of the global economy, China's economy will be increasingly affected by the international economy.
- With the growing tendency for countries to protect their own industries through such means as anti-dumping, anti-subsidy, and the protection of intellectual property rights, China's exports will face greater challenges.
- China's efforts to protect intellectual property rights still leave much to be desired. For example, more severe punishment for violation of property rights which meet the requirements of TRIPS needs to be established.

China's position in the Doha round

After 15 years of arduous talking, China eventually became a WTO member in late 2001. This reflected China's power and potential, and also indicates China's readiness to pay certain costs in exchange for its due position in international economic affairs. As the third largest trade power and the largest developing country, China plays a unique role in international trade negotiations. As pointed out by Zhang et al (2004), China needs a stable, standardised and orderly international market, which is in line with the interests of developed countries. At the same time, China lags behind developed countries in terms of economic development level, corporate and industrial competitiveness and therefore is unable to match them in the commitment to open the market, which means China shares some interests with other developing countries. Without knowledge of China's unique status, it might be difficult to understand China's position in the Doha round of negotiations.

In what is to follow, China's position or the position China should take in the issues of government procurement, agricultural trade and international investment will be examined.

Government procurement

Background   China's government procurement did not start until the 1980s when the country initiated tender invitations in the field of public construction projects, mechanical and electrical equipment,   and research projects (Zhu and Jin 2000). Large-scale government procurement appeared in the 1990s. In 1996, China started a pilot scheme in government procurement, followed by an expansion of the range of the pilot scheme. In 2000, government procurement was practiced throughout the country.

In 1998, China's Ministry of Finance issued "Interim Regulations on Government Procurement", which was formulated in the spirit of the WTO Agreement on Government Procurement (GPA), on the basis of the provisions in the United Nations Model Law on Procurement of Goods, Construction and Services, and with reference to laws and rules of other WTO members concerning government procurement. The Government Procurement Law of the People's Republic of China was approved by the 28th Standing Committee of the Ninth National People's Congress on 29 June 2002.

Figure   5.3   demonstrates   the   growth   pattern   of   China's   government procurement.

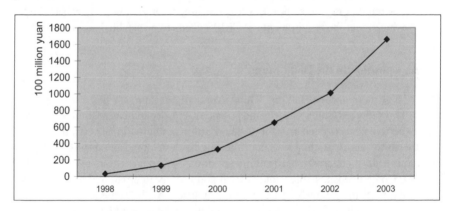

Figure 5.3   Growth in government procurement

Source: "Report on the statistical analysis of government procurement in 2003"
www.ccgp.gov.cn/tongji/2003fifth.htm

It is expected that in 2005 the volume of government procurement will reach 250 billion RMB,[15] or about US$30 billion.

After a decade of development, a Chinese government report[16] indicates the implementation of Government Procurement Law has made significant headway, and breakthroughs have been made in key areas. In 2003, 37,9 percent of government procurement was conducted with fiscal capital, and the rest with self-raised funds. Government procurement expanded a great deal in scale. Government procurement in commodities, construction projects and services increased by 43,3 percent,

115 percent and 34,3 percent respectively over 2002. Various modes of government procurement were developed, including centralised government procurement, centralised public sector procurement and decentralised procurement

China's general position on Government procurement

Since the opening-up of the government procurement market is an inevitable trend in economic globalization, and China has already committed itself to the accession to the Government Procurement Agreement, it is generally believed that it is in China's own interest to take a positive attitude toward the issue and actively participate in the formulation of relevant rules.

According to the Report of the Working Party on the Accession of China, upon China's WTO entry, it became an observer of the WTO Agreement on Government Procurement (GPA), and started the negotiation to become a GPA member after two years. China has committed itself to opening its government procurement market to all GPA members in 2020.

GPA, in its essence, paves the way for the participation of enterprises around the world in government procurement on the basis of equality. If China obligates itself to adhere to transparency in government procurement, Chinese enterprises will also benefit from the opportunity to participate in government procurement under the transparency agreement. However, given that China is still a developing country and that many Chinese enterprises are less competitive in certain aspects than their overseas counterparts, Xue et al. (2004) maintain that China will only make commitments that it will be able to honour.

As it stands now, since China's commitments to government procurement cover the principles of transparency and most favoured nation status but does not touch on market entry and national treatment, Zhang et al. (2004) believe China stands little chance of signing the GPA in the next few years. The government is therefore advised to utilise the period of time to expand domestic demand and develop domestic enterprises that will meet the requirements of government procurement so as to build a secure foundation for their future role in the international market of government procurement.

Sun Zhengyu, China's ambassador to the WTO, said in an address to Beijing University on 24 November 2003 that China maintains a cautious attitude toward the transparency of government procurement.[17] As a rapidly developing country, China has many government-initiated projects. If all these projects are opened to suppliers around the world, domestic enterprises will experience a great shock.

Discrepancies between domestic law and GPA

An analysis of the disagreements between China's Government Procurement Law and the GPA may help us better understand China's position on this issue. Zhang (2003, 397–399) identifies four inconsistencies between the two.

1. Procurement procedure   The Government Procurement Law has an open bidding procedure as the principle procedure and other procedures (including tender invitation procedures) as exceptions, whereas GPA has open or selective bidding as the principle.

2. The examination of the qualification of suppliers or contractors   It is stipulated in Article 23 of China's Government Procurement Law that 1) only domestic suppliers and contractors can participate in government procurement with only a few exceptions, and 2) the eligibility of the suppliers and contractors will be examined based on the facts and legal features of government procurement items. It can therefore be concluded that a scientific eligibility examination system needs to be developed. On the other hand, according to the analysis of Xiao (2003), GPA features more elaborate stipulations on this issue.

3. Release of information   Government Procurement Law, in principle, calls for the release of certain information; however, it is not clear what kind of information falls into this category.

4. Challenge procedure   In this aspect, the Government Procurement Law differs from the GPA on two points. First, the former stipulates that the institution to handle the questioning of the supplier is the procurer, whereas according to GPA, a court of examination institution independent of the procurer plays this role. Second, as is stipulated in the Government Procurement Law, a supplier will not be able to continue to file a complaint, apply for administrative review or lodge an administrative prosecution without going through the questioning procedure first. By contrast, the GPA stipulates that a supplier can file a challenge as long as it is the conviction of the supplier that its interests in government procurement are harmed.

These differences again indicate that it might take some time before China joins the GPA, as China needs time to foster the competitiveness of domestic industries so as to protect domestic interests while not violating the GPA at the same time.

Agricultural trade

Background   In discussing China's position in agricultural trade, it is important to bear in mind that China finished its WTO negotiation in September 2001 and started the Doha round of negotiation in November 2001. The majority of WTO members, however, started the negotiation after the Uruguay round of negotiation completed in 1994. As the Agricultural Agreement of the Uruguay Round took effect in 1995, developed countries had had six years to complete tariff cuts, and domestic support and export subsidies by 2000, and developing countries also had had 10 years to complete the tariff cut by 2004. Therefore, when China became a WTO member in 2001, it was deprived of initial conditions in the negotiation of

Agricultural Agreement, and had to pay an extra entrance fee and had to make a stricter commitment than that required prior to 1995.

China's general position on agricultural trade

As a new member of the WTO, China submitted an agriculture negotiation bill in September 2002. Generally speaking, China's stand in agriculture negotiations shares many similarities with that of the Cairns Group. The following is China's general stand in the negotiation of agricultural trade: The negotiation should abolish trade barriers, reduce agriculture protection, raise the chances of market entry for the developing members of the WTO, and promote fair trade in agricultural produce. The reality of and need for agricultural development in developing countries and the least developed countries should be taken into consideration to ensure that the final agreement will reflect the interests of different members. New members of the WTO should receive special treatment and should be immune from commitment to new cuts.

Tariffs

With regard to high tariff and tariff escalation in developing countries, it is the position of the Chinese government that developed countries should abolish their tariff protection, lower the tariff level substantially so as to pave the way for the entry into their markets of agricultural produce from developing countries, especially those produce with significant export interests (Xue et al. 2004). Zhang (2003) suggests that the Chinese government advocate the abolition or restriction of non-ad valorem tariffs and the implementation of advalorem tariffs for all agricultural produce.

Zhang et al. (2004) maintain that China should advocate drastic cuts in bound tariff rates. They further point out that tariff cuts and the abolition of non-tariff barrier should proceed side by side, so as to ensure that non-tariff issues will not offset the benefits brought about by tariff cuts.

Export subsidy

On 17 June 2002, in the agriculture negotiation of the Doha Round, China expressed its support for quick abolition of export subsidies. China's position was made with reference to the stand of the Cairns Group, namely, that export subsidies should be cut by 50 percent within the first year of the implementation of the Doha Agreement, and the developed countries have three years and developing countries six years to abolish the rest of the subsidies. As China is already committed to the abolition of export subsidies, to create an environment of fair international market, the Chinese government should advocate the acceleration of reform of export subsidies and of the abolition of export subsidies. This is a view shared by many WTO experts in China.

Domestic support

The following should be China's position in negotiation of the issue of domestic support (Zhang 2003, 80–81):

- Re-examine the "green box" policy to define policy standards, standardise the employment of the "green box" policy, and restrict the support for the "green box" policy;
- Oppose the "blue box" policy;
- Substantially cut the domestic support that hampers trade – such as "amber box" and "blue box".

To sum up, as Du Qinglin, Minister of Agriculture, states, China maintains the following position in the new round of agricultural negotiations:

- The negotiation should follow the principle of equitable competition to abolish trade barriers, cut agricultural support, improve the chances of market entry for developing countries, and promote the fair trade of agricultural products.
- The negotiation should take into consideration the reality of and need for agricultural development in developing and the least developed member states, so as to ensure that negotiation results reflect the interests of different parties in a balanced manner.[18]

International investment

Currently, scholars in China are divided with regard to the position China should hold toward multilateral investment (Zhang 2003).

Some support the negotiation of a multilateral investment for the following reasons:

- As the international community has never given up the attempt and efforts to establish a unified international investment code, the trend has been to standardise international investment. Therefore, an active participation in the formulation of rules will better serve China's interest than a passive acceptance of rules.
- An active participation is in conformity with the strategic goal set during the 16th National Congress of the Chinese Communist Party.
- China's investment overseas has met with some restrictive measures in other countries, which therefore calls for an enhancement of investment liberalisation and market entry level through our participation in the negotiation of multilateral investment framework.
- An active participation in the negotiation is consistent with China's international image as a "responsible power" and will enhance China's influence in the WTO.

Others, like Zhang (2003), maintain the opposite position. They believe that:

- Although global economic integration will be conducive to the improvement of world well-being, it does not ensure equal distribution of economic fruits as the interests of underprivileged countries will be harmed.
- The future multilateral investment policy will focus more on the obligations of host countries toward foreign investors than the other way round. At the current stage as a foreign investment receiver, we will shoulder more obligations and responsibilities. China's rapid development means we will become investors in the future, but that will take about ten years. Therefore, delaying the start of the negotiation of the multilateral investment framework will bring more benefits to China, as China will then have enough time to develop its economy.
- At the present stage, it is difficult to foresee the significance of engaging in investment negotiation. Without a multilateral investment framework, China made great achievements in utilising foreign investment. It is questionable if China will continue to enjoy a high foreign investment once China becomes a member of the framework.

China's efforts in the direction of free trade agreement

While WTO multilateral trade talk is faced with many difficulties, FTA (Free Trade Agreement) talks are in full swing. Since 2004, China has been engaged in a number of FTA talks:[19]

- 23 May 2005: the first round of China-Australia Free Trade Area talks started in Sidney.
- May 18–20, 2005: the third round of China-New Zealand Free Trade Area talks were conducted in Wellington and positive headway was made. The negotiation started in December 2004.
- April 29, 2005: the second round of China-Chile Free Trade Area talks finished in San Diego. The first round of talks were held in Beijing in January.
- April 23rd and 24th, the first round of free trade talks between China and the Gulf Cooperation Council was held.
- March 20th, the Non-government feasibility study of Sino-Korean Free Trade Agreement was initiated.

It is expected that China will start Free Trade Agreement talks with an increasing number of countries. Xu (2005) suggests that China should start FTA talks with both neighbouring and distant countries, with both developed and developing countries. An FTA with neighbouring countries will benefit regional trade and investment, thus laying the foundation for the deepening of regional economic cooperation. An FTA with distant countries should aim at exploiting markets for export and carrying out trade with oil and special metal producers. An FTA with developing countries is conducive to cooperation with countries with similar development levels and ensures a steady importation of key resources, while that with developed countries will help the improvement of corporate and industrial performance and the improvement of institutions and management.

Conclusions

Since China implemented reform and opening-up policies in the late 1970's, China's economy has witnessed rapid, sustained and steady growth. Chinese people's living standard has also improved dramatically. Along with economic growth, China has established a socialist market economy and is now in the process of continuously improving it. China's industrial structure has also experienced upgrading, with its manufacturing and service function being further strengthened. In the meantime, great changes have taken place in China's economic ownership structure. Private businesses, which were non-existent prior to the 1980s, have been booming in the past decade.

Despite the impressive achievement in China's economic development, problems still exist in the following areas: energy and resource strain, widening income disparity, blind or overspread investment with low efficiency, deteriorating environment, and aggravated poverty in certain areas, etc.

China's impressive economic success is related to the growth in its export and foreign investment, which provided China with new demand, new management experience and new technology. In the 20 years from 1985 to 2004, China's exports increased almost 22-fold, and foreign direct investment increased 32-fold.

The continuously growing exports have played an important role in boosting China's economic development, and in driving economic growth, bringing new ideas and technology, fostering the development of private enterprises, township enterprises, and creating more job opportunities, etc.

The increasing foreign direct investment in China has brought about tremendously positive changes in China, such as inducing institutional reform and improvement, promoting the accumulation of capital, helping to develop the concept of investment in human capital, and improving technology and management, etc.

With a view to ensuring a stable international trade and investment environment, China began its efforts to enter the WTO in 1986, and officially became a WTO member on 11 December 2001. In order to be admitted to the WTO, China made substantial concessions and serious commitments. Since the entry into the WTO, China has made great efforts to honour its commitments in the following areas: substantial cut in tariffs, removal of non-tariff barriers, opening up of the service sector, and strengthening the protection of intellectual property rights, etc.

2005 marks the end of the transitional period for most sectors gained in China's WTO entry negotiation. According to China's commitments to the WTO, China will open its market further in the post-transitional period and is now faced with a series of challenges in the areas of international economic risks, trade disputes, intellectual property rights protection, etc.

In the future, China will continue to play an important role in the world trade negotiation. China will strengthen the economic and trade relationship with other countries, and will be further committed to free and fair trade. In the meantime, as the largest developing country in the world and a new member of WTO, China will agree to make new commitments under the condition that domestic interests will not be jeopardised. It is always China's position that WTO rules should raise the chances of market entry for the developing members of the WTO. Hence China maintains the view that the interest of developing countries and the least developed countries should be taken into consideration to ensure that the final agreement in Doha round will reflect their requirements.

References

Breslin, S. (2003), 'Reforming China's Embedded Socialist Compromise: China and the WTO', *Global Change, Peace & Security* 15.3, pp. 213-227.

Chen, JY and Xiao, GG. (2004), *A Study of the New Development in International Direct Investment and Foreign Direct Investment in China* (Beijing: People's Press).

Fung, HG. (2005), 'China's Foreign Trade and Investment: an Overview and Analysis', *China and World Economy* 13.3, pp. 3-16.

Gong, W. (2001), 'History Will Remember This Day—a Memorandum of China's Negotiation for Accession to the WTO', *People's Daily*, Nov. 11th, 2001, 2nd page.

Lai, PY. (2005), 'China's Foreign Trade: Achievements, Problems and Future Policy Options', *International Economic Review* May-June, pp. 12-16.

Li, AF. (2005), 'China's Foreign Trade Policy Calls for Strategic Changes', *First Financial Daily* March 3rd, 2005.

Li, JS. and Zhao, YQ. (2005), 'The Three Channels Through Which China Promotes the World Economic Growth', *Economic Information Daily* June 22, 2005.

Liang, YF. 'China's Fulfillment of WTO Commitments and Their Impacts', 2004 <http://www.ce.cn/ztpd/tszt/hgjj/2004/zgrssnh/snrslxc/200412/06/t20041206_ 2495758.shtml>, accessed 18 June, 2005.

Liu, GX and Chen, TF. (2005), 'WTO Effects: Opening Up Promotes Reform and Development—an Examination of China as a WTO Member at the 3rd Anniversary of China's WTO Entry', *Review of Economic Research* 1872.8, pp. 2-7.

Ma, K. and Li, J. (eds.) (2003), *China Business* (Beijing: Wuzhou Chuanbo Press.)

National Bureau of Statistics of China <http://www.stats.gov.cn>

Pei, CH. (2005), 'Analysis of China's Foreign Trade Growth and Discussion of Related Policies', *China and World Economy* 13.2, pp. 26-38.

Premier Wen's 2005 Government Work Report, <www.chinadaily.com.cn/ english/ doc/2005-03/15/content_424826_2.htm> accessed 9 July 2005.

Ran, Z. (2005), 'Developing Countries' Anti-dumping Cases Against China: Reasons and Countermeasures', *Journal of International Trade*, pp. 122-126.

Report on the statistical analysis of government procurement in 2003 <http://www. ccgp.gov.cn/tongji/2003fifth.htm> accessed 28 June 2005.

Shen, L. (2005), "An Overview of China's Utilization of Foreign Investment," in: Xiao (ed.) (2005), *Economic Analysis and Outlook,* (Beijing: Economic Science Press).

Tang, HT and Hu, LF. (2005), 'System Cultivating of China's Foreign Trade Innovation', *Journal of International Trade* Issue 6, pp. 9-13.

The UN Trade and Development Report, 2004 <http://www.unctad.org/ en/docs/ tdr2004_en.pdf>, accessed 27 June 2005.

USTR General Counsel on China's "Imminent" WTO Accession (Testimony Aug. 2 to U.S.-China Security Review Commission) <http://usinfo.state.gov/ei/ Archive/2003/Dec/31-865405.html> accessed 18 March 2006.

Wang, QH. (2005), 'Outlook of China's Foreign Trade', in Xiao (ed.) (2005), *Economic Analysis and Outlook,* (Beijing: Economic Science Press).

WTO Commitments, Market Profile on Chinese Market http://www.tdctrade.com/ main/china.htm, June 27, 2005.

WTO Economic Guide, www.wtoguide.net/Get/meeting/chinawto/2005042105421 19185365428.htm, 6 July, 2005.

Xiao, B. (2003), *A Comparative Study of Government Procurement Rules of International Organizations,* (Beijing: China Fangzheng Press).

Xiao, Z. (2005), 'Stick to Road of Rapid Development and Construct a Harmonious society," in Xiao (ed.) (2005), *Economic Analysis and Outlook,* (Beijing: Economic Science Press).

Xiao, Z. (ed.) (2005), *Economic Analysis and Outlook,* (Beijing: Economic Science Press).

Xu, Q. (2005), 'Basic Strategies of China's FTA action', *Reference News* June 16th, 2005.

Xue, R and Fan, Y. et. al. (2004), *WTO Doha Round and China,* (Beijing: Foreign Trade University Press).

Zhang, Y. (ed.) (2003), *A Study of Legal Issues of WTO New Round,* (Beijing: China Commerce Press).

Zhang, Y et al. (2004), *Development Agenda of Doha Round: Issues and Countermoves,* (Shanghai: Shanghai People's Press).

Zhao, X. (2005), 'International Investment in China' 2005, <http://chinadatacenter. org/cdc/papers/investmentChina1998.pdf>, accessed 9 July 2005.

Zheng, J. (2005), 'Efforts Are Called For to Take the Course of Scientific Development—an Interpretation of Statistical Communiqué of National Economy and Social Development, 2004," *China Statistics* March, 1.

Zhu, J. and Jin, L. (2000), *The Bidding and Tender Invitation in Government Procurement,* (Beijing: People's Court Press).

Notes

1   See Zhao, X.D. (1998) "International investment in China", available at: http://chinadatacenter.org/cdc/papers/investmentChina1998.pdf.
2   "The top priority for the government is to further strengthen and improve macroregulative policy and measures in order to maintain a steady and fairly rapid economic growth." Premier Wen Jiabao, addressing the National People's Congress 2005. Premier Wen' Government Work Report, www.chinadaily.com.cn/english/doc/2005-03/15/content_424826_2.htm.
3   The amended Foreign Trade Law is available at: http://www.cacs.gov.cn/DefaultWeb App/showNews.jsp?newsId=300840000009.
4   These laws and regulations are available at: www.fdi.gov.cn/ltlawpackage/index.jsp?cu rrentPage=1&category=0140&app=1&language=en.
5   The complete articles of the Catalogue are available at: http://english.mofcom.gov.cn/aarticle/topic/lawsdata/chinaforeigntradelaw/200501/20050100015843.html.
6   The list of Encouraged Foreign Investment Industries is available at: www.macrochina.com.cn/english/laws/investment/20010416000186.shtml.
7   Available at: http://www.unctad.org/en/docs/tdr2004_en.pdf.
8   Shen's view is cited in the report "FDI continues to be hotbed of debate" at http://english.people.com.cn/200411/16/eng20041116_164042.html.
9   See Gong (2001) "History will remember this day—a memorandum of China's negotiation for accession to the WTO", available at: www.people.com.cn/GB/jinji/222/6755/6757/20011111/602478.html, also available at the website of the Central Government of People's Republic of China www.gov.cn/ztzl/content_87675.htm.
10 The simplified version is cited from: http://www.tdctrade.com/main/china.htm.
11 The interview was conducted on Dec. 8th, 2004 and the English version is available at: http://english.people.com.cn/200412/08/eng20041208_166528.html.
12 The full text of Peter Davidson's testimony is available at: http://usinfo.state.gov/ei/Archive/2003/Dec/31-865405.html.
13 The online version of the report is available at www.cacs.gov.cn/DefaultWebApp/showNews.jsp?newsId=300840000008.
14 Yanfeng Liang is the director of WTO Research Center, Research Institute, Ministry of Commerce. Her review is available at: www.ce.cn/ztpd/tszt/hgjj/2004/zgrssnh/snrslxc/200412/06/t20041206_2495758.shtml.
15 Government procurement data for 2004 is not available.
16 "Report on the statistical analysis of government procurement in 2003", www.ccgp.gov.cn/tongji/2003fifth.htm.
17 *WTO Economic Guide*
     www.wtoguide.net/Get/meeting/chinawto/20050421054211918536548.htm.
18 People's Daily, 9 September 2003.
19 See 16 June, Reference News (Cai Kao Xiao Xi).

Chapter 6

Back from the Future?
Brazil's International Trade in the
Early Twenty-first Century[1]

Luiz Estrella Faria[2]

To the States or any one of them, or any city of the States,
Resist much, obey little,
Once unquestioning obedience, once fully enslaved,
Once fully enslaved, no nation, state, city of this earth,
ever afterwards resumes its liberty.

Walt Whitman, *To the States*

Introduction

Brazilians used to perceive their motherland as a land of the future. Stefan Zweig shared this confidence in the country's future and recorded it in his writings when he immigrated to Rio de Janeiro escaping from the Nazis. The faith in a brilliant prospect of upcoming socio-economic development was deeply rooted in the nation's spirit after the outcome of two historic events. The first event was the modernist movement in the arts, which produced a new self reference for national culture, opposed to the colonial heritage and its old oligarchies of European imprint. Meaningfully, and in a reference to the former Indian inhabitants, its radical wing named itself as "anthropophagic". In politics, the new ideas of modernisation first inspired the *Tenentismo*, from the Portuguese word for lieutenant, a progressive movement of young officers from the Brazilian Army in the 1920s. Thereafter, there came the second event, the Revolution of 1930, whose victory led to the fall of the Old Republic and the seizure of power by a new social bloc which, despite being heterogeneous, initiated political, social and economic reforms of a democratic and progressive kind. These two cultural and political revolutions changed the way Brazilians looked at themselves. The quiet agrarian man committed to his harvest work and the duty of feeding the world left his place to become an aroused urban citizen devoted to build a nation. After 1930 and armed with the weapons of planning, the state led a successful process of catching up via fast economic growth. The shape of the future they wished to attain had already been seen in the history of Western Europe and North America. Economically, this process involved a focus on industry, domestic markets and self-sufficiency. Socially, it entailed urbanisation, and politically it was a breaking with the colonial inheritance and taking control of the direction of the nation's fate, thereby achieving real independence.

It was a long road, but the means existed. There were natural resources, a huge territory, a large labour force and, after the World War II, an international environment permissive of nationalistic developmental experiences. After forty years of fast growth, Brazil had built an almost complete industrial estate and had linked its economic dynamics to the domestic market. Its international trade, formerly the main economic activity, had a complementary role. The country had taken on a new role in the international division of labour. The former exporter of raw materials and agricultural products, although preserving its peripheral situation, became an industrialised economy of an intermediate income level.

Nevertheless, the future was full of many promises that had still to be fulfilled. There was still poverty, inequality and a great distance from the central economies to be overcome. Unfortunately, at the beginning of the 1980s, there was a deep crisis, the longest in Brazilian history. Its ideological effects were considerable. Brazilians stopped dreaming of the future and started to look at the past searching for answers for this situation. Then, old habits of thinking emerged from a hidden part of the national soul and reshaped the ruling classes' beliefs. Political and economic leaders began to listen to advice from Washington, London and New York. The very understanding of crisis changed. It was perceived not as a lack of economic growth, but as a lack of economic stability. The higher growth rates of import substitution development were blamed for instability, inflation and fiscal crisis. It was seen as an artificial development. Thus, the issue was to reverse this development via free trade, free capital flows, and an agenda of reforms to guarantee economic openness, deregulation and state shrinking. The centre of economic dynamics had to be moved from the domestic to the external market, changing the country's international insertion back to an exporting economy, whose comparative advantages are mainly primary and semi-manufactured goods. It was also pointed out that there is a savings gap to be filled by foreign investment. Dependency on international finance happened to be up to date. Back from the future after a long journey, Brazil's development and trade policy landed in the past.

An outline of the Brazilian economy and foreign trade[3]

Brazil's economic performance during the first 80 years of twentieth Century has to be described as exceptional. This long period can be divided in two stages. The first one lasted until the 1940s and was that of a primary export economy, whose main product was coffee. From 1900 to 1942 the average annual growth rate was 4,2 percent with a large standard deviation and many episodes of a negative value. The second stage, the import substitution industrialisation, lasted until the 1980s. Its annual growth rate was 7,9 percent from 1943 to 1980, with a small variance, no negative rates and just three episodes less or equal than 2,4 percent. At the end of this period, Brazil was an industrialised country and had the 8th highest GDP in the world.

This impressive development away from underdevelopment, as is noted by many Latin-American researchers (Palma, 1978), built a strong economic structure with an embedded dynamic centre whose growth engine was the manufacturing sector producing for domestic consumption. Its "decision nucleus", as it was called by Celso Furtado (1966), had become endogenous since the main economic choices of investment, consumption and saving were taken by resident agents. Financing investments necessary for these high growth rates was a problem resolved in an *ad hoc* manner. Direct investment of transnational corporations, credit from public banks and public expenditure were handled in a permissive way by flexible monetary and exchange rate regimes. Permanent and more or less high inflation were tolerated. The developmental strategy of this period can be compared to what Immanuel Wallerstein named "technique of mercantilist semi-withdrawal" (Wallerstein, 1974). It had the same state-led pattern, except that it was being performed by a peripheral country.

As statistics show, its dynamics can be viewed as very similar to the ones of core economies in the so-called Golden Age of Capitalism in the post- World War Two years. It was this perspective that inspired Alain Lipietz to name it "Peripheral Fordism" (Lipietz, 1985) and, following him, I myself called it "Tropical Fordism" (Faria, 1996). The picture was of an intensive accumulation regime led by an automobile and home appliance industry stabilised by a monopolistic mode of regulation centred on state economic intervention. A growing rate of urbanisation, rising state expenditure and spreading of wage labour ensured demand for an increasing productive capacity, in spite of great income inequality and poverty. This specific arrangement formed the virtuous circle of economic development. An economy of "mass consumption without consumption of the masses", as Oliveira (1990) said.

The year 1981 witnessed the onset of a crisis that has not yet been overcome. From 1981 to 2004, annual growth rates suffered from a sharp slowdown to an average of 2,1 percent, with five years showing negative values. As the data show, this long crisis can be viewed as the end of an era. The slowdown of the rates of urbanisation and salaried employment growth, the financial exhaustion of the state and foreign debt default abruptly stopped economic growth. The end of the dynamic role of these combined conditions led to Brazil facing a crossroads. Continuing development needed new horizons to overcome this situation in at least one of two alternative ways. The first one was to face the obscene social and income inequality and implement a distributive policy to raise domestic consumption. And the other way was to turn to the outside to preserve social fracture and explore the opportunities of globalisation, and improving exports.

The first alternative could not surmount the distributive veto of the rich (Borón, 2004). Despite the end of the military dictatorship and the return of democracy in 1985, the ruling classes were able to handle the political situation of rising social conflicts and popular struggle. Crisis and unemployment disciplined the working class and permitted the choice for an outward strategy. The neo-liberalism of the

Washington Consensus has given direction to economic policies since 1990. Three steps were taken on a road towards a new insertion into the world economy: the first was an agreement on external debt following the Brady Plan, the second was commercial liberalisation, opening of the domestic market and the exposure of national firms to international competition; and the third one was the opening of financial markets to free capital flows. This option had to face two main drawbacks. On the one hand, the burden of productive and technological gaps on many industrial branches implied the risk of a regressive specialisation and deindustrialisation.[4] On the other hand, foreign direct investment was concentrated in short term operations, favouring speculative moves, exchange rate oscillations, growing indebtedness and balance of payments constraints.

Despite all these changes, Brazil's economic structure still bears the imprint of the Developmental Epoch and, in spite of the many years of liberal reforms, the main characteristics of its economy remain the same. Taking the year of 2002, agriculture accounted for 8,8 percent of GDP, industry for 38,3 percent (where 3.4 percent was oil and mining and 11,6 percent of public utilities and construction) and services for 59,2 percent (including government, 16,3 percent, real estate and rental 11,3 percent, finance 7,7 percent and trade 7,7 percent as well). The figure is for an industrialised country and shows how far the so-called inward development went. The falling growth rates put Brazil in the 11th position in an international comparison of GDP.

Economic openness, as measured by the arithmetic average of commercial in- and outflows, was calculated by the Ministry of Development and External trade as 11,7 percent of GDP and exports reached 13,1 percent in 2002. This outline is a result of recent trade improvements during the 1990s, where openness had an average of about 7,0 percent of GDP and exports of about 7,5 percent. In spite of this commercial expansion, Brazilian exports were 0,96 percent of the world total in 2002. In comparison, in 1984, when Brazil reached another peak in a good period, the country's exports accounted for 1,47 percent of the world total and reached a proportion of 14,2 percent of GDP. The improvement of international trade has been erratic in the last quarter of the century. It had to face the many difficulties of a crisis environment where exchange rate oscillations and financing shortages were frequent.

It was in the last period of import substitution that a process of export substitution took place. As is shown in Figure 6.1, composition of exports had deeply changed since 1960. In 1964, primary products such as coffee or iron ore accounted for 85,4 percent of the total. Semi-manufactured products such as cane sugar and soybean oil accounted for 8 percent and manufactured goods for 6,2 percent. Manufactured products have been the major part of exports since 1980, when they reached 44,8 percent of the total, followed by primary goods (42,2 percent) and semi-manufactured (11,7 percent). In 2000 the figure was 59,0 percent, 22,8 percent and 15,4 percent for manufactured, primary and semi-manufactured products respectively. As will be analysed in the following pages, the first four years of this century witnessed a preoccupant regression in the composition of Brazilian exports. The primary goods share rose to 30,8 percent in 2004. The share of manufactured goods dropped to 53,8 percent.

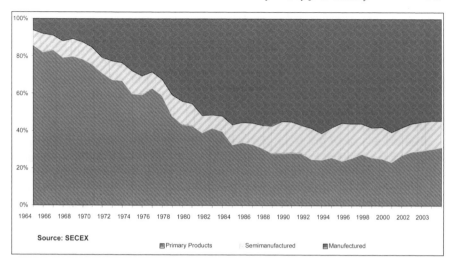

Figure 6.1   Components of Brazil exports

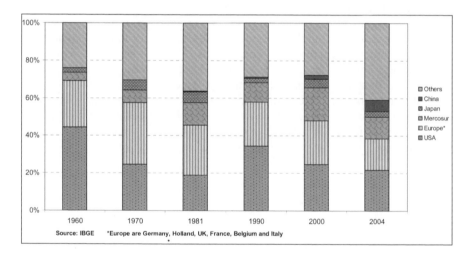

Figure 6.2   Destiny of Brazil exports

When looking at the partners of the country's foreign trade, there can be observed a visible shift as industrialisation proceeded. As seen in Figure 6.2, in 1960 when primary products accounted for the main part of exports, the most important destination was the US (44,4 percent of total exports in 1960). Europe was the second one, since Germany, the UK, France, Belgium, Italy and the Netherlands accounted for 24,7 percent in that year. Argentina bought 4,4 percent of Brazil's exports and Japan 2,4 percent. As the composition of exports changed, the partners changed as well. The share of the US fell to 24,7 percent and to 18 percent in 1970 and 1981, as the one of today's MERCOSUR states rose to 11,6 percent in 1981 and the "others" also rose. This spreading of the destinations of exports revealed a new condition of the country's international trade, that of a global player. In 1990 the USA recovered its importance to reach a total of 33,6 percent, as the share of semi-manufactured goods rose. Notwithstanding this, the other partners maintained their significance as the condition of global player was kept. This shift was also a reaction to the oil crisis and trade deficits of the 1970s, as seen in Figure 6.3. The needs of financing oil imports forced Brazil to look for new markets for its exports.

The last decade of the twenty-first century brought two significant changes: the unilateral decision for foreign trade openness and economic integration into the MERCOSUR which was formed jointly with Argentina, Paraguay and Uruguay. They had the effect of increasing the importance of the South American neighbours as a destination for Brazil's exports. Their share rose from 12,8 percent in 1990 to 19,9 percent in 2000, while that of the USA declined to 23,9 percent. At the same time, as Figure 6.3 shows, a huge deficit was created in the wake of openness, the stabilising Real Plan and its overvalued exchange rate regime. The new century began with a new environment of a floating exchange rate regime, started in 1999, and new commercial partnerships, with the importance of China having increased. As a sole trading partner, China ranked third in 2004, after the USA and Argentina.

Macroeconomic effects of foreign trade can be summarised in the measure of trade balance deficits or surpluses. Looking at Figure 6.3 it can be seen that there was a long period of equilibrium from 1950 to 1973 with an almost permanent, though small surplus. After 1973, the oil price shock produced several years of big deficits. The Brazilian government reacted by launching two programmes which resulted in a large phase of consistent trade surplus. On the one hand, the energy substitution programme of sugarcane methanol, the Pro-alcohol, and the growing domestic production of oil in the deep ocean fields reduced imports. On the other hand, an export promotion policy gave rise to a fast increase in foreign sales. The

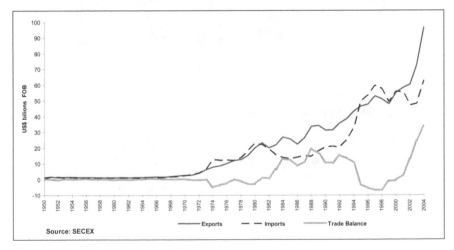

Figure 6.3   Trade balance of Brazil

administered exchange rate regime with permanent devaluation contributed to the improvement of the trade balance as well.

From the 1940s to the 1970s, the function of exports was to make possible the purchase of capital goods and other requirements of the industrialising processes. Since 1980, external indebtedness has made trade surpluses necessary to confront the huge debt servicing requirements. Export promotion policies and the administered devaluation of exchange rates, as well as debt renegotiation facilitated the handling of the situation of the balance of payments. After 1994, the fixed exchange rate regime associated with tariffs cuts produced another huge deficit. This disequilibrium could temporarily be sustained because of capital inflows of foreign direct investment (FDI) in those years. When there was euphoria in the markets, FDI was readily available, and when risk evaluation rose after the Asian and Argentine crises, there were IMF loans. Whilst exchange rate started to float in 1999, commercial surpluses returned.

The pendulum of foreign policy, the commercial issues and the MERCOSUR

All through the 20th Century, Brazil's foreign policy oscillated between moments of close alignment with the US and some moments of independence. Those moments cannot be seen in isolation. In reality they were two aspects of the dialectics of Brazilian diplomacy. Only in this way can one understand the "Responsible Pragmatism" of the Military Government in the 1970s. Born from a *coup d'état* sponsored by the US Embassy, the deeply anti-communist regime then adopted a new independent orientation for its foreign policy that situated Brazil as an ally of the Third World nationalist movement, joining the 77 Group. Trade interests were important in this shift, for Brazil was facing the consequences of the oil crisis and had to handle an uncomfortable situation concerning its balance of payments. The partnership with the non-aligned countries was important as new destinations were opened up for exports, mainly of industrial products, as suppliers of oil that were ready to exchange their oil for Brazilian goods were found.

This shift was to endure when democracy returned in 1985. The civil government and the new Constitution of 1988 echoed the social movements' position blaming dependency and external indebtedness for the economic crisis. However, in 1990 a right-wing president was elected and the political situation changed. On change was the return of a US alignment as a new orientation to foreign policy, following the adoption of a neo-liberal course in economic policy. Subsequent to an agreement with the creditor banks for external debt restructuring, unilateral trade opening through a radical cut back in tariffs was a second step of the new policies. As will be seen, this unilateral choice became a burden in trade negotiations, mainly with the developed countries, for it reduced bargaining capacity since there was little left that the Brazilian government still could offer in terms of tariff reduction.[5] At the same time, deregulation and privatisation compounded the new political orientation and were followed by a financial liberalisation and free capital movements. Once more, as will be seen, this opening of the domestic capital market represented another burden for international trade because of its effect of an initially appreciating exchange rate as it engendered an important inflow of capitals.

The dialectics of foreign policy had its antithesis in these last years of the 20th Century. It came in the form of the integration process that gave birth to the MERCOSUR and then went even further through consolidating alliances within South America. Since Argentina and Brazil initiated the rapprochement process, it was regarded with suspicion by the US, who feared for its interests in the region.[6] In the spirit of that moment in the mid-1980s, the two new democracies, haunted by economic crisis and looking to consolidate their civil power, were anxious to find the lost path to development and economic growth. They realised that it could be better achieved together. Notwithstanding the political shift, integration process went on and the Treaty of Asunción was signed in 1991 by the initiator of the neo-liberal era, Collor de Melo.

In the point of view of the neo-liberals, MERCOSUR was a necessary step for free trade. In the opposite corner of political spectrum, it was seen as a safeguard protecting the partners from the bad effects of globalisation and improving their capacity to pursue a sustained and independent course of development. These two views made regional integration a consensual issue. As the process of integration went on, it created its own interests. And, until now, its most powerful partisans have been trusts and big corporations seeking advantages in exploiting an enlarged market within the customs union. MERCOSUR has been constructed via sector agreements regulating competition within the regional market favouring domestic firms by rules of origin such as, for example, in the automobile industry. The Common External Tariff came into force in 1995 and consolidated many interest groups, not only in the industrial sector, but also agricultural producers. It was an outcome of the Protocol of Ouro Preto which provided an institutional structure and a legal personality to the MERCOSUR, consolidating the economic bloc.

Brazil stated that the MERCOSUR is "a backbone for further regional integration and negotiation of extra-regional agreements" in its report to the WTO (WTO, 2004, 14). This position provides evidence of the importance of the bloc for trade negotiations. And if it shows the prevalence of the economic interests mentioned above, it also indicates the massive political support for the process of integration. Beyond corporations that benefit from the common market, social movements as Trade Unions, NGOs, intellectuals and artists are deeply engaged in the process, for the scope of integration, as defined in the Treaty of Asunción, goes far beyond free trade and includes free movement of people and services, as well as cultural and social integration. This more ambitious scope of the integration process has social and political implications and concerns many social forces.

In spite of all limitations, the MERCOSUR echoed deep feelings of the people of the countries concerned: the dream of Latin-American union. But the longing for this integration under the spirit of the Treaty of Asunción has a great obstacle to overcome: neo-liberal economic policy. As I argued in another work (Faria, 2004), the process of integration needs a common and autonomous project of development for the region in order to endure. It is not just a matter of brushing away the national borderlines, crossed by capitals and commodities in order to create a continuous space for economic activity, which is an expected outcome of globalisation. This would represent a mere integration of things and will result in a disintegration of societies, for the powers ruling these things are beyond the reach of the local or even national social forces. These impersonal forces of capital, once commanding integration process, could manage it in a way that goes against social interests. Milton Santos (1997) described this process as "the transformation of national territories in national spaces of the international economy" (p. 50).

These powers, the beneficiaries of neo-liberalism, are international finance and the big business of multinational corporations. Their local partners broke away from any national development strategy and expect to profit from the liberalised movements of capitals and goods. And for this reason, they prescribe to governments the economic policies that are in their interest. Bankers, shareholders of internationalised industrial corporations, shareholders of privatised companies of public services, proprietors of natural resources (often illegally acquired) are represented by the "economic team", as the media call the officers in charge of economic policy, and set their agenda. Neo-liberal reforms gave them new opportunities to profit without economic growth, changing relative prices and functional income distribution from wages to surplus, as well as the very property of capital assets. As they benefit from a valued currency because of their liquidity, inflation targeting, high interest rates and exchange rate appreciation are the key goals of economic policy; all of this is supported by fiscal responsibility[7] for, as usual in capitalism, public debt is the security of private finance.

While in the last fifteen years, foreign policy has followed its pendulum pattern, economic policy was characterised by steadiness, though lacking any popular support. The election of Lula in 2002 was, on the one hand, a confirmation of the unpopularity of this policy. On the other hand, his government confirmed this steadiness, keeping the economic team in charge. Changes were limited to some adjustments in social policies and to the foreign policy. In regard to the latter, its independent side was reinforced with the definition of three priorities: South America's integration, South-South alliances and a tougher position in trade negotiations.

Social forces and foreign relations

The most powerful economic interests in Brazil have abandoned their belief in national development. To them, prosperity is not necessarily dependent upon fast economic growth, as was seen all through the 20th Century. Although the crisis that began in 1981 was perceived as being long-lasting, they managed to profit in the middle of stagnation. When inflation, its most afflictive component, was finally overcome after 1994, the new macroeconomic environment gave birth to a set of new opportunities. The novel business concerning privatisation and trade and financial openness consolidated a new bloc within the indigenous bourgeoisie that took over the dominant position of the formerly hegemonic industrial entrepreneurs. This new block of the ruling classes assembles interests from finance to agribusiness and has the most prevailing influence upon the Brazilian government. As it succeeds in what concerns the general economic policy, this interest bloc intends to control the agenda of external negotiations as well.

In identifying the social forces related to trade negotiations, it is quite obvious to begin with the groups arranged within the dominant bloc. The first one is agribusiness, and is well-organised to influence negotiations. This group consists of landowning producers of agricultural commodities such as cattle, soybeans, sugar cane, coffee or cotton; agro manufactures of meat, sugar, soy oil or tobacco; and trading companies and other activities related to exports. Although it strongly influences trade negotiations, the group was very uneasy with the overvalued real, for it is the only sector in the dominant bloc harmed by this key aspect of economic policy. As an inheritor of the old oligarchies, it is very influential in the National Congress and acts upon the judiciary authorities as well, which is visible in its successful opposition to agrarian reform and its preserved status of tax exemption. The prominence of the market access issue in the external agenda of Brazilian government and the offers related to it, as will be seen below, showed the influence of the agribusiness lobby.

A second group is the one of producers of semi and manufactured standardised goods. Differently from agribusiness, the group shows a very high level of economic concentration and is formed mainly by monopoly corporations of iron mining and other minerals, steel industries, cellulose or chemical and plastics. It is an arrangement of a few huge corporations, some of which were formerly state owned, such as in the mining, chemical and steel sectors, and, after privatisation, are controlled by local capitalists, banks and pension funds. Others are multinational corporations. These firms act as monopoly powers. They are price makers in the domestic market. They also export an important part of their production, are price takers in the international market and face many barriers protecting their competitors within the markets of the US and Europe. Because of its monopoly position and international scope, exchange rate appreciation is of less concern to this group.

A third group are the producers of manufactured durable goods such as automobile, farm machinery and household appliances. This group is formed mainly by multinational corporations and joint ventures of foreign and local firms. These industries are structured as monopoly competition markets in the regional arena. Therefore, its central interest is MERCOSUR and South America integration because firms established in Brazil have competitive advantages within the regional market. To them the exchange rate is less of a concern. Instead, the sector agreements in the MERCOSUR and between the bloc and its neighbours are strategic. In this way, the group invokes government actions on behalf of its interests, negotiating shares of the South American market for its production.

Within this group, the aircraft industry is in a particular situation. As for the nature of this industry, the market is worldwide and very dependent upon government procurements. It is a case of strategic commercial policy and its branches: subsidies, intergovernmental bargains, and claims within the WTO etc. It was the subject of the case taken Brazil against Canada within the WTO dispute settlement mechanism.

A fourth group is the nondurable goods industries, such as food products, footwear, textile and clothes. Its aims in trade negotiations are, on the one hand, to preserve the domestic market and, on the other hand, to overcome trade barriers in Europe and the USA. The group is very sensitive to the exchange rate revaluation and it suffered severe losses in the 1990s when Brazil decided unilaterally to open its domestic market. With a lower level of economic concentration and with an important part of its production accounted for by small firms, the group has a less prominent position in the discussions.

On the other pole of society, popular forces are present in the process of negotiation through three groups. The first one is that of family farmers and peasants. They are led by the CONTAG (the National Confederation of Agriculture Workers) and the MST (The Movement of Landless Peasants) and fight to preserve or to achieve land ownership and corresponding agricultural jobs. The group aims to feed the people by means of its productive work. Hence, their core intention is to preserve the domestic market and Brazil's offers in the negotiations are carefully examined. They are aware also of issues like intellectual property rights and trade of services as they intend to preserve their technologies and natural resources and fight against monopolies. The case of market access is of less concern, as this group has no significant export activity. Differently than in the developed countries, in many subjects of trade negotiations, agricultural farmers' interests are opposite to those of agribusiness. Ideologically, they are militantly against the free market and globalization, while agribusiness is supportive of it. In this sense, they tend to tolerate European protectionism.

The second group is the trade unions. They ideologically oppose the free market and globalisation as they see it as a threat to their jobs and as a process that intensifies dependency. Trade unions support transparency in negotiations and are very sensitive to issues like intellectual property rights, anti-dumping measures, services and government procurements, as they perceive them as limits to an independent development policy. They are inclined to support industry groups' positions in the market access issue, defending the domestic market and seeking to overcome barriers abroad. Historically internationalists, trade unions are comprehensive in regard to the position of their peers in developed countries seeking to preserve their jobs.[8]

The third group is a large array of NGOs and social movements related to trade negotiations via an also large array of issues like environment conservation, access to medical care for victims of illnesses such as AIDS, support for fair trade or the taxation of international financial flows. Since President Lula has been in office, NGOs have strengthened their capacity to influence government decisions. Although they suffered important defeats, like in the matter of legalisation of transgenic seeds or in their opposition to the neo-liberal policies of the economic team, they are an important support for the independent positions of the Foreign Ministry representatives in international trade negotiations.

These contradictions within the civil society are reflected in the state. With their belief in the virtues of free trade, neo-liberal fundamentalists in the Central Bank and the Ministry of Finance are in accordance with both the wishes of the ministers of agriculture, development and foreign trade and the interests of the agribusiness and standardised goods industry. They have decisive influence on offers in the sensitive area of exchange of market access improvements. Integrationists in the Ministry of Foreign Affairs are supported by popular forces and NGOs and by the industrial bourgeoisie of durable and non-durable goods industries, interested in strengthening MERCOSUR and South America integration.

The three arenas of trade negotiations and their agendas

The present strategy of Brazil's foreign policy intends to link regional integration, international trade and development. This approach is followed in three arenas of negotiations. The first is multilateral and has its most important playing field in the WTO rounds, although other forums as the UNCTAD are of relevance as well. The second is that of bilateral trade agreements involving developed and less developed countries, such as FTAA and MERCOSUR-EU negotiations.[9] And the third arena is that of regional integration of the MERCOSUR and the South America Community of Nations.

Before dealing with these three arenas, it is necessary to have a look at the negotiating position of Brazil and many of its allies. The first issue relevant for evaluating this position is the balance of claims and offers presented. In other words, what Brazil intends to gain by the negotiations and what it is willing to concede. And for this position, the last decade of economic reforms inspired by the Washington Consensus was a burden and a handicap. The rank of "good student" of neo-liberal policies is a very weak one for trade negotiations, as the offers necessary to bargain were very limited. The unilateral cut back of tariffs in the early 1990s reduced the scope for further concessions. The same applies to privatisation and the deregulation of public services, some of the new issues included in the Uruguay Round of the GATT agenda, as these activities were unilaterally opened for exploitation to foreign persons and companies. The opening of financial markets and the termination of almost all restrictions to economic activities for foreign citizens or corporations (also unilateral decision as well) reduced the negotiation options, weakening the bargaining position for further offers.[10]

A second issue is what agenda for which arena. Brazil wishes to restrict what I here call bilateral negotiations - or bi-regional as Brazilian officers call it – to market access and to remit to the WTO the sensitive issues of intellectual property rights, trade related investment measures and trade in services. This is so because Brazil thinks of the WTO as more friendly to its negotiating stand point and realistically conceives the multilateral arena as favouring its position as it permits it to act as a bloc with other developing countries. In the case of South America's regional integration, the scope is much broader as it goes far beyond a free market zone. The matter is that of a community of nations, which implies the building of common rules and institutional and political convergence, and the formation of a common infrastructure, etc.

Explaining Brazilian foreign policy strategy, Ambassador José Bustani (2004) contradicted what he called a contemporary myth, the one of an imperial world order imposed on less developed countries like Brazil and of "recommending shyness in the international scene and the acceptance of supposed realities of power". Since 2003, under Lula's administration, Brazilian diplomacy has intended to play a relevant role in the world and has defined its foreign policy as to realise this purpose. Bustani (2004) defined the four principles commanding Brazil's strategy targeting a new position of importance within the international community: the priority to South America; the strengthening of alliances with big developing countries; the awareness of the special links with Africa and the importance of the Arab countries; and the relevance of political dialogue and the opportunities for national development that could emerge as a result of a responsible relationship with developed countries. These principles command trade negotiations, the setting of its agenda and the choice of its arenas.

The multilateral negotiations in the WTO

Beginning with the multilateral arena, to Brazil and its allies the central point of interest is to get through the Uruguay Round agenda and its inclusion of new themes in trade negotiations. Issues like trade related intellectual property rights (TRIPs), trade related investment measures (TRIMs) and trade of services (GATS) were novelties added to multilateral negotiations under the influence of the neo-liberal ideological turn within the Uruguay Round of the GATT pushed by the USA and many of the OECD countries. To Brazil, these new themes ought to be dealt with by considering the differences between countries and their stages of development. Any agreement ought to support and favour a country's development and it should not produce more obstacles to it. A major concern for developing countries is, as has been pointed by many authors (e.g. Rodrik, 1999), that the new rules under these agreements strongly limit the possibilities for a national brand of development strategy for they impose uniformity of rules. Worse, these rules hamper forcefully the possibility of an autonomous development by forbidding some measures indispensable to it.[11] The second point of importance is that of agricultural trade. In this field, the aim is to overcome the protectionism and export subsidies of the US and European domestic markets.

If national interests are broadly the same from the time when the negotiating processes had started and their agenda was defined, Brazil's attitude has changed since 2003, under the characteristic pendulum of its foreign policy. Instead of the former general conformity with the US propositions, only broken in a few specific topics such as in the well known case of generic pharmaceuticals and AIDS medicine,[12] the new attitude is to strengthen the alliance with a group of developing countries in order to form an active bloc for negotiations. This new attitude was present at the origins of the G-20 group, organised within the Doha Round and blamed for the failure of the Cancún meeting by the US and in other developed countries' versions of the events. The central point of discord was agricultural trade and the two items under dispute were: market access for developing countries products and subsidies of developed countries that hamper competition and bring down prices. Neither the European Union nor the US was able to make any significant advance on those subjects at that meeting.

For Brazil, agricultural issues are significant in trade negotiations for three reasons. First, in what concerns the negotiations, the claim for market access and the concern about subsidies unify a very large number of developing countries and consolidate a powerful bloc of nations. Second, the Brazilian government pays attention to the demands of the agribusiness sector due to its political importance. And third, Brazil has a reason to be intransigent in the negotiation of the other topics.

It is realistic to look forward to small and delayed advances on the issue of agriculture. At the same time, as the other arenas show, developed countries are pressing for the so-called Singapore issues, especially investment, competition and government procurement, and the matter of intellectual property rights. It will be very hard for Brazil and its allies to sustain the linkage of those subjects to the issue of development. At the same time, they intend to deal with them exclusively within the multilateral arena of the WTO for they see the Doha Round as an opportunity to overcome the way the Uruguay Round addressed these sensitive issues.[13]

After the collapse of the Cancún conference, negotiations restarted in the meeting of the General Council of the WTO on 31 July 2004, which decided a general text with four annexes defining a framework for future negotiations. The annexes dealt with agriculture, services and trade facilitation. From the point of view of Brazil and other developing countries, they achieved removing the Singapore issues from the agenda, except for trade facilitation,[14] at least for the time being. As for the demands of developed countries under the TRIPs agreement, they succeeded in securing concessions with regard to the exceptions on licensing for medicine.

Until now in balance the WTO negotiations have been mainly positive in that they have permitted the developing countries to organise themselves (Drábek, 2004), putting away their usual shyness, as Ambassador Bustani has said. Well-organised and led by the bigger countries – Brazil, China and India – they have prevented until now the repetition in the Doha Round of what happened at the end of the Uruguay Round when the interests of developed countries were promoted regardless of the developing ones. The coalition under the G-20 consolidated the influence of some social groups on the Brazilian negotiating position, especially the agribusiness and the standardised goods producers seeking market access. Nevertheless, multilateral negotiations are the arena less affected by groups of interests. Consequently, it is there that diplomatic officers have the opportunity to act in a relatively autonomous manner as public servants committed to what they perceive to be the national interest in the long run.

The bilateral negotiations for free trade agreements

European Union and MERCOSUR   The more difficult arenas are those I here refer to as bilateral negotiations: the FTAA and MERCOSUR-EU. The expectation for the concretisation of a free trade zone between the European Union and the MERCOSUR has become more positive over the last years. Discussions have been accelerated since 2003 so as to compete with the FTAA calendar. Starting with a less ambitious agenda focused on market access, one of the biggest stumbling blocks is agriculture, the issue of most importance for the South-Americans, which represents 48 percent of MERCOSUR exports to the EU and only 3 percent of the European exports. In 2003, the EU had a commercial deficit with MERCOSUR of 10,2 billion Euro. Its interests in market access are for industrial goods to reduce the deficit. In the last round of consultations, in the second semester of 2004, the Europeans maintained their position for very small quotas for agriculture products and the South-Americans reduced their offers in industrial goods for they were sensitive to durable and equipment goods producers and family farmers demands, as was the case for dairy products.

Aside from the market access issue, the EU is also pressing for some Singapore items such as services, investment and government procurement that have the connotation of a counterbalance for the trade deficit. Nevertheless, MERCOSUR wants to deal with those themes only within the multilateral arena of the WTO and intends to restrain the bi-regional agenda to trade. The main obstacle was the insistence of the Europeans on their meagre agricultural offer proposing extremely reduced quotas for sensitive products such as chicken meat and pork. MERCOSUR negotiators saw this position as a strategy to safeguard their quotas policy and create a precedent for the multilateral arena of the WTO. At the same time, the South-Americans do not intend to renounce any sovereign right to regulate investment or services within the bi-regional arena for they intend to discuss this subject exclusively in a package with development issues within the Doha Round of the WTO. The negotiations reached an impasse and the schedule has been delayed.

The Free Trade Agreements of the Americas   The second and more complex arena is the FTAA discussions. The negotiating process started at the Summit of the Americas in Miami in 1994. At that moment, the project of a hemispheric economic integration had an agenda that went far beyond a free trade agreement. The heterogeneity of the 34 countries - including the richest and some of the poorest in the whole world, with their different levels of development, and consequently different social and economic needs, and their cultural and political differences - was perceived as an important challenge to continental integration. Asymmetries are challenging if economic integration has to produce reciprocal benefits. Topics like political and financial support to social development, cooperation in such important areas as education and health, and the needs of financing the infrastructure of transport, energy and telecommunications were addressed in the final statement of the meeting with the same relevance as trade liberalisation.

Nevertheless, ten years after the spirit of that summit was lost. As Ambassador Bahadian, the Brazilian co-chair of the negotiations said, "it survived just the FTAA project, separated of any more comprehensive notion and point of view of how we can and what we have to do to accomplish the social and economic development of the hemisphere" (Bahadian, 2004). The original FTAA proposition was delivered by the US government as a replication of the NAFTA, the free trade agreement of the US, Canada and Mexico. Very ambitiously, it intended to regulate issues like intellectual property, competition, investment, government procurement, and many others that are under discussion within the WTO agenda. The original proposition included some highly controversial provisions as the "investor-state" and the "dispute settlement" issues. The dispute settlement provision was to prevent a disagreement being tried by any judiciary authority in the light of the national law. And the investor-state provision was to permit a foreign investor to question every government decision or even a legal stipulation - for example, an environment protection rule- that may produce an alleged economic prejudice. This claim will be reviewed by the dispute settlement unit that may decide that monetary compensation should be paid by the state to the demanding investor without any regard to the relevant provision of the disputed country's national law. The criticism of this principle alleges that it erodes state sovereignty and subverts national law.[15]

As soon as negotiations started, groups of interests and social forces organised themselves to intervene - with agribusiness and standardised industrial goods producers on the one side, and trade unions and NGOs on the other. The latter form an anti-free trade coalition and demands that the country withdraw from the negotiations. These groups joined with their counterparts from other countries in the Hemispheric Social Alliance, which is a network of civil society organisations, mainly trade unions, and proposes that another kind of integration is possible, a social integration based on fair trade. As for the former, they desire that the Brazilian negotiating team assume a compliant position *vis-à-vis* the US demands in exchange for advances in market access. As the chief Brazilian negotiator argues, the process reached an impasse due to the considerable imbalance of concessions the two main parties were willing to admit. The US pushed for rigid rules on investment, and intellectual property and services far beyond what is being considered in the WTO round but refused any progress on topics of MERCOSUR interest like reducing barriers for agriculture or discussing their anti-dumping measures (Bahadian, 2004).

In order to continue discussions, MERCOSUR suggested two tracks: first, to resolve a framework for a general agreement, shifting the sensitive items to the WTO; and second, to negotiate further advances in market access in a bilateral way (the 4+1 formula). These principles, however, only could operate in an environment of a general reduction of tariffs. Quoting Bahadian (2004): "the intent to leave agriculture or part of it out of the tariffs cut down shows how shameless became the free trade rhetoric". As the US refused to consider MERCOSUR demands on agriculture and insisted on the intellectual property topic and, at the same time, they made MERCOSUR their worst offer in the bilateral mode, negotiations reached an impasse. The co-chair of the US and Brazil in the last round of consultation has the hard job of surmounting this stagnant state of affairs. The prospect is of modest results, for advances seam only to be possible as a consequence of progress in the WTO arena.

The two bilateral negotiations seem to be intimately linked. When the FTAA negotiations stalled, EU-MERCOSUR negotiations were deadlocked on similar issues.

The regional integration of South America

This third arena seems to be the most hopeful. All social forces interested in international trade and related matters unanimously support it. But, and at the same time, there are reasons for caution because attempts at regional integration, except for MERCOSUR's contradictory steps forward, have been a matter of a wealth of rhetoric and a poverty of tangible advancement since the middle of the twentieth century. The customs union of the South Cone runs the danger of suffering the same fate. The beginning was enthusiastic. Intraregional trade grew spectacularly from 1991 to 1997, when its share of total exports rose from 11,1 percent to 24,3 percent. Thereafter, the integration process assumed an almost lethargic state.

This situation was a consequence of a deep crisis that finished the period of economic growth which had ensued after stabilising policies had managed to overcome inflation. Price stability was based on a fixed exchange rate anchor. Growing indebtedness and balance of payments deterioration was an expected outcome of this political option. On the path of successive financial crisis in emergent markets, Brazil devaluated its currency in 1999 and Argentina froze bank accounts and defaulted on its debt in 2001 and finally devalued its currency in 2002. The whole region suffered from economic turmoil. Recent economic recovery of the two biggest economies of the South Cone did not instil a renewed dynamism into regional trade. These circumstances reduce the concern for the integration process and have led to protectionist measures and other attitudes undermining it. In 2004, Brazilian exports to MERCOSUR had fallen to about the share of 1981, 11,6 percent.

When it was signed in 1991, the Treaty of Asunción had in view the consolidation of a common market with free movement of commodities, capital and people, and pointed to an institutional common ground and to a coordination of macroeconomic and sectoral policies. Its principles were gradualism, flexibility, reciprocity and equilibrium. Gradualism was a necessity given the complexity of such an undertaking; flexibility responds to a characteristic tradition of Latin American diplomacy. The basic instruments of the integration process are broadly defined, leaving more precise provisions to protocols on specific issues. The principle of equilibrium intends to impede economic specialisation within the bloc. It works as an anti-Ricardian mechanism and is materialised in sector agreements that intend to promote intra-sector trade and prevent an economic downfall of any industry in any participant country. Reciprocity is the only of those principles defined explicitly in the Treaty, and it requires any outcome of the integration process to have the same economic and social effects to each participant.

The spirit of the Treaty points necessarily to a large agenda that includes infrastructural integration of transport, energy and telecommunications as well as institutional integration. Differently from what happened in Europe, South

American nations built their infrastructure in a secluded way. Railroads, power lines and pipelines were engineered so as to prevent any connection with neighbours. Historical feelings of suspicion and competition led governments to not explore opportunities for economies of scale and other advantages of joint projects. The spirit of today would favour this kind of integration, which is a frequent subject of official meetings. Unfortunately, its realisation is constrained by economic policies where finance shortage and fiscal austerity are characteristic. Consequently, hardly any advances have been realised.

The second large item on the integration agenda, the institutional one, has another historical obstacle to overcome: thoughts of national sovereignty as selfishness. Any process of integration that intends to go beyond a free market zone is not possible if states involved are not able to limit to some extent their sovereign power. Reordering of the levels of regulation is a requirement for integration and this implies institutional redesign and transfer of national authority to regional authority. In other words, the powers have to be ceded to an upper level. Actual progress in the institutionalisation of integration has not been made until now. In fact, as Werter Faria (2002) said, the four states in MERCOSUR confounded this necessary cession of power to reassignment of sovereignty. Institutions of integration have to be supranational in order to achieve the scope necessary to implement the integration processes. In contrast, actual institutions are of an intergovernmental kind. This sort of institution is appropriate for cooperation and not for a process that has its own determinations and its specific level. Nation states and its bureaucracies have commitments not compatible to integration requirements. As designed by the Ouro Preto Protocol, MERCOSUR institutions are interstate institutions "their members have no independence, are submitted to the pressure of national interest and cannot be devoted to their international charges but sporadically" (Faria, 2002, 32). In the final part of this article, the author concludes: "The precarious construction of the MERCOSUR, shown by the impasse that it reached, will only disappear by a drastic transformation of its organic structure" (*ibidem*, 45).

Within MERCOSUR, economic integration continues to be reduced to trade and trade related matters. The agenda is filled with quarrels on commercial imbalances, claims for safeguard measures and charges of dumping, which are nothing else but the music accompanying the decline of intraregional trade. In the intraregional negotiations, durable and non-durable industrial goods producers are the most important interest groups. For these sectors, the regional market is the main destination of their exports and that is why they complain against their neighbours time and again as economic growth expectations diminish.

At the same time, the successful action in other arenas of negotiation reflects the comparatively growing importance of other markets for bloc exports. These best results have been made under the provision of a common foreign trade policy affirmed in the Pact of Asunción. This stipulation forces MERCOSUR to play as a bloc in the international arena. The necessary coordination of the national interest of the four countries has consolidated an agenda of one overwhelming issue: market access for primary products. The prominence of agribusiness interests is clearly visible. This group forms the most powerful social force influencing the MERCOSUR standpoint in trade negotiations. Its influence in Brazil was already mentioned and looking at Argentina, agribusiness is the lone economic survivor after neo-liberal fundamentalism and its devastating crisis of 2001.

While economic integration reached a lethargic state, the bloc has made important political advances: association of Chile and Bolivia, advanced negotiations with the Andean Pact and the recent launch of the South American Community of Nations. Recent political advances on regional integration are a result of political change in three important countries: Brazil, Argentina and Venezuela. The disagreements of Venezuela with the US and of Argentina with the IMF and international finance have been very important in strengthening the regional alliance, although Brazil, which carefully preserves good relations with both the US and the IMF, has taken a low profile position.

Nonetheless, the continuing of regional integration depends on the definition of a regional brand of development strategy, as I argued more profoundly in my recent book on MERCOSUR (Faria, 2004). Summing up, integration has to get a purpose. It is not just a matter of trade improvement, good neighbourhood and peacekeeping. The economic meaning of continental integration in these times of globalisation and for countries like those in MERCOSUR is to find a common way of development. This shared development requires the reindustrialisation of Argentina, investment in backward regions and consideration of small countries' special needs. Though there have been political changes in recent years, like the rise of leftwing governments in many countries of the region, how to start walking towards development is an unanswered question.

The quest for development when formerly put forth, though at a national level, had a reference in the industrialised countries as a vision of the future and reckoned with an international environment friendly for autonomous national development projects. These two conditions do not exist any more. Worse, globalisation is pushing for what can be called market integration. This process is of a specific significance for countries like Brazil. It leads to financial dependency resulting from free capital flows, to lost self-determination via internationalisation of productive chains, to missing national economic integration by way of subordinately linking parts of the productive structure and regions of the national territory to international markets.

Concluding remarks

At the beginning I quoted an ancient self image of Brazilians, when, long ago, they dreamed of a brilliant future to come as a natural consequence of a kind of uniqueness of their country. They started to build this future when they held the tiller of their fate in the great industrialisation adventure. The brightest of Brazilian economists, Celso Furtado, called it "the interrupted construction". Social forces interested in this brand of national oriented development had not the strength to go further in their way. Economic growth was missed for the last 25 years, when foreign debt and financial dependency consolidated another arrangement of social forces ruling the nation's destiny. Economic policy was reshaped in the light of these interests and set new objectives: market oriented reforms and price stabilising macroeconomics.

The triumph of neo-liberalism consolidated not just the empowerment of finance as the main group in the ruling class. It also undermined the compromise of big business in the productive sector with a national brand of development. The top segment of what once was called the national bourgeoisie is now resigned to a secondary role, waiting for foreign investment to lead its movements. As for international trade, the new powers-that-be echoed a Ricardian point of view on the comparative advantages of agribusiness and standardised industrial products exports. As seen above, the most important groups of interest concerned with trade negotiations are the exporters of these products and they allege that their interests are the national ones. In this sense, I argued that trade negotiations may force Brazil, coming back from the future, to land in the past of a primary exports economy.

In the multilateral and bilateral arenas of negotiation, claims from big business exporters are reflected in Brazil's position. At the same time, coordination of developing nations tends to favour these interests, for many of them are just primary products exporters as well. So, what appears as a Third World oriented stand point in negotiations, in defence of the poor, may contribute to crystallising the development gap between North and South. Other items on this agenda, such as textile or even steel, do not change the picture because they are not capable of helping to reduce national economic distances. To poorer countries, endowment for development is economic diversification, which still means that industry requires access to new technologies and is the opposite of exploiting comparative advantages. This is the purpose of the equilibrium provision in the Treaty of Asunción.

South American regional integration and the MERCOSUR are some of what might be the last achievements of the Developmental Era, dreams of the future. The course of action has entered in a semi-lethargic state as it has been challenged by neo-liberal policy and its bias favouring finance that results in economic stagnation. Without a change in the very direction of the economic policy, the prospect of sustainable growth, which is a requirement for continuing integration process, is doomed to failure. For this reason, regional negotiations have an enormous difficulty to go beyond political talks and intention statements. Brazilian government officially declared "FTAA is a possibility, but MERCOSUR is a destiny", in the words of the former President Cardoso. If this destiny is to be fulfilled, the helm of economic policy must get into other hands; policies need to be given a different direction.

References

Bahadian, A. G. (2004), *ALCA: um balanço das negociações*. Rio de Janeiro: September 22, 2004 (lecture at the Superior School of War). http://www.mre. gov.br/portugues/politica_externa/discursos/discursos_autoridade.asp?ID_ AUTORIDADE=11.

Borón, A. (2003), *Estado, capitalismo y democracia en América Latina*. Colección

Secretaria Ejecutiva, Clacso, Consejo Latinoamericano de Ciencias Sociales, Buenos Aires. p.320. http://www.clacso.org/wwwclacso/espanol/html/libros/estado/estado.html.

Bustani, J. M. (2004), *Mitos e desafios da política externa*. Folha de São Paulo. São Paulo: September 9, 2004.

Castro, A. B. (2003), *El segundo catch-up brasileño: características y limitaciones*. Revista de la CEPAL. n. 80, agosto.

Chang, H. W (2003), *Kicking away the ladder: the "real" history of free trade. Foreign Policy In Focus (FPIF)*, Silver City, NM: Interhemispheric Resource Center, December 2003. http://www.fpif.org/papers/03trade/index.html.

Drábek, Z. (2004), *The potential of Doha development agenda. In: Diversity in development: reconsidering the Washington Consensus*, (The Hague: FONDAD), www.fondad.org.

Faria, L. A. (1996), *Fordismo periférico, fordismo tropical y posfordismo: el camiño brasileño de acumulación y crisis*, (Ciclos, Buenos Aires), v. 4, n. 10.

Faria, L. A. (2004), *A chave do tamanho: desenvolvimento econômico e perspectivas do Mercosul*, (Porto Alegre: Editora da UFRGS).

Faria, W. R. (2002), *O impasse do Mercosul. Revista de Informação Legislativa*. Brasília, ano 39 nº 155, jul/set.

Furtado, C. (1966), *Subdesenvolvimento e estagnação na América Latina*, (Rio de Janeiro: Civilização Brasileira).

Gonçalves, R. (1999), *Globalização e desnacionalização*, (São Paulo, Paz e Terra).

Lipietz, A. (1985), *Miragens e milagres: problemas da industrialização no Terceiro Mundo*, (São Paulo: Nobel).

Oliveira, F. (1990), *Os protagonistas do drama. In: LARANJEIRA, S., Classes e movimentos sociais na América Latina*, (São Paulo: Hucitec).

Palma, G. (1978), Dependency: a formal theory of underdevelopment or a methodology for the analysis of concrete situations of underdevelopment. *World Development*, v. 6, pp. 881-924.

Rodrik, D. (1999), *The new global economy and developing countries: making openness work*, (Washington: Overseas development Council).

Santos, M. (1997), *Técnica, espaço, tempo: globalização e meio técnico-científico informacional*, (São Paulo: Editora Hucitec).

Wallerstein, I. (1974), The rise and future demise of the world capitalist system: concepts for comparative analysis. In: *The Essential Wallerstein*, (New York: The New Press).

WTO (2004), *Trade Policy Review: Report By Brazil*. WTO Document WT/TPR/G/140. 1 November 2004.

Internet references

www.ibge.gov.br
www.mict.gov.br/secex
www.asc-hsa.org

Notes

1   Dedicated to the memory of Werter R. Faria, my father, who died on 22 Jnauary 2005. He was a pioneer of Latin American integration and for many years devoted his wise scholarship to Brazilian foreign relations.

2   From the Fundação de Economia e Estatística (FEE) and the Universidade Federal do Rio Grande do Sul (UFRGS) in Porto Alegre. I am very grateful to Joachim Becker for his helpful comments on a first draft. Remaining mistakes are my own. I also thank the Research Assistance Foundation of the State of Rio Grande do Sul (FAPERGS) for its financial support.

3   The sources of data mentioned in this section and to the end of the chapter are, for GDP growth rates and compositions, as well as for exports destination, the Brazilian Institute of Geography and Statistics, IBGE, and for foreign trade, the Secretary of External Trade, SECEX, of the Ministry of Development, Industry and External Trade, MDIC.

4   There is controversy on this point for some authors sustain that the most important part of national firms succeeded in filling this competitive gap (Castro, 2003) and others don't (Gonçalves, 1999).

5   This point is commonly neglected in literature. I think it is a consequence of the neo-classical view of free trade as a good in itself, capable of improving a nation's welfare *per se* and without any negative consequences of importance.

6   It was not surprising that an agreement for a peace zone in the South Atlantic was induced by the US so as to prevent any military consequence of the integration. The Argentina-Brazil approach had sector agreements; one of them was for nuclear cooperation, a very sensible issue to the USA.

7   "Fiscal responsibility" is understood as a budgetary primary surplus, as defined by the IMF, which implies a total deficit, for the interests of public debt are bigger then the primary surplus. If the deficit does not matter anyhow, responsibility intends nothing more then some limit to the public debt/GDP relationship.

8   As will be referred to below, Brazil's larger federation of trade unions, the CUT, joined the Hemispheric Social Alliance, a continental network founded to fight against free trade and the FTAA project, alongside labour federations of other American countries, including USA's AFL-CIO and Canadian trade unions.

9   Brazil and the MERCOSUR countries tried to adopt a strictly bilateral framework within the FTAA negotiations under the formula of 4+1, the bloc plus the US, but the Americans rejected it. To them, bilateral means 1+1 and the USA went on signing free market agreements with many Latin American countries individually, as was the case with Chile.

10   Another handicap, not related directly to trade negotiations is the effect of the reforms on the Balance of Payments, as they raised to the moon the transfers of factors services, and profits sent back home. Besides foreign debt payments, it represents another burden to be carried on by the trade surplus that then needed to be even larger.

11   Let me refer to two things on this subject. First, as Chang (2003) argued, developed countries try to prevent developing ones from doing what they have done to achieve their higher level of development. Second and most importantly, there is a theoretical issue. Institutions are a result of social history; they come to light specifically in the transforming evolution of any social formation. So, to transfer or to impose from abroad an institutional arrangement from one society to another results in artificiality and malfunctioning and different effects will necessarily ensue.

12   Under Brazilian law, in cases of public interest, the Ministry of Health can compulsory license the production of drugs in generic form without payment of intellectual property rights. The public interest was evoked when pharmaceutical companies refused to reduce the prices of some drugs purchased by the government for anti-AIDS purposes and other programmes of public health in the middle of the 1990s. The World Health Organization applauded this policy and urges other nations to follow Brazil's example, considering it a necessary step to fight against the AIDS epidemics in Africa.

13   In fact, this is an optimistic expectation of the Brazilian negotiators, for the actors in the Doha Round are almost the same as in the Uruguay one. Nevertheless, there is a best coordination of developing countries within the WTO and, undoubtedly, in a multilateral arena the balance of power is most favourable to these countries *vis à vis* a bilateral negotiation.

14   The opposition of developing countries on the subject of trade facilitation is more a matter of suspicion then of real interest. It seems as if bureaucracy and its impeding practices were necessary to defend national interests in international trade.

15   On February 16, 2005, a Subcommittee of the Canadian Parliament passed a motion recommending to the Standing Committee on Foreign Affairs and International Trade that it undertake a complete review of NAFTA Chapters 11 and 19, corresponding to the investor-state and the dispute settlement provisions, which are viewed as eroding Canadian sovergneinty. NAFTA Ch.11 is also being challenged in the Canadians courts as unconstitutional.

Chapter 7

Join my Value Chain!
South Africa's Regional Trade Policy

Gottfried Wellmer

Introduction: Rupture and continuity

The struggle for democracy in South Africa imprinted itself on social and economic structures and radiated into the whole of the Southern African region, which also struggled for an end to colonialism. The resistance to apartheid was a very broad movement, embracing local, national and international protesters, national democratic and socialist revolutionaries. It stretched from civil rights movements to non-racial class struggles. The resistance achieved a negotiated compromise that contains both rupture and continuity with the old system. For example, regarding the future state two broad options were articulated by different interest groups (Maré 2004:33ss).

If the majority in the resistance against apartheid understood the state as racially exclusive and – on second though – also economically exploitative, then the democratic restructuring might aim to make the new state reflect the racialised demographics of South African society. It would therefore enable a new racialised black bourgeoisie to emerge as the prime beneficiary of new state policy – a repetition of what the Nationalist Party had done 60 years earlier for the Afrikaner versus the British.

If the dominant interpretation of the past struggle had been that the system was capitalist, within which racial discrimination served to strengthen particular forms of exploitation, then the working class would have carried the whole liberation movement to a complete rupture with corporate capitalism and the embedded racism within it in favour of an alternative system of production.

The South African Communist Party deferring to the African National Congress wrote in the mid-1970s: "the main content of the *immediate* struggle for change is the national liberation of the African people and, with it, the destruction of all forms of racial discrimination". (Slovo, 1977, 134) The SACP's concept of the two-stage national-democratic revolution saw to it that radical demands were kept out of transitional negotiations. Recently the secretary general of the communist party, Blade Nzimande, lamented the small number of people able to profit from the Black Economic Empowerment programme. He said: "it is a deliberate attempt to rapidly create a layer of black bourgeoisie by both the state and incumbent capital".

(Malefane 2005). With the end of the Cold War and the collapse of the Soviet Union, the first option had won the day. The state – whose legality was not questioned – was inherited at most levels, even though apartheid laws were cancelled and a new democratic constitution installed. Some state structures were abolished, like the Bantustan authorities and the tricameral parliament. Most structures were merely reformed to meet new demands.

When the ANC was unbanned in 1990, it needed an economic policy outline as a bargaining position for negotiations on a future economic dispensation (Ismail 1994, 50–59). The Economic Trends Group of the Trade Union Federation COSATU had already made serious efforts to chart an economic strategy. The first ANC attempt was a 1990 "Discussion Document on Economic Policy" that reflected much of the thinking of its allies in the labour unions. It envisaged an active role for the future state in planning industrial strategy and overcoming social inequalities. Its overriding theme was 'growth through redistribution'. The state should take a strong role in redistributing wealth and income. This was to be achieved by developing domestic industry's production to meet the demand for the basic needs and better living standards of the masses and growing the economy on the basis of an expanding domestic market while seeking simultaneously to diversify production and increase the competitiveness of export industries. The left wing of the ANC alliance wanted a growth path resting on both inward industrialisation and export promotion, aiming at expanding domestic demand and social infrastructure, a Keynesian programme (Marais 2001, 124–126). Industrial production of goods for poor consumers was expected to have a higher labour component and a lower imported content; it would boost output and employment more than the capital intensive production in most of the industries of South Africa. The Macro-Economic Research Group expanded this approach into a coherent policy framework (MERG 1993).

South African corporations started a massive campaign against this first discussion document, denouncing it as "macro-economic populism". It warned that such a programme would soon run into budgetary, monetary and balance of payments constraints; depreciation of the currency and inflation would soon follow. The IMF backed the argument by declaring that the remedy for structural unemployment was to increase the productivity of labour and to lower the real wage (IMF 1992). Already in May 1992, the revised economic policy guidelines of the ANC no longer made reference to the formula of growth from redistribution. Even COSATU economists ended up arguing for South Africa's economic revival through an export-led growth strategy (Joffe, Kaplan, Kaplinski, Lewis 1994). Before taking office, the ANC on the insistence of the IMF and local corporations had endorsed a policy of fiscal and monetary austerity, restricted the role of the state in regard to income redistribution and supported the liberalisation of trade in line with an export-led growth strategy. The ANC had hoped that local and international capital would reciprocate and launch the economy on a new growth track that would enable government to reduce poverty and the high rate of unemployment. The first part of this article examines the outcome of this strategy.

From 1980 to 1993 per capita gross domestic product in South Africa suffered an average annual decline of almost one percent. During the second half of the 1980s, South Africa's industrial policy attempted to shift from import substitution to export orientation and liberalised trade. This took place shortly after the debt crisis, when the whole country was under martial law. When South Africa initiated trade liberalisation, the outside world had imposed economic sanctions against Apartheid. The prolonged recession set the terms for democratic South Africa's re-integration into the global economy. The European Union was and still is South Africa's main partner in foreign economic relations, both in terms of trade and of investment. The urgent need to recuperate from economic sanctions, capital flight and negative GDP growth rates and to regain creditworthiness and investment flows made an agreement with the EU the most important task of the new democratic government. After the lifting of sanctions, South Africa applied to join the EU's Lomé IV accord with the ACP in order to implement its Reconstruction and Development Programme (RDP) under favourable trade conditions. The RDP aimed to increase the rate of economic growth, of investment and of wage employment. It also wanted greater equality in the distribution of income and wealth. The European Union rejected this application and persuaded South Africa to negotiate a free trade agreement instead. The South African negotiators learned quickly that their main trade partner was set to abolish non-reciprocal trade preferences and funds to stabilise deteriorating terms of trade for primary exports of ACP members. Hoping for increased investment flows and expanding exports in industrial products, South Africa negotiated a reciprocal FTA.

There were concerns, though, that the inequality of the parties concerned would increase the trade imbalance in the EU's favour. South African producers would also face high adjustment costs for having to liberalise trade faster than agreed to in the WTO and for having to compete in their domestic market against more competitive EU producers. South Africa wanted to add to the trade chapter further agreements on financial aid, technological co-operation and support for industrial restructuring. The EU pressed for the inclusion of issues that went beyond WTO agreements. These included investment protection, trade development, competition policy, government procurement and also the free movement of capital. Apart from confirming WTO obligations towards intellectual property protection and the strict observance of GATS, parties also endeavoured "to extend the scope of the agreement". Signing these WTO-plus demands of the EU, South Africa in fact undermined the position of the ACP in negotiations of a post-Lomé accord and of the WTO's so-called Doha Development Agenda.

Apart from the impact of an EU-SA FTA on the revenues of the other members of the Southern African Customs Union (SACU), it was acknowledged that the FTA would impact negatively on intra-SADC trade and the chances of other SADC states to increase their exports to South Africa. During negotiations there was an agreement in principle that SADC exporters should temporarily enjoy preferential access to the South African market over competitors from the EU. But this concession was small, when considering existing supply side constraints of SADC producers.

In order to support industrial transformation, South Africa also initiated a homemade structural adjustment programme, misleadingly called Growth, Employment and Redistribution (GEAR). It aimed to decrease the fiscal deficit and the inflation rate in order to reduce the real bank interest rate from 7,0 percent (1996) to 3,0 percent in 2000. The authors of the programme predicted that a fall in interest rates would provoke a rise in private investment. That was to lend 93 percent of the stimulus to achieve a higher GDP growth rate. This was based on the assumption that when the state borrowed to finance a deficit, it competed with the private sector for saving and thus raises interest rates. However, no empirical evidence was provided to demonstrate that the assumed "crowding out effect" was an important factor in the mid-1990s. Gear's scenario also projected an increase in the ratio of the external current account deficit as a consequence of increased imports from the EU, causing a net depression of domestic demand. The real exchange rate should devaluate on average by – 1,8 percent. The scenario did not foresee the possibility that a stronger weakening of the Rand could provoke the Reserve Bank to act independently to raise interest rates. That is what happened. The actual real bank rate increased to an average of almost 10 percent (1996–2000). That could have been avoided, if Government had continued with the commercial and the financial rand system to control forex flows. In hindsight, GEAR was not at all necessary, because inflation was relatively low at the time and the foreign debt was manageable. The Reserve Bank did not need to defend the Rand by raising interest rates, because the external current account deficit was more than balanced by long term capital inflows (Weeks, 2000). GEAR was actually harmful, because inflation and deficit reduction was achieved at the cost of very low GDP growth rates and a substantial loss of employment.

Before the TDCA was signed the EU proposal to the ACP group to negotiate regional free trade economic partnership agreements was well known. This raised questions concerning the policy of both the EU and South Africa towards the future of SADC. How would the EU's neo-classical concept of market integration relate to the SADC concept of development integration? Would the EU have a separate FTA with the rest of SADC excluding South Africa and other members of SACU? If so, how would that be compatible with SADC's own FTA? Would it be the intention of the EU and South Africa to extend the TDCA to the rest of SADC, despite the fact that half the SADC members were LDCs and had a very different economic/industrial structure than South Africa? If so, would the TDCA be re-negotiated? Would the new TDCA be based on the trading strengths of South Africa or the weaknesses of the SADC-LDCs? Would SADC have a future at all after the TDCA, the new round at the WTO and the conclusion of EPAs between the EU and assorted ACP groups?

In 1994 the EU institutionalised a political dialogue with South Africa and the other regional SADC member states trying to convince them of the merits of "open regionalism" versus collectively determined regional development. Opening up regions for the EU's non-agricultural goods and services is one objective the EU follows up in both bilateral and WTO negotiations. The FTA between South Africa and the EU was the first step in opening the SADC region by picking out the economically most potent member state. The second step was the EU's offers of an FTA with the rest of the SADC states according to the Cotonou agreement. Negotiations on the so-called Economic Partnership Agreements (EPAs) caused a break up between those states structurally very dependent on South Africa – mainly SACU and Mozambique - and the others. In negotiating EPAs the EU again raised demands regarding the Singapore issues and specific measures in trade liberalisation which go far beyond current WTO agreements (Wellmer 2005, 20–28).

The EU also influenced Pretoria's policy change towards the Southern African region. The South African government did a) impose the EU's rules of origin on to the SADC-FTA, and b) adopt a protectionist attitude towards competitive SADC producers. In 2000 trade politicians in South Africa could still assert: "Regional integration must be developmental … Trade agreements must be asymmetrical and …be accompanied by effective programmes … to address supply capacity constraints and infrastructural deficiencies" (Davies 2000, 25). That was a reaffirmation of the old SADC concept of 1992. But in October 2001 South Africa also formulated together with Nigeria and Senegal the New Partnership for Africa's Development (NEPAD) and made this second edition of GEAR a programme for the African Union. NEPAD sees SADC as one out of five regional economic communities (RECs), which are to evolve from FTAs to Custom Unions. These would later unite in an African Common Market with a single currency. That is a neo-classical concept following the example of the European Union (RSA 2003). In NEPAD South Africa plays the intermediary offering to help open up Africa's markets to global corporations. Simultaneously, South Africa does invite its regional neighbours to integrate their industries into the primary production end of the value chains of its own corporations. To examine this process a look at South Africa's Strategic Development Initiative is of interest. The investment into aluminium smelter MOZAL operated on a tri-lateral level outside the SADC institutional framework serves as an example. There are fears that this integration into South African corporate accumulation strategies would exacerbate the acute imbalances in regional economic relations and increase polarisation within the region. South Africa's corporations may just continue to play their traditional role as agents of global capital's interests.

South Africa's shift towards export orientated industrialisation policy

One may distinguish roughly between four periods: initial industrialisation 1911–1925, import substitution led industrialisation 1925–1975, stagflation and transition 1975–1994, and attempts at export led growth since 1994. South Africa's early robust growth performance in manufacturing reached its peak between 1960–1965 with an average GDP growth rate of 6,3 percent, a value added growth in manufacturing of 9,9 percent and an employment growth rate in manufacturing of almost 7 percent. In difference to South Korea or other NICs, South Africa's economic growth deteriorated since the early 1970s and has been poor during 1982–1994 (Table 7.1). South Africa's industrial policy was forced by a debt crisis in the mid-1980s to abruptly shift from import substitution to export orientation. Various economic sectors in the economy reacted very differently to the shift. Since this process sets the perimeters of the political space in which a newly elected democratic government had to move and make decisions from 1994 onwards (and even before), we must sketch the main events and factors which came to shape developments.

Table 7.1   **Average annual growth rates of GDP, manufacturing valued added (MVA) and manufacturing employment in South Africa 1960–1995, in percent**

Period	GDP growth	MVA growth	Manufacturing Employment
1960-1970	5.71	8.61	4.87
1970-1980	3.37	5.20	2.91
1980-1990	1.51	1.27	0.78
1990-1995	0.86	0.15	-1.25

Source: Bell, Madula, 2001: 7

The international currency crisis between 1968–1972 unsettled the marketing of South African gold, then at a stable international price of US$ 35 per fine ounce. It also unsettled the South African Balance of Payments. This came at a time, when post World War II gold exports, which had been boosted by the opening up of the deep level OFS gold- and uranium mines, suffered a decline during 1965–1970 of 0,9 percent a year anyway. The Reynders Commission was set up in 1969 to inquire into South Africa's export trade and proposed that the state should start to promote the diversification into non-gold exports, including manufactures.

Table 7.2   **Average annual growth rates in South Africa's external trade, 1960–1995, percent**

Period	Merchandise exports	Net Gold Exports	Total Exports	Merchandise Imports
In constant (1995) US Dollars				
1960-1970	4.04	3.10	3.70	7.12
1970-1980	9.49	16.39	12.37	7.52
1980-1985	-8.93	-14.24	-11.43	-13.06
1985-1990	10.38	-2.11	5.77	7.46
1990-1995	5.16	-3.80	2.88	8.13

Source: Bell, Madula, 2001: 31

From 1971/2 to 1981 there was a new commodity price boom, during which the price of South Africa's gold, for example, increased from an average US$ 52 in 1972 to $ 613 per fine ounce in 1980 – reflected in strong net gold exports

(Table 7.2). This boom in fact delayed the strategic shift from import substitution to export orientation.

A major effect of that boom was a real appreciation of the foreign exchange value of the rand. The real effective exchange rate in 1982–1983 was 28 percent higher than in 1970–1972. This appreciation caused the exports of natural resource based manufactures to grow at almost 12 percent a year during 1970–1980 (Table 7.2), while the downstream durable goods group of industries saw their export growth rate reduced from about 8 percent a year (1960–1970) to only 2,1 percent (1970–1980). But the output of the durable goods producers increased because of high rates in gross fixed capital formation especially in the resource based group of industries led by private mining corporations and parastatals like Iscor, Eskom and Sasol. During 1973–1983 total manufacturing output increased by 50,1 percent because domestic demand increased by 44,6 percent and South African firms displaced imports and increased the share in the home market by an additional 3,0 percents of output growth, while export growth increased by 2,5 percent. (Belli, Finger, Ballivian 1993, 26–27).

Table 7.3   **Shares of Industrial Sectors in South Africa's Total Manufacturing Value Added in Constant 1995 Prices. Manufactured Exports and Export Growth Rates (percent)**

	Value Added, shares in total MVA%			Shares in manufactured exports %			Annual export growth rate %
	1980	**1985**	**1990**	**1980**	**1985**	**1990**	**1980-90**
Chemicals	11.98	15.86	14.14	14.56	15.80	13.44	2.09
Iron and Steel	7.23	6.25	5.89	13.62	18.21	19.82	6.84
Non-ferrous basic metals	1.49	1.75	1.73	7.52	5.77	7.52	4.64
Pulp and Paper	3.99	4.91	4.85	2.53	4.52	4.59	9.23
Total Natural Resource-Based Group	**24.70**	**28.77**	**26.61**	**37.07**	**50.60**	**45.37**	**5.01**
Fabricated Metal Products	8.28	6.98	5.13	1.84	1.66	3.27	9.00
Machinery and Equipment	9.52	8.28	6.86	4.36	4.35	5.65	5.61
Electrical Machinery	3.85	3.88	2.73	1.01	0.80	1.24	5.02
Motor Vehicles	9.28	6.86	7.54	1.71	2.20	3.28	9.85
Other transport equipment	1.29	1.10	0.71	0.68	0.58	0.72	3.59
Total Durable Goods Group	**32.21**	**27.10**	**22.98**	**9.60**	**9.59**	**14.16**	**6.99**
Textiles	3.95	3.28	2.43	3.38	4.03	3.77	4.05
Clothing	2.71	2.77	2.84	1.74	1.93	1.65	2.41
Total labour-intensive group	**11.18**	**10.75**	**9.74**	**7.26**	**8.27**	**8.04**	**3.96**
TV, Radio and communication equipment	0.53	0.71	1.20	0.21	0.34	0.46	10.96
Professional & scientific equipment	0.11	0.21	0.28	0.30	0.35	0.45	6.92
Other manufacturing sectors	**31.26**	**32.46**	**39.19**	**45.55**	**30.84**	**31.53**	**-0.81**

Source: Bell, Madula 2001, 61–64

With the collapse of the commodity price boom (especially of the gold price) and in the context of the OECD recession of 1980–1983, South African exports of mined minerals fell and the natural resource based group in manufacturing decreased its average annual export growth from 10,5 percent to 5,01 percent (Table 7.3). Between 1983-1990 domestic demand increased by a meagre 1,6 percent, local companies lost domestic market shares to imports, which caused an additional decline in output by -3,3 percent. The national currency (Rand) began to depreciate in late 1983, and fell rapidly from mid-1984. This culminated in the debt crisis of August 1985 and the rescheduling of foreign debt. Together with the domestic recession, growing resistance to apartheid, the declaration of a state of emergency, martial law and foreign sanctions, investment fell by 20 percent between 1984 and 1986, and there was a sharp reduction in gross domestic expenditure.

In response to the crisis, the state initiated a system of incentives for exports. Quantitative restrictions on imports were reduced and in early 1989 schemes of duty-free imports for export production were introduced in the motor vehicles, textiles and clothing industries. In April 1990 a General Export Incentive Scheme (GEIS) was initiated as well. Between 1990 and 1995 import surcharges, which had been imposed during the debt crisis, were removed again. Thus, in conditions of economic crisis, the long delayed shift towards export-oriented industrialisation began.

If one looks at the average annual rates of growth of manufactured export during the 1980s (Table 7.3), it is striking that the total durable goods group enjoyed an annual export growth rate of almost 7 percent (from 0,72 percent in 1970–1980). The resource based industry group had a diminished export growth rate. In general, the ratio of manufactured exports to the total sales of manufacturing industry increased from 9,1 percent in 1983 to 12,7 percent in 1990. As the World Bank economists put it: "Exports expanded after 1983 mostly because, in the face of the contraction of domestic demand, firms sought exports as a vent for surplus capacity" (Belli, Finger, Ballivian 1993, 27).

On the other hand, the other industry groups suffered stagnation if not reduction in their value added. This also showed up negatively in a loss of places of employment (Table 7.1). The question for the future democratically elected government was then whether the abrupt shift towards increased export orientation during domestic crisis may not have been a sign of some deeper problem? Trevor Bell named it the problem of *export orientated stagnation*.

The impact of trade liberalisation under a democratically elected government

The end of the Cold War offered the people of South Africa a window of opportunity to rid themselves of the apartheid system. The negotiating power of the ANC was, however, weakened by a number of factors. It had not gained any decisive victory over the security forces of the Apartheid State, so could not dictate the agenda or terms of negotiation. Secondly, having struggled since 1912 for rights and freedoms of the discriminated majority, the ANC was about to gain political power at a time when socialism had collapsed and with it a host of future options. The space for decision making became narrow. Thirdly, with structural adjustment in full swing in indebted developing countries, it would be difficult to develop a welfare state model for the racially discriminated, politically oppressed, and chronically poor. Finally, with the end of the Cold War, the OECD was fast losing its former strategic interests in the Southern African region.

Even before the first democratic elections, the ANC raised the right to private property to the level of a constitutional principal. The ANC's policy documents indicated a readiness to privatise state owned enterprises and public corporations. At the end of 1993, the ANC was ready to guarantee the independence of the Reserve Bank: the central national bank was to be free from parliamentary control and did not have to follow government's political directions. This meant that the oligarchs of the private sector, which owned 80 percent of the country's mines, industries and finance houses gained increasing influence over central bank policy. (Marais 2001, 133). In November 1993 the transitional government entered into a $850-million balance of payments loan agreement with the IMF, committing itself in a letter of intent to reduce in future the government budget deficit. In 1993 South Africa signed the Agreement on the GATT Uruguay Round. When it joined the WTO as a member in 1995, it shaped its tariff structure, reducing the number of tariff levels from ten to six. The range of export promotion options open to the government was sharply reduced. This meant in particular the ending of the general export incentive scheme (GEIS) at the end of 1996. On the other hand, South Africa was granted the status of an "economy in transition", placing it between "developed" and "developing" economies, so that South Africa gained some flexibility in the timetable for restructuring its trade regime. Therefore, import tariff liberalisation could potentially become less onerous and destructive to national producers (EIU 2001, 50).

The World Bank's 1993 examination of South Africa's trade policies came to the conclusion that the trade regime was far too complex and also biased against exports. What irritated the World Bank economists the most was that South Africa's tariff schedule appeared extraordinarily variable, changing from week to week. The bank saw two sources of an anti-export bias: firstly, protection made sales in the domestic market more profitable than exports, and secondly, protection increased the cost of inputs for all producers. The World Bank therefore recommended to 1) reduce the number of rates, 2) eliminate quantitative restrictions, and 3) to levy tariffs on an *ad valorem* basis while simultaneously reducing the highest rates. The World Bank warned that a tariff reduction would not have any positive impact on employment or output growth. It would merely simplify the system. The World Bank quoted the South African Chamber of Business' complaint that South African manufacturing costs were 15 percent higher than the OECD average, because exporting firms had to pay 24 percent more than OECD competitors for their inputs and also because their capital costs were higher. The World Bank stressed that it was possible to achieve export neutrality while maintaining protection for the domestic market. The World Bank economists were of the opinion that there was a statistically significant association between growth in total factor productivity and export expansion - rather than general output growth.

Table 7.4   Changing levels of protection in selected sub-sectors, (percent)

	1994	1995	1996	1997	1998	1999	2000	2001	2002	GATT binding
Clothing	74	72	67	62	57	51	46	41	36	41
Motor vehicles	51	42	40	37	35	33	31	29	27	40
All Industry	15	11	10	9	9	8	8	7	7	16

Source: Roberts, 1998: 12

The ANC led government offered GATT a one-third decline in the average tariff level over five years, the abolition of surcharges on certain imports and the removal of quantitative restrictions on imports. These moves merely continued trade liberalisation trends started by the previous administration. However, over and beyond GATT binding levels, the ANC led government did undertake tariff reductions more profoundly and rapidly than originally agreed (Table 7.4). Despite negotiating longer phase down periods for clothing, textiles and motor vehicles, the ANC government decided not to make use of the full transition period and to reduce tariffs to below the GATT binding. To give an example: a 12-year period had been negotiated in order to reduce the maximum tariff for clothing imports to 45 percent. The Government decided to implement an eight-year schedule, during which the maximum tariff was to be reduced to an average of 40 percent. Table 7.4 shows the steepest tariff reductions in sectors previously most heavily protected.

The Director General of the DTI viewed tariff reductions as part of a general restructuring of industry. The process was to be based on investments in new technologies, on human resource development and an increase in total factor productivity (TFP). He anticipated that the restructuring process could involve shifting low-skill/low-wage industries to other countries in Sub-Saharan Africa (a continental division of labour, securing South Africa the high-skill, high-wage industries). The DG expected that tariff reforms would also help bring down the inflation rate and ease the cost of living for the poor. The DG maintained that tariff reforms were not pursued merely because of the GATT agreement, but that they were rather required as a precondition for South Africa's development (Rustomjee, 1977).

During the period 1991–1995, exports of sub-sectors in manufacturing increased markedly (Table 7.5). Of 26 recorded sub-sectors, 14 increased their exports by more than 15 percent, a further 6 sub-sectors increased their exports by between 5–14,9 percent. Only in three sub-sectors did exports actually decrease. Yet, the growth in manufacturing value added (MVA) was negative (-1,6 percent), reflecting the fact that exports constituted only 11,1 percent of manufacturing output, and had therefore too small a share to contribute decisively to growth. The GDP was almost stagnant with a growth rate of 0,86 percent, and overall the manufacturing industries demand for labour decreased by 2,3 percent. In the early 1990s there was only one sector – that of non-metallic minerals – with an increase of total factor productivity by 5,7 percent, an increase in value added by 2,6 percent, and in employment by

4,2 percent, and an increase in exports by almost 15 percent (Cassim et al. 2003, Tables 17–18). Therefore, initial effects of trade liberalisation offered no evidence for the assumed link of export led growth to employment and development. The spectre of 'export orientated stagnation' had not been dismissed.

Table 7.5　　**Revealed comparative advantage (RCA) and average growth rates in exports, value added and employment of South African manufacturing sectors**

SIC Code	Sector	Change in RCA 1991-96	RCA 1996	Growth rates in % 1991-1995			RCA 2004
				Exports	MVA	employment	
301-304	Processed Food	-0.29	-0.15	5.9	- 1.2	- 2.8	-0.09
305	Beverages	+0.27	+0.27	+ 24.4	1.6	- 3.6	+0.54
306	Tobacco products	+0.80	+0.49	- 2.9	- 0.2	- 7.1	+0.59
311-312	Textiles	-0.03	-0.32	4.9	4.8	- 7.7	-0.35
313-315	Clothing	-0.08	-0.08	0.1	- 2.8	3.2	-0.43
316	Leather products	+0.34	+0.11	+ 29.6	- 0.4	- 5.3	-0.44
3170	Footwear	+0.07	-0.79	+ 45.1	- 4.8	- 1.2	-0.92
321-322	Wood products	-0.09	-0.43				-0.22
391	Furniture	-0.11	+0.54	+ 58.8	2.9	+ 3.0	+0.45
323	Pulp and paper	-0.05	0.22	+ 20.6	2.8	0.2	+0.33
324-326	Printing & publishing	+0.55	-0.24	+ 29.0	2.3	+ 0.6	-0.59
331-333	Petrol, Coal products			- 1.3	1.1	- 3.6	+0.16
334	Industrial Chemicals	+0.35	+0.02	+18.1	0.1	- 2.4	+0.02
335-336	Other chemicals	+0.09	-0.60	+ 29.3	3.5	- 1.7	-0.45
337	Rubber products	+0.17	-0.42	+ 18.8	2.6	- 0.5	-0.21
338	Plastic products	+0.16	-0.51	+34.4	4.8	+ 0.2	-0.39
3411	Glass products	-0.16	-0.43	+1.8	4.8	+ 0.8	-0.26
342	Non-metallic mineral products	+0.06	-0.27	+ 14.9	2.6	+ 4.2	-0.29
351	Basic iron & steel	-0.02	+0.77	+ 7.9	0.3	- 6.2	+0.79
352	Precious NF metals	-0.05	+0.74	- 3.1	6.6	- 5.9	+0.57
353-355	Metal products	+0.18	+0.04	+ 14.0	- 0.1	- 1.5	-0.10
356-359	machinery & equipment	+0.23	-0.68	+ 26.5	- 1.3	- 0.5	-0.46
361-366	Electrical machinery	-0.19	-0.76	+ 29.1	3.0	+ 0.5	-0.42
381-383	Motor vehicles, parts,	-0.01	-0.71	+ 13.2	- 0.6	- 0.6	-0.32
384-387	Other transport equipment	0.35	-0.43	+ 21.7	- 4.1	- 10.7	-0.795
371-373	TVs, radios, communication			+ 24.2	- 0.9	0.0	+0.66
374-376	professional equipment	+0.08	-0.78	+ 12.4	- 6.7	+ 1.4	-0.70

Source: Roberts 1998, 21 and DTI, manufacturing trade by SIC for 2004. Note: RCA= trade balance divided by total trade. A value of +1,0 indicates exports with no imports; zero indicates balanced trade; a value of minus 1,0 indicates imports only with no exports

There is an overall deficit in the net export ratio of manufacturing industry. It was -0,21 percent in 1991 and -1,17 in 1996; it sank to -0,11 in 2001 and in the first half year of 2005 it was back to -0,16 percent. 18 sub-sectors within manufacturing industry have a negative revealed comparative advantage. However, there are 15 sub-sectors that show a positive net export ratio.

If economic sub-sectors with improved net export ratios (Table 7.5) nevertheless show less employment, less real output and use less than full productive capacity, what then is meant by the concept of competitiveness or export-led growth as distinct from liberalisation? Sub-sectors with positive but decreased net export ratios indicate a higher growth of imports compared to export growth: domestic producers may be losing ground to foreign producers.

If export bias was to be removed in order to facilitate increased exports and new growth in output, then one should expect the effects to be greatest in those manufacturing sub-sectors, where the original tariffs had been highest. Between 1993 and 2000 tariffs on textiles decreased by an average 67,4 percent, tariffs on clothing by 75,2 percent (Table 7.7). While the textile sub-sector increased exports by 4,9 percent during the first half of the 1990s, employment decreased by 7,7 percent. Clothing is the most labour intensive sub-sector and accounted for about 10 percent of manufacturing employment; this sub-sector is important for possible employment generation. But clothing exports had only a 0,1 percent growth in the first half of the 1990s, while employment increased by 3,2 percent, reflecting the impact of government support programmes. During the second half of the 1990s the picture changed. Textile exports turned negative, while clothing exports increased by 11,3 percent. However, in both sub-sectors places of employment were cut: in textiles by 9,5 percent and in clothing by 1,5 percent. Value added was negative for clothing throughout the decade of the 1990s. A developmental effect of trade liberalisation cannot be observed.

In the transport equipment sector, tariffs were decreased by 98,9 percent between 1993 to 2000. The sector improved exports by 21,7 percent and 15,9 percent for the two halves of the 90s, but output decreased slightly between 1991 and 1996 as did value added. Employment in this sub-sector fell by more than 10 percent in the decade. The increase in exports may have been a reaction to both falling domestic demand as well as government incentives for exports. Unfortunately, statistics on the demand of the domestic market are not available, even though domestic demand must be decisive for the growth of a sub-sector, if manufacturing exports make up only 21,1 percent of manufacturing output during 1995–2001 (11,1 percent for 1989–1994). During the second half of the 1990s output increased by 15 percent and so did imports, but value added decreased and so did employment (see also Table 7.7). This reinforces doubts over the hypothesis of an export led growth and development concept.

All manufacturing sub-sectors shed places of employment during the 1990s, regardless of skill levels (Table 7.6). Temporarily (1989–1994) there was a new demand for high-skilled labour. But this was limited to the transition phase. In general, low economic growth was achieved by maintaining output while reducing the labour force. At the same time, the informal sector with its shadow labour grew exponentially. Now a whole series of activities could only be done in the informal sector, because they found no market under the existing formalised conditions.

Table 7.6   **Shares (percent) in demand for labour in selected sectors**

Sectors	Highly skilled labour		Medium Skilled		Low Skilled		Overall Share	
	1989-94	1995-01	1989-94	1995-01	1989-94	'95-01	'89-94	'94-2001
Community Services	60.2	62.5	33.9	37.2	26.1	29.1	33.1	37.1
Manufacturing	12.5	11.7	15.4	14.2	22.7	22.6	18.9	17.8
Agriculture	0.9	1.2	1.1	1.2	20.0	20.9	11.0	10.7
Trade	9.7	9.6	23.5	23.3	5.4	5.8	12.3	12.8
Mining	1.7	1.6	2.8	2.6	13.1	10.9	8.1	6.4
All industries	2.8	-1.3	-0.4	-0.5	-2.4	-2.3	-1.1	-1.5

Source: Cassim, Onyango et al., 2003:19–25

There may be other factors apart from trade liberalisation that may have had a higher impact on exports and general macro-economic performance. The exchange rate fluctuations give a few pointers. In the second half of 1997 there was a strong depreciation of the Asian currencies; a little later (2nd quarter of 1998) there was turmoil in South Africa's financial market. Reduced demand in Asia led to a decrease of commodity prices in 1998. Commodity producers like South Africa saw significant declines in export earnings, which led to a deepening deficit on the current account of its Balance of Payments. South Africa witnessed an outflow of capital during the 3rd quarter of 1998. Foreign trade was discouraged by the high cost of forward cover. A substantial depreciation of the Rand took place: minus 19,4 percent against the Euro, 21,4 percent against the UK Pound and 20,1 percent against the US$. This raised the price of tradable products. Also import prices rose from 0,8 percent (2nd quarter of 1998) to 26,9 percent (3rd quarter 1998). There was an increase in interest rates and in the domestic markets demand for durable goods declined. According to South Africa's Reserve Bank there were inordinately high levels of job losses in late 1997 and early 1998. As a consequence, the number of man-days lost to stoppages and strike action rose from 310 000 in the first three-quarters of 1997 to 1,85 million in the corresponding period of 1998 (SARB, QB: December 1998). An even stronger depreciation of the Rand took place between 2000 and the 3rd quarter of 2002.

Of interest are also the investment activities of the South African private sector. Between 1997 and 2001 the net capital formation of private business in South Africa added up to 118.086 million Rand. During the same period corporate savings amounted to 172.911 million Rand, whereas the outflow of capital owned by South African residents of the private non-banking sector ran up to 170.104 million Rand. (SARB, QB March 2000; September 2005). During the last three years the outflow of private capital out of South Africa became less of an issue, which favoured net capital formation and corporate savings.

During the second half of the 1990s, output in manufacturing increased by an average of about 1,8 percent, a relatively slow growth rate. A few sub-sectors have performed better than average. Higher export growth rates were recorded (Table 7.7) in the car industry (31,4 percent), TV and communication equipment (29,2 percent), machinery and equipment (16,4 percent) and other transport equipment (15,9 percent). Of the natural resource based industries, four sub-sectors within the chemical industries showed an export growth of more than 8 percent (rubber, plastic products, glass products). Iron and steel, however, as well as basic chemicals were mostly stagnant, probably influenced by the currency turmoil described above. As a result, even more labour was getting the sack than in the first half of the 1990s. Compared to the rest of the economy, manufacturing's export performance with a 7,4 percent growth rate was better than the average export growth of the total economy (4,1 percent). However, growth in value added was only 1,2 percent in manufacturing, compared to 2,3 percent for the economy as a whole.

Looking back, the Department of Trade and Industry remarked in 2002:

> The ANC and COSATU had undertaken substantial trade and industrial policy investigations, such as the Industrial Strategy Project and the Macroeconomic Research Group. Between 1992 and 1994, the groundwork for an agreement on trade policy reform was laid in the context of South Africa's negotiation in the Uruguay Round. The interventions made prior to 1994 were inadequate for the task at hand ... While at the time the (new) government did not clearly articulate a coherent industrial policy framework ... significant trade reforms took place in order to open the economy and create opportunities for growth and improved competitiveness ... In general the tendency was towards a lowering and simplification of tariffs. This process took place from 1995 and was largely completed in 2002.   (The DTI 2002, 9–12)

Industrial policy's shift to export orientation happened about 20 years ago. The latest census on manufacturing industry occurred in 2001, there is none more recent. Some simple observations on the effect of export orientation may be drawn:

- Trade protection was judged to have had a negative effect on industrial growth in the past. Now that tariffs have been lowered and simplified, it is surprising that manufacturing industry has not gained more from liberalisation (Table 7.5).
- Exports of goods and services have increased (with the exception of 2003) and imports of goods and services have also increased (with the exception of 1999). However, the gross value added of manufacturing actually decreased in 1998 and 2003. Similarly, the share of manufacturing in the gross value added of the total economy decreased from 26,4 percent (1981) to 22,8 percent (1991), 19,0 percent (2001) to 17,9 percent (2004). In terms of classification of world merchandise exporters, South Africa lost its 16th place (1980) and was ranked 27th in 2001 (WTO 2003, A4-219; Bond 2000, 38).
- Despite export growth in some sectors, manufacturing's net export ratio has been slightly negative over the last 15 years.

Even in 2001 the group of natural resource based industries still had a 42 percent share of value added in manufacturing. It makes this group the anchor of manufacturing value added since 1980 (Table 7.3). The same group maintains also a leading share in manufactured exports. This industrial group reveals a high degree of capital concentration, strong sub-sector linkages (Innes 1984, 166–219), and close co-operation with the state that intervened to help develop iron and steel, the

Table 7.7   Effect of trade liberalisation, 1996–2000

Manufacturing Sector	Tariffs change 1993-2000 (%)	Tariff 2000 average %	MVA change %	Exports change , %	Employment change, %
301-4 Food	- 37.3	8.4	-2.3	-1.6	-3.6
305 Beverages	+23.8	17.7	-1.2	+2.4	-1.9
306 Tobacco	+54.0	42.8	-3.6	+15.3	-4.6
311-2 Textiles	-67.4	16	+2.2	-1.4	-9.5
313-15 Clothes	-75.2	20.1	-5.5	+11.3	-1.5
316 Leather products	- 36.6	15.2	+1.5	+4.1	+7.6
317 Footwear	- 27.4	27.6	-16.2	-12.6	-11.4
324-6 Print, Publish	-90.5	0.9	+1.6	-0.3	+4.7
391 Furniture	-26.1	16.6	-1.9	-1.2	-2.1
331-3 coke, petrol	-69.3	2.8	-9.3	-1.0	-6.9
334 basic chemicals	+11.0	2.2	+6.0	-0.1	+2.0
335/6 other chemicals	-83.6	2.8	+6.1	+8.1	+2.5
337 rubber products	- 15.3	16.9	+3.6	+8.1	-4.8
338 plastic products	- 45.9	9.7	+12.3	+ 9.8	+6.9
341 glass products	- 26.3	8.2	+2.7	+ 10.8	- 9.7
342 non-metal minerals	-52.4	5.2	-6.5	+2.0	-3.5
351 basic iron & steel	-43.9	4.1	-1.6	+1.6	-11.7
352 precious NF metals	-88.5	0.9	-2.1	+0.5	-5.2
323 pulp & paper	+26.9	7.1	-2.4	+4.7	-2.3
353-5 metal products	-45.0	7.7	-1.0	+2.8	-5.7
356-9 machinery+equip.	-68.1	2.0	+ 2.4	+ 16.4	-3.0
361-6 electric machinery	-55.3	6.1	+ 0.9	+ 9.9	- 5.0
381-3 cars, parts	-74.6	9.4	+ 5.2	+ 31.4	- 1.4
384-7 other transport eq.	-98.9	0.1	-8.0	+ 15.9	-10.5
371-3 TV &com mobiles	-80.1	2.8	+6.9	+ 29.2	+ 2.4
374-6 scient.,prof.equip	-96.1	0.5	-10.9	+ 5.9	- 4.9

Source: IDC, quoted by Rashid Cassim et al., 2003: Tables 17.18; MVA = manufacturing value added

petrochemical complex and non-ferrous metals, amongst other means by supplying electrical energy, water and transport infrastructure (Fine, Rustomjee, 1996). Given the present strong demand for natural resource based products by countries like China and India, South Africa could make the most of its comparative advantage, increasing its resource based output, while upgrading the skills levels of its workforce in order to promote the further diversification of the economy.

As of May 2005 the production capacity of large enterprises in the manufacturing industry is under-utilised by 15,3 percent. This is an improvement compared to previous years. The reason given for under-utilisation is insufficient demand rather than the shortage of skilled and semiskilled labour (Statistics South Africa P3043, 2005,1). Since the export-output ratio of manufacturing had been 11,1 percent (1989–1994) and 21,1 percent (1995–2001), it is the domestic demand and the purchasing power of domestic markets that seem to count more than export growth.

Since the initiation of a fully democratic system in South Africa, foreign direct investment in South Africa was on average about 1 percent of GDP (WTO 2003, A4-220). The repayment of apartheid's odious debts, the opening of financial markets and rapid trade liberalisation or the permission in 1998 for major corporations like Anglo American Corp., Liberty Life, South African Breweries and Old Mutual to relocate their headquarters to London – all of these efforts failed to persuade foreign capital to increase its direct investments in South Africa. A discussion paper on South Africa's position for the Doha WTO ministerial remarked on trade in industrial products: "... further liberalisation may be frustrated by the lack of demonstrable gains in productive investments in value added sectors or in areas that have comparative advantages. The situation will be compounded if enhanced market access in areas of our export interest is not realised".

More importantly, there have been major reductions in employment in the formal sector of the economy (Table 7.6). For example, between 1990 and 1998 the mining industry lost 347.308 jobs or 45 percent of the 1990 mining labour force. Job losses and casualisation of labour in textiles and clothing have also been substantial. According to the Labour Force Survey of 2003, 70 percent of the officially unemployed South Africans were youth aged 15–34; of these some 87 percent were black (SARB 2005, 11). There has been no increase in labour intensive employment inside South Africa. No regional industrial strategy was developed to ensure that jobs lost in South Africa could be gained in countries within the SADC region as part of a programme of balanced and sustainable regional co-operation and development.

Since 1994 GDP per capita has been growing at a slow pace. Measured at constant 2000 prices, per capita income has not yet recovered to the level of 1975. The poorest 40 percent of the population receive a lesser share of national income (6 percent) than ten years ago. The purchasing power of those population groups that had been discriminated against previously has not sufficiently increased to be driving domestic demand, or else the output of manufacturing industry is not geared to satisfy the needs of poor consumers.

"South African producers are entirely uncompetitive internationally in 'low-end' products for poor consumers", a World Bank study stated while stressing that wages in South Africa were ten times higher than those in Bangladesh (World Bank 1994, 13). The state did engage in efforts to develop basic needs industries such as clothing, footwear and furniture, but so far results have been disappointing. The majority of households are now provided with electricity and clean water; however, the question whether poor households can afford these public services is still a troubling concern (Wellmer 2004,72–83).

Looking at the economy as a whole, its export-output ratio has only reached 13,7 percent during 1995–2001. As the WTO admitted in 2003: "Significant reduction of unemployment and poverty remains to be made" (WT/TPR/S/114/ZAF March

2003, A4-237). It seems to be evident that the demand of domestic markets must be understood as the basis for growth in industrial output and development, rather than import substitution or export orientation. Exports might either serve as a dynamising factor or as an escape valve in times of domestic recession. To interpret export growth as the only motor for economic growth and development seems to entirely miss the point in South Africa's case.

The impact of negotiating a free trade agreement with the European Union

The European Union (EU) has historically been South Africa's most important source for foreign direct and indirect investments. In the 1970s the EU's investments focused mainly on the manufacturing industry (31 percent of total in 1980). But by 1995 this had declined to about 25 percent. Since 1980 finance, insurance and business services (FIRE) attracted 26,5 percent of total EU investment in South Africa; by 1995 it had captured a share of 36 percent. Direct investment decreased from 48 percent of all EU investment in 1973 to almost 30 percent in 1989. From September 1986 to February 1992 the EU had recommended a ban on new investments and suspended iron and steel imports from South Africa.

Europe also was and is South Africa's most important trading partner. These relations suffered a setback, when the international anti-apartheid movement managed to persuade parliamentarians in the USA and in Europe to impose sanctions against the apartheid system, even though governments were against it. Academics still fight over the effectiveness of sanctions. The political leaders of South Africa, however, do not doubt that international sanctions (October 1986 to September 1993) coming on top of South Africa's debt crisis of 1985 did impact on South Africa's financial prospects. Firstly, there was a substantial outflow of foreign capital out of the South African economy. This amounted to R 52,7 billion during 1985 to 1993. One has to add to this figure the unrecorded capital flight through mechanisms of transfer pricing. Secondly, the costs to attract fresh foreign loans or even to re-schedule old loans became very expensive. Thirdly, the obligations to repay rescheduled debts were a burden on the balance of payments. Fourthly, the average real growth of GDP over the two business cycles from March 1982 to March 1994 was 0,9 percent against a population growth rate of 2,4 percent. All of this forced the South African government to re-introduce foreign exchange controls (financial rand) and fiscal austerity measures that had the potential to cause further waves of labour protests and of resistance.

In order to rescue the economy, the minority regime had to restructure the political framework within which South African corporate accumulation strategies were played out. Once an agreement had been reached on the principles of the new constitution and the first universally democratic elections had been held peacefully, the new legitimate government needed urgently to reopen lines of trade and investment flows in order to back up the new political dispensation. During the period 1998 to 2003 South Africa's exports into the EU averaged annually 31,8 percent of total exports. During 1998–2003 the European Union supplied on average a share of 42,5 percent of South Africa's imports. It explains why South Africa not only devoted a lot of skilled manpower and time on trade and development negotiations with the EU, but also why the process of negotiating with the EU and its member states did inform and shape the future trade policy of South Africa overall.

Traditionally, South Africa's incorporation into the global economy rested on three functions: as a minerals exporter (some minerals processed to the intermediate stage) as an importer of capital goods and technology, and thirdly as a net recipient of portfolio investments and direct foreign investments by multinational corporations. For the manufacturing industry, it was a real problem that following the banking and currency crisis of 1985, South Africa had become a net exporter of capital. No doubt, mineral exporters themselves contributed to capital flight through manoeuvres like false invoicing and transfer pricing. Overall, manufactured products share of total exports had declined from 31 percent (1970) to 12 percent (1988-MERG 1993, 241).

South Africa's largest corporations had already exhausted local avenues for expansion. They saw global corporations driving on liberalised, transnational routes of capital accumulation, while they themselves had been isolated by sanctions and held captive by an inward industrialisation policy. South African capital had been shunted to a neglected siding of the world economy, which had lost its strategic importance since the end of the Cold War. National corporations faced the prospect of a sustained devalorisation of capital. Now that in 1994 the political crisis had been overcome, the big corporations in the financial and mining sectors wanted out and into the global mainstream. For them liberalisation of financial markets was essential, if they were to be free of the restrictions of a national economy (Marais 2001, 155). That urge to relocate away from home was no advertisement for foreign investors. Government on the other hand wanted fresh and productive investments from the EU to compensate for the disinvestment of local capital and was persuaded that the opening of the financial market would serve as an incentive.

Shortly before the 1994 democratic elections, the General Affairs Council of the EU had sent a strong signal to South Africa offering a package of immediate support measures. The EU offered to unilaterally grant the benefits of GSP and a special programme of financial aid. The newly elected government in South Africa wanted a non-reciprocal preferential access to EU markets preferably via "the closest possible relationship with the Lomé Convention". This would be a more stable base for trade than GSP. In general, South Africa wanted to have a favourable transition period of 10-15 years, in which to make its stagnant industry fit for global competition.

In order to achieve this objective, South Africa joined the Southern African Development Community (SADC) in August 1994. There was now a triangular relationship between the EU, South Africa and SADC. In a policy paper of 1992, the ANC had already expressed its vision of the "development of a prosperous and balanced regional economy in Southern Africa based on the principles of equity and mutual benefit" (ANC, 1992). The ANC's department of International Affairs declared that it wanted to base its regional policy on three principles. 1) The *collective nature* of the construction of a new regional order, transforming the currently exploitative and undesirable features of the existing regional economy; 2) An anti-militaristic and *development-oriented* approach to regional security cooperation; 3) Renouncing South Africa's former hegemonic regional ambitions. In 1994, the Reconstruction and Development Programme (RDP), reiterated the need for reconstruction and development in the region and to "negotiate with neighbouring countries to forge an equitable and mutually beneficial programme of increasing co-operation, co-ordination and integration, appropriate to the conditions of the region" (ANC 1994, 116s.). The ANC was concerned about the unbalanced regional trade pattern and stated: "A democratic government must develop policies in *consultation* with our neighbours to ensure more balanced trade." In particular, the RDP proposed a *social charter* on the rights of workers in Southern Africa to organise, so that a process of regional integration would embrace decently high standards regarding the rights and working conditions of workers. Very importantly, the RDP proposed that the capacity of the *region as a whole* be enhanced to effectively interact with international financial and trade institutions (Zarenda 1997, 62).

All other SADC member states were members in the African, Caribbean and Pacific group of developing countries (ACP) which at the time enjoyed the most favourable non-reciprocal preferential access to European markets (under the Lomé IV convention). Having been accepted by SADC, South Africa applied to ACP members to join the group and the Lomé agreement. On November 30, 1994 South Africa's trade minister argued at an ACP/EU ministerial in Brussels that being granted market access by the EU under Lomé IV would enable South Africa to restructure its vulnerable and uncompetitive national industries. It could develop a regional integration programme at the same time without having to fear serious economic or social risks. South Africa added in March 1995 that any free trade agreement with the EU would *seriously endanger* South Africa's industrial transformation and any efforts for regional integration. In May 1995 the ACP and even the EU parliament supported South Africa's application to join the Lomé IV convention. But the EU Commission rejected it in June 19, 1995. Instead the EU proposed to South Africa to negotiate a bilateral free trade agreement.

What had made SADC special had been its objective to create a development community that would aim to overcome inherited colonial structures of dependency. SADC did not want a region polarised between enclaves of prosperity and vast seas of chronic poverty. SADC had since 1980 survived by continually transforming itself to meet wars, droughts and debt crises. Since political communication functioned well, SADC member states were confident that they could control market forces through a close political dialogue co-ordinating regional economic policy, transforming regional industrial production, regional infrastructure, services and trade. Trade was not supposed to be the only tool for regional integration. This development approach to integration stressed the need for a fair distribution of advantages resulting from regional integration. The Windhoek agreement of SADC 1992 included a range of initiatives to secure the structural transformation of regional production patterns. The region had to reduce transaction costs of regional producers and to design the physical infrastructure for the movement of goods. Regional communication networks had to be expanded. There were to be institutions for the exchange and harmonisation of technical standards and regulations. The linkages between regional industrial sectors needed strengthening. Poor areas needed easier access to credits from a regional bank. Regional strategies were to increase the value added of traditional export products, to restructure regional production, to create new jobs, and to sharpen the comparative advantages of regional industries. "Southern African approach to regionalism is not to use it as a quick launching pad to globalisation as the WTO and the EU prefer. Neither is it to seek 'autonomous development' by retreating behind protectionist walls. It is instead a practical means of working collectively to overcome economic marginalisation, while at the same time gradually integrating into the global economy" (Thompson 2000, 55). Being heavily indebted after decades of war, SADC states knew that regional co-operation would not defeat the agendas of international capital, inside or outside the region, but they hoped to perhaps modify them.

The EU was in favour of open regionalism, where regional integration was just an interim step to globalisation. The EU gave South Africa this basic choice: either to be singled out through a bilateral FTA with development aid and private investment flows attached to it or regional integration along the guidelines of the failed Lagos Plan of Action and the "African Alternative Framework to SAPs". South Africa decided to go for a bilateral FTA with the EU. Indeed, this decision was to endanger, if not revoke SADC's concept of regional co-operation and development integration. From 1996 onwards SADC itself aimed for a Free Trade Area. The SADC trade protocol had a number of deficiencies compared to the original SADC vision. The SADC trade protocol does not respect the fact that half of the SADC members are LDCs. There is an asymmetrical approach in the timing and content of tariff liberalisation, but fair play would demand that the strongest regional economies open their markets where the weakest economies have comparative advantages and competitive products. The protocol also does not consider that the major barriers to intra-regional trade are not primarily tariffs or non-tariff regulations, but underdeveloped production structures and inadequate infrastructure, especially in the LDC of SADC. Measures to develop supply-side capacities in favour of regional integration are not seriously elaborated. Finally, the protocol does not define measures that would pool regional resources for an equitable spatial allocation of industries across the region. By narrowing the focus on tariff liberalisation the potential for polarisation remains great. By selecting South Africa for a bilateral FTA without regard to South Africa's original commitments to the SADC region, the EU seems to have forced its own concept on the whole region. Even if "the basic argument for a development integration programme within SADC remains incontestable" (Davies 2000, 10), it no longer enjoyed the political support of South Africa.

The South African government also had to take into account the transition from the GATT to the WTO in 1995. Whereas the GATT was mainly about market opening for trade in goods and services, the WTO mandate expanded into new policy areas. The WTO linked foreign trade with investment protection, trade related intellectual property, mechanisms of conflict resolution and demanded that the whole package be accepted as a "single undertaking" (UNDP 2003). These policy areas were formerly regulated by national governments, because they have great influence on development processes, regarding employment, education, health, the flow of capital investments and access to new technologies. South Africa joined the WTO. It was aware that trade and development negotiations with the EU would, on a bilateral level, tend to even expand the agreement signed at the WTO multilateral level.

In October 1996 an official of the South African department of trade and industry (DTI) explained how the recently self-imposed structural adjustment programme GEAR complemented the desired Trade and Development and Co-operation Agreement (TDCA) with the EU (Hirsch 1997, 70–77). To ensure the success of GEAR, the DTI expected from the future TDCA assistance to improve manufacturing's productivity, a diversification of South African exports to the EU and long-term direct investments of EU companies in outward oriented industrial projects of South Africa. On its part GEAR was to contribute to a success of the TDCA by reducing trade protection, removing the state's demand-side intervention, expanding supply-side support including export facilitation through, for example, a credit guarantee insurance, and by reducing government deficit before borrowing, reducing domestic interest rates and stabilising the currency. In regard to both the TDCA and GEAR, the DTI saw its main tasks to increase gross domestic fixed investment and to increase manufactured exports by an annual average of 10 percent.

The Trade, Development and Co-operation Agreement (TDCA) was signed by South Africa and the EU in October 1999 after 21 rounds of talks in five years. The chapter on trade provided for asymmetrical trade liberalisation between the two contracting parties. South Africa will liberalise around 86 percent of its imports from the EU during a 12-year transition period, while the EU will liberalise 95 percent of its imports from South Africa in ten years. During the negotiations South Africa managed to reduce the EU's percentage of agricultural products *wholly* excluded from liberalisation from 46 percent of South Africa's current agricultural exports to 28,5 percent. But the EU will only *partially* liberalise 11,5 percent of that agricultural trade, in which South African products are especially competitive (canned fruits, fruit juices and wines, cut flowers), and where some gains have been made despite quota limitations (Table 7.8).

EU quota restrictions impose on potential South African exporters more bureaucracy, slowing down trade. They have to apply for export licences supplying proof that sanitary, phyto-sanitary and other technical requirements of the EU are being met (SAG 2003, 40–52).

EU protectionism becomes especially glaring in the chapter on sugar and confectionery products. It is clear that South Africa is a much more 'efficient' sugar producer than the EU and has the capacity to expand its exports to the EU at a moment's notice if it had unhindered access. However, between 2002–2004 South African sugar exports to the EU decreased by 62,2 percent and sugar imports from the EU increased by 37 percent. It is here that South Africa's complaints at the WTO level over the EU's common agricultural policy with its export subsidies and high import barriers are most understandable.

Table 7.8   South African Net Export Rate in trade with EU

	NET EXPORT RATE			
Section	2002	2003	2004	Aug 2005
1. animals, animal products	0.67	0.66	0.59	0.53
2.vegetable products	0.71	0.73	0.84	0.86
3.animal/vegetable Fats and oils	-0.38	-0.54	-0.72	-0.79
4.prepared food, beverages, spirits	0.38	0.40	0.32	0.34
5.mineral products	0.93	0.88	0.79	0.82
6. chemical products	-0.56	-0.61	-0.57	-0.55
7.plastic and rubber products	-0.59	-0.55	-0.54	-0.56
8.hides,fur,leather articles	0.66	0.66	0.69	0.65
9.wood, articles of wood, cork	0.18	0.15	0.13	0.08
10. pulp & paper	-0.05	-0.15	-0.21	-0.27
11. textiles, cloth, clothes	0.14	0.18	0.09	-0.01
12. shoes, hats, umbrellas	-0.18	-0.20	-0.37	-0.48
13.ceramics, cement, asbestos products	-0.37	-0.34	-0.26	-0.21
14. pearls, gems, jewels	0.44	0.49	0.64	0.94
15.base metals, articles of base metals	0.31	0.39	0.46	0.43
16.mechan. & electrical machinery	-0.48	-0.51	-0.50	-0.47
17. vehicles, planes, ships, railway	-0.21	-0.45	-0.54	-0.53
18. optical, photographic and measuring instruments	-0.78	-0.78	-0.81	-0.81
19. arms & ammunition	-0.04	0.58	0.11	0.73
20 miscellaneous manufactured articles	0.52	0.53	0.48	0.35
21. art works	-0.43	0.14	-0.57	0.09
22. other unclassified goods	0.83	0.82	-0.73	-0.57
23. special classification on origin	-0.99	-0.99	-0.99	-0.99

Source: www.dti.gov.za/econdb/ Note: +1,0 indicates exports with no imports, zero indicates balance in flow of goods, minus 1,0 means imports with no exports

South Africa hoped to gain market shares in the EU in the exports of iron and steel products, ferroalloys, aluminium products, furniture and automotive products. Base metals did indeed increase market share (Table 7.8), but both the net export ratios of furniture and automotive products declined.

Because of back-loaded schedules, it is at present not yet possible to fully evaluate the effects of the FTA on the development of industrial sectors of South Africa. Looking at the low GDP growth rate, low FDI and negative net job creation, South Africa has merely been muddling through. In Table 7.8 South Africa shows its traditional strength in its exports of mining products and base metals. It imports from the EU mainly machinery, transport and chemical products. The FTA with the EU certainly was no kick-start into a bright future. South Africa's balance on the current account turned negative in 1995 after having been positive during the 10 previous years. In 2004 the balance on the current account was negative again and amounted to R 44,3 bn or 3,2 percent of GDP (SARB, QB Sept. 2005, 86–152). South African producers and employees face high adjustment costs for having to liberalise trade tariffs faster than agreed to at the multilateral level of the WTO and for having to compete in their own domestic market against more competitive EU producers.

The non-trade aspects of the negotiations were fairly easily agreed upon. South Africa wanted to add to the trade chapter further agreements on financial aid, technological co-operation, and support for industrial restructuring. The EU pressed for the inclusion of new issues that went beyond WTO agreements. One issue was investment protection and the free movement of capital. According to Table 7.9 the agreements here did help to increase the EU's share of direct investments in total capital flows to South Africa from 33,4 percent (1995) to 52,2 percent (2003).

The shift in European investment patterns in South Africa took place *before* the TDCA had been signed. But in the 4 years between January 2000 and the end of 2003 *after* the TDCA had been signed, the European capital flow at all levels declined by an annual average 8,7 percent. Also, the capital of South African residents increasingly left South Africa and found its way via portfolio investments and loans, deposits and trade credits to European capital markets. In 1995 the net investment balance between the EU and South Africa was in favour of South Africa by about 9,5 billion Euro. In 2003 the net investment balance favoured the European Union by a margin of two billion Euro. Between 1989 to 2001 investment rates in electricity, mining, business services, and transport were all higher than that in manufacturing industries (Cassim, Onyango et al. 2002, 18). Investment rate is defined as gross domestic fixed investment divided by the value added of an industry.

Competition policy and government procurement was another trade-related issue on the EU's to-do list. Article 41.1 of the TDCA states that public aid favouring certain firms or the production of certain goods, which distorts or threatens to distort competition, and which does not support specific public policy objectives of either party, is incompatible with the agreement. Annex IV outlines that environmental protection, employment and training could be considered compatible and Annex IX adds another set of acceptable public aid objectives: regional development, industrial restructuring and development promotion of SME or affirmative action programmes. Under the apartheid regime a competition board had occupied a Cinderella status in industrial policy since 1980. In 20 years there was no instance of a successful prosecution of an uncompetitive practice by either state-owned or private conglomerates. Corporate power, reinforced through simultaneous control of the financial sector, reached to potentially all activities within mining and manufacturing. The resistance movement had long argued for strong anti-trust legislation. When coming into power, the ANC-led government met with strong opposition not only by private conglomerates like Anglo-American but also by public enterprises, who argued that their services (energy, telecommunication, water etc) might be unduly constrained by the operation of effective competition law. The new competition laws of 1998/9 tried to link traditional competition objectives – efficiency and consumer welfare – with broader social objectives like employment creation, ownership diversity, and the promotion of small and medium enterprises

(SME). The Law explicitly states that these objectives have to be taken account of as public interest criteria in a merger evaluation by the competition commission, the tribunal and the appeal court (Lewis, Reed, Teljeur 1999, 11–15). Thus, the proposed merger between SASOL and AECI, South Africa's two largest chemical companies, was prohibited. The state-owned broadcaster SABC was hindered in achieving dominance in TV film production.

Table 7.9   South African liabilities towards, and assets in, Europe, 1995–2003 in millions of Euro

	1995	Share percent	2000	2003	Share percent	growth p.a. 1995–2003	growth p.a. percent 2000–2003
Direct Investments							
Liabilities	9, 323	33.4	45, 777	28, 817	52.2	23.3 percent	-9.3
Assets	16, 120	87.6	32, 684	16, 102	28.1		
Net direct investment	-6, 797		13, 093	12, 715			
Portfolio investments							
Liabilities	9, 920	35.6	25, 550	16, 873	30.5	7.8 percent	-8.5
Assets	135	0.7	45, 798	26, 957	47.1		
Net portfolio investments	9, 785		-20, 248	-10, 084			
Other investments							
Liabilities	8, 641	31.0	13, 372	9, 545	17.3	1.2 percent	-7.2
Assets	2, 136	11.6	4, 403	14, 203	25.0		
Net other investments	6, 505		8, 969	-4, 658			
Total liabilities	27, 884	100	84, 699	55,234	100	10.9 percent	-8.7
Total assets	18, 391	100	82, 885	57, 261	100		
Net investment balance	9, 493			1, 814	-2, 027		

Source: SARB, QB Supplement June 2001; QB June 2005. Note: Data do not allow identifying the EU as distinct from the rest of Europe

On the other hand, the TDCA does not explain, how the agreed upon competition policy would harmonise with the EU's partial liberalisation and even exclusion of major markets in bilateral trade or with the strict adherence of the WTO's TRIPs.

The anti-dumping measures, safeguard clauses and procedures also tend to restrict competition. Insofar as bribes aimed at winning a government tender do violate competition policy, the EU did not impose obligations on itself in the TDCA to prevent this common practice of European TNCs (Stang 2002; Honey 2003). Stung by public perceptions that watchdog institutions investigating an arms procurement connived with the executive in a cover up, the South African Parliament passed a "Prevention and Combating of Corrupt Activities Act" in early 2004. The Act threatens heavy penalties for offences in respect of *inter alia* procurement of any contract (Wille, 2004; Sole 2005).

The TDCA also reaffirms strict observance of the GATS principle of MFN treatment and their respective commitments concerning basic telecommunications, financial services as well as access to the international maritime market. Two years later, the EU requested of South Africa to open up markets in all 12 service-categories. (Joy, Hardstaff 2003). Between 1993 and 2004, South Africa's balance on the current account was negative in eight years because of the constantly negative balance on services, payments of income earned from the provision of financial capital, and current transfers including insurance contributions and benefits (SARB, QB 2002, 2005).

The EU and South Africa acknowledged that their FTA would reduce the revenues of the other members of the SACU and also diminish the chances of other SADC states to increase their exports to South Africa improving their trade balance. In late 1997 the head of the EC negotiation team stated: "SADC countries have undertaken to treat each other better to how they treat outsiders. In this context, the EU is the outsider ... The SADC Trade Protocol only needs to be ratified ... We have already agreed with the South Africans who are negotiating another FTA within the SADC that it would be legitimate for them to open their market first to their neighbours and only later to us. This is what they call 'SADC first'..." (Boidin, Percival 1997, 6s.). The EU proposal to the ACP group to go after Lomé IV for reciprocal FTAs was well known before the TDCA was signed. This raised questions regarding the future policy of both the EU and of South Africa towards SADC. Article 22 of the TDCA states that either party may expand its custom union or establish free trade areas with third countries. Consultation between the contracting parties is provided for in such cases. The exception is if trade policy with third countries (like SADC member states) alters the rights and obligations of the TDCA parties. This provision would have made it even more important to outline the space, in which SADC could develop.

As to the "SADC-first" approach, an advisor to the SADC Industry and Trade Division in Tanzania made a preliminary comparison of South African tariff liberalisation offers to the EU and to the non-SACU SADC states (Pallangyo 2000, 81). He concluded that in strict tariff terms South Africa's offer to SADC was indeed superior to its offer to the EU. However, these SADC preferences are only valid for a limited number of products and a rather narrow time frame of three to five years. The tariff concessions towards SADC are small considering the development gap between South Africa and other SADC states. Given the existing supply side constraints and limited access to capital, it is doubtful whether SADC industries can exploit a temporary preference at the word go. In addition, South Africa's list of sensitive industrial products is more or less similar in relation to both SADC and the EU. It is highly unlikely that South African imports originating in SADC could compete with imports from the EU and pose as much of a threat to South Africa's industry as imports from the EU would.

The TDCA provides that products will be considered as originating in the EU or South Africa, if they have been wholly obtained in the area of the trade partners or if they incorporate foreign materials that have undergone sufficient processing. To define what sufficient means, a list was attached of processes required for non-originating materials in order to gain originating status. The TDCA protocol provides for two types of cumulation of materials relevant for the rules of origin. *Full cumulation* can only be allowed between members of a single customs territory that is within and between members of the EU or of SACU. *Partial cumulation* is allowed in a case by case approach for South Africa processing materials from ACP members outside of SACU. That includes SADC member states. It is also allowed for South African processing materials imported from the EU. Unless EPAs are concluded, SADC states cannot partially cumulate South African inputs in products destined for export to the EU (Lowe 2000: 44). This lacuna deprives SADC members not only of the opportunity to increase their market share in South Africa. Europe's rules of origin (RoO) actually hinder regional integration insofar as they discriminate between SACU and non-SACU SADC members and prevent full cumulation within SADC. It is the EU, which determined by its RoO that SADC will have to turn into a custom union if it wants full cumulation of their raw materials or intermediate products in South African value chains destined for export to the EU. EU rules of origin push for a neo-classical concept of a customs union and are a barrier to regional integration.

Since colonial days the centre of capital accumulation in Southern Africa has been the mining industry and the related processing and engineering industries. The growth pole of the regional economy was situated in South Africa, whose neighbours had subordinated functions in the regional economy. They offered cheap migratory labour, they supplied services (water, energy, railway transport, and harbours), and they were dependent markets for South Africa's processed goods and capital. Trade patterns in Southern Africa mirror somewhat the one between the EU and South Africa.

In 2004 South African exports to SADC amounted to R 26,3 billion and imports from SADC to R 6,5 billion. According to Table 7.10, total regional trade is heavily in South Africa's favour. SADC's only revealed comparative advantage in its trade with South Africa lies in sections 8 (leather articles), 9 (articles of wood), 11 (textiles and clothing) and 14 (precious stones). There are two other sections, where SADC countries have managed to steadily better their position: section 5 (mineral products) and section 15 (base metals). This may be due to the fact that South Africa's considerable FDI into SADC has concentrated on mining, mineral beneficiation and metal products. In only 17 out of 99 chapters does the region have a competitive edge to capture market shares in South Africa and SACU (Lee 2003, 171–241). Looking at South Africa's exports of (durable) capital goods, it is evident, that Africa, and SADC in particular, is of strategic importance. SADC imported up to 35,1 percent (2002) of all capital goods exports of South Africa. The EU followed with 26,6 percent (2002), decreasing to about 24 percent (Aug. 2005), NAFTA followed in

3rd place by purchasing 14,5 percent (2002) and 11,4 percent (August 2005). Thus, South Africa is trying to sharpen the competitive edge of its capital goods sector by competing with the OECD exporters first in SADC markets, then in other developing regions. Achieving a massive surplus in its trade with SADC and the rest of Africa, South Africa aims for a more or less balanced trade account overall.

We already observed a decrease of South African food exports to the EU. Table 7.10 also indicates that food exports to non-SACU SADC countries decreased by 41 percent. SADC partners, on the other hand, managed to increase their share in South African markets in regard to fish, fruits, coffee and tea, oilseeds, meat and fish preparations and sugar and tobacco. South Africa refused during negotiations on the SADC FTA to allow free access to the SACU sugar market. South Africa does not want to compete with the more cost-effective sugar producers in Zimbabwe, Zambia, Malawi, Mozambique and Swaziland. The decision whether or not the SADC sugar industry will be fully liberalised by 2012 will be determined only in 2006 according to the Sugar Co-operation Agreement. That means: the potential for SADC exports to South Africa cannot be fully exploited. That has more to do with South African protectionism than with SADC supply restraints.

The DTI reported in 1999, during the negotiations on a SADC free trade agreement: "Increases in SADC exports are unlikely to have much impact on our economy, because current exports are at such low levels that even if they were to increase four-fold, the impact would be marginal." Imports from SADC "account for a mere 2,1 percent of South Africa's total imports. In category C (sensitive products) where SADC has the highest level of exports to South Africa relative to the rest of the world, the products that comprise that category will continue to be protected under special dispensations." (DTI 1999, 3–4). During SADC FTA negotiations, South Africa declared four of its sectors as very sensitive: automotive, footwear and leather, clothing and textiles and the sugar industry. In all sectors some SADC products are competitive, as Table 7.10 indicates. From its negotiations with the EU about an FTA South Africa had learned that "rules of origin are not only about customs control, but, more importantly, about economic development, jobs and investment" (Smalberger 2000, 50). In applying this "lesson" to SADC FTA negotiations in order to protect national textiles and clothing in particular, South Africa not only lost its image as benign hegemonic partner in Southern Africa; it also polarised relations among SADC member states and impeded regional integration.

The impact of restrictive rules of origin is to raise costs and prices of traded goods, to impede regional trade creation and deprive consumers of the benefits of SADC free trade. These higher costs reduce the competitiveness of downstream producers and make SADC irrelevant for international markets. South African negotiators were captured by special interests and abandoned thinking regionally. South Africa required for instance that all downstream textile and garment products be made of regional yarn and regional fabric. South Africa will agree to regional free trade in textiles and clothing only if regional competitors forego access to most international inputs. This forces SADC orientated producers into production patterns that are completely different from competitive producers elsewhere. It is bound to cripple them in global markets. Only if RoO are used simply to authenticate that imports from the region arise from fundamental economic activity in the region, SADC could help promote the regional and international trade of member states. But if South Africa insists on using EU RoO for protection, SADC might become irrelevant for the region's development (Flatters 2002). Having no coherent industrial policy itself, South Africa also failed to give direction to the transformation of productive capacities of SADC industries. The result favours rent seekers, mercantilist and protectionist interests.

Table 7.10 South Africa's net-export ratio in trade with SADC, 1995 to August 2005

Source: *www.dti.gov.za./econdb/ See also tables 8+9 in Wellmer 2000, 34s.*

SECTION selected chapters under sections	August 2005	2004	2003	2002	1998*	1995*
1.animals,animal products	0.70	0.80	0.77	0.78	0.72	0.49
Ch.3 fish, crustaceans	0.24	0.35	0.14	0.24		
2.vegetable products	0.78	0.61	0.74	0.83	0.63	0.57
Ch.8 fruits	0.52	0.76	0.80	0.90		
Ch.9 coffee, tea	- 0.56	- 0.38	- 0.39	- 0.28		
Ch.12 oilseeds	-0.01	-0.18	0.15	0.49		
3.animal, vegetable fats and oils	0.995	0.96	0.88	0.86	..	0.93
4. prepared food, beverages, spirits	0.65	0.69	0.70	0.68	0.44	0.46
Ch.16 preparations of meat, fish	0.38	0.33	0.39	0.82		
Ch.17 sugar	0.73	0.70	0.72	0.84		
Ch.24 tobacco	- 0.25	- 0.07	- 0.14	- 0.20		
5. mineral products	0.17	0.14	0.48	0.58	0.79	0.90
Ch.26 Ores, slag, ash	- 0.987	- 0.978	- 0.97	- 0.91		
Ch.27 fuels	0.46	0.38	0.95	0.82		
6.chemical products	0.985	0.984	0.97	0.98	..	0.89
7.plastic and rubber products	0.97	0.95	0.94	0.96	0.34	0.89
8.hides, furs, leather articles	0.03	- 0.27	- 0.32	- 0.36	- 0.20	- 0.42
Ch.41 hides, skins and leather	- 0.67	- 0.64	- 0.71	- 0.73		
Ch.42 articles of leather	+ 0.44	- 0.08	- 0.07	- 0.03		
9.wood, articles of wood	- 0.13	- 0.08	0.02	0.14	-0.25	- 0.11
10.pulp and paper	0.97	0.96	0.92	0.95	..	0.89
11. textile, cloth, clothing	- 0.23	- 0.35	- 0.14	- 0.11	- 0.34	0.00
Ch.52 cotton	- 0.84	-0.82	- 0.60	- 0.47		
Ch.60 knitted fabrics	- 0.67	- 0.29	+0.81	+ 0.55		
Ch.61 clothing articles	- 0.36	- 0.22	+0.03	- 0.16		
Ch.62 clothing, not knitted	- 0.36	- 0.21	- 0.24	- 0.35		
12 shoes, hats, umbrellas	0.67	0.54	0.57	0.59	0.44	- 0.14
13.ceramics, glass, cement	0.76	0.82	0.76	0.75	..	0.82
14.pearls, gems, jewels	- 0.81	- 0.44	0.27	0.67	- 0.20	- 0.74
15.base metals, articles of	0.49	0.64	0.72	0.75	0.74	0.82
Ch.74 copper	- 0.81	- 0.74	- 0.40	- 0.56		
Ch. 75 nickel	- 0.99	- 0.99	- 0.98	- 0.95		
Ch.79 zinc	+ 0.25	+ 0.32	+ 0.23	+ 0.62		
Ch.81 other base metals	- 0.48	- 0.47	- 0.36	- 0.79		
16 mechanical, electrical machinery	0.90	0.93	0.91	0.94	..	0.92
17 vehicles, planes, ships, railways	0.93	0.96	0.95	0.98	..	0.94
18 optical and measuring instruments	0.92	0.95	0.91	0.91	..	0.90
19 arms and ammunition	0.91	0.90	0.86	0.88	..	n.a.
20 misc. manufactured articles	0.61	0.71	0.73	0.76	0.66	0.51
21. art works	0.58	-0.09	0.36	- 0.04	0.43	0.08
22.other unclassified goods	0.36	- 0.05	- 0.61	- 0.53	1.0	0.80
Total Trade	**0.61**	**0.60**	**0.73**	**0.77**	**0.70**	**0.75**

Note: *Data from 1998 and 1995 refer to SACU trade with rest of SADC*

The fact that South Africa negotiated with the EU without the other SADC members has further negative consequences. The TDCA modified the basis on which SADC now has to negotiate an Economic Partnership Agreement (EPA) with the EU (Wellmer 2005). The other SACU members cannot deviate much from the TDCA already signed, unless they dissolve SACU. The non-SACU SADC members have different economic structures than South Africa and can therefore not just join the TDCA. "SADC cannot sign as a unit because South Africa already has an EPA, which incorporates all the SACU countries … It is not clear whether splitting the region is part of a South African agenda or if it is the result of EU initiatives." (Mpande-Chuulu, 2004, 93). Apart from Lesotho, the other LDCs in SADC have little incentive to opt for free trade with the EU, if they are not negotiating as part of SADC. Zimbabwe, Mauritius, Zambia, Malawi and the DRC all have joined COMESA for the EPA negotiations. Furthermore, fragmenting the trade regimes applying to imports from the EU impedes the adoption by SADC of common external trade policies; it also makes it difficult to formulate coherent regional industrialisation strategies. Thus, the EU has effectively split SADC. South Africa may be able to market its capital goods exports to the SADC region regardless, because of established dependency structures. But the other SADC states may no longer be in a position to grow new industries and create new places of employment.

Turning from regional trade to regional investments, South Africa has invested about 96 billion Rand in the period 1997–2001 in African countries. Some 80 percent of this amount went into SADC member countries. Of the SADC investments about half of them were direct investments, only 5 percent were portfolio investments. But foreign African companies have invested about 104 billion Rand in South Africa. Only 10 percent went into direct investments, while 42 percent percent went into portfolio investments. Almost 90 percent of the total investment came from SADC member states (Naidu, Lutchman 2004, 13). In seven SADC countries South Africa is the top foreign investor. In four additional SADC countries South Africa ranks 2nd or 3rd place. The country receiving the highest amount of direct South African investment within SADC is Mozambique, where R 22,8 billion were either invested between 1994 and 2003 or where such investments were firmly announced. The Mozambican case might offer useful information on the nature of such investment.

Between 1990 and 2003 some 67 percent of all FDI and half the total private investments were allocated to six manufacturing industries in Mozambique (aluminium, energy, natural gas, heavy mineral sands, sugar, beer and cement). In this period, South African corporations have absorbed 85 percent of total FDI and 73 percent of total loans accruing to Mozambique. The so-called mega-projects allegedly "developing" Mozambique correspond most closely to the accumulation strategies of South African corporations. If other private foreign capital flows into Mozambique, it is because it is attracted by the regional strategies of South African corporations. To make this point clearer, one detailed example is provided next.

MOZAL is a large aluminium smelter built during the end of the 1990s at the outskirts of Maputo, Mozambique's Capital City. It has the capacity to produce 512.000 tons of aluminium ingots per year. The cost of this project amounted to about US $ 2,4 billion. Production started in 2000. Main markets are in the EU and the automobile industry in Asia. The South African controlled MOZAL is exempted from paying duties on imports of material inputs (the ore), equipment and services required. Mozal need not pay value-added tax and corporate taxes are limited to one percent of sales. The company may import and export capital freely after communicating with the central bank of Mozambique. Mozal consumes for its operations more energy than the rest of Mozambique. Because of Mozal, the energy grids of South Africa, Mozambique and Swaziland were linked through a newly founded joint company called Motraco. Its sole function is to supply South African energy produced by ESKOM to Mozal. ESKOM is also the main customer of the energy produced by the hydroelectric dam of Cahora Bassa at the Zambezi in northern Mozambique. ESKOM is also urging Mozambique to construct another hydroelectric dam on the Zambezi at M'panda Uncua. ESKOM is also negotiating contracts for supplying electricity to the energy intensive projects to exploit Mozambique's heavy sands, possibly even a new iron and steel factory near Maputo. There are doubts about the viability of the iron and steel project, because such an industry will demand more drinking water than the citizens of the Capital City can afford to offer. Mozal is called a mega-project because this one factory contributes 75 percent of Mozambique's manufacturing exports and 42 percent of the total export revenue of Mozambique. But after accounting for production costs and profit repatriation, Mozal's net balance of payments gains are reduced to about US$ 100 million annually. Of this sum, Mozambican workers receive about $17 million, purchases in the national economy may amount to about $14 million, social programs cost about $ 4 million and the fiscus gets about $10 million – much a do about little (Castel Branco 2004, 42). Mozal is an enclave in the Mozambican economy. It has a capital-intensive production and is therefore in no way designed to combat high unemployment. Fiscal incentives prevent the Mozambican State to gain much. Mozal has not caused a significant upgrading of local industrial capacities; little real technology transfer takes place. Raw materials and energy are imported, and the product is exported instead of serving as an intermediate input for Mozambican manufacturing industries. Such an enclave industry does not contribute much to Mozambique's development. In fact, the massive incentive package of the State increases the social cost of FDI and reduces the industry's social benefits. Mozal is not a substitute for a national or regional industrialisation strategy that creates locally productive and managerial capacity, capability and a qualified workforce. Castel Branco (2004, 36) concludes: the Mozambican economy will become an extension of the minerals-energy complex of South Africa and growth in other areas will be precluded because of the destabilising effect (of mega-projects) on Mozambique's balance of trade. The country's trade deficit with South Africa has increased by 300 percent in 10 years in parallel with the increase in South Africa's FDI in Mozambique.

During an investor's conference to support the Nacala Development Corridor in northern Mozambique, the South African Minister of Trade and Industries said in February 2003, that the South African manufacturing industry was interested in the corridor because it may link them to the required raw materials of Southern African countries. SADC member states could thus become part of the value adding chain built up by South African corporations. Linking infrastructure developments with clusters of dynamic industrial activity in South Africa will make the infrastructure profitable. Already, South African engineering firms were heavily involved in implementing the Nacala Corridor Strategy in Zambia, Malawi and Mozambique while South African capital would be involved in investment projects related to the corridor in relation to the forests and mineral resources within the 'catchment area' of the corridor (Castel Branco 2004, 37).

According to this perspective regional integration would mean for SADC member states to fit into the accumulation strategies of South African corporations, mainly related to the resource based industrial group. This group sees the region as a springboard for its integration into world markets. Dependent industrialisation may be developing around production chains controlled by South African capital. That is a concept very different from the original SADCC concept of equitable regional development. The original regionalism of SADC(C) aimed at combining economies of scale derived from developmental integration (including, but not exclusively derived from the market) with a collective effort to regulate capitalist corporations at a regional level (Tsie 2001). This original concept wanted SADC as a structure for regional political co-operation to promote the region as a viable economic, cultural and ecological unit. The region was to gain a measure of freedom from the accumulation strategies of big corporations in order to lead the majority of its population out of chronic poverty. Free trade agreements may be just what it costs to destroy regional policy cohesion.

If you can't beat them, ... NEPAD

The Industrial Development Decade for Africa (IDDA) was proclaimed in 1980, based on the Lagos Plan of Action (LPA) of the Organisation of African Unity. The LPA focused on industrial development as a means for the structural transformation of African economies. Long term objectives of this process were the self-reliant and self-sustained development of Africa. A Framework and Guidelines were worked out between the Economic Commission for Africa, the OAU and UNIDO that specified action programmes relevant for the development of indigenous technology, human resources, planning capacities and entrepreneurship in order to progressively reduce Africa's dependence on external factors. Intersectoral and intra-industrial linkages were to be maximised. African sub-regions like SADC were to develop their supply capacity and a core of industrial projects of importance for the structural transformation of the whole region. The IDDA framework and guidelines did not specify programmes for LDCs, in contrast to middle income countries. Its vision may have been too diffuse to be easily operationalised. IDDA's assumptions may have been too optimistic in counting on investment flows without taking into account possible external shocks such as the collapse of the prices of Africa's primary commodity exports, increasing fluctuations in the exchange rates, sudden rises in interest rates and subsequently an unmanageable debt crisis.

The 1980s were a decade of rapidly shifting international economic relationships; while defending itself against regional destabilisation by the Apartheid regime, SADC ended up in the debt trap. In that decade, over thirty African countries were forced to embark on Structural Adjustment Programmes (SAPs) organised and defined by the IMF and the World Bank. The objectives of the first generation of SAPs was the restauration of budgetary and balance of payments equilibria, without addressing the structural weaknesses of production. Regional integration in the context of IDDA was justified by achieving economies of scale, enlarging and integrating national and sub-regional markets, and creating an indigenous growth engine. The World Bank and most of the creditor states looked at regional integration only as a stepping stone to achieve international competitiveness on the world market. Economists like Adedeji argued that "both the design and implementation process of orthodox SAPs are not relevant to the long-term development objectives of African countries as spelt out in the Lagos Plan of Action" (Adedeji 1992, 66). It is, however, a fact that not a single country in Africa set up a coherent industrial planning machinery, none developed a core industrial investment programme or mobilised funds specifically for industrial development. Sadly, this is true for Africa's sub-regions as well. During the 1980s, as crisis management for economic survival was given priority attention, the vision of self-sustained development faded away. This is not to deny that regions like SADC had some success, for instance in ending the apartheid system, in expanding transport and communication infrastructure, and in engaging in regional research, which led to improved, drought-resistant sorghum and millet strains for all areas of the SADC region. SADC built up a regional information network, which included an early warning system and a drought monitoring system as well as co-ordinated meteorological services and pest control. It is merely to state the obvious. SADC at the end of the 1980s was severely in apartheid caused debts; SAP caused currency devaluation, increased the cost of imported spare parts, the liberalisation of competitive imports from the EU and the inability to secure finance for the rehabilitation of national industries contributed to the closure of local industries.

Notwithstanding the failure of IDDA during the 1980s, the OAU reformulated its industrialisation strategy in the context of Africa's Alternative Framework to Structural Adjustment Programmes for socio-economic Recovery and Transformation (UN-ECA 1989). Again, it did not gain the support of the World Bank, which now started to argue that the crisis of governance in SSA had to be the overriding theme. Economic efficiency had to play a more important role in industrial policy reform than the outdated concept of self-sustainment. One knows now that the response of domestic as well as foreign industrial investment to SAPs remained insignificant, so that the prospects for employment and productivity growth and structural changes remained very poor.

NEPAD is based on the premise of attracting increased private capital flows, more debt relief, especially for middle income countries, and a reform of official development aid for the promise of good governance and macro-economic stability. It sees the liberalisation of trade and financial markets as an opportunity to "lift millions of people out of poverty" (§ 32). The task ahead is to achieve and sustain a GDP growth rate above 7 percent per annum for the next 15 years (§ 68) and to make African industries more competitive (§ 28.33.50.64.69.94.98), so that the continent arrives at an "effectively managed" (§ 28) and "rapid" integration (§ 35.52.189) into the world economy. Integration will be achieved through increased exports (§ 69.168–173) and "better market access" (§ 97.170). The implementing agency is the democratic state in co-operation with private capital (§ 39.66.84–88). Leo Panitch formulated earlier:

> Capitalist globalisation is a process, which also takes place in, through, and under the aegis of states. It is encoded by them and in important respects even authored by them. And it involves a shift in power relations within states that often means the centralisation and concentration of state power as the necessary condition of, and accompaniment to, global market discipline. (Panitch 1994,14)

NEPAD does lightly touch upon the "absence of fair rules" in the multilateral trade system (§ 33), regrets "unfavourable terms of trade" for Africa (§ 34) and the instability in world commodity prices (§ 132). It nevertheless calls for "active participation" in the WTO (§ 169) to ensure "open, predictable" market access for Africa's exports (§ 170) and demands "more equitable terms of trade for African countries within the multilateral framework" (§ 188). Already articulated positions of the Africa Group in the WTO are ignored by the NEPAD document. NEPAD is more interested in offering a deal: "Transparency and predictability for increased investment in return for boosting supply capacity and enhancing the gains from existing market access" (§ 170). Assistance in capacity building for implementing the rules and regulations of the WTO is requested, even though that assistance is never neutral.

NEPAD allegedly wants African countries to "enhance regional development" and to strengthen "the five subregional economic groupings of the continent" (§ 94). NEPAD will focus on rationalising the institutional framework for economic integration "so as to improve the continent's international competitiveness and to enable her to participate in the globalisation process" (§ 98). But Nepad project finance is being paid out directly to individual national governments, not to the five regional economic groups. Planning and financing such continental projects is done in parallel structures, circumventing the regional organisations already in place.

One straight criticism of NEPAD came from the trade union federation COSATU. It said that the "plan has been developed through discussions between governments and business organisations, leaving the people far behind … the transformation of Africa can only happen if it is driven by its people" (http://gate.cosatu.org.za). The NEPAD initiative of July 2001 is the first AU document, in which – to the dismay of many African intellectuals of the left wing – the political elites of African states like South Africa, Senegal and Nigeria, formulate a clearly neoliberal development strategy. What the bilateral FTA between South Africa and the European Union did to the demise of SADC's long-term objective of self-sustained development, NEPAD is now doing to the plurilateral relationship between the African Union and the G-8 group. With NEPAD the last principled protest of a group of states against the neo-liberal Washington Consensus has collapsed (Tetzlaff, Jakobeit 2005, 209). If you can't beat them, join them.

Strategies at the multilateral level of the WTO

South Africa has been a founding member of the General Agreement on Tariffs and Trade (GATT) since 1947. Democratic South Africa joined the WTO. When negotiating within the WTO framework, South Africa initially did not join the Africa group or the ACP in the WTO ministerials. At the 6th WTO ministerial in Hong Kong for the first time all developing country groups held a meeting renewing their call for a comprehensive development outcome of the Doha round. South Africa's tactics changed.

At the first WTO ministerial in Singapore, the delegates of the European Community had pushed to extend the coverage of the WTO by proposing new agreements in investment, competition and government procurement together with trade facilitation. South Africa supported proposals for a new round of WTO negotiations including the new Singapore issues even before the 1999 Seattle Ministerial. It did not consult with other African governments on the new issues before defining its own position. In the Seattle and Doha ministerials, South Africa's trade delegation tried to play the intermediary between the leading trading nations and the underdeveloped nations instead of supporting out of solidarity the concerns and demands of poor African nations. In Seattle, South Africa's strategy was to trade off the 'new issues' against implementation issues and technical assistance. It risked a divided African stance on the new issues and another round of industrial tariff reductions. Reportedly, Kenya, Mozambique, Tanzania, Uganda, Zimbabwe and Zambia had submitted a joint paper explaining that they did not want a new round of negotiations to begin in Doha. Instead they demanded a study on the impacts of previous liberalisation on domestic firms, employment and government revenue for developing countries and on tariff escalation for developed countries. They were supported by Egypt, India and Brazil in this position, but not by South Africa (Jawara / Kwa 2004, 25). Before and during the Doha ministerial, the South African delegation "embarked on a broad drive to get African countries to consider a new round of WTO trade negotiations. [It] ... managed to take the SADC along with it, but failed to reach consensus with other African countries." (Mail & Guardian, 2001, 16th November). African ACP countries finally accepted the "Doha Development Agenda", because otherwise they would not have received a waiver for their Cotonou Agreement with the EU. To some of the other African delegations South Africa appeared too defensive and accommodating towards the leading global actors pushing the new Singapore issues, further tariff reductions in trade of industrial products and a widening of trade in services.

South Africa did probably see its re-integration into the global economy more as a chance than as a threat. If it had hopes that following the economic policy lead of the US and the EU would bring an increase of FDI, it discovered that these were not realised. It is doubtful whether one should see AGOA as a US "reward" for "good governance". AGOA aims for full free trade agreements. South African preferential exports 2001–2005 under AGOA constitute at an average about 15 percent of its total exports to the USA. For NEPAD the AGOA policy has also not worked out. In 2003 it was noted that while preferential exports under AGOA had increased, the value of total exports to the US from Sub-Saharan Africa had declined by 18 percent to $ 18,2 billion since AGOA's inception (*Financial Mail* 1.8.2003).

South Africa also forged an alliance with India and Brazil concerning issues in trade related intellectual property rights (TRIPs). The USA and the pharmaceutical industry have been promoting strong patent protection for pharmaceuticals. Pharmaceutical corporations took the South African government to court in 2001 to prevent it from introducing a law allowing compulsory licensing for the national production of generic (and cheaper) medicines. In Doha the highest profile issue was the effect of the TRIPs agreement on the affordability of anti-retroviral medicines for HIV-Aids patients. The final wording of § 4 read: "We agree that the TRIPs Agreement does not and should not prevent members from taking measures to protect public health." The TRIPs agreement allows a government to issue a licence to a local generic manufacturer for producing a copy of a patented medicine. But article 31(f) requires the generic drug to be sold "predominantly" on the local market. The exact way in which developing countries without manufacturing capacity could have access to generic drugs remained unresolved. § 6 of the TRIPs and Health declaration therefore states: "We instruct the Council for TRIPs to find an expeditious solution to this problem and to report to the General Council before the end of 2002." This deadline was missed. The USA, the EC and Japan insisted that intellectual property protection was the best way to promote pharmaceutical research and development. Developing countries are therefore still vulnerable to the high price dictates of pharmaceutical corporations (Jawara/Kwa 2004, 123). The South African Minister for Trade and Industries, Erwin, consistently refused to use his regulatory powers in terms of the 1997 Medicines Act to lower drug prices. According to the most active social movement in South Africa – the Treatment Action Campaign (TAC), Erwin even rejected offers by countries like Brazil to transfer technology for the manufacture of generics. The TAC campaign received massive popular support in South Africa itself and worldwide. It is here that South African trade and health policies were criticised most severely by the public. On 30th August 2003, a WTO deal was signed empowering the WTO secretariat and the TRIPs Council to review individual licenses, oversee the use of compulsory licenses of patents on medicines, and evaluate national manufacturing capacity. The Indian pharmaceutical Alliance was of the opinion that "no generic manufacturer would be able or willing to comply with its provision". Other critics described the WTO solution as "largely symbolic" (Correa 2004).

Driven by the interests of its agro-business, South Africa initially joined first the Cairns Group in the WTO, which argues for agricultural trade liberalisation. Australia, New Zealand and Canada dominate the Cairns group. The Cairns group leaders do not share the developmental interests of states like India or South Africa. In the run-up to the WTO Cancun Ministerial, South Africa joined a new country grouping, which counts Brazil, India and China among its lead members. The new alliance, established in August 2003, is called the G-20. Hugueney, a Brazilian official, stated that the G-20 was born "to open up a space for negotiations on agriculture at Cancun" as an alternative to just passively accepting the agreement between the EU and the US as the basis for the results on agriculture. Whereas the Cairns Group is more focused on trade liberalisation, market access and an end to trade distorting subsidies, the G-20 support special and differential treatment of developing countries in the area of market access (a dual approach to market access). The G-20 wants to combine trade liberalisation with development objectives. Even though agricultural trade is dominated by OECD protectionist policies, the G-20 realise that developing countries may in this round on market access obtain greater gains in agriculture than in services or manufactured products. "No one could lightly dismiss a group that represented almost 60 percent of the world population, 70 percent of the world's farmers and 26 percent of world trade in agriculture", according to Hugueney, speaking at world social forum in Mumbai (FES Berlin, Briefing Papers 2004, 3).

The G-20 supported the African group's initiative on cotton and integrated it in its platform. Both jointly demanded the elimination of domestic support measures and export subsidies for cotton producers in the USA and elsewhere no later than the 6th WTO ministerial in Hong Kong. In Hong Kong it became apparent that 2006 will only see the cutting off of export subsidies in cotton, but no commitment was to be made for an immediate ending of domestic subsidies for cotton. Thus the dumping of subsidised cotton will continue. The G-20 also proposed urgent development assistance (or an emergency fund) for developing countries that are net cotton exporters. In November 2005, the US trade delegate R. Portmann proposed a 'West Africa Cotton Improvement Program' worth US $ 7 million – an amount that the US pays its own farmers in about 10 hours of domestic subsidies. This $7m programme was offered only to 5 of the 33 cotton producing countries of Africa. It would compensate only a minimal part of the losses incurred by African producers. The decision of a WTO arbitration board declaring the US cotton subsidies illegal and demanding a reform of the system was not respected by the USA during the Hong Kong negotiations.

Concerning export subsidisation in general, the G-20 and the ACP, LDC and the Africa Group proposed a five-year deadline for a credible end to the elimination of all export subsidies. The LDC and the Africa Group add here that the end to export subsidies should not prejudice the Special and Differential Treatment in the LDC's market access or of the Net-Food Importing Developing Countries. In terms of market access, there is a joint interest in special safeguard mechanisms (SSM) to protect developing countries against dumping. (See also Faizel Ismail, Sept. 2002). The Hong Kong ministerial agreed to end export subsidies only in 2013, and regarding excessive domestic agricultural subsidies, no clear decision was reached.

There are also differences between the positions of the G-20 and the LDC/ACP and the Africa Group. They stem partly from the fact, that the G-20 agricultural exports are controlled by corporate agriculture, whereas in the LDC the majority of farmers are small scale and struggling against chronic poverty. G-20 agriculture does not enjoy the same preferential access to the EU markets as the ACP/LDC countries. It is therefore not preference dependent. The G-20 recognises, however, that for the LDC the dismantling of the special preferences poses real risks that no sensible government with a weak economic base could take lightly. But the G-20 is generally opposed to granting special treatment on market access to *specific* products when addressing preference erosion (South Centre, 2005). This may contain potential for a future conflict of interest or tough competition between producers in the G-20 and the LDC/ACP, for example competition for cane sugar- or beef exports to the EU. Finally, the G-20 is very much interested in subjecting agricultural trade to the disciplines of the multilateral trading system. This can be seen by the G-20 efforts in July 2004 (WTO document WT/L/579 of 2 August 2004).

Since the EU already passed its 'Everything but Arms' initiative for the LDC, it was mainly the USA and Japan who were asked to follow suit in Hong Kong. Whereas the Doha mandate included a duty-free, quota-free market access for LDCs, in Hong Kong the USA and Japan were only willing to allow the LDC free market access for 97 percent of their export products. This allows the USA to continue to protect their textiles and clothing sector against cheap imports.

In Hong Kong, South Africa participated actively in negotiations on tariff cuts for industrial products, demanding together with Brazil, India, Argentina, Indonesia, the Philippines and Namibia that rich countries end tariff escalation and tariff peaks against industrial exports of poor countries – an issue already vigorously discussed in Seattle. At the same time, this so-called core group wanted to defend some flexibility for developing countries. The question of formulae and figures on cuts in industrial tariffs have not yet been finalised.

When negotiating services, the poor countries suffered a setback. During the Uruguay round developing countries had agreed to the GATS under the condition that each WTO member would have the right to decide which services sector, if any, they would open, the pace and extent of market opening, and the limitations to liberalising each sector (Jawara,Kwa 2004, 31). This is the so-called 'bottom up' approach. The EU, dissatisfied that until July 2005 only 92 of the 147 members had presented offers for liberalising services sectors, started a 'benchmark offensive': members should present a minimum offer to liberalise a certain number of sectors and commit themselves further more to continue liberalisation in plurilateral negotiations (Hachfeld 2005). Brazil pointed out that the GATS does not oblige countries to take commitments in any sector and that plurilateral negotiations would be a deviation from the MFN principle. In Hongkong developing countries were pressured to aim for 'qualitative benchmarks' and to participate in plurilateral negotiations on services liberalisations.

Concluding remarks

South Africa's democratic constitution of 1996 was the outcome of a negotiated compromise containing rupture with racist legislation and continuity with many aspects of the capitalist system of production. There was never a welfare state before, but, even after democratisation, the early commitment to neo-liberal policies will not allow for it. The deliberate creation of a black bourgeoisie, in a sense a replay of 1930s policies by the NP, has exchanged solidarity among the exploited for competitive individualism. Even pan-Africanism, strong during the struggle decades, has been replaced by a chauvinist xenophobia against black foreigners from poor neighbouring states. It makes rhetoric of an "African Renaissance" appear as an irrelevant flight of fantasy. Patriotism may be a fine sentiment of valuing one's culture and origin, but nationalism, apart from being an imported concept, contains always an element of hostile contempt of "the others". It is a cultural barrier to regional integration.

Recent South African foreign economic policy was formulated in a general framework characterised politically by the end of the Cold War and economically by the accumulation strategies of transnational corporations. Nationally, South Africa had to overcome a 30 year long history of economic decline. A great part of the population, incorporated by imperialism's brutal force into a system of racial capitalism, had become, and still is, captive to chronic poverty. The democratic state and 'old' incumbent capital enabled a small layer of black bourgeoisie to emerge as the prime beneficiary of new state policy. Society experienced a shift in power relations. State policy as announced in GEAR or in multilateral agencies like the WTO is no longer the outcome of long and popular political debates between social forces, but reflects a concentration of state power as a necessary condition of falling in step with global market discipline. The change from import substitution towards an export oriented industrial restructuring and growth strategy, initiated by the outgoing apartheid regime, has been reinforced with new vigour by the democratic government. Export bias has largely been eliminated, and import tariffs have been reduced, faster and exceeding that which was agreed to at the WTO level. At the start of negotiations with the European Union in 1996 on a free trade agreement, a self-imposed structural adjustment programme called GEAR backed this up. However, a coherent industrial strategy has not been formulated for South Africa or for the SADC region, of which South Africa became a member. Unemployment and the informal sector grew rapidly, productivity and value added less so. The opening of the financial markets has made the economy vulnerable to speculative attacks from outside. Fluctuating exchange rates may neutralise export growth. In addition, local private capital invested more outside South Africa than into new production and places of employment inside the country.

The early debates on import substitution versus export-led growth tended to ignore the importance of the domestic market. Its potential purchasing power languishes from the fact that 40 percent of the population receive a lesser share of national income than ten years ago. Notwithstanding slow economic growth rates, the mass of the population may become poorer, resulting in the further erosion of previously stable social relations. Crime is on the increase. To turn economic growth towards the creation of new places of employment – not an automatic process – a socio-economic decision has to be taken by state, social forces and capital. They have to agree to the mechanism which would facilitate the invigoration of the domestic market, including places of employment for production by the poor for the poor, and a limitation/reduction of the informal sector which already has absorbed more than 30 percent of all employees.

The European Union has long styled itself as the champion of free trade, although it practices managed trade. Protectionism is rife in the EU's Common Agricultural Policy and shows itself in tariff peaks against industrial exports of developing countries. The EU nevertheless actively encouraged its former colonies in Africa to develop regional trade organisations. While it refused for a long time to impose sanctions against the apartheid state, the EU was the main funding agency of overlapping regional organisations. It funded *inter alia* SADC(C), the PTA (later COMESA) and the World Bank's Cross Border Initiative (since 2000 called the Regional Integration Facilitation Forum and "owned" by COMESA). The EU wanted open markets in Africa - and a preferential access to them, in comparison to the US or Asian traders. The EU supported trade integration of African regions. Even so: it did not matter to the EU, that there was no real progress in African regional trade integration, that intra-regional trade in COMESA, for an example, amounted only to 4,9 percent of total trade in 2000 (Wellmer 2005, 31). The EU still encouraged COMESA to form a Free Trade Agreement and a Customs Union. Real inter-African trade facilitation was of no direct concern to the EU, in difference to trade facilitation as a 'new issue' at the WTO. As long as the regional label can later be used by the EU as the leverage for enforcing WTO style market discipline later on, when the EU itself has signed FTAs with these regions in 2008 according to the Cotonou Agreement.

In June 1996 the EU agreed on a mandate to negotiate a FTA with South Africa only. At the First WTO Ministerial in Singapore (Dec. 1996), the Commission pushed aggressively to extend the scope of multilateral trade by introducing new agreements in investment, competition, government procurement and trade facilitation. Essentially these 'new issues' are to deal with any national legislation in developing countries that favours local companies over foreign ones, in order to concur with the WTO principle of national treatment and the MFN principle. Most developing countries rejected the idea of launching a new round of multilateral negotiations, particularly on the new issues, because they were still struggling with losses and adjustment costs in implementing the agreements of the Uruguay Round. However, Singapore, South Africa, Mexico and South Korea supported the 'new issues'. At the end of 1996 South African officials had a formal position on impending bilateral talks with the EU. Thereafter, South Africa was co-opted by the EU in WTO talks in Seattle and Doha to get other SADC countries to back the new round of WTO talks. South Africa's strongly wished to conclude a favourable bilateral trade deal with the EU. To this end, it supported EU positions at the multilateral talks. In Doha SADC fell in with the South African position because it feared that the Cotonou Agreement would otherwise not get WTO approval. Most recently, Peter Mandelson, the EU trade commissioner, criticised South Africa:

> The EU has made an ambitious services offer in the DDA negotiations but is dismayed that South Africa has not. We have yet to see an initial offer, or request, tabled by South Africa and I hope this will be rectified soon...South Africa can also give a lead to developing countries by playing its full part in the DDA. An early post-Hong Kong services offer will help to do this.   (EC Press Release 13/02/2006)

Even before being elected into power, the ANC had attended SADC meetings. South Africa joined SADC in 1994 with the objective of making regional development integration a priority concern of external economic policy. Trade was to be one of the tools for regional development integration, but not the only one. Every member of SADC was aware that a neo-classical approach to regional integration would result in polarisation between states of different economic potential. After 30 years of regional wars, claims to regional hegemony and economic polarisation were to be avoided at all costs. Therefore, market integration had a back seat. Development integration had to tackle the sensitive task of finding a common strategy in the allocation of regional industries, the pooling of regionally available technology and resources and of industrial restructuring. Before any progress had been made, the European Union intervened. For its own purposes of trade expansion, the EU wanted regional market integration in Southern Africa, not development integration. To manage this, it was decided to break up SADC, select its strongest member state and conclude with it a FTA. The European Union, having been too greedy to decide itself in favour of sanctions against apartheid, was also unable to consider the possible outcomes of its FTA offer for the common weal of co-operation between a South Africa free of *Herrenvolk* ideology and the subcontinent of Southern Africa.

During the seven sanction years, South African TNCs had observed how the global economy had been sidelining them. They put enormous pressure on the government to accept the EU challenge and go all out for trade and financial markets liberalisation with South Africa's most important trading partner. In order to gain access to investment capital and new technology and to send a political message to the rest of the global actors, South Africa accepted to negotiate with the EU on a bilateral FTA with WTO-plus attachments. It also started on FTA negotiations with the USA, EFTA, Mercosur, India and China. SADC was not present in any of these negotiations. None of these other negotiations has been concluded because of the caution exercised by the other SACU member states.

Internally, South Africa exchanged a Keynesian policy for a neo-liberal GEAR agenda. Regionally, a co-operative development approach to integration was turned into a mercantilist call of the leading economy to the others in the region: "Join my value chain at the lower primary producer end." Having been driven into heavy debts by previous regional wars and having to accept structural adjustment programmes by the IMF/WB, SADC passed a trade protocol, which now made free trade the only means to regional integration. When the EU started to negotiate FTAs with all African ACP states under the title of "Economic Partnership Agreements", it finally dawned on all member states of SADC that the EU had managed to effectively break up the original SADC concept and with it the region itself.

References

Adedeji, A. (2002), Africa's Alternative Framework and a New Industrial Strategy for Africa. In: *African Development Perspectives Yearbook 1990/91* Vol. II, Münster: pp. 56-72.

Amin, S. (2002), Africa: living on the fringe. In: *New Agenda. South African Journal of Social and Economic Policy* N° 7, 2002: 20.

ANC (1990): *Discussion Document on Economic Policy.*

ANC (1992): *Ready to Govern. ANC Policy Guidelines for a Democratic South Africa.* May.

ANC (1994), *The Reconstruction and Development Programme.* Johannesburg.

Bauer, G., Taylor, S. D. (2005), *Politics in Southern Africa. State and Society in Transition.* Boulder, Colorado 2005, pp 404.

Bell, T., Madula, N. (2001), *Where has all the Growth Gone? South African Manufacturing Industry 1970-2000.* NIEP/TIPS. Johannesburg, September.

Belli, P., Finger, M., Ballivian, A. (1993), *South Africa. A Review of Trade Policies.* The World Bank Southern Africa Department, August 1993, Discussion Paper 4.

Boidin, J.C., Percival, D. (1998), EU/South Africa negotiations: What consequences for South Africa's neighbours? In: *European Commission, The European Union and South Africa. Building a framework for long term co-operation.* Brussels, February.

Bond, P. (2000), *Elite Transition. From Apartheid to Neoliberalism in South Africa,* (London, Pietermaritzburg).

--------- (2001), Thabo Mbeki and NEPAD. Breaking or shining the chains of global apartheid? In: Jacobs, S. & Clalland, R. (eds.), *Thabo Mbeki's World. The Politics and Ideology of the South African President,* (Pietermaritzburg: London), pp. 53-81.

--------- (2004), *Talk Left, Walk Right. South Africa's Frustrated Global Reforms.* Scottsville 2004.

Cassim, R., Onyango, D., Skosana, Z. and D.E. van Seventer (2003), *A Review of the Changing Composition of the South African Economy.* TIPS, (Johannesburg), www.tips.org.za.

Castel-Branco, C. N. (2004), *What is the Experience and Impact of South African Trade and Investment on the Growth and Development of Host Economies? A View from Mozambique.* SARPN/HSCR Pretoria March 2004, pp 28-54.

Correa, C. (2004), Access to Drugs under TRIPs: A Not so Expeditious Solution. In: Bridges 1, *International Centre for Trade and Sustainable Development,* (Geneva).

Daniel, J., Naidoo, V. and S. Naidu (2003), *The South Africans Have Arrived: Post-apartheid corporate expansion into Africa,* (Johannesburg), www.hsrcpress.ac.za.

Davies, R. (2000), *Situating the Trade Challenges facing the SADC.* Keynote Address SARIPS Conference on "Emerging Trade Relations in the 21st Century", (Harare), p. 27.

Du Toit, A. (2005), *Chronic and Structural Poverty in South Africa. Challenges for Action and Research.* CSSR Working Paper 121, July.

Economist Intelligence Unit (2001), *South Africa. Country Profile,* (London).

Fine, B., Rustomjee, Z. (1996), *The Political Economy of South Africa. From Minerals-Energy Complex to Industrialisation,* (London).

Flatters, F. (2002), SADC Rules of Origin: Impediments to Regional Integration and Global Competitiveness. In: *Southern African Update. A Trade & Industrial Strategies Publication*, September 2002, Volume 15.

Hachfeld, D. (2005), *Neues vom GATS: Die Daumenschrauben werden angezogen. Eine Analyse der Benchmark Offensive der EU in den aktuellen GATS Verhandlungen.* Attack.

Hirsch, A. (1997), The Role of Growth and Development in South Africa's Trade Policy. In: R. Houghton (ed.), *Trading on Development. South Africa's relations with the European Union*, FDG, FES, (Johannesburg).

Honey, P. (2003), Arms Deal Investigation. In: *Financial Mail* 30 May 2003.

Hugueney, C. (2004), The G-20: Passing Phenomenon or Here to Stay? In: *FES Briefing Papers 'Dialogue on Globalisation'*.

IMF (1990), *South Africa – Recent Economic Developments*. Article IV consultations, SM/90/176, (Washington).

IMF (1994), *Key Issues in the South African Economy*, (Washington).

Industrial Development Corporation (1996), *Manufacturing Trading Conditions. Pretoria*, Vol. 1 May 1996, Vol.2 October 1996.

Innes, D. (1984), *ANGLO. Anglo American and the rise of modern South Africa*, (Braamfontein).

Ismail, F. (1994), Industrial Strategy and Economic Development in South Africa 1990-1993. In: *Review of African Political Economy* N° 59, pp. 50-59.

Ismail, F. (2002), *On the Road to Cancun: A Development Perspective on EU Trade Policies*. Two Parts.

Jawara, F., Kwa, A. (2004), *Behind the Scenes at the WTO: the real world of international trade negotiations. Lessons of Cancun* – updated version, (London).

Joffe, A., Kaplan, D., Kaplinski, R., Lewis, D. (1996), *Improving South Africa's Manufacturing Performance*, (Cape Town).

Joy, C., Hardstaff, P. (2003), W*hose Development Agenda? An Analysis of the European Union's GATS Requests of Developing Countries*, (London).

Keet, D. (2003), *Proposals on the role of trade within the New Partnership for Africa's Development (NEPAD) – Challenges and Questions*, (Johannesburg).

Lee, M. C. (2003), *The Political Economy of Regionalism in Southern Africa*, (Cape Town, London).

Lewis, D., Reed, K., Teljeur, E. (1999), South Africa: Economic Policy Making and Implementation in Africa: A Study of Strategic Trade and Selective Industrial Policies. In: IDRC (ed.), *The Politics of Trade and Industrial Policy in Africa*.

Lowe, Ph. (2000), Main Parameters of the EU-SA Partnership. In: Bertelsmann-Scott, T., Mills, G. and Sidiropoulos, E. (eds.), *The EU-SA Agreement*. SAIIA. Pretoria 2000: 39-45

Malefane, M. (2005), SACP accuses state of enriching elite. In: *Sunday Times* (South Africa) December 4, 2005.

Marais, H. (2001²), *South Africa. Limits to Change. The political economy of transition*, (London, New York, Cape Town).

Maré, G. (2003), The state of the state: Contestation and race-reassertion in a neoliberal terrain. In: Daniel, J., Habib, A., Southall, R. (eds.), *State of the Nation: South Africa 2003-2004*, (Johannesburg), pp 25-52.

Mbeki, T. (2003), Letter from the President. www.anc.org.za/ancdocs/ anctoday/2003/ at 33.

McCarthy, C. (2000), *South Africa and the Region. Reconciling the Benefits and Costs of Integrating Unequal Economies*, (Leipzig).

Mistry, P. S. (2000), *Africa's Record of Regional Co-operation and Integration. In: African Affairs*, 99, pp. 553-573.

Mpande-Chuulu, Ch. (2004), Harmonising Trade Relations between Regional Economic Communities: the case of SADC and COMESA. In: SARPN, *Stability, Poverty Reduction and South African Trade and Investment in Southern Africa*, (Pretoria), pp. 92-94.

Naidu, S., Lutchman, J. (2004), Understanding South Africa's Engagement in the Region: Has the Leopard Changed its Spots? In: SARPN (ed.), *Stability, Poverty Reduction and South African Trade and Investment in Southern Africa*, (Pretoria), pp. 12-23.

OAU (1981), *Lagos Plan of Action for the Economic Development of Africa*, (Geneva: International Institute for Labour Studies).

Palotti, A. (2004), SADC: A Development Community without a Development Policy? In: *ROAPE* N°101, pp. 513-531.

Panitch, L. (1994), *Globalisation and the state*. (paper), (Mexico).

Portfolio Committee on Trade and Industry (1996), *Report to Parliament on Public Hearings. Tariff Protection in the Context of Industrial Policy*, (Pretoria).

Roberts, S. (1998), A *Preliminary Analysis of the Impact of Trade Liberalisation on Manufacturing Or: Will trade liberalisation generate export-led growth in South Africa?* (London).

Rustomjee, Z. (1997), Economic Growth hinges on tariff reform. In: *Business Day* 14-2-1977.

RSA, Department of Foreign Affairs (2003), *The Role of Regional Economic Communities as the Building Blocs of the African Union*, (Pretoria).

Saul, J. S., Gelb, St. (1981), *The Crisis in South Africa. Class Defence, Class Revolution. Monthly Review Press*, (New York and London).

Slovo, J. (1977²), South Africa – No Middle Road. In: Davidson, Slovo, Wilkinson, Southern Africa, *The New Politics of Revolution*, (Penguin Books), pp 103-210.

Smalberger, W. (2000), Lessons learnt by South Africa during the Negotiations. In: Bertelsmann-Scott, T., Mills, G., Sidiropoulos, E., The EU-SA Agreement: South Africa, Southern Africa and the European Union, (Pretoria).

Sole, S. (2005), Arms Report Sanitised. In: *Mail & Guardian* 7 January 2005.

South African Government (2003), "Procedures for the application, administration and allocation of export permits under the TDCA between the EU and South Africa", Department of Agriculture, *Government Gazette*, 3 October 2003, pp. 40-52. Notice 2509 of 2003.

South African Reserve Bank (2005), *Labour Market Frontiers*, 25 November.

South African Reserve Bank, *Quarterly Bulletin*, various issues.

South Centre (2005), *State of Play in Agriculture Negotiations*. Country Groupings Positions. SC/TADP/AN/AG 10, (Geneva).

Stang, B. (2002), Anklage wegen Bestechung. Lesotho bezichtigt deutsche Firma der Schmiergeldzahlung. In: *Süddeutsche Zeitung* 14./15. August 2002.

Tetzlaff, R., Jakobeit, C. (2005), *Das nachkoloniale Afrika. Politik-Wirtschaft-Gesellschaft*, (Wiesbaden).

The Department of Trade and Industry (2002), *Accelerating Growth and Development: The Contribution of an Integrated Manufacturing Strategy*, (Pretoria), www. dti. gov.za.

Thompson, Carol B. (2002), Regional Challenges to Globalisation: Perspectives from Southern Africa. In: *New Political Economy*, Vol.5, N°1, 2000.

Tsie, B. (2001), International Political Economy and Southern Africa. In: P. Vale, L. A. Swatuk and B. Oden (eds.), *Theory, Change, and Southern Africa's Future*, (London).

UN (1982), *A Programme for the Industrial Development Decade for Africa*. Jointly Prepared by ECA, OAU, and UNIDO, (New York: UN).

UNCTAD (2005), *Erosion of Preferences for the Least Developed Countries: Assessment of Effects and Mitigating Options*. TD/B/52/4, (Geneva).

UNDP (2003a), *Making Global Trade work for People*, (Geneva).

UNDP (2003b), South Africa Human Development Report 2003. *The Challenge of Sustainable Development in South Africa: Unlocking People's Creativity*, (Oxford).

UN Economic Commission for Africa (1989), *African Alternative Framework to Structural Adjustment Programmes for Socio-Economic Recovery and Transformation*. E/ECA/CM.15/ 6/ Rev.3.

Weeks, J. (2000), *Stuck in Low Gear? Macroeconomic Policy in South Africa, 1996-1998*. SOAS, CDPR Discussion Paper 1300, (London).

Wellmer, G. (1992), Regional Labour Flows. In: S. Vieira, W. G. Martin and I. Wallerstein (eds.), *How Fast the Wind? Southern Africa 1975-2000*, (Trenton), pp. 83-97.

--------- (1998), *On the effects of European beef exports to South Africa on communal farmers in Namibia. A case study on the coherence of European Policy*, (Stuttgart).

--------- (2000), *SADC between regional integration and reciprocal free trade with the European Union. A Study on future trade relations between the EU and SADC States*, (Bielefeld).

-------- (2004), *Vulamanzi! Municipal Service Partnerships and the Poor*. Situation Report, (Bielefeld).

-------- (2005), *Tragen wirtschaftliche Partnerschaftsabkommen (EPAs) zur Beseitigung der Armut bei? Die Handelspolitik der Europäischen Union mit den AKP Staaten am Beispiel der Entwicklungsgemeinschaft des Südlichen Afrika (SADC)*, (Bielefeld).

Wille, C. (2004), Act will target white-collar crime. In: *Business Day* 15 January 2004.

World Bank (1994), *Reducing Poverty in South Africa. Options for Equitable and Sustainable Growth*, (Washington).

WTO Trade Policy Review (2003), SACU-South Africa March 2003.

WTO (2004), *Doha Work Programme*. Decision Adopted by the General Council 1-8-2004 WT/L/579, (Geneva), 2 August 2004.

Zarenda, H. (1997), Regional Integration Policies in Southern Africa. In: Michie, J., Padayachee, V. (eds.), *The Political Economy of South Africa's Transition. Policy Perspectives in the late 1990s*, (London), pp. 55-69.

Chapter 8

Turkey: WTO Negotiations in the Shadow of the European Union

Gaye Yilmaz

Introduction

Turkey is a particular case among the middle powers in that it already began to look for a close alignment with one of the emerging regional blocs about 45 years ago. In 1959, the then Turkish government declared its intention to seek a close association with the European Economic Community (EEC). The first agreement between Turkey and the EEC was negotiated in 1963. Over the next forty years, closer bonds were forged, though occasional disagreements have emerged, especially in regard to Turkish-Greek and Turkish-Cypriot relations. Presently, the officially declared aim of Turkey's full accession to European Union (EU) is a subject of considerable and acrimonious debates in the EU, and it does not go uncontested in Turkey either. While this longstanding alignment with a major regional bloc is unique among Third World middle powers, the phases of Turkey's economic development are in line with middle powers in Latin America or with South Africa. After the great crisis of 1929, a long phase of import substitution industrialisation was started. This model reached some limits in the 1970s. It was increasingly politically contested. In 1980, a more extraverted development was initiated and was vigorously propelled by a military regime. Whereas the 1980s were characterised by the attempt to achieve a positive trade balance, the 1990s have seen a financialised development model built upon volatile inflows of capital. The changes in the development model have affected the trade and investment policies of the successive Turkish governments, but they did not put into question the fundamental orientation towards the EU. Therefore, an analysis of Turkey's trade policies is of particular interest.

In this chapter, the economic structure of the country is historically analysed from a social and political perspective. This is followed by evaluations of the foreign direct investment regime and Turkeys' foreign trade and trade policies.

The economic structure of Turkey

Background from a historical perspective

From 1927 to 1979, the underlying political and economic basis of the Import Substitution Industry (ISI) strategy was one of grand, yet delicate, alliance between the bureaucratic elites, industrial capitalists, industrial workers, and the peasantry (Boratav and Yeldan 2001, 6). Accordingly, private industrial profits were fed from three sources: first, the protectionist trade regime, often implemented through strong non-tariff barriers, enabled industrialists to capture oligopolistic profits and rents originating from a readily available, protected domestic market. Second, the existence of a public enterprise system with the strategic role of producing cheap intermediates through artificially low, administered prices enabled the private industrial enterprises (and the rural economy) to minimise material input costs. Third, a repressed financial system (supported by undervalued foreign currencies) enabled cheap financing for fixed capital investments in manufacturing. In turn, industrialists "accepted" the conditions of a general rise in manufacturing wages, and an agricultural support programme which biased the domestic terms of trade to favour agriculture (Boratav and Yeldan 2001, 6). The ISI strategy suffered from chronic external constraints.

On 24 January 1980, the Government announced a huge reform package to liberalise the whole economy including labour, goods, money and capital markets, foreign direct investment and public enterprises. On 12 September 1980, the third military coup was realised as a response to the resistances of the masses against this very comprehensive liberalisation program.

Besides several legal changes in the Constitution which were necessary to introduce these anti-social laws, privatisation was the most vital item of this package. This also implied that the state put an end to Keynesianism. All mines and other public enterprises were opened to privatisation regardless of the nationality of buyers. As part of a regressive incomes policy, the wages and salaries were frozen for the first year and bonuses were totally removed; corporate taxes were reduced and a new value added tax was introduced. Financial markets were established and improved. In order to facilitate this process, the law to protect the value of Turkish currency (TL) was radically amended. As a consequence of foreign exchange liberalisation, TL became quite vulnerable to external financial shocks.

These steps opened the way for an unstable, more indebted and volatile economic process in the country. The relationship between the military coup in September 1980 and the liberalisation steps taken soon after the coup was expressed by Turgut Özal, the architect of the January 24 measures, in his address to industrialists: "We wouldn't get the results of the reform program of January, 24 if we didn't have the military coup in September 1980" (cit. in Ercan 2004, 158).

The first stage of neo-liberal reforms initiated by Turkey in 1980 was characterised by enhanced efforts to achieve a surplus in the balance of trade. In 1989, the Turkish government decided to de-regulate the capital account and to fully liberalise its financial markets. This opened the way to a financialised development model which was predominant in the 1990s, when there was again international excess liquidity and financial institutions looked for investment opportunities in the semi-periphery in order to unload their excess liquidity. As a consequence of financial market liberalisation, the Central Bank lost its control over the money markets. It was deprived of the option to pursue active policies in regard to the exchange rate and the interest rate, which actually became an exogenous variable, totally dependent on the decisions of international arbiters (Yeldan 2003). The dramatic effects of deregulating the flows of capital which opened a way for hot money speculations were to be seen in the financial crisis that started in 1994 and continued with the further devastating bouts in 2000 and 2001. Financial instability was aggravated by the high degree of currency substitution which drastically curbed the policy options of the Central Bank. The predominant objective of fiscal policies has become servicing rising levels of public debt and reducing the risk of default. This is to be realised by targeting the primary surplus of the public budget. Ruling classes gradually have fallen in line with this way of thinking. National policies are guided increasingly by the criteria of the International Monetary Fund (IMF) because this is perceived as the only way "respectability" (as it is defined by international finance) can be acquired and economic stability and "reasonable growth" can be achieved (Boratav 2003, 10). Today, this vicious circle is increasingly used as a tool to blackmail in international trade negotiations.

The foreign direct investment regime

Foreign trade and investment have started to become an important topic on the agenda, particularly in advanced capitalist states, since 1970s. This renewed attention to foreign trade and investment was due both to the crisis in the Organisation for Economic Cooperation and Development (OECD) countries and to the lack of investment in developing countries. The reduction in transport and communication costs has facilitated the relocation of production. Successive Turkish governments have banked on the attraction of foreign capital. In a letter of intent to the IMF dated 18 January 2001, the Turkish Government summarises the present investment policies in the following way:

> For the purpose of promoting the role of the private sector in the economy it has been considered to speed up the privatisation, to develop a business friendly environment including to establish an Investor Council and to encourage domestic and foreign direct investment.
> (cit. in Karahanogullari and Dikmen 2002, 1)

This project was developed and realised in 5 June 2003, with the active support of the Foreign Direct Investment Advisory Service (FIAS) which had been founded by the International Financial Corporation (IFC) under the patronages of the IMF and World Bank (WB) in 1985. FIAS has been functioning in more than 120 countries in order to improve the environment for foreign direct investors in these countries (FIAS 2004). In the legislation in Turkey, it is advocated that a "rational balance between the interests of the country and foreign investors should be achieved in order to promote and maximize Foreign Direct Investment (FDI) inflows" (Karahanogullari and Dikmen 2002, 2). The privileges to be conceded to foreign investors include also portfolio investments which will be made through the Istanbul Stock Exchange. Another target of the legislation is to eliminate some provisions existing in the current law, aiming at preventing foreign investors from having the majority of votes in state monopolies. Foreign investors have the right to sue the government in international dispute settlement mechanisms in the case of disputes (Karahanogullari and Dikmen 2002, 3).

According to foreign trade and investment experts, it is a must to attract "high quality" FDI on the one hand, and to adopt domestic business friendly policies on the other hand in order to overcome the problem of capital insufficiency and structural bottle-necks. Here, the term of "high quality" means that the capital inflows have a long-term perspective, are aimed at exportation, are wholly integrated into the national economy, increase social and environmental standards, bring high technology, invest in R&D and increase the productivity and competitive power of the country (Caliskan 2003). However, some of the criteria that qualify FDI as being of "high quality" are not necessarily the type of environment that foreign companies are seeking. For example, this is the case with high social and environmental standards. In this field, it can be noted that the ruling circles in Turkey did rather anticipate the potential investors' desires for low social standards and eliminated constitutional and other legal provisions that stipulated social rights that might be regarded as barriers to free trade. In addition, factors like political and economic stability and general economic performance play a key role in investment decisions. In view of the high degree of economic volatility and the recurrent political crises in the 1990s, it is not surprising that "the FDI stock of Turkey has developed at a quite low level in comparison with its equivalents" amounting to US$ 9.650 billion as of December 2005 (AnsesNet 2006).

Recent signals illustrate that the "business environment" in Turkey has continuously improved and this tendency has received strong applause from interest groups inside and outside of the country. For these groups, the major problem is the large extent of informal economic activities, which account for more than 50 per cent of total employment and lead to a narrowing of the tax base. Furthermore, a special strategy which should include less onerous regulations in product and labour markets and shifting the burden of tax and social security charges away from labour is also suggested by these interest groups (Gonenc 2004, 2). Social security charges which are jointly paid by employer and employee are de facto part of the "social wage". Thus, it can be argued that the main target of the proposed and ongoing changes in the social security and tax legislation is to eliminate the burden of tax and social security charges away from capital rather than labour.

In regard to the sub-title "investment" of the "Singapore Issues", the Turkish Government declared in the Doha negotiations that Turkey is in favour of a multilateral approach instead of plurilateral approach which has been strongly defended by many developing countries (TCDTM 2001)[1]. Parallel to this position taken in the Doha negotiations, the Turkish Government has now begun to draft its future plans for the third generation of investors' rights. Although they are not being seen as determining factors to attract foreign investors, tax incentives, free trade zone and/or export processing zones and reduced bureaucracy are seen as facilitating factors for FDI inflows (Caliskan 2003, 7).

The efforts to attract FDI have not yielded the results the Government had hoped for. In the field of FDI, the main competitors for Turkey are Central and Eastern

Europe Counties (CEECs), Russia and Euro-Asia region, which is defined as a bloc of countries with intensive energy sources and scarce high-tech resources. They are a cause of concern to both the Government and bourgeoisie in Turkey. According to the Economist Intelligence Unit (EIU), for instance, as long as Russia is getting closer to the standards of the business climate in Europe, it will be able to attract an additional US$ 10 billion FDI inflows per year (Caliskan 2003, 6).

The number of foreign companies which are economically active in Turkey reached 11685 by the end of 2005. 6153 of them are European companies (AnsesNet 2006).

There are not only inward flows of FDI into Turkey; Turkish capital does invest abroad as well. Regarding Turkish capital invested in foreign countries, US$ 7 billion outflows were realised in the last 8 years. While US$ 3,9 billion of this investment was being made in EU countries, the export of Turkish capital to neighbouring countries amounted to only US$ 400 million. In 2004, the biggest share of the export of Turkish capital was to Azerbaijan totalling US$ 580 million. Total Turkish investment in Azerbaijan over the last 8 years amounts to US$ 1,6 billion and US$ 1,5 billion of it was in the energy sector. Other countries where Turkish capital was invested in the last 8 years were Kazakhstan, the Netherlands, Germany, USA and China. There are also capital exports from Turkey to neighbouring countries including Greece, Bulgaria, and Georgia, but they are at very low levels. The leading sectors which are preferred by Turkish companies are the energy and banking sectors (Hurriyet 2005).

Turkey's foreign trade and trade policies

Turkey's exports have shown a quite strong increase from US$ 23 billion to US$ 73,3 billion between 1996 and 2005. However, when one looks at the progress in import figures it can clearly be seen that the increase in exports did not solve the chronic problem of foreign trade deficit because the imports also increased from US$ 43,6 billion to 116 million over the same period (Pamuk 2006). As of the end of 2004, Turkey's leading export markets were Germany (US$ 8,6 billion), the USA (US$ 5,8 billion), Great Britain (US$ 5,5), Italy (US$ 4,2 billion), France (US$ 3,6 billion), and the Netherlands (US$ 2,1 billion). The following sectors have the largest shares in exports: automotive engineering, machine and equipment, transport vehicles, textile, iron and steel, chemicals and agriculture (food) (TCDTM 2004). As it can easily be guessed, the leading countries for Turkish exports are also the countries where Turkey incurs a deficit in the trade balance. Thus, similar to the situation for exports, the "import champion" is Germany with US$ 12 billion. It is followed by Italy (US$ 6,5 billion), France (US$ 6 billion), the USA (US$ 5,5 billion), Republic of China (US$ 4,2 billion) and Great Britain (US$ 3,8 billion US). Major exporting and importing manufacturing sectors overlap. The machine and equipment, transport vehicles and automotive sectors account for more than 70 per cent of total imported manufacturing goods (TCDTM 2004). This picture also sheds light on the fact that while Turkish Governments expect the transfer of high-technology from FDI, Turkey serves as an assembly centre for manufacturing goods relying on inputs produced in advanced capitalist states.

Moreover, a quite important share of industrial exports and production is still generated from the low-technology products. The share of the products with medium and high technology, in terms of the value added to the manufacturing industry in the country, is only 38 per cent (Tanyilmaz 2004, 27). Accordingly, it can be suggested that Turkey may concentrate on its comparative advantage on cheap labour by promoting labour-intensive industries in the country. The economic policies followed by the Governments actually point in this direction even though this is not clearly expressed in policy documents. Today, it is being widely argued in the country that Turkey displayed a preference for creating a paradise of cheap labour in the name of gaining a competitive advantage through developing labour intensive sectors (Muftuoglu 2004, 61). It is not unusual to find similar metaphors such as "Turkey is becoming China of Europe" being made by the foreign press also (Marchand 2005).

In general, two main factors greatly contributed to pursuing a liberal foreign trading system on the principles of "free and fair" competition, non-discrimination and elimination of barriers to trade. The first factor is the obligations to be fulfilled under the World Trade Organisation (WTO) and the second factor is the negotiations with the EU aiming at full membership of Turkey. Since some regional blocs like the EU have been used to convincing member states to adopt a global neo-liberal agenda, it is not surprising that the completion of the Customs Union between the EU and Turkey coincides with the commencement of the implementation of the Uruguay Round outcomes and the establishment of the WTO.

> Within the wider WTO framework, the Customs Union has been continuing to be the main determinant formulating foreign trade policies of Turkey. The steps that Turkey has taken, or will take, in compliance with its commitments for the proper functioning of the Customs Union are parallel to its commitments vis-à-vis the WTO. This situation certainly facilitates Turkey's implementation of the provisions of the Uruguay Round Final Act. In this respect, Turkey has been implementing the provisions of the Final Act without encountering serious difficulties since they closely follow the EU legislation.
>
> (WTO/Restricted 1998)

On the other hand, in order to meet its commitment of harmonising its trade regime in line with that of EU, Turkey has signed free trade agreements with many countries and negotiations with some others are still underway. The regional trade agreements that Turkish Governments have viewed as complementary elements to the multilateral trading system and integration into the EU have been given considerable importance. In a way, Turkish regional integration initiatives reflect the intermediary economic position of the country. On the one hand, Turkey receives FDI, especially from advanced capitalist countries. On the other hand, Turkey is a source of FDI. Some countries of the region are the major destinations of foreign Turkish investment. The long-term project of integration into the EU can be described as a "subordinate integration", because the accession process is clearly asymmetrical. This is reflected in the EU document from the end of 2004 that details the EU negotiation strategy towards Turkey.

In the other regional groupings, Turkey is a major player. Two regional initiatives with major Turkish participation are the Black Sea Economic Cooperation (BSEC) which was turned into a regional economic organisation in June 1998, and the Economic Cooperation Organization (ECO). Under the BSEC (1992), Turkey aims to improve its bilateral economic relations with 10 states: Albania, Armenia, Azerbaijan, Bulgaria, Georgia, Greece, Moldova, Romania, the Russian Federation and Ukraine covering a vast economic area from the Adriatic to the Pacific with a total population of 325 million inhabitants. The charter of the BSEC on economic cooperation was signed in June 1998 in Yalta. In a prior meeting, the Ministers responsible for Economic Affairs adopted the Declaration of Intention for the Establishment of the BSEC Free Trade Area on 7 February 1997 in Istanbul. Turkey defines this huge project as the step that will prepare BSEC to become an integral part in a larger European economic space (WTO Restricted 1998, 24). Another indicator which shows how regional blocs facilitate internationalisation of trade is the Free Trade Agreement (FTA) between Turkey and the European Free Trade Area (EFTA) states which was signed in 1991 as an adaptation of preferential agreements concluded between the EU and third countries. Thus, the EFTA is part of the process of accession to the EU. In the framework of this FTA, Turkey started to give priority to the following preferential agreements: Israel, Hungary, Bulgaria, Poland, Romania, Slovakia, the Czech Republic, Estonia, Latvia, Lithuania, Morocco, Tunisia, and Egypt and the majority of these agreements have already been signed (WTO/Restricted 1998, 19, 20). After the eastward enlargement of the EU, the European Union obliged Turkey to extend the customs union to the new EU members. Cyprus is part of that group. However, there are major unresolved points regarding the Cypriot issue, which has turned the extension of the customs union into a politically highly significant issue.

The ECO was established in 1985 as a trilateral organisation including Iran, Pakistan and Turkey. Later, it was expanded to include six Central Asian Republics as well as Afghanistan in order to promote regional cooperation. With the adhesion of these countries, the ECO has become a major regional organisation encompassing an area of 7 million square kilometres, inhabited by nearly 300 million people (WTO/ Restricted 1998, 23). The Standing Committee for Economic and Commercial Cooperation (COMCEC) is one of the three standing committees established by the Third Islamic Summit Conference held in Mecca and Taif in 1981. Its main target was defined as the strengthening of economic cooperation among member states (WTO/Restricted 1998, 24).

Another regional economic integration project that Turkey is involved in is the Euro-Med Partnership Project (EMPP) (1995). Among a total of 27 member countries, there are 15 EU member states and 12 Southern and Eastern Mediterranean states in the EMPP. The main target of the project is to reach a progressive free-trade area in the region. In the final declaration of the first Euro-Med Business Summit in Valencia on 24–25 October 1995, business partners of the project, including the Turkish Industrialists' and Businessmen's Association (TUSIAD), the most influential business organisation of Turkey founded in the early 1970s, agreed that a common Euro-Med area would be based on a future Free Trade Zone in accordance with the WTO guidelines in that respect (TUSIAD 2002, 21).

Moreover, in the commitments to the WTO, Turkish Governments have declared that "considering their positive overall impact on international trade as well as on the multilateral trading system and its regulatory framework, regional integration arrangements will also be the key elements in Turkey's future agenda" (WTO/ Restricted 1998, 25).

World trade negotiations and Turkey

It is almost impossible to argue that there are states which negotiate trade agreements independent from domestic interest groups. There are also internal actors and ways including the pressures from domestic interest groups to impose something on the Governments. The IMF's loans and stand-by agreements are one of the most efficient ways that external pressure can be exerted. However, it should be noted that usually the demands of particular domestic interests coincide with the interests of external actors. External pressures might increase the leverage of certain domestic actors. In the following section, Turkey's position in international agriculture and services negotiations are examined together with external and internal impositions.

Agriculture in WTO and Turkey

Particularly since the third ministerial WTO meeting in Seattle in 1999, agriculture has become the major conflict issue not only between south and north, but also inside these blocs. Doha was seen as the crucial step to overcome this conflict and to restart world trade negotiations. Despite the rhetoric of a "Development Round", Malhotra concludes that "overall Doha should be viewed only as the first step in what remains a long struggle to create a genuine trade and development agenda" (cit. in Young 2003, 5). Young argues that while developing countries did achieve some successes on intellectual property rights and public health, they still face many battles with industrialised countries on market access in agriculture, transparency, textiles, anti-dumping measures, and the implementation of the agreements in the Uruguay Round on Textiles (Young 2003, 5).

Similar to other developing and less developed countries, agricultural policies have usually taken the shape of intervention in the markets in Turkey. Intervention into price formation, subsidies, state control over product or input markets are among these policies. The liberal policies imposed on Turkey (like on other developing countries) since the beginning of the 1980s have been targeted at phasing out all these state subsidies to the agricultural sector. The WTO categorised the subsidies given on a product basis as "amber". This implied that they were regarded as distorting free trade and, therefore, had to be eliminated. In contrast to this, the subsidies given directly to the agricultural population have been accepted as "legal" by international institutions. This type of subsidy is not subject to elimination. Since these subsidies got the green light by the WTO, they have been taken into the so-called green box. Traditionally, the share of the amber category in total state subsidies is quite high in less developed countries. For example, it was close to 100 percent in Turkey in 1999, while it was 25 per cent for the USA and 55 per cent for the EU (Boratav 2004, 223). In contrast, green box subsidies are highly relevant in the USA. Advanced capitalist states which have transposition flexibility can relatively easily modify the character of subsidies in order to make them compatible with international rules. Contrary to industrialised states, less developed and developing countries which are under pressure from international financial institutions lack such flexibility (Boratav 2004, 222).

Turkey made tariff reductions on its own long before an eventual agricultural agreement in the WTO. It committed itself to reducing its tariffs rate in general by an average of 24 per cent and by a minimum of 10 per cent on the basis of each product until 2004 (Akder and Dogruel 1998, 13). This is to say that Turkey cannot increase protection beyond the levels of 2004, but it is free to further reduce these protection levels. In the framework of the negotiations in WTO Agreement on Agriculture (AoA), Turkey made commitments to limit its export subsidies for 44 products. These commitments were made separately in regard to budgetary subsidies and in regard to the quantities of these products. Another important commitment is that the exports of these 44 products will not be subsidised (Akder and Dogruel 1998, 15). Diversification in the production patterns, which has occurred over the last 10 years, has also led to problems regarding the newly defined products since they are not subject to past regulations. Turkish negotiators have complained that there is no clarification in the agreement as to the conditions under which countries can impose a quota on agricultural imports. The second criticism is related to different protection levels. Thus, Turkey will reach the zero point level before the states with higher levels of protection. This will make Turkey an attractive export destination. In response to this argument, Turkish officials were told that high protection levels were settled to provide flexibility and developed countries do not use these ratios in practice. Reduction in export subsidies is not seen as an important problem for Turkey because a systematic export subsidy does not exist in the country (Gunaydin 2005).

The basic criticism directed at Turkey is related to internal supports. Some member states argue that the Turkish government declared a lesser level of subsidies than the one that really exists. Some Turkish negotiators explain it as a technical difference which stems from different interpretations of the concept of internal subsidies. According to the interpretations of the WTO, if the price in the domestic market is higher than the price in the world market, an internal subsidy exists. From the perspective of the biggest agricultural organisation in Turkey "if this topic (reduction in internal subsidies) will be executed, Turkey will have to face a decrease in its internal subsidies that are not sufficient even now, especially in premium for butter plants" (Gunaydin 2005). As a result of the criticisms made by other WTO member states, Turkey, finally committed itself to providing only minimal subsidies. Another criticism addressed to Turkey was that advantageous loans were provided by state banks to agricultural cooperatives and associations (Akder and Dogruel 1998, 40, 41). However, this is not the case anymore, as state subsidies have been removed gradually over the last six years.

For the future of agriculture in Turkey, another important issue is market access. The WTO wants to open all protected markets in developing countries soon. Many products in developing countries are not subsidised but only protected by tariffs. If subsidies do exist in developing countries, they are relatively low:

> EU's agriculture budget is 43 billion Euro and the USA's agriculture budget is US$ 74 billion but on the contrary, Turkish agricultural budget is nearly US$2.3 billion. It means unequal powers will compete in the same market. And this process can be destructive for Turkish agricultural policy.   (Gunaydin 2005)

Beyond all these technical dimensions, the complaints made by Turkish governments and negotiators on agricultural policies in the WTO can be interpreted rather as crocodile tears, particularly if the positions taken by negotiators in ministerial meetings are considered. In fact, Turkey has never become a part of alliances established by some developing states to protect their comparative advantages in the agricultural sector. This is not because Turkey sees herself in the camp of developed states, but rather results from the pressures from dominant classes inside and outside the country. However, the Turkish government presents them in a different light. Turkish policy makers are quite successful in associating potentially unpopular actions with popular symbols. In this sense, symbols mask realities, and they provide the option of "window dressing" (Greven 2003, 32). The popular symbol for Turkey in the globalisation process has become the EU. Turkish industrialists see their future in the membership of Turkey in the EU. The EU orientation has not been without consequences for Turkey's stand on agriculture in the WTO and the EU symbolism has been invoked in justifying the Turkish position in WTO negotiations. For instance, in Cancún, Turkey exactly echoed EU arguments which go against a reduction of subsidies to agriculture and aim at maintaining its protectionism against developing countries.

In Turkey, leading industrial and financial groups, with the exception of textile industrialists, support the process of cutting subsidies to the agricultural sector in return for more state support to the manufacturing industry in general, although they argue that Turkey should follow a path free from external pressures in this particular field (TUSIAD 2003, 15). Similar fault lines have started to become apparent in Europe and the USA, too. While ministers of agriculture, member states and agri-business in the EU are resisting WTO agricultural policies, the international business stakeholders including the European Service Forum (ESF) have declared that agriculture subsidies must be eliminated in order to permit a revitalisation of world trade negotiations (International Business Stakeholder, 2004).[2]

According to the view of the Textile Employers' Organisation, however, cotton is the most strategic agriculture product in Turkey, with its annual production amounting to 900 thousands tones, and this product must be supported by domestic policies (Tekstil Isveren 2005). Moreover, there are also agricultural products which have been protected with tariffs higher than 150 per cent like meat, milk, wheat, sugar beet, sugar cane, tobacco products, fruits and vegetables (TC Basbakanlık Gumruk Must. 2006).

Services in the WTO

International negotiations on services show that Turkey will do its best to play its cards in the game depending on its growing economic weight in world trade. In terms of the rules of the game, in the framework of the General Agreement on Trade of Services (GATS) 2000 negotiations in the WTO, for instance, in July 2004 Turkey declared its commitment list to be temporary. Its final stand is to depend not only on the commitments of the others, but also on the evaluation of the overall behaviour of other states in the Doha Development Round (TC Hazine Must. Letter 2003). TUSIAD argues that in the coming period, it would not be proper for Turkey to adopt a negotiating position that goes beyond its prior commitments to the EU in those sectors where the EU does not intend to open up to third countries (education, audiovisual, health) (TUSIAD 2003, 24). On the other hand, it should be noted that the number of cards in the hand of Turkey is much more limited than the cards that the EU could play, and this might narrow the bargaining position of Turkey.

It is also possible to guess the areas of negotiations imposed upon Turkey through the demands of powerful states. In the GATS 2000 negotiations, for example, the USA has demanded from Turkey that it liberalise education, energy, mining, transmission and distribution of electricity, environmental services, and engineering and architecture services. The demands in these areas are not limited only to the USA. Likewise, there are demands from countries like Switzerland, Canada, Malaysia, Norway, China, Egypt, Jordan, and Tunisia. In turn, Turkey has tabled its own demands. They concern the following countries and services:

- Education: Tunisia and Malaysia
- Health: India
- Land transportation: Egypt, Tunisia, Norway and Pakistan
- Overseas transportation: Jordan and Pakistan
- Air transportation: Egypt, Switzerland, South Korea, China, Tunisia, Jordan, Pakistan, Malaysia, Norway and India
- Energy: Tunisia and Pakistan
- Environmental services: Tunisia, Egypt, Malaysia
- Engineering and architecture: Pakistan, Tunisia, Egypt, Taiwan, China, Switzerland, Jordan and Malaysia (TC Hazine Must. Letter 2003).

As it can be seen from the demands and offers, with only a few exceptions, Turkey has usually addressed demands to countries that have a weaker position than it in world trade. In other words, power relations are clearly reflected in the structure of liberalisation demands addressed to Turkey and formulated by Turkey.

The regulation of basic infrastructural sectors covered by international service negotiations is a subject of controversial debates both at the national level and in international fora. Particularly big business stakeholders in Turkey, for instance, complain about the insufficiencies in public infrastructure and use them as an excuse for further liberalisation in that field. One of the two conflicting claims on that matter is that sectors like electricity, natural gas and telecommunications have remained underdeveloped because they are provided by the State and therefore services are being offered at high costs, especially for business users (Gonenc 2004, 2). Indeed, although domestic and foreign investors positively evaluate the general progress in liberalisation achieved by Turkish governments again they consider that the high costs that they have to pay for these public infrastructural facilities are highly problematic for the interests of the private sector. Small business stakeholders, on the other hand, raise their concerns about liberalisation in these sectors by intentionally using the sovereignty question in order to guarantee that the Turkish Military takes the same position as them.

Moreover, since sectors like telecommunication, electricity or energy are the areas of high rent and return, both a group of capitalist classes inside and outside the country and also the state authority in Turkey are very sensitive regarding the liberalisation of these sectors. Liberalisation consists of two basic elements: privatisation of services and the introduction of a new form of regulation. Both elements are controversial. The state has been faced with a serious dilemma between the general interests of the ruling class and the interests of a group of domestic and foreign capitalists. This tension has emerged on the issue of private and state ownership in some specific service sectors. Turkish negotiators' positions in international trade negotiations clearly reflect these tensions and the efforts of the ruling classes to ensure that the state holds the majority of shares in state monopolies. Telecommunications is one of various examples in that field. Indeed, in the revised GATS commitments made by the Turkish Government, for instance, foreign natural and legal persons have not been allowed to hold more than 45 per cent of Turk Telecom shares and they have been prevented from owning the majority shares of that company (TC Hazine Must. 2003). Another example is the Banking sector. Again under Turkey's revised GATS commitments on Banking Services for Mode 3 : a) 'permission to establish a bank which has to be established in the form of a joint-stock company or to open the first branch of a foreign bank in Turkey, shall be given by a decision taken by the Banking Regulation and Supervision Board (BDDK) and b) for the establishment of capital market institutions the permission of the Capital Markets Board (SPK) is required. If bank or insurance companies apply to the SPK to form a mutual fund or to increase fund capital, the approval of the BDDK and the Under-secretariat of the Treasury have to *respectively* be obtained to finalize applications (TC Hazine Must. 2003). The sensitivity shown by the ruling classes in that field can be interpreted in three ways: first, public infrastructure administrations have also been the areas of rent for bureaucrats. Secondly, these fields are defined as "strategic" for the security of the state. And thirdly, this sensitivity showed by Turkish state reveals once more that some local business groups are not willing to relinquish privileged positions hitherto conceded to them by the state.

There are also pressures from the EU for the liberalisation of postal services. In the Regular Report/2004 of the EU Commission on Turkey's Progress Towards Accession, Turkey was asked to adopt a comprehensive programme for the liberalisation of postal services and also to establish an independent national regulatory body for the postal market (TC Hazine Must. 2004, 129).

Sectoral regulation is a second area of considerable controversy. The main change in the area of regulation has been the replacement of the traditional bureaucracy by autonomous authorities. This process was first started by the military regime with the establishment of SPK in 1982. It has accelerated over the last 5 years. Today, the number of these institutions is more than ten covering several sectors from telecommunications, banking, competition and energy to the sub-sectors of agriculture like sugar or tobacco. These boards are mainly manned by the representatives of major entrepreneur organisations. They can act completely independently from state authorities in terms of their decisions and responsibilities. In some cases, the state transfers its regulation rights to these boards, particularly as a consequence of international trade agreements as was exemplified above on telecommunications, banking and postal services.

By these new formations, today, dominant classes are trying to get rid of the legacy of populism. Populism seeks legitimacy from the popular masses. Provision of infrastructure might be part of strategies to gain legitimacy. Removing infrastructure from the direct realm of the state bureaucracy might reduce pressure from the people. Establishing supervisory boards might lower the expectations of the working classes of both the politics and organs of representative democracy in terms of the provision of infrastructure (Boratav 2004, 175). According to the Independent Social Scientists (BSB), speaking in broad terms, these independent boards are related to the *transfer of decisions relating to the public sphere from constitutional institutions of respective countries to "independent" supreme bodies of regulation working under global rules* and further *commercialisation* of the public sphere. BSB defines this process, whose legitimisation is presented as "dissociating politics from economics" a policy which enhances the hegemony of global capital and its domestic extensions on society by keeping large sections of people and working masses far from political processes. Political leaders in all countries where these reforms are being implemented commonly agree that the "old" state and bureaucratic structures are *working clumsily* and are also tainted by *corruption,* and that the new model is superior due to its efficient, strong, rule-abiding and accountable features.[3]

The following view of TUSIAD is in line with the thinking of international organisations on regulatory boards: "particular attention should be given to the privatisation of the Public Economic Institutions (PEIs) and the adoption of policies by regulatory bodies to be established after the privatisation of such state monopolies towards the protection of the competitive environment in the market" (TUSIAD 2003, 25).

According to liberal economists who claim that this process is a must for transparency, the bureaucracy to some extent resists governance boards and does not accept transferring its authority over public resources. The main argument of liberals is that every area that is subject to state license or authorisation is a source of corruption. In what follows, the only remedy to prevent corruption according to liberals is to eliminate these state regulations or to transfer the authority held by the state to so-called autonomous boards. It is true that every step taken to protect the general interest of society in closed capitalist economies, particularly in developing countries, from environmental regulations to general public interest, at the same time represents a potential rent for those who are officially responsible for ensuring this protection and who must achieve their goals with minimum cost. When social regulations prevented the interest groups from making or increasing profit, they resorted to bribery and corruption. Corrupt practices have even been condoned by developed countries. An example of this phenomenon is that until a few years ago German companies had a right to claim a tax deduction from the German state of the same amount as the bribes they had to pay for their investments in developing countries.[4] In the liberal capitalism of today, domestic and foreign companies know that they do not need to engage in bribery anymore to make profit. In this context, the impacts of international institutions in forming regulatory boards cannot be underestimated. Almost in each stage on international trade, governments have been asked to commit to establishing an independent Regulatory Body to rule and supervise the domestic market. The two most striking examples of strong pressures from the EU and the WTO for establishing independent regulatory boards in Turkey are the following: in a conference jointly organised by the International Bars Association and Turkish Bars Association, Jean François Pons, the vice president of DG Competition stated that the full membership process of Turkey is dependent upon the performance of the country in the field of competition policies. Pons also warned state authorities that if the state does not transfer its whole authority of control to the competition board then its membership process would be frozen (Esin 2001).[5] Indeed, today, there are even legal cases that have been directly opened by the competition board against the state monopolies like Turkish Telecom. Claimant companies in these cases are both domestic and foreign. One of the most common reasons for legal cases is the claim that state monopolies abuse their privileged positions and violate the rules of free competition (Rekabet Kurulu 2004). Secondly, in this global war between state and private monopolies under the name of "liberalisation in public procurement" and/ or the "GATS", Turkey signed the 4th Protocol on Telecommunication Services on November 1997. In the voice telephony services part of Turkey's offer for instance, it is stated that, by 1 January 2006 the voice telephony services market in Turkey will be open to both domestic and foreign investors and Turkey will also try to establish an independent "Regulatory Body" to rule and supervise the domestic telephone market (WTO/Restricted 1998, 12).

The external imposition has been made through reference papers which show what member states should do in that specific field. Telecommunications is only one of the contentious areas imposed on Turkey. In this particular field for instance, a WTO Reference Paper states that:

any Member has the right to define the kind of universal service obligation it wishes to maintain. Such obligations will not be regarded as anti-competitive per se, provided they are administered in a transparent, non-discriminatory and competitively neutral manner and are not more burdensome than necessary for the kind of universal service defined by the Member.   (WTO Reference Papers for Telecom Services 1996)

The very friendly language used in these papers does not change the nature of the imposition, however. As a member state, Turkey has the right to define the kind of universal service obligation it wishes to maintain, but it has to comply with the conditions stated above. For instance, it is not clear what are *more burdensome* or what are *the necessary* levels or for whom.

Over the last decade, Turkish governments have taken a number of steps to liberalise services in the framework of commitments made in WTO-GATS and for EU membership. In this context, a comprehensive reform package composed of three separate acts has gradually been ratified by the Great Assembly of Deputies since 2004: Act for the Reform in Public Administration; Act for the Reform in Local Administrations (Municipalities, Governorships and City Administrations); Bill for the Reform in State Personnel Regime, which determines the working, pension and social conditions for public employees. By these two acts and the bill, governments have aimed at transferring public services to local administrations jointly with their properties and equipment. This initiative was interpreted as a new democratic opportunity by some political groups at the beginning of the debates. This debate was based on the definition of the process as localisation and it was argued that de-centralisation of the State would be more democratic than the centralised one. Regarding this misunderstanding of the concept, Sancar cites the following quotation from the WB: *Globalisation and Localisation are twins* and defines localisation as an economic project in the line of the liberal route of capitalism. She also argues that the social and political dimensions of this project have consciously been polished, particularly for veiling economic consequences (Sancar 2002). Then, after the bills had started to circulate, the real intentions behind the veil of "democratic opportunity", summarised in the following three points, became clear:

1. The State will not finance these basic services anymore.
2. Local administrations have to sell these services according to the rules of competition and in the return for market prices.
3. Employees have to be employed in a flexible and more productive manner, totally deprived of job security, according to performance and total quality management criteria (TBMM[6] 2004).

Regarding the strategic service sectors for Turkish Governments it may be argued that following services are in the list of strategic service sectors which are still defined as unbound or selected for derogations: broadcasting, where foreign shareholders' equity participation is restricted to 25 per cent; aviation, maritime transportation;

and telecommunications services (WTO 2004, 6). On the other hand, when one looks at the requests made by government officials it can easily be seen that Turkey's demands from some other member states mainly concentrate on construction, education, health, engineering and transportation services (TC Basbakanlik 2003).

International trade negotiations and Turkish interest groups

The positions taken by Turkish Governments in global and regional trade negotiations are influenced by the organised interest groups of labour and capital. In this section, we shall first deal with labour organisations and occupation chambers and then turn our attention to employers' organisations.

Two dimensions are at the centre of contradictions in the reactions of different unions and occupation chambers to globalisation and its implications: first, the positions taken on the EU membership process of Turkey and, second, class conflicts among the members of each single occupation chamber.

Positions of labour unions, occupation chambers and employers' organisations

Labour Unions   Some Turkish Trade Unions, including DISK and KESK,[7] are traditionally close to Europe and these friendly feelings mainly stem from the solidarity displayed by the unions in Europe during and after the military coup in 1980. The problem is that these feelings have more and more turned into a general support for the EU itself. In this sense, social gains, democratic rights and freedoms in Europe have been identified by the existence of the EU as a "social bloc". Therefore, these unions in Turkey have ignored the negative developments in the EU to some extent. Some of them view the EU's variety of capitalism as a "different capitalism" in comparison with its Anglo-Saxon form. Ironically, the EU, WTO and IMF have insisted on demands which are almost the same but pursued under the separate schemes.

These unions voice their oppositions to the neo-liberal agenda in general without establishing the necessary links with the nature of the capitalist system, and/or by confining their critique to global organisations like the WTO, IMF and the WB for not being disputing the EU (KESK 2004).

The general opposition tendencies in these unions to the reforms in public services have mainly concentrated on protecting most basic services instead of opposing the whole agenda. It can be suggested that this position, which is based on bargaining over single issues like education, health or water, has been influenced by the policies and tactics used by international organisations like the European Confederation of Trade Unions (ETUC), Education International, Union Network International (UNI), European Federation of Public Service Union (EPSU) or Public Services International (PSI) (KESK 2004). In regard to the EU, the most recent political behaviour of these organisations has changed once again towards a slightly more critical position, particularly after they had realised that there is a roll-back in social achievements in the EU. Of course, the desire showed by Turkish unions for democracy and freedoms is to be seen in the perspective of the very anti-democratic process that they experienced for many years. Beyond all internal contradictions and limitations, these organisations do their best to turn this integration process to the benefit of their members. Sometimes they act individually, sometimes under alliances like the "Labour Platform". This particular platform, which consists of trade unions and occupation chambers, was established to form a common front against the attacks coming from the state or bourgeoisie in January 1999. The organisations within the Labour Platform, for instance, asked for information from the government on GATS commitments and requests in a letter formulated in March 2003 (TMMOB 2004)[8]. The government has still not responded to this letter.

There are also unions which support the EU accession with arguments based on a supposed "social market economy". According to them, the EU is the best example of a well-functioning social market economy with its strong social norms as well as a complete free market system (Uslu 2004). The organisation that has most constantly voiced this view is HAK-IS.[9] At this point, it is equally important to analyse the political relations between the parties and unions. HAK-IS is known for its close relation to the political party Adalet ve Kalkinma Partisi (AKP), which is in power today (2005). These relations have helped the AKP to ensure that official state policies take root inside the working class, which represents the most important section of the electorate. In line with this alliance, HAK-IS usually defends the policies of the AKP Government. For example, in an evaluation of the EU Summit in Brussels on 17th December 2004, the President of HAK-IS made the following statement:

> Particularly over the last two years, my Confederation has been very actively involved in the campaigns in favour of the EU membership of Turkey and these efforts jointly with very sincere efforts of the Government have become highly effective in regard to the final decision of the EU on 17 December ... For us, the most important dimension of EU membership is "Social Europe". (Uslu 2004)

It should be pointed out that there are also unions that strongly oppose both neo-liberal policies and to some extent also the EU membership of Turkey. However, this opposition is based on national arguments like sovereignty, independence and indivisible unity of the state rather than on a class perspective. These organisations have made several declarations on international politics to get support from public opinion for an independent Turkish State in Cyprus and conditional support for EU membership (Turk-Is 2004). In that sense, the conditions put forward by these organisations for EU membership, for instance, include Cyprus and the sovereignty question (Turk-Is Inquiry on EU 2004).

The other factor which has influenced the positions of the unions on neo-liberal policies and institutions is of a financial nature. The funds provided for some unions mainly by the EU Commission on a project basis have helped some of these unions to continue their most vital activities, e.g. trade union education, which had almost ceased just before these projects started. However, these relations based on funds may also create a kind of dependency on the institutions providing these funds. This type of project funding sets the EU apart from institutions like the IMF and WTO. Such funds have been provided during the East European accession process as well. It seems that it was not without consequences for the stance taken by trade unions on some sensitive issues. For example, Czech trade unions refrained from participating in the protests against the IMF and WB in Prague in autumn 2000. According to some Czech trade unions, they were warned not to take part in these demonstrations, otherwise the EU integration process of the Czech Republic might be frozen and these unions would be accused of having caused this unpleasant result (Antimai 2000).

Occupation chambers   In regard to the second dimension of contradictory stances by organisations, occupation chambers represent the most striking example. Occupation chambers organise persons in specific professions regardless of their social status (employer, self-employed or employee). They were established to blur class conflicts at the time when corporatism as a state ideology was popular at the beginning of 1950s (Quataert and Zürcher 1998, 145). Thus, these organisations have members from both classes, i.e. engineers who are employers and engineers who are wage earners and so on. Because wage earners form the majority in these chambers, they account for more than 80 per cent of the members of executive and steering committees. Due to the strong leftist traditions in the universities for many decades as well as to the good relations established with young university students, the leftist members are still dominant in occupation chambers. Though the occupation chambers are not labour organisations in a narrow sense, they represent their members – like trade unions – in the Labour Platform.

However, this mixed structure in occupation chambers has privileged some organisations, particularly those involved in the international trade agenda, in getting information on trade negotiations on time and in voicing overall demands when necessary.[10] The government invites occupation chambers to express and exchange their opinions on some international negotiations, probably because employers are represented in them as well. Some executives, experts or members of these organisations have been invited to take part in international meetings held under the auspices of the WTO in Geneva, while workers and public employee unions are not even able to get involved at the national level. Thus, they have at least relatively good access to information on international trade negotiations. Professional chambers differ in the way they participate in the public debate. Some of them limit themselves to informing their members or the broader public in a rather "neutral" tone since they have to take into account that part of their memberships consists of employers who strongly support the neo-liberal agenda. In an overall evaluation, however, it should be stressed that occupation chambers in general have mobilised an important part of their resources to create a consciousness on international trade and capitalist institutions, sometimes by organising conferences, sometimes by lobbying and sometimes even by representing their members in critical international fora like social forums and/or manifestations abroad (Antimai, 2000).

Peasants and agricultural workers hardly have a say in regard to international trade negotiations. There exists neither an organised peasant movement nor a powerful agri-workers' union in Turkey, though there are very small and recently started initiatives to establish agriculture workers' unions on a product basis. The only organised structure in the agricultural sector is the Association of the Chambers of Agriculture Engineers. The official views of the Association on the negotiations on agriculture can be summarised as follows:

> In regard to the demands of the EU to Turkey (these demands are almost the same as the ones made by the IMF and WTO), it points out that there are serious differences in the size of agricultural populations in the EU and Turkey. 33,8 per cent of Turkish employment is in agriculture. At worst, Turkey must retract this number to 10 per cent. Thus, about a fourth of the workforce would be under the threat of losing its employment. Turkey needs a project for these people. Turkey should plan an agricultural structure, which can fit with the EU's Common Agriculture Policy (CAP) for a probable accession day. Turkey has to increase its agricultural sensibility; it should establish competitive, a powerful agriculture structure by eliminating the factors that cause increasing costs of products and by pressing for productivity increases

> Turkey has to solve its agricultural and rural infrastructure problems. 4 million hectares lack adequate irrigation. We cannot talk about productivity without irrigated agriculture. Turkey has to complete public investments and establish enterprises for developing technology in agriculture. These structural changes should be implemented in Turkish agriculture with or without the EU. These structural changes are indispensable. The EU foresees a single food authority, but, at the moment, the Turkish Ministry of Agriculture does not (yet) have enough qualified human resources (Gunaydin 2005).

Employers' organizations   Capital organizations are on the other side of the social divide. The reactions of employers' organisations to the ongoing process of liberalisation differ depending on the company size of their members. The Associations and Unions that represent the small and medium sized enterprises (SMEs) have approached this process with doubt and, to some extent, criticism particularly after consecutive financial crises since 1999. The member companies of these organisations have faced a serious dilemma in the globalisation process: on the one hand, they are convinced that they must find foreign partners abroad in order to be able to survive in fierce competition inside and outside of the country. Parallel to this view Muftuoglu argues that *SMEs believe that the only way out for them in order to overcome the crisis is to integrate into international markets more and more* (Muftuoglu 2004, 61). On the other hand, even if Turkish SMEs can find foreign partners, they still have to face competition from other foreign companies and their larger Turkish competitors taking advantage of the very advantageous conditions provided by the Government. For this perspective, the most striking example of an organisation for small and medium sized enterprises is USIAD.[11] When one asks the members of this association – which opposes globalisation with nationalist arguments – what their problems are they usually say that *the state protected the big industrialists in 60s and 70s and then these companies became powerful on international level. Now this is our term, state should provide protection for us too* (Turkay 2004, 6). This Association has strong relations with nationalist-left wing parties as well as right-wing. However, there are also organisations of small and medium seized employers which support the neo-liberal policies which have been implemented by several governments over the last decade. The TOBB[12] for instance asserts that the model of free market economy chosen by Turkish governments is correct and must continue (Hisarciklioglu 2004).

The biggest employers' organisation in Turkey is TISK[13] even though it is not the most powerful organisation ideologically. Principal demands of employers' associations refer to the reduction in capital taxes and social insurance contributions paid by the employers, to the reduction of the costs of workforce, the flexibility in working conditions and the cutting of collective rights. Furthermore, they would like to have more support for a more competitive domestic market, lower barriers to trade, a reduction of bureaucratic red tape for establishing new companies and, finally, measures that make Turkey the most attractive country for foreign investors (Baydur 2004, 63, Isveren 2004, Pirler 2004/1 and 2). Many of these demands relate to the increasing competitive power of the companies (Belen 2004).

According to the employers, the most basic reason for the comparatively large informal economy, for high unemployment and low FDI levels is the extreme tax and social insurance burden. TISK, for instance stresses that the informal economy could be accepted to some extent as a factor which protects the economic system against shocks, but at the same time views it as being in an 'unfair competition' with the formal sectors. Therefore, it demands measures against informality, particularly under the conditions when unemployment increased to unsustainable levels (Pirler 2004/2). The way that TISK suggests fighting against informality is to make the formal economy more attractive for informal companies by eliminating taxes etc. Thus, they in fact propose to bring formal (registered) functioning of the economy closer to the conditions prevailing in the informal economy.

Regarding the opinions of employers' organisations which are more influential on international trade politics, the best example is TUSIAD which is the only Turkish nongovernmental organization accredited by the WTO and supportive of the liberalisation process since the very beginning (TUSIAD 2003, 11). This Organisation is exceptional in its definite interest in international trade negotiations. TUSIAD argues that mega-tariffs provide only a temporary protection since tariffs are bound to be reduced eventually. It also defends the fact that export subsidies are not advantageous for developing countries like Turkey, which are unable to make necessary budgetary allocations. Considering that it is the developed countries that benefit from export subsidies on real terms, they should be required to make additional and comprehensive tariff reductions (TUSIAD 2003, 16–17). The organisation also believes that the WTO Agreement on Agriculture offers an unbalanced structure that works against Turkey and many other developing countries. Therefore, it holds the opinion that Turkey can act in international agricultural trade negotiations independently from the EU since it is not yet a part of the CAP (TUSIAD 2003, 15 and 17). Regarding GATS, TUSIAD argues that further openings in the services sector would be an important factor contributing to the planning of development strategies for developing countries (TUSIAD 2003,

20). It also proposes for Turkey to have a more coordinated negotiation approach particularly for those sectors where it has requested a transition period from the EU. According to TUSIAD, while determining its sectoral position towards the third countries, Turkey should take the EU negotiation position into account, rapidly establish coordination with the EU on the negotiations at the WTO, and the Turkish Government should try to have its views included in the EU's GATS position as much as possible (TUSIAD 2003, 24). In the field of waste management, too, TUSIAD's stand seems closer to the reaction of the alliance of developing nations who were under the leadership of India before the Hong Kong Ministerial Meeting (2005) of the WTO. Therefore, it warns Turkish negotiators about the danger of completely turning into a toxic waste dump in the future and thinks that it is important for the developing countries to form a single voice, engaging in effective activities aimed at persuading the developed countries to solve the problem at its source (TUSIAD 2003, 30). One of the negotiation topics which seems to be irreversible for TUSIAD is that it believes that there must be a cooperation which can be materialised through international organisations such as the International Chamber of Commerce (ICC) or OECD (TUSIAD 2003, 35). However, the Organisation has also criticisms of some clauses in GATT[14]/ WTO agreements such as national treatment and it argues that providing foreign companies more advantageous conditions than those imposed on domestic companies through the "national treatment" clause is also a form of discrimination (TUSIAD 2003, 35).

Irrespective of their size, employers associations follow the trade agenda very closely as they can address their demands directly to the government.

Empirical consequences of free trade and investment regime in Turkey

According to the economic indicators given below (Table 8.1) the overall picture of Turkey today is clear: despite strong real economic growth, unemployment is quite high and public debt and current account deficit are rising sharply.

According to the pre-accession economic programme of 2004, the government intends to keep the rate of unemployment around 10 per cent throughout the period 2005–2007. It is expected that this high rate of unemployment makes for more flexibility in both public and private sector employment, presses down wages and forces workers to seek informal employment. Moreover, the basic scenario of the Pre-accession Economic Programme envisages the reduction of the proportion of total public debt to GDP from 75 per cent in 2005 to 68 per cent in 2007 (BSB July 2005, 15). However, while total external debt stock was US$ 170 billion (TC Hazine Must. 2006), foreign trade balance also was minus US$ 42,9 billion or 24,9 per cent higher than the deficit in 2004 at the end of 2005 (Capital 2006). Export revenues made a jump by 15,8 per cent in 2005 and reached US$ 73 billion. But since the increase in imports was 19 per cent (total US$ 116 billion) in the same period, the foreign trade deficit virtually exploded (ESKH 2006).[15]

The economy has grown by 5,8 per cent in 2005 according to the OECD (Milliyet 2006/1). Inflation in 2005 continued to fall and the average annual increase in prices receded to 7.72 per cent on CPI, to 2.66 per cent on WPI basis (Yapi Kredi 2006) and to 5,89 per cent average (Capital, 2006).

Table 8.1   Macroeconomic Developments in the Turkish Economy
(*): As of 3rd quarter 2004: (**): As of November 2004
Source: Central Bank of Turkey (www.tcmb.gov.tr); Undersecretariat of Treasury (www.treasury.gov.tr)
(BSB, 2005)

	2002	2003	2004
GNP Growth Rate (%)	7.8	5.9	9.7*
GNP ($ billion)	181.7	238.9	283.9*
Inflation (CPI, %, p.a.)	29.7	18.4	9.3
Inflation (WPI, %, p.a.)	50.1	25.5	11.1
Debt Stock of the Consolidated Budget ($ billion)	148.5	202.7	226.8**
Domestic Debt Stock ($ billion)	91.7	139.3	159.1**
Foreign Debt Stock ($ billion)	56.8	63.4	67.7
Total External Debt Stock ($billion)	130.3	145.8	153.2*
Merchandise Trade Balance ($ billion)	-15.6	-22.2	-34.5
Exports ($ billion)	35.9	47.1	62.7
Imports ($ billion)	51.5	69.3	97.2
Current Account Balance ($ billion)	-1.5	-8.1	-15.6
Current Account Balance/GNP (%)	-0.8	-2.8	-5.3
Open Unemployment Rate (%)	10.3	10.5	10.0

A detailed analysis of the balance of payments statistics from Turkey shows that hot money inflows of non-resident origin amounted to US$ 11,5 billion in 2005 (ESKH 2006). It is well-known that the major economic variable that stimulates these monetary flows is the interest rate differential between domestic and foreign financial markets corrected for the rate of (expected) currency depreciation.

The IMF and government maintain that the net public debt stock is decreasing in its proportion to national income. Indeed, this proportion receded from 78,7 per cent in 2002 to 67,5 per cent during the AKP government period. However, it is also known that the high level of PSBR resulting from the chronic debt problem of the state was still one of the major concerns stated in the 2004 Regular Report of EU Commission on Turkey's Progress towards Accession. Beyond these criticisms, a comparison based on the proportion of net public debt to national income may be extremely misleading, since the 11,2 percentage point fall in net public debt burden may almost entirely be attributed to the 12,8 percentage point fall in the foreign public debt burden. Net internal debt stock, on the other hand, remained around 56 per cent in its proportion to national income and even displayed a slight increase by 1.6 per cent. It is clear that in a period when national income displays an extraordinary growth, internal debt stock keeps up with this pace. In other words, the government has only succeeded in maintaining internal debt burden as constant rather than actually reducing it. Meanwhile, the *external debt* stock of the public sector is rising in terms of foreign exchange. The external debt stock of the public sector increased from US$ 70 billion immediately after the 2001 crisis to US$ 89,2 billion in the third quarter of 2004 (BSB 2005, 34) and to US$ 170 billion at the end of 2005 (Milliyet 2006/2).

Conclusions

In the context of a closed economic system lasting more than 50 years, the basic actors were the owners of productive capital or – in a word – "industrialists". It was they who benefited most from the protections provided by the state before the 1980s and gave a liberal shape to the state structure from the beginning of the 1980s.

When the situation today is considered, the employers and government officials agree that Turkey should achieve a technologically intensive development by concentrating on high-tech sectors. The leading companies in these sectors seek incentives and encouragement from the state. Sometimes this could be seen as a contradiction i.e. to praise neo-liberal policies on one hand and to expect protection from the state on the other hand (Ansal 2004, 82). It may be argued that this contradiction stems from the transposition of the concept of protectionism. The second generation liberal reforms that emphasise the importance of the state, particularly as an actor that guarantees that national markets function according to the requirements of global markets (re-regulation) (BSB, March 2005) also confirm that there is a transposition on the concept of "protectionism". Arrighi, Silver and Brewer argue on this point that polarising tendencies are still at work but *within* rather than *between* countries. "Core-periphery" – in Ankie Hoogvelt's (1997, 145) words: "is becoming a social relationship, and no longer a geographical one" (in Arrighi et al. 2003, 4).

Particularly for the countries which engage in both global (WTO) and regional (i.e. EU) trade negotiations in the same period of time and have high level expectations from membership in a regional bloc like EU, the arenas of negotiations have usually been imposed rather than selected. Not surprisingly, contentious arenas in global trade negotiations are almost the same as the ones in regional negotiations. In other words, even if Turkish negotiators resist the liberalisation of government procurement in the WTO for instance, they cannot reject any demand coming from the EU in the same field. When Turkey accepts liberalising its government procurement in negotiations with the EU, this implies to accept liberalisation in that field for all third countries that have agreements with EU already. This is also a device to convince recalcitrant public opinion: the measure is not something to be done for the highly criticised WTO, it is only for

EU membership. It is equally evident that the increased level of participation of the countries in world trade will have an impact over the bargaining positions of those in international negotiations.

References

Akder, A. H., Dogruel, F. (1998), Agreement on Agriculture of WTO and Turkey (Dunya Ticaret Orgutunun Tarim Anlasmasi ve Turkiye), (FES-Friedrich Ebert Stiftung Publications: Istanbul), pp. 13, 15, 40-41.

Ansal, H. (2004), Digital Division (Dijital Bolunme), *Iktisat Dergisi*, Volume. 452. (Istanbul), p. 82.

AnsesNet (2006), FDI Inflow has reached to 9.6 billion $, (Yabanci Sermaye Girisi 9,6 milyar $'a ulasti) *AnsesNet*, (20 February 2006) in www.ansesnet. com/goster_2.php?sira_no=3952.

Antimai (2000), Report on protests in Prague against World Bank and IMF 5th, October, (Prag Raporu), www.antimai.org/rp/rpprag.htm.

Arrighi, G., Silver, J. B. and Brewer D. B. (2003), Industrial Convergence, Globalization, and the Persistence of the North-South Divide Studies in *Comparative International Development*, (Ohio State University), Spring, Vol. 38, No. 1.

Baydur, R. (2004), Industrialization Adventure and Working Life in Turkey from 1980s to today (1980'lerden Gunumuze Turkiye'nin Sanayilesme Seruveni ve Calisma Hayati), *Iktisat Dergisi*, No. 452.

Belen, E. (2004), Transformation in Industrial Relations in the World and Working Life in Turkey (Dünyada Endüstri Ýliþkilerinde Dönüþüm ve Türk Çalýþma Hayatý), *Isveren Dergisi-Ankara 2004*, www.tisk.org.tr/isveren_sayfa.asp?yazi_ id=240.

Boratav, K. (2003), Some Recent Changes on the Relations Between the Metropoles and the Periphery of the Imperialist System, Delhi Presentation, www. bagimsizsosyalbilimciler.org/Yazilar_BSB/Delhi%20presentation_Boratav.doc

Boratav, K. (2004), *The History of Turkish Economy1908-2002* (*Turkýye Iktýsat Tarihi 1908-2002*), (Ankara: Imge Publications), 8th ed.

Boratav, K. (2004), *Agricultural Structures and Capitalism* (*Tarimsal Yapilar ve Kapitalizm*), (Ankara: Imge Publications), 3rd ed.

Boratav, K. and Yeldan, E. (2001), *Turkey, 1980-2000 Financial Liberalisation, Macroeconomic (in)stability, and Patterns of Distribution*, December 2001, www.bilkent.edu.tr/~yeldane/B&YCEPA2002.PDF.

BSB (2005), *Evaluations on Economic and Political Life in Turkey in early 2005* (*Basinda Turkiye'nin Ekonomik ve Siyasal Yasami Uzerine Degerlendirmeler*), Bagimsiz Sosyal Bilimciler Ankara, www.isletme-finans.com/BSB2005.htm.

BSB (2005), *On Economic and Social Life in Turkey in Early 2005*, www. bagimsizsosyalbilimciler.org/Yazilar_BSB/BSB2005July.pdf.

Caliskan, O. (2003), *An Evaluation on Foreign Direct Investment* (*Dogrudan Yabanci Yatirimlar Uzerine Bir Degerlendirme*) www.treasury.gov.tr/english/ybs/ulkeink.htm.

Capital (2006), Capital Infocard: Latest figures on economic indicators (Ekonomik Verilerin Son Durumu) March, 2006, *Capital Monthly Business and Economy Magazine* No: 2006/3, (Istanbul).

Ercan, F. (2004), *An Essay in the Frame of Science and Theory, Variation of capitalism in continuality in Turkey (1980-2004)* (*Turkiye'de Kapitalizmin Sureklilik Icinde Degisimi (1980-2004). bilgi-kuramsal bir cerceve denemesi*), Iktisat Dergisi, No. 452.

Esin, A. (2001), In Finansal Forum, *Daily Newspaper*, 01, June, 2001 http://66.249.93.104/custom?q=cache:dnOjq1FAPNYJ:www.nethaber.com/haber/arsiv/haberler/0,1106,120667_4_12103,00.html+%22Arif+Esin%22&hl=tr&ie=UTF-8&inlang=tr.

ESKH (2006), *Economic and Social Development Movement* (*Ekonomik ve Sosyal Kalkýnma Hareketi*) 15 February 2006 http://kalkinma.org/?sayfa=haber&id=2571.

FIAS (2004), downloaded in December 2004 from www.fias.net/services.html.

Global Corruption Report (2001), 5 www.globalcorruptionreport.org/download/gcr2001/gi_oecd_convention.pdf.

Gonenc, R. (2004), Policy Brief, OECD October, 2004 Economic Survey of Turkey, www.oecd.org/bookshop.

Greven, T. (2003), *Clash of Globalizations? The Politics of International Labour Rights in the United States*, European University Studies Series XXXI Political Science Vol./Bd. 463.

Gunaydin, G. (2005), *Turkey Must Refine Agricultural Structure That Was Transferred from Ottoman Empire, The Diplomatic Newsbridge*, in www.zmo.org.tr/odamiz/bizden.php?kod=1654.

Hisarciklioglu, R. (2004), Stable Growth Depends on Reforms (Ne Kadar Reform O Kadar Istikrarli Buyume), *Iktisat Dergisi*, No. 452.

Hurriyet, 2005, *Daily Newspaper*, 21 Feb. 2005, www.hurriyetim.com.tr/haber/0,,sid~4@nvid~539892,00.asp.

International Business Stakeholders (2004), *Petition from International Business Stakeholders to National Leaders and WTO Members on the Doha Development Agenda*, April 30, 2004, www.esf.be/pdfs/Joint%20Business%20Petition%20on%20the%20Doha%20Agenda%20April%202004%20final.pdf.

Isveren (2004), *TISK - Increased Cost of Workforce and its Consequences: Report on Diminished competition power, increased Unemployment and Informal Economy* (*TISK-Artan Isgucu Maliyeti ve Sonuclari: Azalan Rekabet Gucu, Buyuyen Issizlik ve Kayitdisi Raporu*), (Ankara), www.tisk.org.tr/isveren_sayfa.asp?yazi_id=1094&id=61.

Karahanogullari, O. and Dikmen, A. A. (2002), *An Evaluation on the Bill for Foreign Direct Investment* (*Dogrudan Yabanci Yatirimlar Kanunu Tasarisi*

Hakkinda Degerlendirme), www.bagimsizsosyalbilimciler.org.

KESK (2004), *Total Quality Management and Flexible Working in Public Services* (*Kamuda esnek calistirma ve Toplam Kalite Yonetimi*), www.kesk.org.tr/kesk. asp?sayfa=egitimgor&id=6, downloaded in December, 2004.

Marchand, St. (2005), in *Le Figaro*, quoted by *Milliyet Daily Newspaper*, 22 June, 2005, www.haberx.com/n/196436/le-figaro-turkiye-avrupanin-cini.htm 22 June 2005.

Milliyet (2006/1), Turkey is on the second rank in OECD Growth List, (Türkiye OECD büyüme listesinde ikinci sýrada), *Milliyet Daily Newspaper* 14 February 2006, www.milliyet.com.tr/2006/02/14/ekonomi/eko03.html.

Milliyet (2006/2), External Debt Stock pf Turkey reached to 170.1 billion US $ at the end of 2005, (Turkiye'nin Dis Borc Stogu 2005 Sonu Itýbariyla 170.1 milyar dolar oldu), *Milliyet Daily Newspaper* 31 March 2006, www.milliyet.com. tr/2006/03/31/son/soneko53.asp.

Muftuoglu, B. G. (2004), Known and Unknown Dimensions of the Relations between Small and Large Firms (Buyuk ve Kucuk Firmalar Arasindaki Iliskilerin Bildigimiz ve Bilmedigimiz Yonleri), *Iktisat Dergisi*, No. 452.

Pamuk, H. (2006), Increase in Foreign Trade will continue in 2006, Pressure generated from oil prices may be relieved, (Dis Ticarette Artis 2006'da Surecek, Petrolun Bakisi Hafifleyebilir), *Reuters* 31 Jan.2006, www.isbank.com.tr/reuters-haber-detay.asp?Document_Header=nPAM157203.

Pirler, Bulent (2004/1) *The Rush of "Flexiblity" in Europe and the World* (*Dünyada ve Avrupa'da "Esneklik" Furyasý Isveren Dergisi)* (Ankara), www.tisk.org.tr/ isveren_sayfa.asp?yazi_id=446

Pirler, B. (2004/2), *Fight Against Informal Economy in Turkey* (*Ulkemizde Kayýtdýpý Sektörle Mücadele/Bulent Pirler, Isveren Dergisi*), (Ankara), www.tisk.org.tr/ isveren_sayfa.asp?yazi_id=1018&id=58.

Quataert, D. and Zürcher, E. (1998), *Workers and the Working Class in the Otoman Empire and the Turkish Republic 1839-1950* (*Osmanlý'dan Cumhuriyet Türkiye'sine Isciler*), (Iletisim Publications: Istanbul).

Rekabet Kurulu (2004), www.telkoder.org.tr/2-decision/RK_KHat.doc.

Sancar, N. (2002), *Cities: As the Residences for Taking Up a Class Position – Collective Bargaining – Governance* (*Bir Sýnýfsal Mevzilenme Mekaný Olarak Kent Agora-Toplu Sozlesme-Yonetisim*), 2002 Evrensel Kültür Dergisi, No. 129, www.evrenselbasim.com/ek/dosya.asp?sayi=129&id=1540.

Tanyilmaz, K. (2004), Turkish Experience of Industrialisation After 1980, (Turkiye'de 80 sonrasi sanayilesme deneyimine bakarken), *Iktisat Dergisi*, No. 452.

TBMM (2004), *The Act on Basic Principles and Restructuring of Public Administration Act No. 5227* dated 15 July 2004 (*Kamu Yönetiminin Temel Ýlkeleri ve Yeniden Yapýlandýrýlmasý Hakkýnda Kanun*), www.tbmm.gov.tr/ kanunlar/k5227.html.

TC Basbakanlýk (2003), Written Reply of Prime Minister Tayip Erdogan, to the Question Proposal asked by deputy Gaye Erbatur (Milletvekili Gaye Erbatur tarafýndan Baþbakan Tayip Erdogan'a tevcih edilen soru önergesine verilen yazýlý yanýt), August 2003, the document can be found in the archive of TMMOB - Union of Chambers of Turkish Engineers and Architects.

TC Basbakanlýk Gumruk Must. (2006), *Tariffs Schedules for 2006* (*Gumruk Tarife Cetvelleri*), www.gumruk.gov.tr/tarife/notlar/01.xls.

TCDTM (2001), WTO Ministerial in Quatar/Doha 9-14 November 2001, Developments, www.dtm.gov.tr/anl/DTO/DOHAGELISME.htm.

TCDTM (2004), *Republic of Turkey - Undersecretariat of Foreign Trade*, www.dtm. gov.tr/ead/ekolar1/Dtgos.htm.

TC Hazine Must., Letter (2003), Turkish Republic Prime Ministery, Treasury Dept. 14.08.03 the letter to TMMOB in www.gatsnedir.org/modules.php?op=modloa d&name=Sections&file=index&req=viewarticle&artid=1&page=1, downloaded in 2004.

TC Hazine Must (2003), Draft Consolidated Schedule of Specific Commitments – Revision quoted from http://hazine.gov.tr/gats/konsolidetaahhutlistesi.doc.

TC Hazine Must (2004), www.hazine.gov.tr/iro_files/Reports-Presentations/rr_tr_ 2004_en.pdf.

TC Hazine Must (2006), Foreign Debt Stock as of 31 December 2005 (31.12.2005 Itibariyla Dis Borc Stoku) No.2006/37 31 Mart 2006 Press Announcement made by Republic of Turkey-Under Secretariat of Treasury, www.hazine.gov.tr/ guncelduyuru/KAF_20060331_disborcstoku.pdf.

Tekstil Isveren (2005), The Advantage generated from local production of cotton which is used as raw material in textile and clothing industry is being lost, Textile Employer Monthly Magazine June 2005 (Tekstil ve Konfeksiyonun Hammeddesi Pamukta Yerli Uretim Avantaji Kaybediliyor, Tekstil Isveren Aylýk Dergi), www. tekstildergi.org/content/view/163/56/.

TMMOB (2004), downloaded in 2004 from: www.gatsnedir.org/modules.php?op= modload&name=Sections&file=index&req=viewarticle&artid=1&page=1.

Turkay, M. (2004), Debates on Industrialisation in Turkey/Round Table Meeting organized by Iktisat Dergisi (Turkiye'de Sanayileşme Tartismalari Yuvarlak Masa Toplantisi), Iktisat Dergisi, No. 452.

Turk-Is (2004), *Turk-Is supports a fair and lasting peace and a solution based on common sense in Cyprus* (*Turk-Is, Kýbrýs 'ta kalýcý ve adýl bir barýstan ve sagduyulu bir cozumden yanadir*), www.turkis.org.tr/yazi.php?yad=48&kat=186.

Turk-Is Inquiry on EU (2004), *An Inquiry on EU membership of Turkey* (AB-Anket), turkis.org.tr/icerik/abanket.htm, 21 May, 2004.

TUSIAD (2002), *Business Views and Actions on the Euro-Mediterranean Partnership*. (Lebib Yalkin Publishing & Printing Co), www.tusiad.org.tr/eng/ homepage.nsf/FRMain?OpenFrameSet.

TUSIAD (2003), *WTO 5th Ministerial Conference Cancun, MEXICO, 10-14, September 2003: Towards Global Development*, TUSIAD Publication No-T/2003/9/361, (Lebib Yalkin Publishing & Printing Co.: Ankara).

Uslu, S. (2004), Speech made by the President of Hak-Is Salim Uslu in the press conference on Turkey's EU membership process, December 2004, www.hakis. org.tr/arsiv/basin_top_22_12_2004.html.

WTO Restricted (1998), Trade Policy Review/TURKEY-PRESS RELEASE, PRESS/TPRB/83, 7 October 1998, www.wto.org/english/tratop_e/tpr_e/tp83_ e.htm.

WTO Reference Paper for Telecom Services (1996) in www.wto.org/english/ tratop_e/serv_e/telecom_e/tel23_e.htm.

WTO (2004), Trade Policy Review Body WT/TPR/M/125/Add. 1 9 February 2004 (04-0497), www.wto.org/english/tratop_e/tpr_e/tp_rep_e.htm#bycountry.

Yapi Kredi (2006), Ekonomi Gundemi, 4th January 2006, www.haber7.com/haber. php?haber_id=145500.

Yeldan, E. (2003), Where we are in globalization? Debt Problem of Turkish Economy and IMF Policies (Küreselleşmenin Neresindeyiz? Türkiye Ekonomisinde Borç Sorunu ve IMF Politikalarý) in Petrol-Is Yilligi, www.bilkent.edu.tr/~yeldane.

Young, B. (2003), *Gender Agenda in der WTO: The Doha Development Round, Gender and Social Reproduction*, (Friedrich Ebert Stiftung: Bonn).

Notes

1   TCDTM: Republic of Turkey – Undersecretary of Foreign Trade.

2   Petition from International Business Stakeholder to National Leaders and WTO Members on the Doha Development Agenda: "...We recognise that fundamental reform and market opening of agricultural markets are of vital importance to developing countries and to the ultimate success of the Doha Development Agenda. We urge the elimination of all forms of export subsidies and of trade distorting domestic support, concomitant with substantial liberalisation of major agricultural markets worldwide."

3   Any reader with further interest in a more elaborate and advanced analysis of these reforms and the *new state* in agenda as well as the *new public sphere* may refer to any website managed by IMF, WB, OECD or EU (BSB July 2005, 9–10).

4   Global Corruption Report, 2001, 5. www.globalcorruptionreport.org/download/ gcr2001/gi_oecd_convention.pdf.

5   In that news, this threat was not only for Turkey, it was valid for all 12 candidates in June 2001.

6   TBMM: The Grand National Assembly of Turkey.

7   DISK: Confederation of Progressive Workers' Unions in Turkey (1967); KESK: Confederation of Public Servants' Unions in Turkey (1996).

8   TMMOB: Turkish Association of the Chambers of Engineers and Architects.

9   HAK-IS: The Confederation of Turkish Real Trade Unions (1976).

10   See the official documents on GATS commitments and offerings of Turkey through the TMMOB web site: www.gatsnedir.org: i.e. official letter of Treasury Dept. to TMMOB dated 14.08.03 / N.50102.

11   USIAD (Ulusal Sanayici ve Is Adamları Dernegi): Association of National Industrialists and Businessmen.

12   TOBB (Turkiye Odalar ve Borsalar Birligi): The Association of Chambers and Stock
      Exchanges in Turkey.
13   TISK: Turkish Confederation of Employer Associations, 1962.
14   GATT: General Agreement on Trade and Tariffs.
15   ESKH: Economic and Social Development Movement.

Chapter 9

Conclusions:
Doha Round and Forum-Switching

Joachim Becker and Wolfgang Blaas

This book is about strategic behaviour in trade policy in general and about forum-switching (arena-switching, forum-shifting) in particular. The latter concept describes the deliberate changing from one negotiation arena to another in order to be able to promote one's trade interests more successfully. Seven important players in global trade negotiations have been analysed: the US, the EU, China, India, Brazil, South Africa, and Turkey.

From these country studies, we can draw a number of conclusions. First, we shall look at the strategy of the US government and the European Commission, which have been the main protagonists in the setting of agendas and switching of fora. Second, we shall compare the counter-strategies of the Third World middle powers. Finally, northern activist strategies and southern defence strategies are placed in the context of forum-shifting.

EU and US strategies

The US government and the EU Commission have been at the forefront in agenda-setting during the Doha Round. Arenas were switched at the multilateral level and from the multilateral to plurilateral and bilateral arenas. Forum switching at the multilateral level has mainly been motivated by the calculus that involving a new arena might increase the chance of pushing through the preferred set of norms. Thus, this strategy was solely linked to norm-making. The switch from a multilateral to plurilateral or bilateral arenas has been motivated by a more complex set of considerations. On the one hand, it has been aimed at furthering the spread of specific norms at least in geographically more circumscribed areas when the chances to get them adopted at a global level were low. On the other hand, plurilateral and bilateral agreements have aimed at gaining specific trading privileges.

Raza (in this volume) points out that the European Union has promoted pro-competitive regulations in the GATS negotiations disempowering and constraining sectoral international bodies like the Universal Postal Union (UPU). It seems that the EU Commission has been even more aggressive than the US government in promoting a liberal agenda in the realm of the WTO. For example, the EU tried to impose a particularly broad agenda at the Singapore Ministerial meeting in 1996 by introducing new topics in investment, competition, government procurement and trade facilitation (Jawara/Kwa 2004, 39) – though largely not successfully. Neither the EU nor the USA has been completely successful in pushing through their agenda. Though they agreed on the general neo-liberal design of trade rules, they have not completely been unanimous. At a number of junctures, they encountered determined opposition to their proposals from groups of Third World states. Their criticism centred on the enlargement of the negotiation agenda and on the issue of agricultural trade. The critical stand of Third World governments was supported by a broad range of NGOs. Twice, key meetings ended in open disagreement. One reaction of the US government and the EU Commission has been to try to co-opt specific key players more closely into the negotiation process with the aim to soften their stand. The other reaction was to switch to other arenas of negotiation. Usually, these arenas were of a bilateral or plurilateral nature. Whereas social movements and NGOs in the USA paid some attention at least to the negotiations with Latin American states due to their experience with NAFTA, European NGOs were late in grasping the significance of bilateralism and plurilateralism.

As they encountered resistance to some of their proposals in the WTO, both the US government and the European Commission have shifted arenas of negotiations. Both have resorted to bilateral trade negotiations with other trading blocs and individual states in order to further their trade agenda over the last decade. In these negotiations, they have pushed for concessions beyond the agenda of the WTO (cf. Chorev and Raza in this volume, cf. also Acosta/Falconí 2005a and Schilder et al. 2005). The demands made by US and European negotiators are variations of the same theme focusing on equal treatment of foreign and domestic investors, government procurement, opening of the service sector, and property rights. In so far as they go beyond the WTO agenda, bilateral negotiations are perceived as a stepping stone for future global trade negotiations. The new trade regulations created at the bilateral level are later to be included into global negotiations and agreements. These bilateral negotiations are characterised by an even larger degree of power asymmetry than the global ones. US and EU negotiators use tactics of carrot and stick. The carrot usually consists of privileged access to some areas of the large US or European market. However, access remains strictly circumscribed in sensitive areas of the US and EU economy, like agriculture. However, trading privileges that are indeed conceded are eroded to the extent that similar agreements are struck with other regional blocs or states.

Promoting a WTO+ agenda has not been the only rationale behind promoting bilateral trade agreements. Both the US government and the EU Commission also seek to gain privileged access to specific markets for US or EU capital. Thus, gaining a competitive edge is a second rationale. At least one free trade agreement has been very high on the agenda of the US government: the project of a Free Trade Area of the Americas (FTAA or ALCA) launched in 1994. In a way ALCA has been a response to the formation of MERCOSUR as a Southern integration project in 1991 (Acosta/ Falconí 2005b, 11). The US government has feared that Brazil might transform MERCOSUR into an alternative pole of attraction for South American states. In order to isolate Brazil, the US government has concluded free trade agreements with Chile and, more recently, with Central American states. In their turn, the European Union likewise started negotiations on a free trade agreement with MERCOSUR in 1999 after having laid the foundations since 1995 (Malcher 2005, 218 ss.). When the ALCA negotiations reached the dead point in 2003, the MERCOSUR -EU negotiations followed suit. Without advances in the rivalling ALCA project, the EU Commission did not feel compelled to be accommodating. As in other continents, the various bilateral negotiations have been clearly interlinked.

In the case of its own continental periphery, the EU proceeded in a way somewhat different from the US. After the demise of state socialism, the EU started to negotiate association agreements called Europe Agreements governing its relations with Central Eastern European states. Essentially, these were free trade agreements. These agreements were loaded in favour of EU interests providing for long transition periods in areas regarded as sensitive by the EU. This negotiation experience made the Central Eastern European countries even more determined to seek full integration into the EU. At the beginning, EU countries were divided on the enlargement issue and the EU adopted a cautious approach. However, with the passing of time, the pro-enlargement stand began to prevail. In 1993, the European Council defined accession criteria. This opened the way to later negotiations (Vachudova 2005, 85 ss.). The accession negotiations provided the European Union with far-reaching leverage to shape policies and future socio-economic and institutional structures in Eastern Europe (Vachudova 2005). The negotiations resulted in the full membership of most Central East European countries and some South East European countries in the European Union. One of the main pillars of the current EU debate on a constitutional treaty concerns the distribution of voting rights in the European Union. There are influential proposals that aim at changing the weighting of the voting rights in favour of the large states – usually the core states of the EU – and reducing the weight of the small states. Many of the latter belong to the East European periphery (Wehr 2006). This would change the balance of forces inside the European Union – to the detriment of its inner periphery. In regard to its outer periphery, the EU has banked on bilateral and plurilateral free trade agreements. In regard to the latter, the EU is close to the US approach to the American periphery which is based on static free trade agreements and not on regional integration having an evolving regulatory framework and an element of supranationality.

Two complementary explanations can be advanced for the particularly aggressive stance in the WTO and the initially slightly stronger emphasis on multilateralism by the European Commission. The first one relates to the regime of accumulation. In the EU, extroverted, neo-mercantilist regimes of accumulation predominate. Extroverted accumulation and neo-mercantilism have a long-term tradition in core EU countries like Germany (Beck 2005, 51 ss.). In the Federal Republic of Germany, even the Fordist regime of accumulation can be described as being supply-side and export orientated. With the crisis and the restructuring since the 1970s, the extroversion has become even more accentuated. The German government actively and successfully pushed for regulations at the EU level that are in line with neo-mercantilism. The fiscal and monetary criteria of the Growth and Stabilisation Pact enshrine restrictive economic policies in the countries of the Euro Zone leaving little space for Keynesian policies at the national level. Since domestic demand is structurally depressed, there is a strong impulse for external expansion. US growth is led more strongly through domestic demand which is based to a larger extent on indebtedness than in the Euro Zone (cf. Pollin 2003). In contrast to the core European states, the US economy relies heavily on capital imports accounting for 76 percent of global capital imports in 2002 (Zeller 2004, 87, graph 2). Thus, the US and core European regimes of accumulation differ significantly in regard to their international insertion. The EU ratio of exports to GDP amounts to ca. 14 percent (2000) – and, thus, is higher than in the USA (12 percent) and Japan (11 percent, Schilder et al. 2005, 4). However, EU strategies of accumulation are more orientated towards exports than is the case with the US due to the different dispositive of regulation. For the stability of the US economy, it is urgent that negative balances (commodity flows and interest payments) with some regions (esp. Europe and East Asia) are compensated by a surplus in international economic relations with other regions in order to shore up the trust in the US as a safe haven for portfolio investment. This is a strong incentive to shore up US influence in regions with a traditionally strong position of US business, especially Latin America, and provides an impulse to negotiate free trade agreements with such regions guaranteeing privileged access for US companies.

The second explanation is institutional. As Raza points out, global negotiations are an opportunity for the European Commission to take over agendas hitherto in the realm of the member states. This seems to have been the case with the issue of investment which used to be in the hands of national governments. European states did individually position themselves in the debates on Multilateral Agreement on Investment (MAI) in the OECD and it was a single national government – France – that gave in to strong protests against MAI and brought the MAI project to a fall in the realm of OECD. Immediately afterwards, the European Commission took up the demands of industry in favour of a multilateral agreement on investment and reaffirmed its will to negotiate the issue in the WTO (Mark-Ungericht/Fuchs 2004, 142 s.). Thus, switching the arena also implied switching the negotiating institution, potentially opening the way to overriding resistances at the national level. Switches from the national to the European level have repercussions for the power relations. Trade negotiations at the European level are well shielded from public interference. At present, the European Parliament has no institutional powers in European trade negotiations. The Commission and the national governments (Council of Ministers) liaise about the trade negotiations in a special Committee which operates behind closed doors. In some areas, ratification by national parliaments still is necessary, though the Nice Treaty reduced the scope of these areas of co-decision (Schilder et al. 2005: 8 s., Monar 2005, 101 ss.). Thus, the European decision structure is clearly biased in favour of executive branches of governance. This favours business lobby groups who have good access to the European Commission. These groups, like the Europe Roundtable of Industrialists or UNICE, usually represent globally acting business (Schilder et al. 2005, 10 ss.). However, agricultural interests enjoy a close relationship with the Commission and are also pressing for continuing protective sectoral dispositives. Europeanised business with global interest has an obvious interest in concentrating the negotiating powers in the hands of the Commission.

US trade negotiations are not as emancipated from parliamentary control and political pressures articulated via parliamentarians as it is the case with the European Union. Nevertheless, the Trade Promotion Act opens the way for the US Congress to limit its role in trade negotiations to approval or rejection of a free trade agreement and restrict the debate to the maximum of 90 days. However, both the approval of this fast track procedure and the final ratification provide at least the possibility of a public debate and parliamentary intervention. These approvals are not necessarily a smooth sailing. At least occasionally, protectionist interests can rally substantial support in Congress. For example, the Clinton government was not able to obtain a fast track for FTAA. This was only obtained by the Bush Jr. government in 2001. Likewise, the passing of the Central American Free Trade Agreement (CAFTA) which was opposed by the textile and sugar industry and trade unions was contested in Congress. The CAFTA agreement was ratified by a majority of only two votes in July 2005 in the US Chamber of Representatives (O Estado de São Paulo, 29 July 2005, B7 s.). From a comparison of the institutional set-up, we can conclude that European negotiators generally have a freer hand in international trade negotiations than is the case with their US counterparts.

The Third World Middle Powers

Export concerns were higher up on the agenda of Third World medium powers than in the past. Nevertheless, they have aimed at maintaining a significant degree of national autonomy in promoting national development. The mixture of export and protectionist concerns has varied from case to case depending on the concrete constellation of interests and forces. In particular, specific manufacturing interests are in favour of maintaining a certain degree of protection and of political space for national development policies. In general, business groups have had privileged access to the relevant decision-making centres of the national states. Social movements from below only occasionally were able to voice their concerns and to have an impact on public debate. Primarily, this seems to have been the case in India and Brazil. Thus, there is an obvious strategic selectivity in the field of international trade policies at the national level.

The higher priority for export interests are linked to the tendentially stronger export orientation. In the case of China and India, enhanced export orientation is built on a consolidated manufacturing sector and is a deliberate choice. In the case of Brazil, South Africa and Turkey, an enhanced export orientation has emerged at least partly as a response to a rather repressed domestic market and a need to service a considerable external debt. In Brazil, Turkey and South Africa, development has been characterised by a slant towards financialisation since the 1990s. Real interest rates have been high or – in the case of Brazil and Turkey – extremely high in order to attract volatile external capital and/or to keep monetary capital within the country.

At the end of 2002 the real prime rate was above 10 percent in Brazil, and slightly below 10 percent in Turkey putting the two countries at the head of the list of real prime rates (Altvater 2004, 49, Tab. 3). This implied even higher active real interest rates in other fields, e.g. in Turkey, they used to be above 20 percent from 1999 to 2002 with the exception of 2000 (Boratav 2004, 281). High interest rates have had a repressive effect on growth. Domestic demand usually has not been strong, capital formation as a percentage of the GDP has considerably declined since the 1970s and has been relatively low in the 1990s (Gelb 2005, 385, Tab. 14.7, Boratav 2004, 271 ss., Faria 2004, 187 ss.). Slack domestic demand has pushed business to resort to exports though the export performance has been affected by exchange rate policies. Brazil and Turkey pursued anti-inflationary policies based on a foreign exchange anchor. This type of policy produced a considerable expansion of foreign debt which, in the Turkish case, has continued until today. High debt service requires increased exports. The neo-mercantilist policies of the Lula government can be linked to the high debt service (Becker 2005, 18). Brazil's and Turkey's vulnerability to financial crisis and chronic foreign debt problems have not been without consequences for their stance in trade negotiations. For example, Brazil promised to continue the policies of trade liberalisation in the 1998 letter of intent to the IMF (Batista Jr. 2005, 108). Turkey agreed to a far reaching restructuring and phasing-out of its agricultural subsidies – one of the most contested areas in WTO negotiations – in agreements with the IMF since 1999 (Aydın 2005, 159 ss.).

All middle powers – with the exception of Turkey – preferred to negotiate in the multilateral realm where the power asymmetries are not as large as in bilateral negotiations. Whereas the US government and the European Commission have aimed at reducing the policy space of national governments through multilateral and bilateral agreements, Third World governments have tried to preserve national policy space. UNCTAD has been the specific venue that they selected for furthering this concern. As Martin Khor (2006) points out, "to the G77 and China, the reference to 'policy space' was the most significant outcome of UNCTAD XI in São Paulo, and the Group proposed that the concept must be operationalised in all of the UNCTAD's future work". With the US government trying to block this initiative, the issue has become highly controversial in UNCTAD. In this respect, the G77 and China have still a way to go in UNCTAD. Attempts to revalorise UNCTAD's General Commercial Preference System do not seem to have prospered too much (Gudynas 2004). The appointment of a former WTO director-general, Supachai Panitchpakdi, as the new UNCTAD secretary-general in spring 2005 is an indication of the obstacles to building UNCTAD as an alternative forum to the WTO (Gudynas 2005a).

While the G77 and China have tried to use UNCTAD as an alternative forum, they have still been deeply involved in the WTO. Brazil, China, India and South Africa have been key negotiators and have been engaged in alliance building in the WTO. Becoming a member of the WTO in 2001 after 15 years of negotiations, China is a relative newcomer to this international organisation. In order to gain membership in this body, China was obliged to negotiate bilaterally with the US government in order to get the "green light" from Washington. In the bilateral negotiations, the Chinese government was obliged to make a number of significant concessions in fields like considerable tariffs reductions for priority US export products, the presence of foreign banks, access to the Chinese telecommunication market, abolition of local content regulations and a transitional import surge mechanism that can be invoked against Chinese exports (Cho 2005a, 189 ss, Saich 2004, 325 ss.). Though there was some opposition to these concessions in China, the Chinese government accepted these far-reaching US demands. It seems that it was basically motivated by three factors. First, it accelerated the negotiations with the US in the moment of a complicated situation in the domestic economy. Slackening domestic demand instilled new vigour into the search for export markets. Entry into the WTO was seen as a means to facilitate exports (Cho 2005b, 614 s.). Second, the Chinese government wanted to participate in rule-making in this crucial arena. "Third, a number of senior leaders seem to have concluded that without some strong external disciplining mechanism, economic reforms might grind to a halt as vested interests resisted further forward momentum" (Saich 2004, 328). Thus, in bilateral negotiations, the Chinese government accepted a number of rules that circumscribe its rooms for manoeuvre in order to gain access to the WTO. However, after having gained membership, the Chinese government is so far in a strong position as China has a continental economy and the interaction with the US is a rather interdependent one, with the US relying to a considerable extent on capital imports from China. This makes China a key player in the WTO. So far, the Chinese government has struck alliances with other key Third World states. South Africa played a rather ambiguous role in the early phase of the WTO negotiations. It was rather accommodating to the US and EU positions in the incipient negotiations and diverged from the position of other African countries. South Africa played a key role in facilitating the success of the Doha meeting (Keet 2002). It hoped for rewards in the form of Western support for its highly ambitious New Partnership for Africa's Development (NEPAD) initiative. This was not to be forthcoming to the extent that the South African Government had hoped for. However, it was rewarded by preferential treatment like the African Growth and Opportunity Act (AGOA), a US initiative holding out preferential access to the US market for African states under certain conditions (Jawara/Kwa 2004, 169 s.). During the 1990s South African trade policies were criticised by a number of African governments, as Gumede (2005, 197 s.) notes. After Doha, the South African government modified its position. It joined hands with the G-20 in Cancún in 2003. In Cancún, Third World countries were able to block negotiations and that strengthened their hand in the further course of the talks. In their stand, they were supported by a broad range of NGOs. Third World countries were able to get most of the Singapore issues (investment, competition, government procurement) off the present WTO negotiation agenda. So far, they have at least been partly successful in their defensive endeavours. Turkey has not been part of these endeavours. It is the overriding concern of the Turkish government to start negotiations with the European Union about eventual future membership. As Gaye Yılmaz points out in this volume, the Turkish integration strategies have considerably narrowed down its choices in the WTO.

In regard to bilateral and plurilateral negotiations, we have to distinguish two groups of countries (excepting the Turkish case). China and India are neither an integral part of significant regional groupings nor have they been engaged in asymmetrical free trade negotiations with the USA and or the European Union. In contrast, Brazil and South Africa are leading members of regional groupings and have taken part in free trade negotiations with both the USA and the European Union.

China and India have quasi-continental economies with a diversified industrial base. On the one hand, the need for them to seek economic integration on economic grounds has not emerged. On the other hand, they would totally dominate any regional grouping they would enter. Vis-à-vis the USA and the EU, they are in relatively autonomous positions. Therefore, bilateral treaties with China and India are not a promising route for the US government and the European Commission to create precedent cases for global negotiations.

Both China and India have intensified South-South cooperation. In particular, the Chinese government has recently struck a number of bilateral and plurilateral trade and cooperation agreements and has developed close links with ASEAN (Association of South East Asian Nations). These do not aim at establishing certain trade norms as a precedence for global negotiations, but aim at creating privileged economic relations. It seems that securing access to raw materials is one of the major concerns for Chinese trade agreements (cf. Bulard 2005, 9). Even in the case of Brazil, a relatively highly industrialised Third World country, the availability of natural resources is a major source of attraction (Gudynas 2005b).

Both Brazil and South Africa are at the centre of regional groupings: Brazil in MERCOSUR and the emerging Comunidad Sudaméricana de Naciones, South Africa in the Southern African Customs Union (SACU) and in the Southern African Development Community (SADC). Both governments have been involved in free trade negotiations with the US government and the European Commission. However, both the strategies chosen by the Brazilian and South African governments and the outcome have differed. Brazilian governments (both Cardoso and Lula) have time and again insisted that existing regional bodies (like MERCOSUR) should be able to formulate a joint position in the FTAA negotiations (Malcher 2005). The Lula government has displayed even an unambiguous resolve in building a South American alliance against the FTAA project. With the EU, Brazil has not negotiated on its own, but as part of MERCOSUR. In both cases, the Brazilian reservations about the proposed free trade treaties have been essential for the deadlock of the negotiations. In contrast, South Africa has negotiated on its own with the European Union (and limited the role of its SACU partners to consultation). In the negotiations with the US which failed in spring 2006, it implicated at least the SACU. The larger SADC grouping has played no role in either of the negotiations. South Africa concluded a free trade agreement with the European Union in 1999. Though the agreement is not as constraining as the originally proposed FTAA agreement would have been, it goes beyond the WTO commitments and the present WTO agenda (cf. Wellmer 2000, Schilder 2005). Thus, South Africa has been somewhat more accommodating in bilateral or plurilateral negotiations than Brazil until today. At first glance, this is rather surprising since Brazil is more vulnerable to external pressures due to its permanent debt problems.

This difference might be attributed to number of factors. First, the FTAA negotiations have more far-reaching implications for Brazil than the free trade agreement with the EU has for South Africa. A change in the agricultural trade regime is one of highest, if not the foremost priority of the Brazilian government in trade negotiations. Giving in to the restrictive position of the US government (or the EU Commission on that count) would prejudice the multilateral stance as well. The original FTAA agreement would have been disadvantageous to a number of Brazilian industries and would have considerably reduced the economic policy options of the Brazilian government. The Brazilian industry is more diversified and seems to be politically stronger than its South African counterpart. Sections of Brazilian business have expressed their reservations about FTAA. Agriculture was not that high on the South African agenda, and the free trade agreement is not as constraining in the industrial and service sectors.

Second, FTAA would de facto imply the demise of MERCOSUR. MERCOSUR is both important for the international weight of Brazil and for some of its industries. Southern African economies are structurally very closely linked to South Africa as part of the colonial heritage. South African business does not need to rely on formal agreements in order to have an economically very strong (if not dominant) position in the neighbouring states. It could maintain its positions even in the face of open political hostility during the apartheid era (cf. Hanlon 1986). Therefore, the regional groupings do not have the same political and economic weight for South Africa as they do have for Brazil.

Third, there are differences in the institutional tradition. Brazil has a history of an autonomous foreign (trade) policy. The Lula government can rely on this institutional tradition, as Faria points out in this volume. The ANC government tried to re-establish its international position on two counts. Firstly, it aimed at re-establishing the international position of the South African state which had been ostracized for many years due to the apartheid regime. Secondly, the ANC as former liberation movement wanted to establish its credentials in western states after the end of the Cold War. Both factors might have contributed to a rather accommodating position towards western states on some issues. However, this is mediated by the stress that the South African government puts on an "African Renaissance" and its aspiration for a leading role among African states and the developing world.

Fourth, the popular movement against the FTAA is stronger in Brazil (and Latin America) than is the case with similar movements in Southern Africa.

Though the interest of dominant Turkish interest groups and of the Turkish government did not completely coincide with EU and US positions in the WTO negotiations, Turkish aspirations for full EU membership restricted Ankara's space for manoeuvre significantly. In addition, Turkey's negotiation position was weakened by concessions it had to make in agreements with the IMF. Thus, Ankara's autonomy was severely circumscribed both by its economic vulnerability and by its strategic orientation towards an EU membership.

Forum-Shifting: Northern activism against southern defence

The US government and the European Commission have actively pursued strategies of forum-shifting combining multilateral, plurilateral and bilateral negotiations. Their strategies have had limited success so far. WTO negotiations have been cumbersome and tortuous. Third World states were able to get some sensitive points off the agenda. In the run-up toward the Hong Kong Conference in December 2005, western governments focused their attention on India and Brazil inviting them to be part, together with Australia, of the "Five Interested Parties". Thus, India and Brazil were integrated into key WTO negotiation process. For the US and the EU, this negotiation strategy paid off. According to Bello (2005), both Brazil and India came to Hong Kong willing to accept a proportionally higher tariff cut for high tariffs in the area of Non-Agricultural Market Access (NAMA) and moving towards a "plurilateral" process of services negotiations eroding the flexible request-offer approach that had marked the GATS negotiations. These were key concessions to the US and the EU and became part of the Hong Kong Ministerial Declaration (WTO 2005, §12, Annex C, § 7). Brazil expected – and achieved – a date for the phasing out of export subsidies in agriculture. Thus, the Southern defence has been weakened in the run-up to Hong Kong. The compromise of NAMA will affect in particular Third World countries who have rather high tariffs in order to build the import substitutions industries. The formula on GATS is likely to step up the pressure on developing countries to open up more service sectors. Thus, the US and EU negotiators achieved some real advances in their WTO strategies in Hong Kong. Nevertheless, they still face stumbling blocks before the negotiation round can be completed.

In a number of arenas, Third World middle powers have blocked negotiations on sensitive points in plurilateral or bilateral negotiations. In this respect, they did have some defensive capacity, though there are differences in the degree of resisting strategies of carrot and stick at the plurilateral and bilateral level. These differences can be explained by the degree of vulnerability to political and economic pressures, the concrete constellation of interests and institutional designs and traditions. Though Third World middle powers successfully engaged in global and regional alliance building, their pro-active capabilities in forum-shifting have been quite limited during the Doha Round.

It seems rather likely that both the US government and the European Commission will lean rather more heavily on plurilateral and bilateral negotiations after the completion of the Doha Round – whatever the results of that round might be. WTO negotiations have proved to be cumbersome. Their leverage is greater at the plurilateral and bilateral level. Third World regional blocs have been weakened by US and EU bloc or bilateral trade negotiation strategies and internal imbalances. SADC has already split into several groups negotiating separately with the European Union (cf. Wellmer in this volume) The willingness of Columbia, Ecuador and Peru to sign free trade agreements with the US made Venezuela announce in April 2006 that it will leave the Comunidad Andina de Naciones (Weissheimer 2006, Ruiz Caro 2006). Thus, this regional bloc is also falling apart. The Uruguayan government is pretending to seek a special deal with the US (cf. Abelando 2006). This attitude is creating tension within MERCOSUR. However, it is doubtful whether the progressive Uruguayan government would be willing to endanger the existence of MERCOSUR. It might be that it uses the talks with the US government as a device to get more leverage on MERCOSUR decisions. Definitely, the Uruguayan government would like to see a more prominent role of small states in MERCOSUR decision-making. In this respect, there seems to be some room for Brazil (and Argentina) to mend the fences.

Regional middle powers are critical to maintaining or losing the cohesion of the regional groupings. They are not always as accommodating to the smaller and economically more vulnerable members as they should be for the sake of maintaining a significant degree of unity. However, Third World states – with the exception of China and India – would be in quite a weak position if they negotiated individually bilateral agreements with the US and the European Union. In international fora, the position of Brazil and South Africa would be weakened in the case of losing their regional groupings. Thus, it would seem that, for governments in the Third World, shoring up regional groupings and forging broader alliances would be crucial for maintaining at least a defensive capacity in the politics of forum-shifting.

References

Abelando, V. H. (2006), La ambigüedad funcional. In: *Brecha*, 31/3, p. 10.

Acosta, A., Falconí, F. (eds.) (2005a), *TLC. Más que un tratado de libre comercio*, (Quito: FLACSO Ecuador/ILDIS-FES).

Acosta, A., Falconí, F. (2005b), Introducción: El TLC, desempolvando el cuento del "libre comercio". In: Acosta, A., Falconí, F. (eds.), *TLC. Más que un tratado de libre comercio*, (Quito: FLACSO Ecuador/ILDIS-FES), pp. 11-38.

Altvater, E. (2004), Inflationäre Deflation oder die Dominanz der globalen Finanzmärkte. In: *Prokla*, 34(1), pp. 41-59.

Aydýn, Z. (2005), *The Political Economy of Turkey*, (London: Pluto Press).

Batista Jr., P. N. (2005), *O Brasil e a economia internacional. Recuperação e defesa da autonomia nacional*, (Rio de Janeiro: Elsevier).

Beck, St. (2005), After the Miracle. The Exhaustion of the German Model? In: Beck, St., Klobes, F. and Ch. Scherrer (eds.), *Surviving Globalization? Perspectives for the German Economic Model*, (Dordrecht, Springer), pp. 33-67.

Becker, J. (2005), *La crisis europea y las lecciones para América Latina. In: Tercer Mundo Económico*, No. 195, pp. 17-19.

Bello, W. (2005), The Real Meaning of Hong Kong: Brazil and India Join the Big Boys' Club. In: *Focus on the Global South*, 22 December, www.focusweb.org/content/view/799/36.

Boratav, K. (2004, 2nd ed.), Yüzyýlýn baþlarýnda Türkiye ekonomisi: bir bilanço. In: Boratav, K., *Yeni dünya düzeni nereye?* (Ankara: Ýmge kitabevi), pp. 263-288.

Bulard, M. (2005), La Chine bascule l'ordre mondial. In: *Le Monde diplomatique*, August, pp. 1, 8-9.

Cho, H. (2005a), *Chinas langer Marsch in den Kapitalismus*, (Münster: Westfälisches Dampfboot).

Cho, H. (2005b), Chinas langer Marsch in die neoliberale Weltwirtschaft. In: *Prokla*, 35(4), pp. 601-618.

Faria, L. A. E. (2004), Aquém da estagnação: 10 anos do Plano Real. In: *Indicadores Econômicos FEE*, 32(2), pp. 175-196.

Gelb, St. (2004), An Overview of the South African Economy. In: Daniel, J., Southall, R. and J. Lutchman (eds.), *State of the Nation. South Africa 2004-2005*, (Cape Town: HSRC Press), pp. 367-400.

Gudynas, E. (2004), Países en desarrollo relanzan un acuerdo comercial. In: *La insignia*, 18/6 (www.lainsignia.org/2004/junio/econ_040.htm.

Gudynas, E. (2005a), Lamy en la OMC, Panitchpakdi en la UNCTAD. In: *La insignia*, 17/5 (www.lainsignia.org/2005/mayo/econ_004.htm.

Gudynas, E. (2005b), *Después del ALCA. Integración y comercio en América latina*, (Montevideo: CLAES).

Gumede, W. M. (2005), *Thabo Mbeki and the Battle for the Soul of the ANC*, (Cape Town: Zebra Press).

Hanlon, J. (1986), *Beggar Your Neighbours. Apartheid Power in Southern Africa*, (London: James Currey)/(Bloomington: Indiana University Press).

Jawara, F., Kwa, A. (2004, 2nd, updated ed.), *Behind the Scenes at the WTO. The Real World of Internation Trade Negotiation. The Lessons of Cancun*, (London: Zed Press).

Keet, D. (2002), *South Africa's Official Position and Role in Promoting the World Trade Organisation*, (Cape Town (Alternative Information and Development Center).

Khor, M. (2006), *UNCTAD Review talks collapse without agreed text*. TWN Info Service on WTO and Trade Issues, 16 May.

Malcher, I. (2005), Der Mercosur in der Weltökonomie. Eine periphere Handelsgemeinschaft in der neoliberalen Globalisierung, (Baden-Baden: Nomos).

Mark-Ungericht, B., Fuchs, M. (2004, 2nd ed.), Vom GATT zur OECD (MAI) zur WTO – Versuche zur Durchsetzung eines multilateralen Investitionsabkommens. In: ATTAC (ed.), *Die geheimen Regeln des Welthandels. WTO-GATS-TRIPS-MAI*, (Vienna: Promedia), pp. 136-149.

Monar, J. (2005), Die Gemeinsame Handelspolitik der Europäischen Union im EU-Verfassungsvertrag: Fortschritte mit einigen Fragezeichen. In: *Aussenwirtschaft*, 60(1), pp. 99-117.

Pollin, R. (2003), Contours of Descent. U.S. Economic Fractures and the Landscape of Global Austerity, (London/New York: Verso).

Ruiz Caro, A. (2006), Comunidad Andina de Naciones. In: mercosurabc (www.mercosurabc.com.ar/notaasp?IdNota=IdSeccion=3).

Saich, T. (2004, 2nd, revised ed.), *Governance and Politics of China*, (Basingstoke: Palgrave Macmillan).

Schilder, K., Deckwirth. C. and P. Fuchs (2005), F*reie Fahrt für freien Handel? Die EU-Handelspolitik zwischen Bilateralismus und Multilateralismus*, (Berlin: eed & weed).

Vachudova, M. A. (2005), *Europe Undivided. Democracy, Leverage, and Integration After Communism*, (Oxford: Oxford University Press).

Wehr, A. (2006), Flagge und Hymne. In: *Freitag*, 26 May, p. 8.

Weissheimer, M. A. (2006), Venezuela sai da Comunidad Andina. Chávez pede apoio a Lula. In: *Carta Maior*, 21/4/2006 (www.cartamaior.uol.com.br).

Wellmer, G. (2000), *SADC zwischen regionaler Integration und reziprokem Freihandel mit der Europäischen Union*, (Bielefeld: Dritte Welt Haus & KOSA).

WTO (2005), *Doha Work Programme*. Ministerial Declaration, Adopted on 18 December 2005 (WT/MIN05/DEC, www.wto.org/english/thewto_e/minist_e/min05_e/final_text_e.htm).

Zeller, Ch. (2004), Ein neuer Kapitalismus und ein neuer Imperialismus? In Zeller, Christian (ed.), *Die globale Enteignungsökonomie*, (Münster: Westfälisches Dampfboot), pp. 61-125.

Index